The POLITICS *of*
WEAPONS INSPECTIONS

The POLITICS of WEAPONS INSPECTIONS

Assessing WMD Monitoring and Verification Regimes

NATHAN E. BUSCH
JOSEPH F. PILAT

STANFORD SECURITY STUDIES

An Imprint of Stanford University Press
Stanford, California

Stanford University Press
Stanford, California

The authors thank Christopher Newport University's Center for American Studies and its donors for supporting the research and publication of this book.

Library of Congress Cataloging-in-Publication Data

Names: Busch, Nathan E., author. | Pilat, Joseph F., author.
Title: The politics of weapons inspections : assessing WMD monitoring and verification regimes / Nathan E. Busch and Joseph F. Pilat.
Description: Stanford, California : Stanford University Press, 2017. | Includes bibliographical references and index.
Identifiers: LCCN 2016029020 (print) | LCCN 2016030198 (ebook) | ISBN 9780804797436 (cloth : alk. paper) | ISBN 9781503601604 (pbk : alk. paper) | ISBN 9781503601628 (ebook)
Subjects: LCSH: Weapons of mass destruction. | Nuclear arms control—Verification. | Chemical arms control—Verification. | Biological arms control—Verification. | Disarmament—On-site inspection.
Classification: LCC U793 .B87 2017 (print) | LCC U793 (ebook) | DDC 327.1/745—dc23
LC record available at https://lccn.loc.gov/2016029020

Printed in the United States of America on acid-free, archival-quality paper.
Typeset at Stanford University Press in 10/14 Minion.

For LIZ *and* MELINDA

Contents

Acknowledgments

We wish to thank a number of organizations and individuals who made this project possible. First, we would like to thank Christopher Newport University's Center for American Studies and its donors, as well as the Dean of the College of Social Sciences, for supporting the research and publication of this book. Thanks also to the Los Alamos National Laboratory for providing research space and other support.

We wish also to acknowledge the enthusiastic support and hard work in researching and editing by the CAS Junior fellows, Cameron Baxter, Ben Coffman, Galen Creekmore, Dani Crowley, Ryan LaRochelle, Ali Nayyef, Zachary Pereira, Bianca Rumbaugh, Nathan Sieminski, and Oliver Thomas. The editorial staff at Stanford University Press, including Geoffrey Burn, Alan Harvey, Anne Fuzellier Jain, and John Feneron, offered helpful suggestions and made the editing process seamless. The insightful comments by reviewers also strengthened the finished product.

Finally, we wish to extend a special thanks to our families for their indefatigable support, love, and encouragement.

The views expressed in this book are our own and not those of the Los Alamos National Laboratory, the National Nuclear Security Administration, or the Department of Energy.

Abbreviations

ABACC	Brazilian-Argentine Agency for Accounting and Control of Nuclear Materials
ANC	African National Congress (South Africa)
AP	Additional Protocol
APS	American Physical Society
BW	Biological Weapon
BWC	Biological Weapons Convention
CBM	Confidence-Building Measures
CBW	Chemical and Biological Weapons
CCHF	Congo Crimean Hemorrhagic Fever
CD	Conference on Disarmament
CISAC	Committee on International Security and Arms Control
CNS	Center for Nonproliferation Studies (U.S.)
CTBT	Comprehensive Test Ban Treaty
CW	Chemical Weapon
CWC	Chemical Weapons Convention
DIQ	Design Information Questionnaire
DNI	Director of National Intelligence (U.S.)
EURATOM	European Atomic Energy Community
FEP	Fuel Enrichment Plant (Iran)
FFCD	Full, Final, and Complete Declaration
FMCT	Fissile Material Cutoff Treaty
HEU	Highly Enriched Uranium
HWPP	Heavy-Water Production Plant (Iran)
IAEA	International Atomic Energy Agency
IFMS	Integrated Facility Monitoring System
INFIRC	Information Circular
INMM	Institute for Nuclear Materials Management
ISG	Iraq Survey Group

ISIL	Islamic State in Iraq and the Levant
ISIS	Institute for Science and International Security (U.S.)
JCPOA	Joint Comprehensive Plan of Action
KEDO	Korean Peninsula Energy Development Organization
LEU	Low-Enriched Uranium
MC&A	Material Control and Accounting
MNSR	Miniature Neutron Source Reactor (Syria)
MOX	Mixed Oxide
MPC&A	Material Protection, Control, and Accounting
MUF	Materials Unaccounted For
NBC	Nuclear, Biological, and Chemical
NDA	Nondestructive Assay
NGOs	Nongovernmental Organizations
NGSI	Next Generation Safeguards Initiative
NLD	National League for Democracy (Myanmar)
NMD	National Monitoring Directorate (Iraq)
NNWS	Nonnuclear-Weapon State
NPR	Nuclear Posture Review
NPT	Nuclear Nonproliferation Treaty
NTM	National Technical Means
NWFW	Nuclear-Weapon-Free World
NWS	Nuclear-Weapon State
OIF	Operation Iraqi Freedom
OPCW	Organization for the Prohibition of Chemical Weapons
PFEP	Pilot Fuel Enrichment Plant (Iran)
PMDA	Plutonium Management and Disposition Agreement
PMDs	Possible Military Dimensions
PNIs	Presidential Nuclear Initiatives
R&D	Research and Development
RRL	Roodeplaat Research Laboratories
SADF	South African Defence Force
SCR	Security Council Resolution
UF6	Uranium Hexafluoride
UN	United Nations
UNIDIR	UN Institute for Disarmament Research
UNMOVIC	UN Monitoring Verification and Inspection Commission
UNSC	UN Security Council
UNSCOM	UN Special Commission (on Iraq)
WAES	Wide-Area Environmental Sampling
WMD	Weapons of Mass Destruction

The POLITICS *of*
WEAPONS INSPECTIONS

Introduction

On July 14, 2015, U.S. president Barack Obama announced what he described as an historic deal that was designed to resolve the ongoing crisis over Iran's nuclear program. The Iranian nuclear crisis, which had lasted well over a decade, was sparked by revelations in 2002 and 2003 that Iran had constructed a covert uranium enrichment facility at a site called Natanz, was building a heavy-water production plant at a site called Arak, and had stated that it planned to construct a heavy-water reactor at the Arak site as well. These facilities raised significant international concerns, since they could be used to produce highly enriched uranium (HEU) and plutonium, both key ingredients for a nuclear bomb. These concerns intensified following reports by the International Atomic Energy Agency (IAEA) stating in November 2003 that Iran had been conducting covert nuclear activities for nearly twenty years.[1] In the years following these revelations, and in violation of UN Security Council (UNSC) Resolutions, Iran continued to press forward with its nuclear program, which many suspected to be part of a nuclear-weapon program, installing nearly twenty thousand centrifuges, producing a significant stockpile of enriched uranium, and nearing completion of the heavy-water reactor at Arak.

The 2015 agreement, known as the Joint Comprehensive Plan of Action (JCPOA), was designed to reduce proliferation risks at key Iranian facilities—particularly the uranium enrichment sites of Natanz and Fordow, and the nuclear reactor at Arak—in return for significant sanctions relief for Iran. The JCPOA also contained requirements to resolve key questions about alleged Iranian weaponization work that had come to light in 2011.[2]

The JCPOA is a complex agreement, spanning more than 150 pages and containing an enormous number of requirements, but the following are some of the most significant elements of the deal. At the Natanz and Fordow enrichment sites, for a period of ten years, Iran was required to reduce the number of operational centrifuges at Natanz from over 19,000 to 5,060, and for fifteen years refrain from using the 1,040 centrifuges at Fordow for uranium enrichment. The agreement also required Iran to maintain a maximum stockpile of 300 kilograms of uranium enriched to a maximum of 3.67 percent U-235 (with the exception of uranium already enriched for use as reactor fuel).

The JCPOA also required Iran to modify the size and operation of the Arak reactor, and thus reduce significantly the amount of plutonium it could produce. In addition, the deal required Iran to use low-enriched uranium (LEU) instead of natural uranium as the fuel for the reactor, which was designed to reduce the quality of the plutonium produced.[3]

The JCPOA also called for the IAEA to resolve outstanding questions about the alleged weaponization work, or "possible military dimensions" (PMDs) of Iran's program. The PMDs had been outlined in some detail in a 2011 report by IAEA (and confirmed in subsequent IAEA reports), and included evidence relating to a possible high-explosive test chamber directly related to nuclear weaponization work at a military site called Parchin. Although the JCPOA itself did not outline what steps the IAEA would take to resolve these questions, it did commit Iran to implement the "Roadmap for Clarification of Past and Present Outstanding Issues," a confidential agreement negotiated between Iran and the IAEA.[4]

In order to ensure that Iran was complying with the terms of the agreement, the JCPOA contained requirements for monitoring and verification, including routine on-site inspections at Natanz and Fordow. Specifically, the deal called for Iran to apply the Additional Protocol (AP) "provisionally" until October 2023, at which point it would "seek" ratification of the protocol. The AP is designed to strengthen IAEA safeguards and expand the agency's ability to detect undeclared facilities and activities.[5] It also expands the agency's toolkit, including the use of wide-area environmental sampling and satellite surveillance. The JCPOA also authorizes the IAEA to conduct daily, routine inspections of Natanz for fifteen years.

Finally, the agreement gives the IAEA the authority to call for challenge inspections of any facility if it suspects undeclared nuclear materials or activities. If, after fourteen days, there has been no progress in alleviating the IAEA's concerns, the matter will be referred to a "Joint Commission," composed of the United States, the United Kingdom, France, Germany, Russia, China, Iran, and the E.U. The Joint Commission then has seven days to decide on appropriate action by consensus, or by a vote of five or more of the eight members. Iran then has three days to implement the Joint Commission's decision or potentially face reimposition of international sanctions.[6]

Heralded by the Obama administration and proponents of the deal as a major breakthrough, the JCPOA did limit or scale back important parts of Iran's program. Despite some early statements to the contrary, Obama officials later stated that the goal of the negotiations was not to achieve a complete dismantlement of Iran's nuclear program but to increase the regime's breakout time—the time required to produce enough fissile material for a nuclear weapon—from a few months to a year.[7] They have maintained that the nuclear deal achieved this goal by limiting Iran's stockpile of 3.67 percent enriched uranium to 300 kilograms, by significantly reducing the number of operational centrifuges at Natanz and forbidding any enrichment at Fordow, and by reconfiguring the Arak reactor.

The president himself, as well as senior officials of the Obama administration, have claimed that the deal closes off all pathways to the bomb. As Energy Secretary Ernest Moniz stated, "We have blocked all of these pathways to a bomb. We should also emphasize this is not a 10 year deal, this is a long-term arrangement. There's no sunset. There will be a lot of phases starting with extremely stringent restrictions on Iran's program. Hopefully they will comply for a long time, build up confidence, but we have 10-year restrictions, 15-year restrictions, 25-year restrictions and we have forever restrictions, so this is a long term program."[8]

A fact sheet issued by the White House elaborated upon the idea that the JPCOA is successful in "blocking the four pathways to the bomb"—including uranium enrichment at Natanz, uranium enrichment at Fordow, weapon-grade plutonium production at Arak, and covert attempts to produce fissile material. Citing the continuous monitoring of the Natanz and Fordow sites, the fact sheet maintains that the deal eliminates the possibility of producing highly enriched uranium at these sites. The fact sheet maintains that Iran would not be able to produce weapon-grade plutonium because "the Arak reactor will be redesigned so it cannot produce any weapons-grade plutonium," "spent fuel rods (which could also be source material for weapons-grade plutonium) will be sent out of the country as long as this reactor exists," and "Iran will not be able to build a single heavy-water reactor for at least 15 years."[9]

The White House has also maintained that the fourth and final pathway to the bomb—nuclear-weapon work conducted at clandestine, undeclared sites—would be closed off because the IAEA would "not only be continuously monitoring every element of Iran's declared nuclear program," from uranium mining to spent fuel from nuclear reactors, "but they will also be verifying that no fissile material is covertly carted off to a secret location to build a bomb." Regarding the possible existence of undeclared nuclear sites, the administration has stated that "if IAEA inspectors become aware of a suspicious location, Iran has agreed to implement the Additional Protocol to their IAEA Safeguards Agreement, which will allow inspectors to access and inspect any site they deem suspicious."[10]

Proponents of this deal, both inside the administration and out, have argued that this deal is unprecedented, providing the most intrusive inspections ever negotiated.[11] Both Susan Rice and Secretary of Energy Ernest Moniz described the verification mechanisms as providing "unprecedented transparency, unprecedented inspections."[12] Obama administration press secretary Josh Earnest and other proponents of the deal have described the Iran deal in even more expansive terms, stating that it includes "the most intrusive set of inspections that have ever been imposed on a country's nuclear program."[13]

While the Obama administration and many in the nonproliferation community have supported the deal, heavy criticism of the deal has emerged from many opponents of the deal, including Israeli prime minister Benjamin Netanyahu and prominent U.S. Democratic and Republican politicians. These opponents of the deal have raised significant questions about the deal and whether it meets its primary objectives. Some have argued that proponents of the deal have engaged in "oversell" of the deal, not only in terms of the stringency of the verification mechanisms but also in the capabilities that Iran is permitted to retain.

• *"Breakout Times?"* Some scholars have questioned some of the assumptions made by the Obama administration in its claim that the deal extends Iran's breakout time to a year. Alan Kuperman has argued that administration's twelve-month breakout timeline makes a number of questionable assumptions, including the number and type of centrifuges that Iran could utilize for enrichment, the levels of enrichment of the starting material, and the amount of enriched uranium required for a nuclear weapon.[14] He argues that the breakout timeline is closer to a few months. Others have argued that the timeline would be closer to seven months if Iran were able to redeploy its already manufactured IR-2 centrifuges relatively quickly.[15]

• *"Most Intrusive Inspections"?* As noted, with several notable exceptions, administration officials and other proponents have most often referred to the deal as providing "the most comprehensive and intrusive verification regime ever negotiated."[16] This careful wording rules out the verification regime in Iraq, which was far more intrusive than the verification regime in Iran but was imposed on Iraq after Operation Desert Storm. Former Pentagon official Michael Rubin points out that the goals of the verification regime in Iran are much more limited than in Libya, since Libya was required to turn over its entire enrichment infrastructure for removal.[17]

• *Not a Long-Term Solution.* Other criticisms have focused on the capabilities that Iran is permitted to retain, especially over time. Given that after fifteen years the vast majority of the intrusive verification mechanisms on Natanz, Fordow, and Arak would be removed, "most of the significant constraints on Tehran's program lapse after 15 years—and, after that, Iran is free to produce uranium on an industrial scale."[18] Critics cite President Obama's statement in an interview on National Public Radio that "[w]hat is a more relevant fear would be that in year 13, 14, 15, they have advanced centrifuges that can enrich uranium fairly rapidly, and at that time the breakout times would have shrunk almost down to zero."[19] As Albright et al. argue, "The JCPOA has many strengths but one of its most serious shortcomings is that it almost ensures that Iran can emerge in 15–20 years as a nuclear power with the potential, at a time of its choosing, to make enough weapon-grade uranium for several nuclear weapons within a few weeks."[20]

• *Mechanisms for Challenge Inspections.* A number of critics have raised questions about the mechanisms for challenge inspections, since the required steps for these inspections could take up to twenty-four days. Although many supporters of the deal have argued that it is not possible to conceal a nuclear facility or significant stockpiles of nuclear materials in twenty-four days,[21] others have still raised questions about this timetable, especially as it would relate to smaller facilities or quantities of nuclear materials. As former IAEA deputy director-general Olli Heinonen has argued, while "it is clear that a facility of sizable scale cannot simply be erased in three weeks' time without leaving traces," the greater risks could likely involve "smaller-scale but still important nuclear work, such as manufacturing uranium components for a nuclear weapon." He notes, "A 24-day adjudicated timeline reduces detection probabilities exactly where the system is weakest: detecting undeclared facilities and materials."[22] This logic also applies to nonnuclear weaponization work.

• *PMDs and Parchin.* Although the JCPOA required Iran to resolve questions about the possible military dimensions of its nuclear program, a critical issue has been the way in which the PMDs, and in particular the issues around the Parchin site, have been addressed. During the inspection of Parchin, the IAEA was not allowed access to the site when the environmental samples were taken, though it apparently had access to video footage.[23] These verification procedures have been sharply criticized by political opponents of the deal and a number of nonproliferation experts as inadequate and potentially setting troubling precedents for other verification activities in Iran. As Olli Heinonen has argued, "You need to be present and see physically the place. Therefore, for the IAEA to do a credible job they need to get to that chamber and take independently their samples."[24]

• *The Significance of Lifting Sanctions.* In return for the set of restrictions outlined above, the JCPOA set the stage for significant reductions in sanctions from the United Nations, the United States, and the European Union. The IAEA subsequently confirmed that Iran had undertaken the required steps for the removal of nuclear sanctions, including the six nuclear-related UN Security Council Resolutions dealing with Iran's nuclear program, as well as U.S. and E.U. sanctions relating to Iran's financial and energy sectors.[25]

There are mechanisms for "snapping back" the sanctions if any members of the Joint Commission have doubts about whether the terms of the JCPOA are being met. If the member's concerns are not resolved within thirty-five days, any member of the Joint Commission can refer the issue to the UNSC. The UNSC must vote to *continue* the sanctions relief. If the UNSC does not pass a resolution within thirty days, the UNSC sanctions will snap back into place.[26] However, critics have raised questions about whether this mechanism would ever be effectively implemented. As U.S. senator Bob Menendez argued, "If anything is a 'fantasy' about this agreement it is the belief that snapback, without congressionally-mandated sanctions, with E.U. sanctions gone, and companies from around the world doing permissible business in Iran, will have any real effect."[27]

Critics have also raised questions about the requirements within the JCPOA and the subsequent UNSC resolution 2231 to remove the embargo on ballistic missiles.[28] As the negotiations over the JCPOA were nearing their end, the news broke that Iran was insisting on the lifting of sanctions on its ballistic missile programs as part of the deal.[29] Western resistance to this requirement largely evaporated after Russia announced its support for this provision. It was subsequently included in the deal, but only after the eighth year. Opponents of the deal argue that the lifting of sanctions on ballistic missiles would allow Iran to work on the delivery vehicles for nuclear weapons and other weapons of mass destruction (WMD) during the period in which there were limits on their fissile material production. These criticisms intensified after Iran tested a long-range ballistic missile on October 13, 2015, which many allege was in violation of UNSC resolution 2231, which codifies the JCPOA.[30]

The JCPOA was formally adopted on October 18, 2015, ninety days after it was signed.[31] However, the debate over the respective benefits or deficiencies of this deal will likely continue for some time. This debate, with radically opposed views among supporters and opponents, has raised or reinforced a number of issues concerning compliance and noncompliance, monitoring and verification, and the importance of nuclear latency—all of which have been discussed or debated in various contexts for more than twenty-five years. How, and the extent to which, this deal is implemented will be critical for its success, but the debate over the Iran deal raises all of these issues.

The Challenges of Verification: Lessons from Historical Cases

The challenges of Iran demonstrate the serious issues associated with verification of WMD rollback in general and remind us of lessons that we should have learned in other instances of monitoring and verification—most notably in South Africa, Iraq, and Libya—from the role of cooperation, to the impacts of deception and denial, to the intrinsic limits of measurement technologies. Monitoring and verification will remain essential tools for international nonproliferation and disarmament efforts for the foreseeable future, both as mechanisms for verifying disarmament in "difficult cases" such Iran, North Korea, Syria, and possibly Myanmar, and as means of detecting covert programs by other potential proliferators in the future. But it is important for the international community to understand both the opportunities and the limits of these mechanisms and the assurances that they are able to provide.

It is clear that a serious study of WMD monitoring and verification regimes is both extremely timely and desperately needed. This book undertakes such a study by examining previous examples of monitoring and verification regimes—including the verification associated with South Africa's dismantlement of its nuclear-weapon program in the early 1990s, the inspection and verification regimes in Iraq in the 1990s and the first decade of this century, Libya's renunciation of its WMD programs in March 2003, and the challenges associated with verification of global nuclear disarmament—to gain a better understanding of monitoring and verification and to explore possible lessons for verification that can be applied in Syria, Iran, North Korea, and elsewhere.[32]

7

As we will see, there are numerous problems that would be encountered by any monitoring and verification regime tasked with confirming that a country had in fact rolled back its WMD programs. Such a verification process would follow one of two basic scenarios. The first, and less problematic scenario would be a "cooperative verification," such as the verification activities that took place following South Africa's dismantlement of its nuclear arsenal in the early 1990s or Libya's apparent voluntary renunciation of its WMD programs in 2003. Despite some lingering questions about the South African case, and more significant questions that later arose about Libya, according to many governmental officials and arms control experts, both regimes were, in many ways, quite cooperative, turning over large amounts of information and equipment and revealing the existence of a number of facilities that had been unknown to international organizations such as the IAEA. In such a cooperative environment, verification efforts would encounter comparatively few difficulties in verifying the rollback of WMD programs—however, as we also saw in the Libyan case, the appearance of cooperation can also be used as cover for a country's concealment of illicit programs.

Nevertheless, questions and difficulties would arise even in an apparently cooperative verification process. For example, will we be confident that all the information, equipment, and materials were turned over? Will we have the expertise to determine how advanced the programs were? Will the state's willingness to renounce one type of WMD (such as nuclear), cause people to assume that it is renouncing all types of WMD (for example, chemical and biological)? How will we be confident that, once a state receives a clean "bill of health," and, presumably, any sanctions on the state are lifted, it will not start up the WMD programs again?

Much more problematic, however, would be a "coercive verification," such as the inspections teams that investigated Iraq's WMD programs following the 1991 Gulf War.[33] Those verification efforts, led by the UN Special Commission on Iraq (UNSCOM) and the IAEA, and later the UN Monitoring, Verification and Inspection Commission (UNMOVIC), were carried out in a largely uncooperative environment, where the Iraqi regime systematically attempted to conceal its extensive WMD programs and materials.[34]

Monitoring and verification regimes in a coercive environment can be plagued by a number of serious difficulties, including:

• effective concealment of illicit programs by the targeted state (via "denial and deception" techniques);[35]

• ambiguities and inconclusive results, which in the absence of a "smoking gun" can merely create doubts about the state's intentions without actually proving the existence of illicit activities or other forms of noncompliance;

• "false negatives," which give the state a clean bill of health—and create a veneer of legitimacy—when the state is actually in noncompliance with international nonproliferation treaties; and

• inadequate enforcement in the event of noncompliance. As Mitchell Reiss notes, "Enforcing compliance with nonproliferation agreements, pledges, codes, and regulations has been a longstanding challenge, even as it has been recognized as essential to the long-term success of regimes." Historically, this has especially been the case with international organizations such as the United Nations, since permanent members of the Security Council can utilize their veto authority to block resolutions and undermine the effectiveness of the monitoring and verification regimes.[36]

Any of these problems can undermine the effectiveness of the monitoring and verification regimes, or even worse, make the regime serve the opposite of its intended purpose by giving the state cover for proscribed activities.[37]

These are important and difficult problems, and it is unlikely that they can be resolved quickly. There is therefore a need for the international community to begin thinking through these issues now, so that it is as well prepared as possible if and when it needs to put a monitoring and verification regime in place, be it cooperative or coercive.

The Outline of This Book

This book will examine the successes, failures, and lessons that can be learned from the cases of South Africa, Iraq, and Libya, as well as the potential challenges of verifying global nuclear disarmament, to help determine how future monitoring and verification regimes can most effectively be established and maintained. These cases all provide important, and sometimes surprising, lessons about monitoring and verification that are essential for the success of future nonproliferation efforts—including in the difficult cases of North Korea, Iran, and Syria. The book proceeds as follows.

Chapter 1: What Are Monitoring and Verification Regimes?

This chapter is intended to set the stage for the substantive case studies in the rest of the book by defining monitoring and verification; explaining the basic capabilities, as well as the issues and challenges associated with these tools; and laying out the monitoring and verification authorities and activities of the IAEA and the Organization for the Prohibition of Chemical Weapons (OPCW), along with various ad hoc arrangements designed to carry out monitoring and verification.

Chapter 2: South Africa

According to David Albright, the case of South Africa provides an important example of verification of nuclear rollback, but it also "highlights the extreme difficulty of verifying disarmament."[38] South Africa is the only country ever to give up a functional nuclear-weapon arsenal, which it unilaterally renounced in the early 1990s. After dismantling its nuclear program, Pretoria invited inspectors from the IAEA in to verify the destruction of the program. It also ended an active chemical- and biological-weapons (CBW) program in 1995, reportedly destroying all deadly agents and dismantling the equipment and facilities. For these reasons, the South African case is often referenced as a potential model for WMD disarmament.

This chapter examines the South African case and the limits to which this case can be a model for disarmament. Although this was a clear success for nonproliferation, there were questions about the declaration that South Africa presented to the IAEA. Because South Africa undertook the elimination process unilaterally and invited the IAEA in only after this process was completed, significant information was lost to international inspectors.[39] There were even greater questions about South Africa's CBW rollback because the reported dismantlement of the programs and the destruction of CBW agents were never independently verified.[40]

Chapter 3: Iraq

The Iraqi case is the most important, and certainly the most controversial of the cases considered. It is therefore very important to get the story straight on the monitoring and verification regimes—both prior to and after the 2003 war. Prior to the war, weapons inspectors were allowed back into Iraq between November 2002 and March 2003 to assess the status of Iraq's WMD programs. The conclusions of the inspectors were mixed. Mohammed ElBaradei of the IAEA reported in January 2003 that that the IAEA had not seen signs of a nuclear-weapon program, while Hans Blix of UNMOVIC reported that, although they had not found any chemical and biological weapons, there were numerous remaining questions that had not been resolved. Indeed, UNMOVIC compiled a list of more than one hundred unresolved disarmament issues shortly before the end of their inspections. Most of these questions were never sufficiently resolved before the war.[41]

Despite these significant questions that remained after the 2002–3 inspections, after the WMD were not found in Iraq following the 2003 war, the monitoring and verification regimes were later described as "a success, a rather striking international success, that stands out in the record of recent decades."[42] The successes of international efforts to detect and destroy Iraqi WMD are indisputable. However, the unqualified praise that many people have given them does little to clarify the situation or to develop the right lessons from this experience. Despite the highly politicized nature of the issue, a careful and sober reassessment of the strengths and weaknesses, the successes and failures, of the inspection and verification regimes in Iraq is desperately needed.

Chapter 4: Libya

Libya's 2003 renunciation of WMD and the subsequent verified dismantlement of large parts of its WMD programs have been hailed as one of the greatest breakthroughs in nonproliferation in the last decades. And while there were again very real successes, especially in verifying the destruction of Libya's nuclear-weapon program, there were still some remaining questions at that time. According to the Commission on the Intelligence Capabilities of the United States Regarding Weapons of Mass Destruction, otherwise known as the Robb-Silberman Report, "[I]t is clear that Libya has been considerably less forthcoming about the details of its chemical and biological weapons efforts than about its nuclear and missile programs." Although noting that most analysts they interviewed believed that any remaining CBW programs would probably be "small-scale," they cautioned that "the mercurial regime may suddenly shift its plans and intentions, leading to a covert resuscitation of these programs."[43] They also cautioned that there is a growing concern in the intelligence community that "shifting priorities" and the belief that "Libya is done" may "leave collectors and analysts without the resources needed to track and monitor future change."[44]

These suspicions proved to be justified, at least to a degree, in October 2011, when Libya's new National Transitional Council announced that they had discovered an undeclared cache of chemical weapons and chemical weapons artillery shells. This discovery was later confirmed as an undeclared stockpile of mustard gas by the OPCW.

This chapter therefore examines the successes, challenges, and lessons that can be learned from the Libyan case of WMD renunciation and verification. As one model of cooperative verification, the Libyan case highlights not only the opportunities afforded by monitoring and verification regimes but also some of the difficulties that any such regime will encounter in real-world circumstances, however positive.

Chapter 5: Verifying Global Disarmament

In April of 2009, President Obama spoke of "America's commitment to seek the peace and security of a world without nuclear weapons."[45] He recognized that this objective "will not be reached quickly—perhaps not in my lifetime. It will take patience and persistence. But now we, too, must ignore the voices who tell us that the world cannot change."[46] This stated goal of complete nuclear disarmament was subsequently underscored by other members of the Obama administration and captured the world's attention, changing the debate over disarmament in important ways.

Despite the appeal of this goal throughout the world, the prospect of its successful implementation nevertheless raises a whole host of challenges that will need to be thought through and addressed. This chapter focuses on one critical element of these challenges: will a world without nuclear weapons be verifiable with enforceable compliance? The limits on verification that are examined in the other case studies in this book are relevant to the challenges of verifying global disarmament, but there are new challenges that are unique to disarmament as well. The most serious of these challenges derive from tensions between secrecy of nuclear-weapon information and the transparency needed for verification. Some verification challenges are increasing as many nuclear weapons, especially in the United States and Russia, are being moved from deployed status to increasingly consolidated storage (which can affect the value of chain of custody procedures for verification). They are also affected by issues of access, by different classification systems, and by other difficulties. These challenges will need to be overcome if the goal of disarmament is to be achieved. As with other issues raised in this book, the time to begin thinking about them is now.

Chapter 6: Lessons for the "Difficult Cases": North Korea, Iran, Syria

This chapter will draw together the lessons learned from the case studies and apply these lessons to the current difficult cases of North Korea, Iran, Syria, and to a limited extent, Myanmar. These cases will demonstrate the essential roles that monitoring and verification play in international nonproliferation efforts. But they demonstrate the significant challenges as well—especially as they apply to these and other potential challenging cases in the future.

All of these cases reaffirm that monitoring and verification, including onsite inspections, will remain critical tools in the international community's ongoing nonproliferation efforts. International inspections provide capabilities, access, and legitimacy that national efforts cannot. But it is important to understand what these inspections can and cannot reliably do.

As it stands, the international community appears to be in danger of misinterpreting what these regimes can and cannot accomplish. In this chapter, we will therefore draw together the lessons that can be learned from the individual case studies and assess what conditions can help make monitoring and verification successful.

Conclusion: Strengthening Monitoring and Verification Regimes

Given the lessons put forward in Chapter 6 and throughout the book, the conclusion discusses what steps might be taken to improve monitoring and verification; examines new technologies and techniques that could be used by the monitoring and verification regimes, as well as the technical challenges that still remain; assesses the impact of latency and ambiguity on the regimes; and provides a forward-looking set of policy recommendations that may help strengthen these regimes in the future.

Ultimately, the success of monitoring and verification regimes depends on both technical capabilities and political factors. When either element is missing, the results from the monitoring and verification can be highly distorted, potentially undermining the effectiveness of this fundamental tool.[47] One particularly disturbing lesson is that too often monitoring and verification regimes have been hamstrung by various technical or political constraints, undermining the legitimacy of inspection teams, and otherwise causing the conclusions drawn from the verification processes to be suspect. Furthermore, the various findings of verification regimes have often been "politicized"—manipulated or twisted to support political positions and arguments that are not sufficiently supported by the evidence gathered. Unless the international community learns from past experiences, it is likely to encounter challenges with any monitoring and verification regimes it attempts to establish in the future.

1   What Are Monitoring and Verification Regimes?

In 1992, after nearly ten years of negotiation, North Korea finally agreed to allow the nuclear watchdog group, the International Atomic Energy Agency (IAEA), to conduct inspections at Yongbyon, the reclusive country's most sensitive nuclear facility. This facility had long been suspected of being the centerpiece of a dedicated nuclear-weapon program. As part of the verification process, DPRK officials declared all their activities at Yongbyon—including, they said, a one-time removal of less than 100 grams of plutonium from "damaged" fuel rods at an operational 25MW heavy-water reactor located at the site. However, after IAEA officials conducted a series of tests on equipment and nuclear waste at the site, they discovered that North Korea had separated significantly more plutonium than it had declared—possibly enough for a bomb or two.[1]

In 1997, vehicles operated by the United Nations Special Commission on Iraq (UNSCOM) rolled up to Baghdad University. This was no sight-seeing mission. UNSCOM inspectors were in search of Dr. al Keedi, an Iraqi biologist of national repute whom UNSCOM also suspected of being part of a secret Iraqi program on the biological agent ricin—a program that Iraqi officials had long denied ever existed. In the confusion of the search, UNSCOM inspector Terry Taylor spotted a man attempting to slip out of the building with a folder concealed under his arm. After stopping him, Taylor discovered that the fleeing man was indeed Dr. al Keedi and that the file he carried contained a progress report on research into ricin as a potential biological-weapon agent, including the results of experiments on a range of animals—a clear indication that the program not only existed but also had made some progress in weaponizing the agent.[2]

On November 8, 2011, the IAEA published its quarterly report on Iran's nuclear activities. Among other troubling activities related to uranium enrichment, the IAEA report stated that the agency had received information relating to "undisclosed nuclear related activities involving military related organizations, including activities related to the development of a nuclear payload for a missile."[3] The information, which the agency assessed to be "credible," came from "a wide variety of independent sources, including from a number of Member States, from the Agency's own efforts and from information provided by Iran itself."[4] According to some reports, some of the most critical information was provided by a Western intelligence agency and was reportedly acquired "from the wife of an Iranian involved in Iran's nuclear program."[5]

All three of these cases are dramatic examples of monitoring and verification activities of international organizations tasked with deterring or detecting covert weapons of mass destruction (WMD) programs in various countries throughout the world. In all these instances, the monitoring process revealed important information about clandestine WMD programs among suspected proliferators—and apparent discrepancies in countries' statements about their programs. These cases, among many others, demonstrate the central importance of monitoring and verification mechanisms for the international community's WMD nonproliferation efforts and for international security generally.

And yet, despite the apparent "smoking guns" that were discovered in each of these cases, the monitoring process did not necessarily produce the political breakthroughs that might have been expected. In the case of North Korea, the crisis of over Pyongyang's nuclear-weapon program is still simmering more than twenty years after this discovery. In the case of Iraq, Iraqi intransigence and opposition by members of the UN Security Council forced UNSCOM to withdraw from the country in 1998, and ongoing questions over the status of Iraq's WMD programs lasted until after a bloody war in 2003 (and some questions have never been answered). And Iran's suspected nuclear-weapon program continued to be one of the most divisive issues facing the international community until the negotiation of the 2015 Joint Comprehensive Plan of Action.

As we will see from these and other cases examined in this book, monitoring and verification is, and will remain, an essential component of the international community's nonproliferation efforts. But these mechanisms also contain significant technical and political limitations that need to be examined carefully, not only to obtain a clear idea of what they can and cannot accomplish, but also to identify potential ways to make them more effective.

This chapter provides an introduction to monitoring and verification. It begins by defining monitoring and verification and by explaining some of the basic challenges associated with these mechanisms. It then describes the specific monitoring and verification regimes, such as the International Atomic Energy Agency (IAEA), the Organization for the Prohibition of Chemical Weapons (OPCW), and various ad hoc arrangements that are designed to carry out monitoring and verification activities. The discussion in this chapter therefore sets the stage for the analysis in the substantive case studies in the rest of the book.

The Challenges of Monitoring and Verification

Defining Monitoring and Verification

How are monitoring and verification defined? Most simply, "monitoring" is the technical process of gathering data allowed under any agreement or regime, or of data available through national technical means. That process can include everything from inspectors physically onsite at a declared facility, to actual readings from sensors placed to observe activity, to the analysis of material samples, to the collection and use of satellite imagery.

"Verification" is a political process that involves authoritative judgments about the data and interpretations provided by the monitoring community collected from monitoring and other sources.[6] With this data, the policy community within the verifying country or the authorities in an international organization must assess whether the treaty-obligated state is or is not in compliance.[7] In principle and practice, then, verification involves monitoring treaty-limited items and activities and assessing compliance on the basis of that monitoring and other relevant information. Aside from this declared purpose of verification, a common goal of verification provisions is to deter the parties from violations. This objective already presumes a reasonable level of effectiveness for the measures. But it is a difficult standard for verification, because like broader deterrence policies, it is difficult to know what deters and under what conditions deterrence operates. What risks is a party to a treaty willing to take? What is their sense of the benefits of cheating? What is their expectation of a significant response?

Whatever the specific verification provisions of treaties and agreements, all of the knowledge a party has about the other party or parties comes into play in the verification process. Intelligence is thus closely related to verification, and intelligence can guide verification by providing an alarm or triggering mechanism for, say, challenge inspections (prompt adversarial inspections called for by a party or parties to an agreement to prove or disprove a suspected treaty violation by another party or parties).[8]

One must not forget that in the long term, greater transparency is critical to increasing the difficulty for those countries that may decide to cheat on an agreement or regime and may provide additional information to assist a verifying country in making compliance judgments. Verification is facilitated by open societies. The activities of closed systems are more difficult to verify. To some extent, on the basis of political and technical factors, we are entering an era of greater transparency, even to some degree in closed regimes. These global trends can be enhanced through specific transparency measures and technological advances (for example, with the use of Google Earth and various forms of social media). Ultimately, they involve obtaining information related to items or activities of interest or concern, in the scope of this analysis from a nuclear nonproliferation or arms control perspective. They may be formal— that is, they could be directly negotiated in the context of a treaty and subject to some means of evaluating the quality of the information provided. Or they may be informal.

Assessing Compliance

A key question confronting the verification process is how to determine compliance and noncompliance. Ultimately this must be a matter of judgment. Because verification often involves sensitive intelligence, charges of noncompliance are difficult to address and assess publicly. Indeed, the consequences of revealing intelligence sources may inhibit the use of available intelligence. This difficulty is compounded by the fact that in some instances, judgments may not be based on clear information, but may themselves be ambiguous.

One of the problems when encountering noncompliance is how to respond, because international organizations, including the United Nations, have not been able to act effectively, especially if permanent members of the Security Council (with a veto) are involved. UN or other collective action, as provided for by treaties and agreements, can be more effective if the violator is a pariah state, a small power, or has been defeated in war. However, even in these cases the results of collective action are by no means certain.

If a violation is clear or probable, diplomacy will certainly be attempted to rectify the problem, but its effects are uncertain. Embargoes, sanctions, and the threat or use of military force in response to violations could be significant in themselves if diplomatic solutions fail, and may even have a deterrent effect. The problem is getting a consensus on action, which is very difficult. Responses are in the hands of the party or parties that are affected by the cheating, a situation that may not provide the aggrieved party many good options, especially if it is a small or weak state. Of course, violations may be ignored by the parties, depending on how they assess their response options, and on the political and security context. A response may be equivalent to abrogating the agreement. Even publicly airing violations has dangers, as it may undermine the agreement, particularly if no action is taken against the violator or violators.

Violations cannot and should not be ignored, but dealing with them is by no means easy. Even if a violation is not significant, it may indicate a pattern of behavior or be a test of a party's resolve. If it is not responded to, the violating party might feel it has carte blanche to violate the agreement further, thereby undermining the legal regime established by the agreement. And it may even lead to repudiation of the treaty or agreement. Violations brought before the public can bring the domestic political forces and the international community into the picture, and indicate to a violator the costs of its actions. Or such publicity, as suggested above, could undermine the agreement.

The Problem of Ambiguity

Ambiguity is almost certain to be a factor in the determination of compliance or noncompliance, and it can derive from:

• uncertainties produced by poor, lost, distorted, or otherwise incomplete information resulting from the passage of time, partial or unreconstructable records, and the like;

• uncertainties caused by active efforts to conceal and deceive by the inspected party, including efforts to hide or destroy documents or evidence;

• uncertainties brought about by limits on the way intelligence can be brought to bear on a problem—sharing or public airing of the information—because of fears of compromising sources or methods or other concerns (for example, revealing to a state the limits of what it needs to own up to);

• uncertainties of political judgments, particularly those made by multiple parties (multilateral, national, nongovernmental), officially and unofficially, in a contentious political environment marked by divergent interests;

• questions about whether apparent violations or anomalies are deliberate or accidental;

- questions about whether political authorities knew about apparent violations or anomalies, or whether any actions were taken by a "rogue" employee or other actor; and
- resource limitations that can reduce actual collection and processing of data germane to some verification (or to related intelligence) efforts can lead to the development of future verification regimes of lesser effectiveness and can jeopardize future technical capabilities by providing inadequate resources for research and development (R&D).

The verification and compliance process is thus deeply affected by ambiguity. Technology can itself introduce ambiguities into both arms control and nonproliferation verification and compliance discussions, but by and large it has been important in limiting ambiguity to some extent. And it has the potential to do so in the future. It can in some cases provide something like "smoking guns" that are difficult (if not impossible) to dismiss. Technological measurements, for example, may provide the only "concrete" evidence of a treaty violation usable in a highly charged political atmosphere. Technology cannot take the place of political judgments, however, and as a tool used by governments or nongovernmental actors it can be "politicized."

There are limits (technical, political, budgetary) that will curb the real application of technologies to the verification and compliance problems in the future. There are potentially significant tradeoffs between cost and other objectives (from governmental and perhaps public perspectives). Increasingly, nongovernmental organizations (NGOs) are able to bring—and have been bringing—technologies to bear to some degree on verification and compliance issues. The emergence of commercial capabilities (such as Google Earth) that have the prospect of rivaling those of governments is dramatically changing the current picture, although with uncertain prospects. What will happen, for example, when the differing views of some activities put forward by certain governments are compounded by dramatically different views among some NGOs and perhaps international organizations, such as the IAEA? These issues will more frequently arise as the increasing role of NGOs, industry, individuals and other nontraditional actors in the verification and compliance process becomes more evident.

A key element in assessing the potential success of monitoring and verification is whether the regime takes place in a cooperative or coercive environment. Clearly, monitoring and verification have a much greater chance of success when a state actively and positively participates in the verification process (though we must be aware that the appearance of cooperation can also be a method of deception). If the state is uncooperative—creating a coercive verification regime—the chances of success are much lower.

The Current Mechanisms for Monitoring and Verification

Monitoring and verification are being carried out at the international, regional, and national levels. The international community has established a set of regimes for monitoring and verification. Some of these regimes, such as those overseen by the International Atomic Energy Agency or the Organization for the Prohibition of Chemical Weapons, have been established through negotiated arrangements with the backing of international law and are carried out by long-standing international organizations tasked with verification responsibilities.[9] Others are carried out by ad hoc groups that are tasked with verifying specific, exceptional cases—such as UNSCOM or the group of American and British experts who oversaw the verification and dismantlement of Libya's WMD programs. Still other monitoring and verification activities are conducted by the intelligence communities of individual nations (known as national technical means), various NGOs, and increasingly on the individual levels. We discuss these various monitoring and verification mechanisms in the following sections.

The IAEA and Nuclear Safeguards

The safeguards system established by the International Atomic Energy Agency has served as the cornerstone of monitoring and verification mechanisms in the nuclear realm. Although the first safeguards system was oriented mainly toward preventing the export of nuclear-related items, nuclear safeguards have evolved substantially over time. The safeguards system was later significantly expanded with the introduction of INFCIRC/153 and "full-scope" safeguards—and then later was modified again with the introduction of the Additional Protocol (INFCIRC/540).

LIMITED-SCOPE SAFEGUARDS (COVERED UNDER INFCIRC/66)

The very first IAEA safeguards system was outlined in INFCIRC/26. The document required inspections of nuclear reactors, but "except in the case of an incident requiring a 'special inspection,' at least one week's notice was to be given of each inspection; the notice must include the name(s) of the inspector(s), the place and time of arrival in the State concerned and the items to be inspected."[10] Although significant for being the first safeguard system, INFCIRC/26 left much to be desired. Its first and most obvious shortcoming was that it applied only to reactors of less than 100MW (thermal). In addition, because of the political battles during its negotiation, the final document was "one of the most convoluted pieces of verbal expression in history."[11] In February 1963, the board of governors of the IAEA unanimously agreed that INFCIRC/26 needed to be clarified, and safeguards extended to cover reactors of any size.[12]

It took until June 1965 to reach unanimous agreement in favor of INF-CIRC/66, which applied safeguards to all sizes of nuclear reactors. It was later revised, so that safeguards would be applied to reprocessing plants (in INFCIRC/66/Rev.1 in 1966) and fuel fabrication plants (in INFCIRC/66/Rev.2 in 1968). INFCIRC/66 established what came to be called "limited-scope" safeguards, which require states to develop a "system of records" and a "system of reports" with the goal of preventing specific facilities from being used as part of nuclear-weapon programs and preventing the export of nuclear materials. These safeguards are placed on individual plants, shipments of nuclear fuel, or supply agreements between importers and exporters of nuclear fuel or technology.[13]

Under INFCIRC/66, it is possible for a nation to have both safeguarded and unsafeguarded nuclear facilities. Limited-scope safeguards are currently still applied to the states that have not signed the Treaty on the Nonproliferation of Nuclear Weapons (NPT): India, Israel, and Pakistan.

FULL-SCOPE SAFEGUARDS (COVERED UNDER INFCIRC/153)

With the successful negotiation of the NPT in 1968 and its entry into force in 1970, the focus of safeguards shifted to include measures to detect (and therefore deter) diversion of nuclear materials from civilian nuclear programs into military ones. Article II of the NPT says that each nonnuclear-weapon state (NNWS) party to the treaty agrees not to receive or develop any nuclear-weapon technologies, either directly or indirectly. In order to verify this commitment, Article III of the NPT says that the nonnuclear-weapon states should undertake to accept IAEA safeguards "for the exclusive purpose of verification of the fulfillment of its obligations assumed under this treaty."[14] The NPT therefore provides the basis for "full-scope safeguards," but it does not specify in detail how the safeguards are to be implemented in each nonnuclear-weapon state or the techniques and methods to use. The specific details for full scope safeguards were laid out in the IAEA document INFCIRC/153.

INFCIRC/153 establishes a system of safeguards to help verify that non-nuclear-weapon states fulfill the commitments they undertook in the NPT not to divert nuclear materials into nuclear-weapon programs.[15] Part I of INFCIRC/153 outlines the general principles governing the rights and obligations of the parties to the NPT. In order to verify that no nuclear material has been diverted into nuclear-weapon programs, it is critical that the IAEA know exactly how much nuclear material a state has at each stage of its nuclear cycle. INFCIRC/153 therefore makes specific requirements for a nuclear material control and accounting (MC&A) system in the nonnuclear-weapon states:

> The Agreement should provide that the State shall establish and maintain a system of accounting for and control of all nuclear material subject to safeguards under the Agreement, and that such safeguards shall be applied in such a manner as to enable the Agency to verify, in ascertaining that there has been no diversion of nuclear material from peaceful uses to nuclear weapons or other nuclear explosive devices, findings of the State's system.[16]

INFCIRC/153 also makes provisions for the IAEA to conduct inspections of declared nuclear facilities in the NNWSs. The agency must conduct an initial (ad hoc) inspection to determine the amount of nuclear materials that a given state possesses in its declared nuclear facilities. After that, the agency can make routine inspections to verify that that state's "reports are consistent with its records" and to verify "the location, identity, quantity and composition of all nuclear material subject to safeguards under the Agreement."[17]

The agency can also conduct "special inspections" if it "considers that information made available by the State, including explanations from the State and information obtained from routine inspections, is not adequate for the Agency to fulfill its responsibilities under the Agreement."[18] In both these cases, the IAEA must give the state prior notification that it will conduct the inspections. For routine inspections, the inspections must occur at least twenty-four hours after notification; in special inspections, the inspections should take place "as soon as possible" after notification.

Shortcomings of "Full-Scope Safeguards." For most of its history, the IAEA was acclaimed as a highly professional and competent technical organization, and was not a target of the criticism directed against many of the other organizations established under the auspices of the United Nations. Its safeguards pioneered onsite inspections and involved unprecedented, albeit limited, inroads into member states' sovereignty.

However, revelations about Iraq's extensive nuclear-weapon program after the 1991 Gulf War threatened the IAEA and its mandate to administer international inspections of peaceful nuclear activities to help ensure that diversions to military programs were not occurring. These revelations about Iraq's nuclear-weapon program resulted in intense criticism of the entire international nuclear nonproliferation regime, including the IAEA's safeguards system. Similar criticisms had appeared after the 1981 Israeli air-strike against Iraq's Osirak reactor. But only after the Gulf War was Iraq found to have violated its safeguards obligations. Despite the insignificant quantities of material (plutonium) diverted from peaceful activities by Iraq's illicit bomb program, this was the first time that a breach of safeguards was confirmed anywhere. More important, perhaps, to a large extent the Iraqi program was based on clandestine, undeclared nuclear facilities that were not covered and could not have been detected under the safeguards system that had developed during the Cold War. For example, Iraq's al Tuwaitha facility had multiple undeclared buildings where nuclear-weapon activities were taking place. Demetrius Perricos, former deputy leader of the IAEA Action Team, stated the problems that came to light at Tuwaitha:

> To our surprise, Tuwaitha was a very, very large center. It was not just the three or four buildings that safeguards inspectors had visited before the war—the two reactors, a small storage facility, and a small laboratory-scale fabrication plant. We found that there was a whole, new area of Tuwaitha where safeguards inspectors had never been before. This area was only known to those people who had access to aerial surveillance. It was in this area, called the new R&D area, where Iraq did most of its clandestine development work.[19]

The post–Gulf War Iraqi program, the terrorist attacks of 9/11, the discoveries of additional states under the NPT developing clandestine programs, and the associated revelation of an extensive nonstate nuclear procurement network have presented new challenges to domestic and international safeguards. Over the last two decades, the IAEA has subsequently been transforming its safeguards system to address these issues.

The Scope and Limits of Implementing Safeguards. As the experience in Iraq suggested, IAEA safeguards have been criticized primarily because they had not realized objectives they were never designed to address. The limits of the agency's safeguards have of course been affected by the agency's organization and culture, but they are largely the result of the limited consensus among IAEA member states in the last thirty years. The agency carried out its members' mandate. Safeguards went as far as those states' limited Cold War consensus on nuclear energy and nuclear-weapon proliferation, along with limits on technologies, would allow. They were not intended to prevent diversion. Indeed, they were designed and administered to deal with only one path to nuclear weapons—that is, diversion to military purposes of material from declared peaceful nuclear activities. Safeguards can in principle deter and, should deterrence fail, detect the diversion of significant quantities of a nuclear-weapon-usable material. But the safeguards put forward in pre-NPT and then NPT authorities looked only upon the "correctness" of a declaration, not upon whether it provided a "complete" picture of the state's nuclear activities.

To state the most fundamental problem with INFCIRC/153-based safeguards, states were required to declare particular facilities (or even particular buildings at given facilities) as part of their civilian nuclear program—and therefore to make those facilities or buildings subject to monitoring and verification activities by the IAEA. However, because it was up to the state to decide what facilities the IAEA could monitor, the IAEA had no authority to carry out routine inspections at any buildings that were *not* declared by the state to be part of civilian nuclear program. As a result, "[T]he IAEA appeared virtually powerless to detect…clandestine activities, even those co-located with safeguarded facilities."[20]

This apparent powerlessness of the IAEA was not quite true, of course, because the IAEA did have the authority granted by INFCIRC/153 to carry out special inspections at suspected declared and undeclared nuclear facilities. However, the agency's board had determined that special inspections would be used only "rarely"—and therefore they were "virtually unused during the agency's 41-year history, and the agency [had] not authorized inspectors to probe for evidence of covert nuclear activities."[21] Thus, although on paper the IAEA had fairly expansive authorities to carry out intrusive inspections at clandestine facilities, "in practice," notes Matthew Bunn, INFCIRC/153 "created an environment in which inspectors were politically constrained to checking the declared information about declared material at agreed points of declared sites, and were strongly discouraged from inquiring into activities elsewhere at the declared sites or at other, undeclared sites."[22]

The expectations surrounding IAEA safeguards, which we now understand were not realistic, developed because of the uniqueness and effectiveness of

IAEA safeguards as they evolved over the preceding decades. IAEA safeguards are the original, and for some decades after their origin, they were the only, multilateral verification instrument. Because they represent a truly international approach, they have developed widespread support in the international community over the years, even after the problems uncovered in the wake of the Gulf War and subsequently. They demonstrated to the world that relatively intrusive onsite inspections could be manageable, not only theoretically but by building confidence in onsite inspections through the experience of states with safeguards that were cost-effective, politically acceptable, and technically workable. Nevertheless, it had become clear that the international safeguards system had significant deficiencies that needed to be corrected.

THE ADDITIONAL PROTOCOL AND EFFORTS TO STRENGTHEN SAFEGUARDS

Over the last two decades, the IAEA has been transforming its safeguards system to address, in part, the limits of its verification mandate and the burden of noncompliance issues, which have raised questions about the value and effectiveness of international safeguards. In this context, the IAEA is adopting a fundamentally new approach to implementing safeguards based on the strengthening measures developed in the 1990s and the lessons learned from Iraq, North Korea, Libya, and Iran. It is recognized that an effective, strengthened international safeguards system, with a strong focus on searching for undeclared nuclear materials and activities, is essential to provide confidence that shared nuclear technologies and expertise, as well as nuclear materials themselves, are not being diverted to weapon programs. "Completeness" as well as "correctness" was critical.

Central to the transformation is the Additional Protocol (AP), which is an important tool and needs to be universally accepted as the basis for safeguards and a condition for exports. Although most states with significant nuclear activities have now brought the Additional Protocol into force, there remain a significant number of states that have not yet ratified the protocol. The agency and member states are trying to remedy this situation, and the problem of the universality of comprehensive safeguards agreements as well.

Implementing the new measures in the Additional Protocol, and integrating them effectively with existing (INFCIRC/153) safeguards, remain works in progress. Fundamental to the new approach to IAEA safeguards is information acquisition, evaluation, and analysis, along with inspections. The new approach is designed to reshape the IAEA's safeguards regime "from a quantitative system focused on accounting for known quantities of materials and monitoring declared activities to a qualitative system aimed at gathering a comprehensive picture of a state's nuclear and nuclear-related activities, including all nuclear-related imports and exports."[23] The AP attempts to accomplish this goal by:

• expanding significantly the amount and type of information that states are required to provide to the IAEA, including "nuclear fuel cycle-related research and development activities work—not involving nuclear materials," and details on uranium and thorium mines;[24]

• increasing the number and types of facilities the IAEA is authorized to inspect, incorporating "pre-approved" access for "any location specified by the IAEA";

• improving the IAEA's capability to perform short notice inspections through expedited visa processes; and

• providing the IAEA with the authority to perform environmental sampling during inspections at declared and undeclared sites and authorizing the IAEA to utilize wide-area environmental sampling to help it detect clandestine facilities.[25]

The new IAEA system that is emerging is more flexible, and should be better suited than the old to allocating scarce resources to where they are needed most in countering proliferation risk. To deal with the growth in nuclear energy use, it is essential that this transformational international safeguards system be both credible and efficient.

There are, however, some ongoing shortcomings with the AP. First, the AP falls short of the universal adoption hoped for by its proponents. Although 127 countries have ratified the treaty (and an additional 19 have signed but not ratified) at the time of this writing, the AP has received a great deal of pushback from many nations.[26] A number of these countries argue that they will not accept any additional nonproliferation burdens, especially since the established nuclear-weapon states still retain their arsenals. Although a number of the countries that object have limited nuclear capabilities, some of the countries that are of the greatest proliferation concern—such as Iran and Syria—also have not ratified the AP, although Iran in the 2015 Joint Comprehensive Plan of Action has agreed to apply the AP's provisions conditionally.[27] As a result, the IAEA does not have expanded monitoring and verification authorities in these countries.[28] This problem was stated clearly in 2011 by Herman Nackaerts, deputy director-general of the IAEA at the time: "In those states without an Additional Protocol, the Agency is not in a position to fulfill its obligation to confirm that all nuclear material is in peaceful activities and that there is no undeclared nuclear material and activities in those countries. You only have to look at Iran and Syria to see how the lack of an Additional Protocol is severely restricting [the IAEA's] ability to look beyond declared facilities and activities."[29]

Moreover, there are significant limits to the IAEA's monitoring and verification capabilities, even in those countries that have ratified the AP. Because the AP provides for IAEA inspectors to have unrestricted "complementary access" at only undeclared buildings *at declared nuclear sites*, the IAEA's strengthened authorities, especially outside of such sites, fall far short of the "anytime, any-place" standard often cited. A 2006 GAO report highlighted the ongoing limitations of IAEA oversight, even with the strengthened authorities established by the AP, arguing that "[t]he IAEA faces a number of limitations that impact its ability to draw conclusions—with absolute assurance—about whether a country is developing a clandestine nuclear program. For example, the IAEA does not have unfettered inspection rights and cannot make visits to suspected sites anywhere at any time."[30] As a result, the GAO concludes, even under the AP, "a determined country can still conceal a nuclear weapons program."[31]

These limits are exacerbated by the fact that the agency does not fully use all of its previous authorities, especially special inspections—which are actually more intrusive than those authorities granted by the AP. In the same 2011 speech quoted above, Hermann Nackaerts underscores the effect of IAEA's largely self-imposed restrictions on using these special inspections:

> The problem is that, over the years, some of these provisions have been interpreted in too narrow a manner, or neglected altogether. An obvious example is "special inspections." The agency may conduct these, inter alia, if the state's explanation and information gained from routine and ad hoc inspections are inadequate. I believe we should now be less wary of deploying this verification tool. It is also important to look with a pair of fresh eyes at the way historically we have implemented some of the other measures contained in the safeguards agreements and whether some of the tools at our disposal have not been fully utilized.[32]

Furthermore, the international verification community also possesses limited technological tools to address such issues as detection of undeclared facilities/activities, especially related to enrichment, bulk handling facilities, and so forth. A victim of oversell in the past, the IAEA along with key member states must avoid creating unduly high expectations in the future. Improvements are being made, but there will always be theoretical and practical limits to the pursuit of this and other forms of verification.

Biological Weapon Verification Mechanisms

Unlike the IAEA safeguards system (including the safeguards system that predated the NPT), there are no verification provisions of the Biological Weapons Convention (BWC). At the time of the negotiation of the treaty in the early 1970s, biological weapons were viewed as having at best only limited military utility, and it was believed that a complete ban on these weapons (unlike the system created by the NPT for nuclear weapons), would be more difficult to verify.[33] Over time, however, biological weapons have come to be viewed as increasingly attractive to certain states, owing in part to advances in biological sciences and lower technical hurdles in comparison to nuclear weapons. In the decades following the BWC's entrance into force, a number of countries have been suspected or proved to have clandestine biological-weapon programs in violation of the treaty.[34]

Although the BWC does establish an international norm against biological weapons—an accomplishment that should not be dismissed—there are significant shortcomings with the convention. The BWC "lacks an implementing body, a verification protocol, an ability to investigate alleged violations, universality…, and industry support."[35] In particular, without any verification mechanisms, it cannot by itself provide any confidence that a state is not violating its prohibitions. According to the terms of the BWC, state parties to the treaty may lodge a complaint with the UN Security Council if they believe that another member has violated the treaty, but this mechanism has never been invoked.[36]

EFFORTS TO STRENGTHEN THE BWC

Over the years, there have been some efforts to strengthen the BWC, most notably in the context of the review conferences held roughly every five years. The biggest push to strengthen the BWC occurred in the lead-up to the fifth review conference, held in December 2001. A number of countries attempted to model a strengthened BWC on the significantly expanded authorities granted to the IAEA by the Additional Protocol. It was believed, and argued directly by many countries, that if it was possible to enhance the monitoring and verification authorities of the IAEA, it would also be possible achieve similar milestones with the BWC.

However, the United States rejected the draft protocol to strengthen the verification mechanisms of the BWC during the fifth review conference, arguing that such steps would be cost prohibitive, unacceptably intrusive—and probably ineffective anyway.[37] In a statement to the Ad Hoc Group of BWC member states on July 25, 2001, U.S. ambassador Donald Mahley presented the Bush administration's case against a BWC protocol.[38] The administration presented three main arguments:

- *The protocol would be unable to uncover illicit activities.* The Bush administration argued that there are too many facilities that could potentially produce BW agents, and BW materials would be too easy to conceal. As Mahley argued: "[O]ur assessment of the range of potentially relevant facilities...indicates that they number, at least in the case of the United States, in the thousands, if not the tens of thousands. In addition, their number and locations change on an irregular but frequent basis."[39] It would be difficult even to catalog all the relevant facilities for declaration, let alone obtain adequate inventories of relevant biological materials or precursors. As a result, the protocol would be unable to identify illicit programs or diverted materials and would therefore fail to meet its key objective of deterring states from embarking on clandestine BW programs.

- *The protocol would be cost prohibitive.* Given the extensive number of facilities that would need to be inspected, this regime would require massive manpower and expertise. "Almost any facility that does biological work of any magnitude possesses the capability, under some parameters, of being diverted to biological weapons work." Visiting even a set of those facilities routinely "would require an international organization of the size and possession of rare skills among its employees" that no member state "would be willing to contemplate."[40]

- *The protocol would be unacceptably intrusive.* The protocol would be unable to protect "proprietary or national security information," and the regular and intrusive inspections would therefore "actually risk damage to innocent declared facilities." Given the importance of protecting proprietary information in the life sciences community (including, for example, in the pharmaceutical industry), the prospect of industrial espionage is a serious one—and the protocol would be unable to provide "no firm assurance proprietary information could not be inferred from what was seen by inspectors."[41] Further, the administration argued, the protocol could inhibit the U.S. biodefense program, which is intended to develop the ability to "protect against those who would violate the norm of abolishing biological weapons—by revealing sensitive information or even by repeatedly delaying the biodefense program through repeated accusations and inspections.[42]

The administration summarized its position by concluding that "after extensive analysis, we were forced to conclude that the mechanisms envisioned for the Protocol would not achieve their objectives, that no modification of them would allow them to achieve their objectives, and that trying to do so would simply raise the risk to legitimate United States activities."[43]

The Bush administration's rejection of the draft proposal effectively killed the initiative to strengthen BW monitoring and verification via an additional protocol to the BWC. Some analysts have argued that there may be other ways to strengthen the BWC's verification mechanisms in more indirect ways—for example, by tying the BWC more directly to the Chemical Weapons Convention (CWC), which has much more stringent verification mechanisms.[44] However, it seems unlikely that there will be an expansion of BW monitoring and verification anytime soon.

RECENT BIOSECURITY INITIATIVES

There is a global interest in pursuing new approaches to biosecurity, following the collapse of the draft BWC protocol. The Obama administration has lauded the BWC as the premier international forum for discussing biosecurity issues and proposed various biosecurity initiatives.

Despite its interest in new biosecurity measures, it has not opted to pursue a protocol to strengthen the verification authorities of the BWC.[45] Their primary justification for this position is reportedly the same as that of the Bush administration: compliance with the BWC would be too difficult to verify.[46] Ellen Tauscher, U.S. undersecretary of state for arms control and international security, explained the administration's position in a 2009 address to the states parties to the BWC: "It is extraordinarily difficult to verify compliance. The ease with which a biological-weapon program could be disguised within legitimate activities and the rapid advances in biological research make it very difficult to detect violations. We believe that a protocol would not be able to keep pace with the rapidly changing nature of the biological threat."[47]

The Obama administration's position on BW threats does differ from that of the Bush administration in important ways. Perhaps most fundamentally, the Obama administration's 2009 *National Strategy for Countering Biological Threats* places a greater emphasis on bioterrorism (carried out by substate actors), rather than biological warfare (carried out by states).[48] As part of their new approach, the Obama administration has emphasized the importance of getting the life sciences community (including doctors, biologists, and the pharmaceutical industry) involved in preventing BW development and use. To begin with, the life sciences community "and its associated infrastructure of high biocontainment (biosafety level 3 and 4) laboratories and pathogen collections, represents a key source of expertise, information, and material that could be used in a bioterrorist attack."[49] As such, this industry could be not only a potential source of trained bioterrorists but also a source of BW materials or production equipment. As one study argued: "[T]he United States should be less concerned that terrorists will become biologists and far more concerned that biologists will become terrorists."[50] By actively engaging the life sciences community—and especially by building strong ties between this community and local and international law enforcement entities, first responders, and the like—the United States could more effectively prevent, deter, detect, or respond to biological terrorism.[51]

As noted, this approach does appear to place a greater emphasis on biological terrorism—especially carried out by domestically grown terrorists—rather than state-led biological warfare or state-sponsored BW terrorism. Considering the number of states that are suspected of having at least rudimentary BW programs, state BW proliferation is surely still an important issue.[52] It is possible, however, that the involvement of life sciences community, especially leaders in the pharmaceutical industry (or "Big Pharma," as it is often collectively called), could potentially help shape a state's desire or ability to proliferate. Not only does Big Pharma control a great deal of the technical expertise and materials that would be necessary for a dedicated BW program, but this industry may also be able to apply leverage by refusing to fund, sell, or produce their products in suspected proliferating states. Because these companies work at the cutting edge of technology, they possess significant leverage for controlling and policing these technologies—and therefore could go a long way in eliminating the worst of the threats. In order for the industry to shoulder these responsibilities, however, it has to recognize that the existence of covert BW programs is not in its economic interest.

As suggested, the broad lines of the Obama administration's approach have been pursued by other governments as well as academics and other nongovernmental organizations. They probably constitute the only reasonable path ahead at this time. In the end, however, because the BWC lacks realistic or effective mechanisms for monitoring and verification, the effectiveness of this treaty will necessarily be constrained in fundamental ways.

The Chemical Weapons Convention and the OPCW

Unlike the BWC, the CWC does have a verification regime.[53] The OPCW is authorized to carry out routine inspections of all declared chemical-weapon production facilities and monitors the destruction of declared chemical-weapon stockpiles by member states. Because many toxic chemicals and precursor agents for chemical weapons have civilian uses, the OPCW also has the authority to inspect commercial industrial production facilities.[54]

The CWC's verification system is based on three "schedules," or lists of toxic chemicals and precursors that have been developed for military purposes. Schedule 1 chemicals and precursors are rarely used for peaceful purposes and may not be retained except in small quantities for research, medical, pharmaceutical, or defensive use. Schedule 2 chemicals and precursors are toxic chemicals that are produced only in small quantities for commercial or other peaceful purposes. Schedule 3 chemicals and precursors are usually produced in large quantities for commercial or other peaceful purposes but could be stockpiled as chemical weapons.[55] Facilities that produce "scheduled" chemicals at higher than specified thresholds must be declared and routinely inspected. Facilities producing more toxic chemicals and precursors are to be scrutinized more closely than those producing less toxic chemicals.[56]

The CWC also includes provisions for "challenge inspections," which can be requested by any state-party to the convention if it has doubts about another state's compliance. As the OPCW indicates, "[U]nder the CWC's 'challenge inspection' procedure, States Parties have committed themselves to the principle of 'any time, anywhere' inspections with no right of refusal."[57] The OPCW undertakes these inspections only upon request of another member state, after verification of the presented proof. In order to avoid misuse, a majority of two-thirds of the OPCW Executive Council can block a challenge inspection request.[58]

These authorities are significant—and in fact are more extensive than those granted to the IAEA, even under the expanded authorities of the AP. However, there are ongoing challenges that pose significant challenges to the CW monitoring and verification regime.

THE DUAL USE PROBLEM

One of the most serious challenges to CW monitoring and verification is the "dual-use" nature of many chemicals and production facilities. Although many chemical production facilities can, and are, used for entirely civilian purposes, these same facilities could potentially be used to produce chemical weapons (or a combination of civilian- and military-use chemicals). It is for precisely this reason that the OPCW is granted extensive authorities to conduct routine and challenge inspections at both declared chemical-weapon facilities and industrial production facilities.

Despite these authorities, however, "at present, the OPCW inspectorate devotes a disproportionate share of its efforts to monitoring the destruction of declared chemical weapons stockpiles."[59] The OPCW has fully inspected these declared chemical-weapon facilities, but to date it has paid comparatively little attention to dual-use facilities and has underutilized such techniques as sampling and onsite analysis (often for proprietary concerns by member states).[60] One of the primary reasons for this is that the OPCW requires full-time monitoring of the chemical-weapon facilities during the CW destruction process—which necessitates an extensive allocation of manpower and resources to the task. As Jonathan Tucker argues, a more effective utilization of remote monitoring of CW destruction would allow the OPCW to expand its monitoring of dual-use facilities.[61]

ADVANCES IN CW PRODUCTION TECHNOLOGIES

Recent advances in chemical production technologies pose new, and particularly difficult, challenges for CW verification regimes. For example, the creation of smaller, multipurpose facilities could enable states to develop CW at undeclared facilities that are much harder to detect. Moreover, equipment at multipurpose facilities could enable chemical plants to shift quickly from producing one agent to another—producing a quick run of chemical weapons amid its more regular production of civilian chemicals. Such techniques would make a state's chemical-weapon production extremely difficult to detect, even in the event of random or challenge inspections, should they ever be used.

Alternatively, a state could utilize "hundreds of small 'microreactors' . . . to synthesize large volumes of chemicals in a small space, minimizing the traditional signatures associated with chemical warfare agent production."[62] As Tucker notes, "Microreactors also offer higher synthetic yields with fewer emissions of tell-tale byproducts and may permit the use of unusual reaction pathways that are not feasible with conventional reactors."[63]

Perhaps even more troubling, advances in chemical production could allow states to develop new types of chemicals that are not currently banned by the CWC. For example, Schedule 1 agents include only those chemicals (and precursors) that had been known to be weaponized or stockpiled as a chemical weapon.[64] As Tucker notes, "[S]everal next generation agents and precursors not listed on the schedules pose significant risks to the treaty and hence warrant greater attention."[65] Although the CWC negotiators devised an expedited process for amending the schedules to incorporate new toxic chemicals and precursors, member states have so far declined to use it.

In sum, these recent technical advances have potentially enabled states to produce new (and unbanned) chemical weapons agents in small or multipurpose facilities that are therefore extremely difficult to detect, even under the most advantageous of circumstances.

CONCEALMENT AND PROHIBITIVE COSTS

The new types of production facilities, combined with the ability to produce new chemical weapons in small, easily concealable facilities, pose serious challenges to effective monitoring and verification. Although there have always been risks that states would be able to conceal CW facilities, the new technologies have made the problem of concealment even more of a challenge.

Even in the most optimistic cases, if verification organizations like the OPCW were to attempt to conduct continual monitoring and verification activities at declared and potential CW production facilities, to give confidence that states were not carrying out covert CW programs, the organizations would quickly encounter severe cost over-runs and personnel shortages. In short, the extensive and extremely intrusive verification activities necessary for reasonable levels of confidence would also likely be cost prohibitive.

RANDOM AND CHALLENGE INSPECTIONS

These issues could, at least in part, be addressed by more extensive use of random, short-notice inspections and the use of challenge inspections. Random, short-notice inspections "could be one of the more effective options available to the OPCW in routinely monitoring compliance."[66] By utilizing the element of surprise, such inspections could reduce the costs of extensive, continual monitoring of declared sites.[67] These methods, however, have not been effectively used.

Challenge inspections would similarly utilize the element of surprise and could be effective in deterring undeclared activities. To date, however, the OPCW has undertaken no challenge inspections, despite the fact that such inspections would be one of the only mechanisms for detecting an undeclared chemical weapon facility. As Jonathan Tucker notes, "[T]he United States has publicly accused China, Iran, Russia, and Sudan of violating the CWC, yet it has not provided specific evidence nor pursued these allegations through challenge inspections, thereby weakening the treaty."[68] Given the advances in chemical production technologies, Tucker argues, challenge inspections should be routinely utilized as part of the CWC verification, but "the longer the challenge mechanism remains unused, the higher the political hurdle to using it will become."[69]

Ad Hoc Verification Regimes

Ad hoc verification mechanisms can also be established to pursue more narrowly focused objectives or to carry out verification activities in exceptional cases, especially when clandestine WMD programs have been discovered.[70] Prominent examples of such ad hoc verification regimes—and ones that receive significant attention in this book—are UNSCOM and its successor, the UN Monitoring, Verification and Inspection Commission (UNMOVIC), which were established to verify the dismantlement of Iraq's WMD programs, and the British and U.S. teams that were sent to Libya in 2003 to verify and dismantle that country's WMD programs after Libyan strongman Muammar Qadhafi publicly renounced these programs.[71]

UNSCOM AND UNMOVIC

In April 1991, after the conclusion of the Gulf War, the UN Security Council (UNSC) adopted Security Council Resolution (SCR) 687, which established a conditional cease-fire agreement with Iraq. The resolution required Iraq to "unconditionally accept the destruction, removal, or rendering harmless, under international supervision" of its WMD and ballistic missiles with a range greater than 150 kilometers.[72] Resolution 687 mandated the formation of a special commission (UNSCOM) to supervise the dismantlement of these programs and designated that the IAEA would provide assistance in the nuclear area.[73]

Although Resolution 687 had foreseen about forty-five days for the work on "destruction, removal and rendering harmless" of proscribed materials and equipment, the verification process quickly encountered difficulties. Iraq began pursuing a policy of systematic obstruction of the inspection process, including deceptive reporting and concealment of its proscribed programs. What originally had been conceived of as a straightforward verification of disarmament became a seven-year game of cat-and-mouse.[74]

Eventually, in December 1998, UNSCOM's executive director, Richard Butler, reported to the UNSC that UNSCOM was unable "to give the Council the assurances it requires with respect to Iraq's prohibited weapons programmes," owing to lack of Iraqi cooperation.[75] Shortly after Butler gave this report, the United States and Great Britain called for the removal of UNSCOM and IAEA inspectors from Iraq and initiated Operation Desert Fox, which was intended to destroy all suspected Iraqi military facilities.

UNSCOM never returned to Iraq and was disbanded in 1999, though a successor verification and inspection regime, UNMOVIC, was created to take its place. In late 2002, faced with the prospect of major military action and a removal from power, Saddam Hussein agreed to allow UNMOVIC and IAEA inspectors back into Iraq. Between November 25, 2002, and March 17, 2003, these organizations conducted an intensive set of inspections in Iraq, with the prospect of war looming in the background. IAEA director-general Mohamed ElBaradei and UNMOVIC executive chairman Hans Blix reported their findings to the United Nations and presented evidence of some Iraqi cooperation, but not the "proactive" support that would provide confidence that Iraq had completely renounced its proscribed weapon programs.[76] Blix also noted numerous questions of substance that had not been sufficiently answered. In the end, the IAEA and UNMOVIC inspectors were removed and the combat stage of Operation Iraqi Freedom began on March 19, 2003.

AD HOC VERIFICATION IN LIBYA

On December 19, 2003, Colonel Qadhafi publicly renounced weapons of mass destruction and announced that Libya had agreed "immediately and unconditionally" to "disclose and dismantle" all of Libya's weapons of mass destruction programs and long-range ballistic missile programs. Qadhafi also agreed to allow international weapons inspectors to verify this dismantlement process.[77] Beginning in late 2003 and through much of 2004, British and U.S.-led teams removed highly sensitive stockpiles and equipment that were part of Libya's WMD and missile programs and conducted verification activities "to better understand the extent of those programs, and the procurement work supporting them."[78] The IAEA and the OPCW were also quickly brought in to assist in the verification of Libya's nuclear- and chemical-weapon programs.

Libya was generally seen to be cooperative in the disarmament and verification processes and, by September 2004, U.S. assistant secretary of state Paula DeSutter announced to Congress that the process was "largely complete"—that the verification teams had "verified with *reasonable* certainty that Libya has eliminated, or has set in place the elimination of all its WMD and MTCR-class missile programs."[79] As we will see in Chapter 4, however, this positive assessment of Libya's disarmament was thrown into some doubt after the 2011 discovery of an undeclared stockpile of mustard agent and associated delivery vehicles, following the toppling of the Qadhafi regime.

Transparency

Transparency, as openness, is not a new concept. Transparency measures are designed or intended to increase confidence or, possibly, to provide warnings through access to information. The development of transparency measures designed to promote openness and confidence in the security realm has long been held as desirable. Although pursued in support of arms control during the Cold War, and modestly furthered in arms accords relating to such provisions as data exchanges, and noninterference with national technical means (NTM), the climate of secrecy in the Soviet Union did not allow major breakthroughs until the mid-1980s. Since that time, amid dramatic changes in the international security environment, the scope and prospects of transparency have broadened, going beyond classical arms control, and appear to be moving toward global security issues, in part because of growing concerns about the security implications of WMD proliferation.

The benefits or incentives for greater transparency are reasonably clear. Transparency can provide confidence that a state is behaving in a certain fashion, or that its activities are in conformance with certain agreements, standards, and norms. In this context, transparency measures presumably can increase confidence in a state's compliance with treaty obligations, especially in political circumstances where other means of reducing suspicions (such as verification measures) are not politically or technically feasible, although poorly crafted measures may not do so at all. And, of course, transparency measures may reveal suspicious behavior within or outside the scope of a treaty's provisions that may affect judgments on verification. But transparency measures can also serve verification by making verification efforts more effective, more efficient, and, perhaps, easier and less expensive to implement.

The risks or impediments to transparency are less well understood, but understanding them is vital to analysis of the desirability of general and specific transparency measures. First, it must be recognized that different states may have very different levels of openness, as a result of cultural, economic, legal, and political factors. This asymmetry may make it difficult to develop effective, mutually beneficial transparency measures. In practice, it limits the prospects of transparency, especially for the countries of the world that are least open. It should also be noted that open societies are capable of keeping secrets as well, and devote considerable energies to doing so. In this context, national security considerations, including the protection of classified or sensitive information, are important and legitimate but can be deemed impediments to transparency measures.

The misuse of transparency to foster disinformation or "spoofing" through incomplete or false information or to improve, for example, the targeting of an adversary based on exchanged information, is a concern that must be addressed. The prospect of proliferation-relevant information being compromised by transparency measures is another problem, one in which national security and international agreements may both argue against certain types of measures. In addition to these concrete national security concerns, the prospect of transparency providing a false sense of security should not be dismissed.

Furthermore, although technological developments have largely been an enabler of transparency, some technologies, including those involving control and accountancy of nuclear materials, have inherent opacities. The properties of these technologies include their statistical nature (measurement uncertainties), the effects of which may accumulate over time and are often misunderstood. These and other uncertainties associated with technological measurements can pose problems for transparency. Uncertainties can often be calculated, but in some cases they are so significant that they may prevent, or reduce the value of, proposed transparency measures, or create mistrust even among the very constituencies the technologies are designed to assist.

While the debate over the risks and benefits of transparency continues to be engaged, trends toward global transparency are occurring. The question is whether these trends have the power to transform the old debate entirely or only to shift its specific terms. At one level, a new openness is being reinforced by transformative political and technological trends. Political developments such as democratization are opening once closed societies. Technology developments, including the information revolution and the surge in commercial surveillance technologies, are also creating a new openness, even in more closed societies. These trends, political and technological, are coalescing to produce a world in which transparency is increasing—irrespective of any transparency initiatives, negotiations, or agreements.

The debate raised over the use of open-source data, crowdsourcing, and social media to enhance monitoring and verification is an extension of the old debate on transparency, and it is not clear that these approaches will change the terms of the debate. The use of open-source data, especially from commercial satellite imagery, has been increasingly used to provide useful information about suspected programs and facilities in recent years.[80] It has also been argued that crowdsourcing could prove useful for treaty verification, both by utilizing "the efforts of citizens to collect and transmit information that is relevant for verification" and by encouraging "people to take public data (satellite imagery, social media posts, etc.) and look for patterns or signals that might be informative about treaty violations or compliance."[81] Although these methods and technologies could provide important supplements to traditional monitoring and verification approaches, this subject is comparatively new, and the potential negatives—from "spoofing," to using crowdsourcing to muddy debates or spread false information—could set back the prospects for decisions on noncompliance at various levels—bilaterally, regionally, and internationally—and by doing so, prevent effective responses.

A key question is the extent to which such transparency can be relied upon in a treaty context, perhaps in place of traditional verification measures. Verification regimes, inspections, and monitoring activities of a variety of types are designed to provide confirmation of compliance. This is an active enterprise that seeks to elicit information useful for drawing conclusions about compliance.

The inherent openness of a society can be a valuable aid in understanding states' actions, and social media provides a conduit through which civil society can broadcast widely. But this is a passive exercise with no guarantee that a concerned and observant citizen will make use of this vehicle. There can be (and certainly have been) instances in which revelations provide valuable information related to verification objectives. Are these to be expected over time? To what extent can and should such events be counted on?

Third-party Information

As noted above, third-party information, including national-level intelligence, NTM, is an important tool for both nuclear- and chemical-verification processes.[82] Indeed, it has proved to be essential in such "difficult cases" as North Korea, Iran, and Syria, where the countries were unwilling to cooperate with inspectors from international verifying organizations. However, there are potential downsides to the use of such information, including potential misinformation by states providing information, politically motivated disputes over the reliability of this information, and risks that a state will reveal its sources and methods when it presents its intelligence findings to verifying organizations.[83]

NATIONAL TECHNICAL MEANS

National intelligence can help guide verification by providing warning of proscribed activities and therefore helping international verifying organizations identify facilities for short-notice (that is, special or challenge) inspections: "For the short-notice approach to have any degree of success it would need to be augmented by supplemental information, presumably supplied by CWC member states," of which NTM would be the primary source of external information.[84]

After the revelations in Iraq following the 1991 Gulf War, the IAEA director-general at that time, Hans Blix, proposed a significant departure from previous safeguards arrangements, arguing for a strengthening of nuclear verification inspections by "(a) incorporating intelligence data supplied by member nations' NTM on possible nonpermitted activities, (b) having free access to any location and wider rights of unannounced inspections, and (c) having the backing of the UN Security Council."[85] The expanded use of NTM significantly bolstered the capabilities of UNSCOM and the IAEA during the inspections in Iraq. "The ability of the Special Commission to obtain as much evidence as it did regarding Iraqi noncompliance with the NPT and the extent and depth of its nuclear-weapon program was greatly assisted by intelligence information provided by the Gulf War coalition."[86] The effective use of NTM enhanced their ability to identify suspected facilities for inspection and to cross-check statements by Iraqi officials.

PROBLEMS WITH RELIANCE ON NTM

Reliance by international monitoring and verification regimes on NTM can create difficulties, however. UNSCOM, for example, became viewed by many as merely a tool of the United States (this was certainly Iraq's argument), in part because of its heavy reliance on U.S. intelligence. This issue becomes especially problematic when coupled with the loss of credibility of U.S. intelligence networks after the predicted stockpiles of weapons of mass destruction were not found in Iraq. For this reason, despite its utility, the IAEA and OPCW may be less likely to rely substantially on U.S. intelligence than they have been in the past.

In the case of the CWC, NTM have been underutilized in part because member states have been reluctant to bring forward evidence from NTM indicating noncompliance by other states. There are several reasons for this:

• Potential exposure of sources and methods. As Ken Apt correctly states, "For all practical purposes, then, providing full intelligence information to the OPCW would be a *de facto* declassification of that information. Member states contemplating providing intelligence information to the OPCW would therefore have to evaluate the resulting loss to national security against the possible constructive uses of the information."[87]

• Loss of credibility if proscribed activities are not located at particular sites identified, not found in the amounts predicted, or not the specific types of agents located. This could be owing to poor timing, inadequate procedures, or incorrect identification of a specific facility (even if proscribed activities are occurring at a different nondeclared site). Nevertheless, states may be unwilling to risk their credibility—especially after the events in Iraq.

• The dual-use nature of specific technologies, which could produce ambiguous results.

• Potential revenge by other states, introducing frivolous accusations in response to an accusation.

In the case of the BWC, in part because there is currently no verification body that could act on intelligence shared by member states, NTM has played little role in verification. As noted above, the BWC does contain provisions permitting state parties to lodge a complaint with the UN Security Council if they believe that another member has violated the treaty.[88] This provision has never been invoked, however, for some of the same reasons that states have not attempted to call for challenge inspections to verify compliance with the CWC: potentially revealing their sources and methods, a potential lack of support in the UN Security Council, ambiguous results, and the like.

CULTURAL PROBLEMS

There has also been a reluctance to share information, including intelligence acquired through NTM, owing to cultures of specific agencies. At times, there have been differences of opinion between verifying organizations and certain states, despite fairly clear evidence provided by that state's intelligence. For example, in the case of Iran, rather than strictly carrying out the IAEA's "nondiplomatic, nonpolitical function dictated by the agency's statute," former IAEA director-general Mohamed ElBaradei "sought to play a more political role and in doing so, undercut not only the agency's credibility, but also the requirements of the Security Council and the two-track strategy of the United States, EU-3, China, and Russia."[89] Indeed, ElBaradei all but admitted in a 2010 interview with Jack Shenker of the *Guardian* that he had downplayed the intelligence on Iran (acquired both by the United States and the IAEA itself) because he did not want a repeat of the events that had led to the war in Iraq.[90] The current director-general, Yukiya Amano, has proven to be more willing to take tough stands, especially on Iran and Syria. It is possible, or even significantly more likely, that the IAEA will be willing to enhance intelligence sharing as it works to strengthen its safeguards capabilities.

The OPCW has long been criticized for its unwillingness to share information, and these concerns remain relevant today.[91] This lack of transparency not only makes it difficult for nongovernmental organizations and the media to play their customary roles as "watchdogs" but also creates a vicious circle that undercuts the effectiveness of the monitoring and verification activities of the OPCW.[92] As well, this behavior deprives member states of critical information that may be useful to their own national assessments. Greater efforts to enhance information sharing could benefit both sides—and better serve the interests of international security as a whole.

Conclusion

For all of the issues with current WMD monitoring and verification regimes, it is not possible to imagine a better situation if they did not exist. They are essential to global efforts to control WMD, but they are not a panacea. It will be necessary to continue to work to strengthen the authorities and capabilities of these regimes, but also to encourage the regimes to fully implement those authorities that they currently possess. If these efforts are successful, they can go a long way toward reducing some of the intrinsic ambiguity of monitoring and verification efforts, though it will never be possible to eliminate ambiguity altogether.

2

South Africa

On March 24, 1993, South African president F. W. de Klerk made a surprise announcement. South Africa had developed "a limited deterrent capability" consisting of six gun-design, uranium-fueled nuclear weapons and a partially completed seventh weapon.[1] De Klerk stated that the decision had been made to dismantle the nuclear weapons early in 1990 and that the weapons, hardware, and design information had all been destroyed by the time South Africa had signed the Nuclear Nonproliferation Treaty (NPT) on July 10, 1991.[2]

This announcement was shocking, not so much because the country had not been suspected of having a covert nuclear-weapon program. It had.[3] Nor was it particularly shocking that South Africa had been a member of the NPT for more than a year and a half, and had undergone numerous inspections by the International Atomic Energy Agency (IAEA), without disclosing the weapon program or having elements of the program discovered by the IAEA. The South Africans, at least, argued that they were under no technical obligation to disclose a program that had been dismantled prior to joining the NPT—and the inspection authorities and capabilities of the IAEA were insufficient to discover signs of a weapon program that a country wanted to keep hidden.[4]

As Mitchell Reiss notes, what was shocking about de Klerk's announcement was that, after developing an operational nuclear arsenal, South Africa had decided, voluntarily and unilaterally, to dismantle it, along with much of the supporting nuclear weapons infrastructure.[5] South Africa thus became the first—and, to date, the only—case of "rollback" of an operational nuclear arsenal.[6] After the declaration the IAEA was given full access to all of South Africa's nuclear sites, and the IAEA determined that "there were no indications to suggest that the initial inventory [provided by South Africa] is incomplete or that the South African nuclear weapons programme had not been completely terminated and dismantled."[7]

In addition to its nuclear weapons, South Africa's apartheid regime had also initiated a chemical- and biological-weapon (CBW) program, code-named Project Coast, in 1981. This program was directed by Dr. Wouter Basson until it was officially ended in 1995.[8] By then, the country's stockpiles of deadly agents had reportedly been destroyed, the CBW programs dismantled, and all technical documents relating to these programs transferred to CD-ROMS that were carefully locked away.

Because of these nonproliferation successes, the South African case is often referenced as a potential model for disarmament—including for such difficult regions as Northeast Asia and the Middle East.[9] For example, the South African case is often used as an example of a "no fault" disarmament that could potentially also be employed in these and other cases. In such an arrangement, if these countries were to dismantle their programs and allow IAEA inspectors uninhibited access to conduct a thorough verification, the international community (including the UN Security Council) would agree not to enact any punishments.[10]

Nevertheless, there are sharp limitations on the extent to which the South African case can be applied as a model for other countries to follow. The South African case was a clear success for nonproliferation, and for the IAEA in particular. However, there remain unanswered, and likely unanswerable, questions about South Africa's rollback of its weapons of mass destruction (WMD) programs—especially relating to the verification process. Because South Africa undertook the elimination process unilaterally and invited the IAEA in only after that process was completed, despite the extraordinary work by the agency a great deal of potential information was lost to international inspectors. The impact of this reality may be debatable in the South African case. However, such a loss could be consequential, especially in countries with large, complex, and long-running programs, where baselining is incredibly difficult. As we will see, even more severe questions remain about the country's rollback of its CBW programs, since there was no formal verification of the CBW disarmament.

Thus, although certain aspects of South Africa's rollback may indeed provide useful lessons to other cases, not all of the lessons are positive. Certainly, it would be difficult to apply many of the lessons from the South African case to monitoring and verification regimes. It is unlikely that claims by any of the "difficult cases," including Iran and North Korea, that they had unilaterally renounced and dismantled their nuclear programs would be believed—or that the subsequent verification would yield sufficient levels of certainty that those countries had in fact abandoned their programs. Indeed, as we will see, unanswered questions about South Africa's nuclear program remain to this day.[11]

In this chapter, we will examine the South African case, including Pretoria's decision to pursue WMD, its subsequent disarmament, and the challenges for monitoring and verification that are revealed by this case. In its analysis, the chapter will explore three primary questions:

• What were the reasons for South Africa's initiation and subsequent rollback of its WMD programs?

• What are the parameters for "success" in cases of monitoring and verification of WMD rollback—and can the South African case be considered such a success?

• Can the South African case be applied to other cases of nuclear rollback?

Although the chapter will examine South Africa's nuclear-, chemical-, and biological-weapon programs, it will place the greatest emphasis on the nuclear program. Not only did that program make further advances on more destructive weapons, but it is also the program that has received the most attention internationally—in part because it has frequently been held up as a model of verifiable nuclear disarmament. As we will argue, however, even more questions arise with the limited verification undertaken of South Africa's CBW dismantlement than with the more systematic verification efforts in the nuclear realm.

South Africa's WMD Programs: An Overview

As noted, South Africa developed an operational nuclear arsenal and made significant advances in its CBW programs before its WMD rollback. The following discussion explains Pretoria's motivations for WMD acquisition and provides an overview of the WMD programs.

South Africa's Motivations for WMD Acquisition

South Africa is believed to have had several motivations for the development of WMD. In 1977, South Africa's Department of Defense published a white paper describing what government officials viewed as a "total onslaught" in virtually every area of society. These threats ranged from the growing presence of Soviet-backed insurgents in southern Africa, to the increasing isolation of the apartheid regime in the world, to significant and growing opposition domestically. In order to address these threats, Defense Minister P. W. Botha initiated a "total strategy" that included the development of advanced weapons, the capability for covert operations, and the widespread use of coercive state power.[12]

As President de Klerk stated in his March 1993, speech, a primary reason for the development of nuclear weapons was the South African regime's fear of "a Soviet expansionist threat in southern Africa."[13] Most directly, the toppling of the Portuguese-backed regimes in Southern Africa led to the independence of Mozambique and Angola. After Angola descended into a bloody civil war, South African forces intervened in a failed attempt to support forces fighting against the Soviet- and Cuban-backed Movimento Popular de Libertacao de Angola (MPLA). This intervention resulted in open hostilities between Pretoria and Angola's new government, and the eventual introduction of fifty thousand Cuban forces into Angola. In addition, a pro-Soviet, Marxist-Leninist government also took power in Mozambique, on South Africa's northeast border.[14] "Suddenly, South African leaders found themselves surrounded by communist forces, which were viewed as implacable and unscrupulous enemies. South African defense experts knew that the Soviet Union possessed nuclear, biological, and chemical (NBC) weapons."[15]

De Klerk also pointed to Pretoria's "relative isolation and the fact that it could not rely on outside assistance if attacked."[16] South Africa's apartheid regime was increasingly criticized internationally. By the late 1970s its membership on the UN General Assembly had been suspended, and in 1977 the UN had placed an arms embargo on the country following the Soviet discovery of underground nuclear test preparations. The United States had also withdrawn support for South Africa's intervention against the MPLA in Angola, despite its initial encouragement.[17] The country was also denied a seat on the International Atomic Energy Agency's board of governors, despite its being the most advanced nuclear country in Africa.[18]

Given these circumstances, a large part of the regime's justification for nuclear weapons was reportedly that a test of a nuclear weapon could force the United States to become engaged in a dispute with the Soviet Union or Soviet-backed forces.[19]

A primary justification for CBW was the reported discovery of potential preparations for chemical-weapon (CW) use by Cuban forces in Angola. After the South African military reportedly confiscated vehicles from Cuban soldiers, the military stated that it found that the vehicles were "fitted with air filters as well as with medical bags containing nerve gas antidotes and gas masks."[20] To defend against a potential CW attack, it was argued, the South African military would need to develop Soviet-style CBW programs in order to understand their capabilities, develop appropriate antidotes, and so forth. However, military discussions soon reportedly began considering the prospects for offensive use of CW as well. "As it became evident that an offensive CBW program was to be developed, discussions began concerning the possible uses for such a program." Magnus Malan, former South African Defence Force (SADF) chief of staff and defense minister from 1980 to 1991, reportedly proposed that "signs of a chemical warfare attack in Angola would force the Cuban and Angolan forces to don suits, which would cut combat effectiveness in half."[21]

It also appears that South Africa viewed its CBW program as a potential means for addressing the significant unrest within the country. On June 16, 1976, thousands of students from the African township of Soweto sparked a wave of rebellion that lasted into 1977. The unrest would continue until 1984, when the Township Uprising sparked the most sustained revolt in South Africa's history.[22] These uprisings "led the apartheid regime to search for ways, including the use of chemical agents, to control or incapacitate large groups of people."[23]

In reality, however, many of the regime's justifications for its WMD programs were tenuous at best. For starters, the prospect of a major attack of Soviet or Soviet-backed forces from the north appears unrealistic, despite the Soviet backing of rebel forces in Angola and Mozambique. Moreover, as Mitchell Reiss notes, a nuclear test would have been unlikely to draw the United States into a conflict with the Soviet Union unless an overarching strategic concern dominated. And if such an overarching strategic concern did exist that would justify a U.S. intervention, a nuclear test would have been irrelevant.[24]

There are also some questions about South Africa's justifications for its CBW programs. Although the captured Soviet-supplied vehicles in Angola did contain air filters and CW antidotes, this equipment reportedly "was standard issue and the allegations about communist CW usage were never actually verified."[25] It also does not appear that SADF troops had been outfitted with proper CW equipment or had received adequate training to defend against CW attacks—steps that certainly would have been taken if the potential CW attacks had been viewed as credible threats.[26] Nevertheless, despite these questions, Magnus Malan's argument that the SADF could have an operational advantage if its adversaries were forced to fight in chemical suits could still have carried some weight.[27] And, more troublingly, the ongoing interest in CBW for domestic use, especially for crowd control or assassination of "enemies of the state," reportedly does appear to have played a significant role in South Africa's development of CBW.[28]

South Africa's Nuclear Program

South Africa's nuclear program began in 1944 after the British government asked South Africa to conduct a survey of its uranium deposits. Within a few years, South Africa was regularly producing and exporting uranium, mainly in support of the nuclear-weapon programs of the United States and Great Britain. The country developed enrichment capabilities by July 1970, ostensibly to improve the value of its uranium exports, and reportedly made the formal decision to develop nuclear weapons a few years later.[29] As noted above, by the time the country decided to dismantle its nuclear-weapon program in the early 1990s, it had developed six gun-design, uranium-fueled nuclear weapons, and had partially completed a seventh.[30]

KEY FACILITIES

South Africa had long been involved with nuclear technology, including uranium enrichment for peaceful export. Because the country possesses very large uranium deposits, it created numerous facilities for mining and milling, as well as fuel fabrication. More recently, the country has expanded its civilian nuclear program and has built several research and light-water reactors for these purposes. However, at the time, South Africa's nuclear-weapon program consisted of a uranium enrichment capability, as well as several facilities for weapon design, fabrication, and testing.[31]

Uranium Enrichment Facilities: Y-Plant and Z-Plant. Before de Klerk called for the end of the nuclear-weapon program, South Africa's uranium production took place at two sites, the Y-Plant and the Z-Plant. The Y-Plant, located in Valindaba, was the country's first uranium enrichment plant and the only site believed to have produced highly enriched uranium (HEU), the fissile material reportedly used in South Africa's nuclear weapons.[32] The first uranium enrichment at the Y-Plant occurred in 1978, one year before South Africa's first nuclear weapon was created, and it produced enough HEU (enriched to 80 percent) after that for one nuclear weapon every eighteen months for the following ten years.[33] By 1989 the Y-Plant could produce around 100 kilograms of HEU annually, which is the equivalent of two crude nuclear devices per year. In 1987 South Africa also completed construction of a larger, semicommercial uranium enrichment plant, often referred to as the Z-Plant. Although initially suspected of being part of the nuclear-weapon program, this plant is believed to have produced only low-enriched uranium (LEU) prior to its closure in early 1995.[34]

Weapon-dedicated Facilities. Other facilities that were reportedly part of South Africa's nuclear-weapon program included the Circle Facilities (Advena), as well as those at Vastrap and Pelindaba.[35] The Circle Facilities, which were operated by the South African government's weapon agency, Armscor, were designated for the design, manufacture, and storage of nuclear weapons in the 1980s and the early 1990s. Vastrap, located in the Kalahari Desert, contained two nuclear test shafts. Pelindaba, which was an AEC facility, was primarily dedicated to making nuclear weapons. This facility reportedly contained a pulse reactor, a critical assembly facility, and machining facilities for uranium metal.[36] Despite having done some research on plutonium production and separation, South Africa's nuclear program relied on uranium enrichment and did not heavily focus on plutonium.[37]

WEAPONIZATION AND DELIVERY SYSTEMS

For the South African strategy of forcing the United States and other Western powers to intervene in a conflict with Soviet or Soviet-backed forces to be successful, Pretoria needed to develop a credible nuclear weapon. According to Armscor officials, if they were to show their nuclear devices to Western powers, "the device would have had to have been deliverable. If the nuclear devices were only test devices, the Western powers might not take South Africa's threat seriously enough to intervene on its behalf."[38]

By 1977 all the nonnuclear components for a gun-design weapon had been assembled, but the Y-Plant reportedly did not produce sufficient HEU for the weapon's core until November 1979.[39] The second weapon was assembled in April 1982, with an additional nuclear weapon added to the arsenal every year and a half until the program was halted in 1989.[40]

South Africa's early nuclear weapons were to be delivered by bomber.[41] The warhead designs were reportedly variations of a gun-design, similar to the U.S. weapon dropped on Hiroshima and with an estimated yield of 10 to 18 kilotons.[42] The first generation design for the bombs themselves was a simple airdrop variety that could be delivered by bomber. Some reports indicate, however, that newer weapons (beginning in 1987, with the third weapon) utilized a targetable "glide" design.[43] South African scientists had also reportedly conducted significant research on more advanced weapons, including "boosted" devices that would have yields of around 100 kilotons, implosion designs, and delivery by ballistic missiles. According to Armscor officials, they had planned to replace the seven gun-design weapons with upgraded weapons, deliverable by aircraft or possibly ballistic missiles, by the year 2000.[44]

Possible Nuclear Test. In July 1977, a Soviet Satellite passing over South Africa reportedly discovered the distinctive configuration of a nuclear test site.[45] Soviet officials quickly notified Washington that South Africa was preparing to test a nuclear weapon, and U.S. reconnaissance satellite provided imagery confirming that these preparations were underway.[46] After strong pressure from the United States and several Western European countries, however, South Africa abandoned the planned test and sealed the shafts.[47] In 1987, South African nuclear experts returned to the site, at the direction of the government, to inspect the shafts and ensure that they could be used rapidly if such orders were given. In order to conceal their activities, the workers constructed a metal building (which they called the "shade") on a concrete foundation over the shaft. Albright and others report that "the site was kept on standby until the end of the nuclear weapons program in 1989, at which point the shafts were sealed."[48]

On September 22, 1979, the U.S. Vela 6911 Satellite detected a double flash, characteristic of a nuclear detonation, over the Indian Ocean. A declassified U.S. document from the time reported that technical data and analysis suggested that it was an explosion of less than 3 kilotons, "produced by a nuclear device detonated in the atmosphere near the earth's surface."[49] The document considered the possibility that it was a South African, an Israeli, or a joint South African–Israeli test, finding that the arguments that South Africa had tested were "inconclusive."[50] However, it did report that "if a nuclear explosion occurred on that date, South Africa is the most likely candidate for responsibility."[51] At the time, South African officials strongly denied that their country was involved with the event. In 1997, however, the South African deputy foreign minister, Aziz Pahad, was reported to have confirmed that the flash was indeed a South African nuclear test, but his office subsequently denied the report.[52]

Project Coast: South Africa's CBW Program

South Africa maintained significant chemical- and biological-weapon programs until 1989 (despite having ratified the Biological Weapons Convention in 1975).[53] In 1981, South Africa's minister of defense, Constand Viljoen, approved plans for the establishment of Project Coast, and by 1982 two front companies had been created to spearhead the research and development of these agents. Delta G. Scientific would conduct research on chemical weapons, while the Roodeplaat Research Laboratories (RRL) would spearhead the country's efforts on biological weapons.[54] As Gould and Folb note, there were multiple purposes for Project Coast, including:

- development of chemical agents that could be used by security forces to control crowds;
- research into offensive and defensive chemical and biological warfare;
- development of offensive chemical and biological weapons for operational use;
- development of defensive training programs for troops; and
- development and manufacture of protective clothing.[55]

According to some reports, some U.S. officials described South Africa's program as the "second most sophisticated program next to the Soviets," though other assessments have downplayed how advanced the program really was.[56] Although the project does not appear to have developed a large-scale BW production capability or to have weaponized standard biological weapons agents, the program did reportedly develop and test several of such agents.[57] These reportedly included "all 45 local strains of anthrax bacteria, *Brucella maletensis*, all four types of *Clostridium botulinum*, cholera bacteria, and *Yersinia enterocolitica* and/or *Y. pestis*."[58]

Although many of these agents were apparently used mainly for defensive research, the South African regime reportedly made some headway in research and development of offensive agents as well. For example, it reportedly produced 20 tons of CR, a crowd control agent, half of which was used by the army to fill munitions.[59] There also appears to be significant evidence that toxic chemicals and pathogens were developed—and in some instances used—for the purposes of targeted killings or assassinations. As Jeffrey Bale reports, "There can be little doubt that several of these toxic materials, items, or devices were subsequently used to murder or sicken opponents of the apartheid regime."[60]

The RRL had also reportedly developed plans to build a large-scale production plant to develop anthrax for use either outside or inside the country. According to testimony of a former RRL scientist, those plans were nearly operationalized in 1985, but Project Coast directors ultimately decided not to fund the site, opting instead to use BW agents "in low-intensity regional skirmishes and assassinations" rather than on a more massive scale.[61] According to some reports, Project Coast also conducted more advanced genetic engineering research, including efforts to produce a "black bomb," which would weaken, kill, or reduce the fertility rates of blacks but not whites.[62] There is no evidence that these agents were ever developed, however, or that any real progress was made on such programs.

Renunciation and Dismantlement

As Frank Pabian notes, "Just as the strategic situation dramatically darkened in 1974, it dramatically brightened in 1989."[63] In 1989, the Berlin Wall fell and the global Soviet presence receded. The war with Angola had also ended in 1988, which not only effectively ended a potential threat from Angola but also brought about a phased withdrawal of all Cuban troops from Angola.[64] As the strategic justifications for South Africa's WMD programs were removed, the stage was set for their reversal.

In addition, the newly elected president, de Klerk, initiated efforts to end South Africa's pariah status and rejoin the community of nations. This involved ending apartheid and removing the ban on the African National Congress (ANC) as a political party. Part of this effort included abandoning their WMD, which were increasingly disapproved of internationally. South Africa therefore signed the NPT in July of 1991 and set the stage for joining the Chemical Weapons Convention (CWC) in 1993. As Reiss notes, the apartheid regime may also have begun working to eliminate its nuclear program prior to a transfer of power because it feared the prospect of having these weapons misused by a black-majority government.[65]

The Decision(s) to Dismantle the WMD Programs

Shortly after entering office, President de Klerk organized a steering committee, consisting of senior officials of the AEC, Armscor, and the South African Defense Force to evaluate the prospects of dismantling the program and joining the NPT. He also ordered that the Y-Plant be shut down by February 1, 1990.[66]

In late February, de Klerk also requested a comprehensive study to determine the best method of dismantling the program, selecting AEC director Waldo Stumpf to oversee the dismantlement and Wynand Mouton to serve as an independent auditor. The results of the comprehensive study were presented to de Klerk in July 1990. At Mouton's recommendation, South Africa's nuclear weapons were dismantled one at a time until the last one was destroyed. Although a slower method, this option would allow South Africa to retain its deterrent capability for a longer time and could allow opponents of disarmament time to get used to the idea. The official dismantlement of South Africa's nuclear-weapon program began in late February, 1990.[67]

Although the nuclear program was eliminated by 1991, South Africa's CBW program was retained several years after that. Upon taking office in 1989, President de Klerk received briefings on Project Coast but reportedly had been told only about the defensive programs, including those intended to produce CBW protective gear.[68] In March 1990, de Klerk reportedly gave orders that no more lethal chemical agents be produced, though he did reportedly authorize continuing development of irritating and incapacitating agents.[69] Certain elements of the CBW programs also appear to have been retained and even accelerated by Basson and others in Project Coast, as "insurance against the ANC/MK and the 'black onslaught,'" and for use in assassination attempts.[70] Also, "[E]xperiments with chemical warfare apparently continued, with an alleged attack on Mozambican troops as late as January 1992."[71]

In November 1992, President de Klerk appointed Lieutenant-General Pierre Steyn to investigate the secret programs of the South African Defense Forces, including Project Coast. The report that Lieutenant-General Steyn produced in 1993 reportedly found that Project Coast was "offensive in nature" and that it had been operating outside of civilian control.[72] "Upon receiving Steyn's report, de Klerk finally ordered the destruction of all lethal and incapacitating CBW agents, as well as an end to such research and operations. He also forced the retirement of Basson at the end of March 1993."[73]

Dismantling South Africa's Nuclear-Weapon Program

Based on the steering committee's recommendations, the de Klerk government began dismantling its nuclear-weapon program on February 26, 1990, dismantling its nuclear weapons, destroying technical documents, and decontaminating its facilities.[74] Throughout this process, South Africa essentially carried out a unilateral disarmament of its nuclear-weapon program, with IAEA verification taking place only once the dismantlement process had been completed.

By July 1991 significant progress had been made, including the dismantlement of all six completed weapons, along with the seventh partially completed one, at Armscor. It is reported that all HEU was extracted from South Africa's nuclear weapons and sent to the AEC by September 6, 1991.[75] The steering committee was also responsible for the decontamination and conversion of all Armscor facilities to conventional-weapon production and nonweapon commercial activities.[76] By July 1991, the weapon production site of Advena had been decontaminated and converted for commercial use.[77] Throughout the process, highly contaminated equipment was also sent to the AEC for safety purposes.

In order to prevent a reconstitution of the nuclear-weapon program, "more than 12,000 technical documents used for designing the Y-Plant and building the nuclear weapons were retrieved and compiled."[78] South African officials reported that "all the technical documents, drawings, design information, computer software, and data associated with the nuclear-weapon program were recovered and destroyed."[79] Some documents and records were preserved, however, including de Klerk's original dismantlement order, the operating and production records for the Y-Plant and Z-Plant, and Mouton's final report on the dismantlement.[80] If the documents and equipment were destroyed as claimed by South African officials, these actions would have made it more difficult to reconstitute the program, although the fissile materials and the human knowledge that are the key factors in reconstitution remained. However, the destruction of those items also increased the challenges of verifying the dismantlement or of reconstructing a precise history of the program.[81]

Upon completion of the dismantlement process, the steering committee was instructed to inform the government when to sign the NPT and the Comprehensive Safeguards Agreement, and to form a preliminary inventory of all nuclear material and facilities.[82] As noted, South Africa acceded to the NPT on July 10, 1991, after the decommission process was complete.[83]

Dismantling Project Coast

In January 1993, de Klerk ordered that all CBW stockpiles be destroyed and that all CBW-related documents be transferred to CD-ROMS, and all hard copies of these documents be destroyed. Despite the order to dismiss Basson, and despite the apparent reports that Project Coast (under Basson) was operating outside of civilian control, Basson and other SADF officials were tasked with carrying out these orders. The CD-ROMS were reportedly stored in a vault that could be opened only by the state president, along with the surgeon general and the head of South Africa's National Intelligence Agency. Basson was also "entrusted with personally supervising the destruction of various Coast-related chemical stores."[84]

In 1994, U.S. and British officials reportedly demanded that South Africa brief their experts on the CBW programs and that all CBW systems and records, including the CD-ROMS, be destroyed. Although South African officials did brief the U.S. officials, they refused to destroy the CD-ROMS, reportedly describing them as a "national asset."[85]

In the end, there are a number of questions about the extent to which de Klerk's orders were completely followed. In sworn testimony, Project Coast officials stated that the CBW agents were destroyed by dumping them into the sea, about 200 nautical miles south of Cape Agulhas.[86] However, some of their testimonies reportedly conflicted over whether the materials were destroyed in January of 1993 or at the end of that year, after South Africa had acceded to the CWC. There are also some reports that South Africa concealed its stockpiles of CR from the verification body of the CWC, the Organization for the Prohibition of Chemical Weapons (OPCW), and continued work on dispersion technologies for the gas even after formally joining the CWC on January 14, 1993.[87]

A subsequent inquiry by the South African Truth and Reconciliation Commission reported that certain elements of the CW programs may have been accelerated after the country's January 1993 accession to the CWC. For example, according to some reports, "R6.6 million were made available in February 1993 for the purchase of starter chemicals from Croatia . . . . These contradictions raise questions about the destruction of the chemical substances, which according to the documents took place on January 27, 1993."[88]

What is certain is that, if de Klerk did order Basson and other Project Coast officials to destroy all CBW-related documents, those orders were not followed. Numerous CBW-related documents were discovered in the possession of Basson upon his arrest and subsequent trial on several counts of murder, conspiracy, corruption, and drug trafficking.[89]

Verification of South Africa's WMD Rollback

The IAEA conducted two rounds of verification and inspection activities in South Africa. The first round occurred in late 1991, after Pretoria signed the NPT and negotiated a comprehensive safeguards agreement with the IAEA. The second round of verification activities began shortly after de Klerk's March 1993 revelations about the country's nuclear arsenal. As we will see, fewer, if any, systematic steps were taken by the international community to verify South Africa's dismantlement of its CBW programs. This section explains these verification activities and some of the questions that remained after the initial verification activities took place.

Verification by the IAEA

On September 16, 1991, South Africa signed a comprehensive safeguards agreement with the IAEA that required South Africa to submit a report including "quantitative data on all types of nuclear material, on a facility-by-facility basis," as well as "the location and the number of items of nuclear material contained in each respective facility."[90] South Africa's "initial report" was purported to have provided "a complete inventory of all nuclear materials and facilities."[91] It did not, however, contain any information on the nuclear weapons or key facilities involved with the nuclear-weapon program.

INITIAL REPORT ON HEU PRODUCTION

IAEA inspections, which began in November 1991, were intended "to verify the correctness of South Africa's declared inventory of nuclear material."[92] In its 1992 report on its verification activities in South Africa, the IAEA outlined its general approach.[93] The IAEA concentrated its efforts on facilities involved in the production of HEU (the Y-Plant) and LEU (the Z-Plant) or in conversion and fabrication of HEU and LEU. To confirm the completeness of South Africa's declaration of HEU and LEU inventories, the IAEA "calculated U-235 balances and carried out an audit of the accountancy records of plants used to produce, convert and fabricate enriched uranium and of the operating records of the Pilot Enrichment and Semi-Commercial Enrichment Plants [the Y- and Z-Plants]." It also charted the flows of imported and domestic uranium throughout the nuclear facilities.[94] In order to confirm the completeness of the inventory of declared nuclear facilities, the IAEA visited the declared facilities as well as a number of other locations that had been identified to the agency by other states.[95]

Based on the accounting data provided by the AEC, the IAEA calculated the U-235 balance of the Y-Plant Pilot Enrichment and found an "apparent discrepancy in this balance."[96] IAEA officials later wrote that "it proved necessary to make a number of corrections to the data included in the initial report" and that "the direction of these 'apparent discrepancies' could be interpreted to indicate that an amount of uranium-235 was unaccounted for."[97] The IAEA did note that the "apparent discrepancy" could have resulted from the material accountancy system used by South Africa, which, among other things, did not measure depleted uranium output from the facility. Other discrepancies appear to have been explained by the suspension of HEU production between August 1979 and July 1981 owing to technical problems at the Y-Plant.[98]

The IAEA did note, however, that South Africa had imported a quantity of natural uranium prior to 1979 to use as feed for the Pilot Enrichment Plant.[99] Although South African officials presumably provided records on the amount of imported uranium, the "AEC wished to keep confidential the identity of suppliers of previously unsafeguarded imported depleted, natural and low enriched uranium and, as a consequence, the shipping documents were not made available to the team for examination."[100]

In the end, the IAEA concluded in its September 1992 report:

> Examination of records of transfers of material between facilities and the plant operating records (including data on electrical consumption; on plant, cascade and stage availability; plant operating parameters; and feed and product registers) showed these records to be internally consistent and consistent with the declared production of enriched uranium over the fifteen year lifetime of the plant.[101]

The IAEA further reported that "the results show that the amount of HEU included in the Initial Report is consistent with the amount stated to have been transferred to the conversion and fabrication plants during the lifetime of the Pilot Enrichment Plant," and that "the amount of HEU declared to have been produced by the Y-Plant was consistent with the plant's production capacity."[102]

The United States, however, remained much more suspicious over the "apparent discrepancies" than the IAEA apparently did. A recently declassified 1992 State Department draft paper on South Africa's declaration to the IAEA argued:

> We strongly believe the collective body of information is ambiguous, and contradictions must be resolved before any firm judgments can be offered with confidence. Some information tends to support the notion of an "honest declaration"; some tends to support the "cheating" scenario; and much is open to both interpretations. There is no basis at present for assigning greater likelihood to the "cheating" scenario. More importantly, we feel it is premature to offer *any* general verdict at present on South Africa's conduct [emphasis in original].[103]

Similarly, a declassified U.S. report from 1993 notes that "the South African case illustrates the difficulty of verifying nuclear-material stocks of a former nuclear-weapons state and of 'closing the book' on past actions." The 1993 report goes on to elaborate significant U.S. concerns:

> South Africa's nuclear-material inventory—declared to the IAEA shortly after the July 1991 NPT accession—is [deleted] difficult to verify given the incompleteness of our own information. The amount of enriched uranium produced at the Valindaba plant (the nation's key HEU producer) [deleted] corresponds to the mid-range of previous US estimates of actual plant production but is well below plant capacity. South African officials have described, in impressive detail, plant operating problems that technically are plausible but were hitherto unknown to the United States."[104]

The report does indicate that the IAEA was satisfied with South Africa's reports and further notes that Pretoria had accepted a long-standing U.S. offer to have U.S. experts directly assist the IAEA in analyzing enrichment plant records, but the IAEA had rejected the proposal.

CONCEALMENT AND DECEPTION BEFORE AND
AFTER NPT ACCESSION (1989–93)

The original South African plan had been to declare that they had produced HEU but not to admit that they had had a nuclear-weapon program or had produced nuclear weapons. As a result, South African officials had to deceive IAEA inspectors about the existence or purpose of certain sites and facilities that were part of the weapon program—including the Kalahari test site and several buildings at the Pelindaba site.

As noted above, South Africa had made preparations for a nuclear test at the Kalahari site 1977 but hurriedly sealed the shafts and temporarily abandoned the site after its discovery.[105] When workers returned to the site in 1987, the first shaft was concealed under a concrete ramp inside the "shade" that had been cast to cover the shaft's opening; the other shaft, located outside some distance away, was covered with dirt.[106] Although South Africa never declared this site to be part of its nuclear program in its initial declaration to the IAEA, the IAEA nevertheless asked to inspect this site based on information from agency member states. Following this inspection, the IAEA reported in September 1992 that, on the basis of information received, the site was used as a military test range and that the building

> was used by the Air force for storage and as a workshop. On the floor at one side of the building was a large concrete ramp, which appeared to have been cast in situ. A number of environmental samples were taken in and around the build-

ing. The team found no evidence that the location has been or is being used for the testing of nuclear weapons.[107]

As Pabian notes, "From the IAEA reporting, it is clear that at no time was there any mention made by the South Africans of the existence of the shaft under the ramp during the IAEA visit in 1992"[108]

Similarly, in 1992, the IAEA visited Building 5000, which is located at the Pelindaba site. Although this had been South Africa's key site for nuclear explosives development, criticality tests, and weapon assembly, South African officials withheld all information about these activities. According to the IAEA report, "The building was stated to have been used as a general-purpose critical facility by the AEC's Reactor Development Group, which was disbanded several years ago. According to the AEC the facility itself was abandoned in the early 1990s."[109]

Despite some reports to the contrary, Pabian notes that "there were absolutely *no* IAEA inspections of South African nuclear weapons production sites prior to South African accession to the NPT. This is abundantly clear from both the recently declassified, previously 'top secret,' South African documentation and the IAEA's own reporting" (emphasis in original).[110]

Why did the South Africans withhold any reports of their nuclear-weapon work—especially since the weapons were reportedly dismantled and the weapon facilities already shut down by this point? Mitchell Reiss indicates three possible reasons:

• Domestic Political Upheaval: Public announcement at the time could have enraged the Conservative Party and white supremacists.
• In the aftermath of the first Gulf War, Pretoria noted the controversies over Iraq's nuclear program and did not want to be linked with Iraq.
• South Africa wanted to garner as much goodwill as possible from its entrance into the NPT.

David Albright suggested, however, that Pretoria may ultimately have come clean about its program because it was becoming increasingly difficult to conceal the regime's previous activities. Albright noted that IAEA inspectors suspected that there had been a nuclear-weapon program. He stated that although the IAEA "kept its suspicions to itself" owing to confidentiality restrictions on safeguards arrangements, information about its inspection activities in South Africa began leaking immediately.[111] Allegations about a weapon program began circulating in the international press and, domestically, in the ANC. As Albright noted, de Klerk alluded to the mounting pressure in his March 1993 announcement, stating that charges were "regularly taken up by both the local and international press" and that they were "beginning to take on the dimensions of a campaign."[112]

If the mounting international and domestic pressure was what actually tipped the scales, it is possible that the regime may not have otherwise disclosed the program. This possibility does potentially point to another additional reason why South Africa might have refrained initially from reporting its nuclear-weapon program. It could be that the country wanted explicitly to retain latent capabilities for developing nuclear weapons beyond those that inhered to their nuclear materials and human knowledge. In the end, it may be that it simply became too difficult to conceal the existence of the program altogether, especially since the IAEA was also receiving reports from the United States about the suspected nuclear-weapon sites, so the decision was made to announce the existence of the weapon program March 1993.[113]

VERIFICATION AFTER SOUTH AFRICA'S NUCLEAR
ARSENAL REVELATIONS (AFTER MARCH 1993)

After de Klerk's March 24 speech, IAEA inspections were extended and the agency conducted additional and more extensive verification procedures. Inspectors made four additional trips to South Africa with a primary objective of "further examin[ing] the apparent discrepancies associated with the high enriched uranium (HEU) produced by the pilot enrichment plant."[114] IAEA inspectors also carried out an assessment of the status of South Africa's former nuclear-weapon program to ensure that sensitive components were destroyed and that all nuclear material was recovered from the program.[115]

IAEA inspectors reported that South Africa provided "extensive co-operation," including "transparency and openness with respect to access to information and locations."[116] After the investigation, the IAEA reported that it did not find evidence of an active nuclear-weapon program, and that it found that South Africa's HEU inventory was consistent with the previous IAEA investigation.

At the Y-Plant, agency inspectors consulted with officials of the AEC and conducted a "detailed re-examination" of the historical records, including "many thousands of records relating to the operation of the plant and intervening shutdown periods."[117] The IAEA reported that it had received clarifications that had significantly reduced the magnitude of the "apparent discrepancy" of the U-235 balance.[118] On the basis of its reexamination, the IAEA reported that "[f]rom the team's assessment of the production capacity of the pilot enrichment plant, on the basis of the operating records and supporting technical data provided to the team by the AEC, it is reasonable to conclude that the amounts of HEU which could have been produced by the pilot plant are consistent with the amounts declared in the initial report."[119]

The IAEA also reported that, by its visit in April 1993, "the dismantling and destruction of the weapons components and the destruction of technical documents had been nearly completed."[120] Based on dismantling records, the IAEA concluded that HEU previously possessed by ARMSCOR/Circle was successfully moved to the AEC and was under IAEA safeguards.[121] IAEA also concluded that the uranium metallurgy process area at ARMSCOR/Circle had been dismantled and decontaminated, and the equipment sent back to the AEC.[122]

The IAEA also visited various facilities that had been declared to be part of the nuclear-weapon program, including the Kalahari test site and AEC and ARMSCOR sites near Pelindaba. At the Kalahari site, the IAEA worked with ARMSCOR officials to prepare and initiate a plan to render the test shafts useless. This plan, which involved back-filling the shafts with sand and covering them with concrete plugs, was completed by July 1993.[123] The IAEA confirmed that the other sites had been decommissioned and reported that it did not find any evidence of working nuclear components or nuclear activity in the declared facilities.[124]

The IAEA reported that South Africa had cooperated significantly with them and helped the IAEA verify the timing and scope of the program. Throughout the process South Africa provided the IAEA with records, documents, interviews, and significant access to facilities.[125]

Verification of CBW Dismantlement?

As noted, there are a number of remaining questions about the destruction of the documents and even the agents developed by Project Coast. As Jeffrey Bale notes, "Unfortunately, there is no proof that the project's toxic materials and documents were all actually destroyed. Basson's reported destruction of Coast's CW and BW agents was never independently verified."[126]

Subsequent efforts to confirm the dismantlement and destruction of the program also failed to yield significant results. In 1993, South Africa reportedly submitted a "confidence building measure" (CBM) to give some assurances that they had rolled back the BW side of Project Coast. U.S. and British officials reportedly found the CBM inadequate and began serious efforts to engage South African officials in order to obtain more sufficient evidence of the roll-back of Project Coast. U.S. ambassador Princeton Lyman reportedly stated that "the South African CBM was not forthcoming on many aspects of the CBW program, including offensive uses, weaponization, and proliferation."[127]

Even within South Africa, it was apparently very difficult to lift the veil of secrecy that had been drawn over the country's CBW programs. In part this arose from the shielding that had long dominated the program with the South African military establishment, along with a lack of civilian oversight. But, initially, de Klerk had reportedly had difficulty ensuring that his orders to dismantle Project Coast had been carried out. In fact, a subsequent inquiry by the South African Truth and Reconciliation Commission found that at least certain elements of the CBW may have been accelerated after de Klerk's order and South Africa's January 1993 accession to the CWC.[128] The Foreign Affairs minister reportedly requested confirmation that the CBW program had been eliminated prior to the country's entrance into nonproliferation treaties.[129] Although President Mandela had apparently been briefed on the Steyn Report (by Lieutenant-General Steyn himself), the details of the report were not made public, possibly owing to concerns about how the report could affect the country's transition from apartheid rule.[130]

As noted, U.S. and British officials reportedly demanded that South Africa provide more information about these programs, including briefing their experts. Although the specific files were reportedly locked away, the South African government did begin briefing U.S. experts about the programs during several trips to the country in 1994 and 1995. According to Burgess and Purkitt, U.S. ambassador Donald Mahley and his British counterpart led teams to examine Project Coast documents in 1994.[131]

In late 1994 and 1995, additional information began surfacing about Project Coast, though mainly in press accounts. South Africa's parliament, however, continued to encounter difficulties in obtaining information on the CBW programs. This, reportedly, was owing to an agreement reached by cabinet members of the Government of National Unity that details of the program should be kept secret. The South African government also reportedly kept details secret because it was preparing a lawsuit over the corruption, excessive spending, and other abuses within the program. Parks Mankahlana, President Mandela's spokesman, reportedly said "an overall lifting can be considered once the OSEO investigation is over .... There is no intention to impose permanent secrecy on the matter."[132]

More information about the programs did come out in 1998, when the South African Truth and Reconciliation Commission held a public hearing into the CBW program, and later in 2000 during a criminal trial of Dr. Basson.[133] During the trial, Dr. Niels Knobel, South Africa's surgeon general at the time of the CW destruction, admitted that he had simply taken Basson's word that the materials had been destroyed, rather than overseeing the process himself or setting in motion an independent verification, whether by the South African government or by international agencies.[134]

There is no evidence of any kind of verification process of South Africa's CBW dismantlement along the lines of the IAEA verification of the nuclear program. Jeffrey Bale summarizes the problems with the verification of CBW dismantlement:

> However justifiable South Africa's pride may have been in regard to the dismantling of its nuclear and missile programs, such pride would have largely been misplaced had it been extended to the dismantling of the country's CBW program. Not only did many irregularities mark South Africa's rather convoluted disarmament process, not least of which was the lack of any independent verification of the alleged destruction of its remaining stocks of chemical and biological agents, but there are indications that certain key personnel associated with Project Coast may have subsequently facilitated CBW proliferation, intentionally or otherwise.[135]

Assessing the South African Case

In total, the IAEA carried out twenty-two inspection missions in South Africa, conducting more than 150 inspections at individual facilities and locations outside facilities between November 1991 and September 1993.[136] In September 1993, the IAEA reported that it was "reasonable to conclude" that South Africa's initial report was consistent with the amount of HEU that could have been produced by the Y-Plant.[137] The IAEA's efforts to verify South Africa's declarations were remarkable, but there were limits to what the agency could do after the dismantlement process had been completed. The IAEA's overall positive assessment revealed that there was at that time considerable uncertainty in the verification process, which left a number of questions about South Africa's rollback unanswered. However, the IAEA's conclusions were often interpreted as being more definitive than they could be under the circumstances.

Unanswered Questions

The verification process that took place at that time was, as suggested, limited by the fact that dismantlement had already occurred and by uncertainties about South Africa's "initial report"—including the operational records for the Y-Plant. Although the IAEA concluded that the report was "consistent with" the amounts of material that could have been produced by the Y-Plant, if South Africa had not emerged as a robust democracy under Nelson Mandela and taken a different political course in the aftermath of its apartheid regime, would we have any confidence at all that they had totally eliminated their nuclear and CBW programs? If any of South Africa's politicians had decided to act differently, requiring a coercive verification process, would we have full confidence in the IAEA's assessment or would the uncertainties have dominated judgments on South African disarmament?

Given the uncertainties of the operational history of the plant and other factors, it is possible that a stockpile of highly enriched uranium could have been set aside with little prospect of detection. If the records delivered to the IAEA were inaccurate or doctored, such a stockpile may not have been detected by the IAEA. More specifically, the following questions may not have been fully answered by the verification process:

• *Questions about the recordkeeping itself.* As noted, by the time that the IAEA began conducting its verification activities, South Africa had stated that its weapons had been disassembled, its facilities had been decommissioned and stripped of equipment, and the majority of the technical documents and components had already been destroyed. The IAEA therefore had to rely mainly on South Africa's operational records for the Y-Plant and other facilities (along with interviews of officials and personnel).

If these records were inaccurate or doctored, however, they might not present a correct account of material flows or the dismantling process and could have created opportunities for concealment. And the official IAEA account and the IAEA's technical report did indicate that numerous corrections had to be made in the record-keeping. "This resulted from the continuing efforts of the SSAC to ensure the accuracy of the data, errors identified during the inspection process, and corrections to estimations resulting from measurements made by facility operators after issuance of the initial report."[138]

• *Questions about the operational history and production capacity of the plant.* According to the IAEA, many of the agency's questions about the "apparent discrepancy" in the HEU balance were explained by an unexpected shutdown of the Y-Plant "between August 1979 and July 1981 as a result of technical problems."[139] IAEA officials indicated that South Africa provided detailed operational records that sufficiently addressed the issue. However, as noted, recently declassified documents reveal that U.S. intelligence agencies were far from convinced about South Africa's explanations—and note that U.S. intelligence had been unaware of the shut-down of the facility. If the plant had actually been operating during some or all of the time that South African officials said it was shut down, a covert stockpile of HEU could have been accumulated without detection.

• *Measurement uncertainties and the "apparent discrepancy."* South Africa claimed that a large part of the "apparent discrepancy" could be explained by uncertainties in the estimates of the "tails" of the enrichment process—the U-235 that is eliminated as waste, along with depleted uranium. A more accurate accounting of the tails, South African officials claimed, would clear up the "apparent discrepancy" between the IAEA's estimated output of the Y-Plant and the actual declared HEU stockpile. The IAEA apparently accepted this argument, stating that "having regard to the normal uncertainties expected to be involved in the plant's historical operating and accounting records, it is reasonable to conclude that the uranium-235 balance of the high enriched uranium, low enriched uranium, and depleted uranium produced by the pilot enrichment plant is consistent with the uranium feed."[140]

However, in a detailed analysis of the tails of South Africa's enrichment process, Thomas Cochran noted that the very large uncertainty in the AEC's estimates—15.6 percent—ultimately results in an uncertainty of about 526 kilograms of HEU.[141] Nor is it at all clear that more accurate measurements of the tails would have explained the "apparent discrepancy." As Cochran points out, "[F]rom a purely statistical standpoint," reducing the 15.6 percent uncertainty could generate an average tails assay that is *either lower or higher* than the declared amount, "and therefore the 'actual discrepancy' in the U-235 inventory could just as readily increase as decrease."[142]

In the end, the IAEA decided that the increased confidence provided by more accurate measurements of the tails "would not justify their considerable expense."[143] And yet, as a result, significant questions remained about South Africa's HEU declaration. As Cochran concluded in his study, "To date, only South Africa knows for certain whether the U-235 inventory difference is 'in the tails,' or whether additional HEU was hidden away."[144]

• *Discrepancies between the operational records and the actual HEU stock-pile.* The IAEA notes that the "apparent discrepancy" could be partially explained by "materials unaccounted for" (MUF)—that is, materials that are lost as part of normal operation of a facility. As the IAEA noted, "The accuracy of the physical inventory was impaired by such factors as the non-availability of suitable instruments to measure process hold-ups [material that gets "held up" in pipes and other places as it moves through a facility], the unwillingness of the plant management to interrupt production in order to drain condensers or transfer material to measurement points, and to the lack of comprehensive measurement control programmes."[145]

Accounting problems arising from MUF are common and in themselves are not necessarily an indication of diversion.[146] But, as with all instances of MUF, there is always a question about whether the "unaccounted for" materials were actually diverted—or in the South African case, retained—as part of a covert weapon program. There are ways to decrease MUF, of course, including shutting down a production plant to clean out pipes, conduct detailed assays of potential hold-ups, and the like, but South African officials were apparently unwilling to take these steps.

• *Questions about the amounts of natural and low-enriched uranium imported.* As the IAEA noted, South Africa refused to show the shipping manifests of imported uranium, ostensibly in order not to disclose what countries had been willing to provide unsafeguarded materials to Pretoria.[147] But an additional reason could have been to hide the true amounts of materials that were actually imported. The materials could potentially have been fed through the system without detection.[148]

• *Are we sure that all technical documents, computer files, and equipment were destroyed?* There are inherent limitations to the level of confidence one can have that a country destroyed documents or equipment. That, incidentally, is exactly what Iraq claimed to have done with large amounts of CBW agents, documents, and equipment, but inspectors viewed Iraqi claims as insufficient proof of destruction. South Africa did provide some dismantlement records to the IAEA teams, but by the IAEA's own account, "[T]he dismantling records comprised brief hand-written listings of component systems dismantled from the deliverable devices." The IAEA also indicated that "no records had been kept documenting the dismantling of components of the demonstration device or any of the pre-production experimental devices or on the destruction of their components."[149] In some cases, therefore, it may have been very difficult to verify South African claims that certain devices, equipment, or components had actually been destroyed.

The IAEA did note that "a number of destroyed or partially destroyed components had been retained and were shown to some members of the [IAEA] team in April 1993."[150] The agency team also examined "build-history" log books and compared those records with the dismantling listings, and they further compared the identification records of the remaining components and found those to be consistent with those shown in the records. However, the comparing of records and testimonial accounts is very different from actually witnessing the destruction. It would take comparatively little to conceal essential components and claim that they (and any ID numbers) were destroyed. If essential equipment, documents, or materials were retained, a state could potentially reconstitute the program more rapidly.

• *Actual evidence of deception and concealment.* It should not be forgotten that South African officials did intentionally mislead IAEA officials during the agency's inspections of the Kalahari test site and several buildings at the Pelindaba site in 1991–92.[151] Under normal circumstances, such a willingness to deceive IAEA inspectors would have been a cause for alarm and would have raised significant questions about the state's willingness to deceive generally.

If the verification process had remained where it was in 1993, these and other questions about the South African nuclear-weapon program might never have been sufficiently answered. For example, Mitchell Reiss later argued that one cannot rule out the possibility that South Africa hid some number of nuclear devices (retaining a "bomb in the basement" capability), or, a somewhat greater possibility, that it retained a stockpile of highly enriched uranium (thereby potentially allowing the country to build some number of nuclear weapons rapidly if it so desired).[152] Indeed, Reiss notes, "[T]he November 1993 U.S. intelligence assessment also could not determine with certainty if South Africa had declared all of its uranium to the IAEA and placed it under safeguards at Pelindaba. A complete accounting of South Africa's enriched uranium inventory may never be known."[153] A primary difficulty with the South African disarmament was that it was done unilaterally.

It is the case that once a country has carried out the disarmament itself, there will be information that will *never* be recovered. However, as occurred in South Africa after 1993, if new information becomes available by undertaking decontamination activities, if long-term verification involves such activities as refining the process for material balance evaluations, and if wastes are recharacterized, at least some information can be recovered.[154] Indeed, Olli Heinonen argues that "there is no reason to indicate that the nuclear material inventory of South Africa is incomplete."[155] This judgment appears overstated. However, even if it is true, it may not apply to other states in the same way as it did in South Africa, especially states with larger and more complex programs.

Potential Scenarios for Nuclear Diversion or Concealment

At the time of the initial IAEA reports, one could have developed a set of scenarios that South Africa might plausibly have pursued with a reasonable chance of avoiding detection. While we are not arguing that South Africa implemented any of these scenarios, they would likely be troubling us now if South Africa's political evolution had been different.

Scenario 1: South Africa Diverted a Small, Undeclared HEU Stockpile. As the IAEA reported, they discovered "apparent discrepancies" whereby South Africa's declared stockpile was smaller than expected. South Africa explained away the discrepancies by claiming that the Y-Plant had to be shut down for some period, that some materials were lost as "MUF," and that the SSAC did not measure certain materials. However, another possibility could have been a diversion of the HEU.

Scenario 2: South Africa Imported Unsafeguarded Natural or Low-enriched Uranium and Enriched It at the Y-Plant. Because South Africa refused to turn over the shipping manifests or reveal what country (or countries) had provided the unsafeguarded material, the IAEA had only South Africa's records as evidence. The IAEA did reportedly verify that certain declared, low-enriched uranium had been fabricated into fuel elements for South Africa's Koeberg nuclear reactors, but it is possible that some was undeclared and therefore untraceable.[156] This scenario assumes either that the Y-Plant was operating at a higher capacity than South Africa admitted, thus allowing for HEU overproduction, or that it was operational when South Africa said it was shut down. (Both of these possibilities would likely involve a doctoring of the operational and electrical records, which would not be difficult to do.)[157]

Scenario 3: South Africa Placed All HEU under Safeguards, but Retained Technical Documents and Equipment That Would Allow for a Rapid Resuscitation of the Program. South African officials claimed that most of the technical documents and equipment (except a few models) relating to the nuclear-weapon program were destroyed. But it is impossible to know that this is the case. Even if the remaining HEU stockpile is under safeguards, the regime could be satisfied that it could seize this material at any point if it chose a rapid breakout.

Scenario 4: Some Combination (or All) of the Previous Scenarios. None of these are mutually exclusive, so any combination, or all, could have been attempted to varying degrees.

WMD Latency

Any of these scenarios, if they were carried out, would have provided a significant latent nuclear weapon capability for South Africa, enhancing the latency that it already possessed and still possesses because of its retention of a stockpile of HEU and its ongoing nuclear-energy program, including uranium mining and enrichment.[158]

Although there are other potential explanations for why South Africa did not report its nuclear-weapon program at the time of its accession to the NPT, one possible explanation was that it had intended to retain a latent nuclear-weapon capability.[159] Nuclear latency can be viewed as the possession of most or all of the technologies, facilities, materials, expertise (including tacit knowledge), resources, and other capabilities necessary for the development of nuclear weapons, without full operational weaponization.

As Scott Sagan points out, one of the most important elements of latency is a country's ability to acquire the fissile material for nuclear weapons.[160] To this day, South Africa has retained a stockpile of 400–450 kilograms of HEU that had been developed as part of its nuclear program. (The original stockpile had been over 800 kilograms.) In this sense, South Africa has already achieved a degree of nuclear latency. Even though its declared stockpile of HEU is under safeguards, South Africa would still be able to seize the HEU if it so desired, especially if it had the technical capability to allow for a rapid nuclear "breakout." Moreover, there have been suspicions that South Africa could be retaining this stockpile precisely for that reason. Because South Africa's research reactor has been converted to low-enriched uranium, the HEU has been used "for a target material to produce molybdenum-99 for medical isotope use." Although "this use could be converted to low-enriched uranium," South Africa has not done so.[161]

On the CBW side, however, South Africa *explicitly* retained a latent capability to resuscitate its programs. Because all the technical documents were merely saved on CD-ROMS and stored away, it could be a fairly straightforward and rapid process to rebuild the programs—assuming that scientists obtained precursor chemicals or bio feedstocks. And if the reports of additional possible acquisitions of CW starter chemicals noted above are true, South Africa may have also acquired latent capabilities to allow for a fairly rapid CW breakout.

Moreover, given the unanswered questions about whether South Africa managed to retain a covert, unsafeguarded HEU stockpile, technical nuclear documents and designs, or nuclear components, it could have achieved additional latent nuclear capabilities. If South Africa did retain any or all of these items, it could potentially cross the nuclear-weapon threshold again rapidly, without even needing to access the safeguarded material (or by keeping the safeguarded stockpile as a hedge).

In the end, we do not know exactly what South Africa retained, and this ambiguity can be part of a strategy of nuclear and CBW latency. The ambiguity can be a strategy for some states who find ambiguity to be an optimal response to security while possibly avoiding international reactions from diplomatic isolation to sanctions to military options. In the South African context, the country was already diplomatically isolated, so it is not clear that this was the South African rationale. It is notable, however, that South Africa's nuclear-weapon program itself was based on a policy of ambiguity—which included, for example, no admitted nuclear test and no open admission of the arsenal—prior to its disarmament.[162]

Neither the Nonproliferation Treaty nor the other negotiated nonproliferation and arms control treaties directly address latency, and the concept is not fully encompassed and explored in the policy debates over nuclear weapon proliferation or the treaties, institutions, and norms designed to address these threats through nuclear nonproliferation, arms control, and disarmament.

Lessons

The lessons from the South African case for both regional rollback and global disarmament efforts involve the limits to international monitoring and verification, the predominance of political constraints, and the potential downsides to cooperation.

The Limits to International Monitoring and Verification

As David Albright notes, "The case of South Africa provides the only example of verification of nuclear rollback and highlights the extreme difficulty of verifying disarmament."[163] However, some descriptions of the South African case may overstate the confidence levels achieved, especially by 1993, and thus draw the wrong lessons from the case.

For example, a study by the Committee on International Security and Arms Control (CISAC) states: "The IAEA experience [in South Africa] illustrates that *high confidence* in the completeness of declarations can be achieved with a high level of cooperation and transparency" (emphasis added).[164] And yet, somewhat contradictorily, in the very next sentence of its report, CISAC notes that the South African case "also demonstrates that uncertainties will exist and may be difficult to resolve."[165] It is unclear how one can simultaneously have "high confidence" and "uncertainties" that are "difficult to resolve."

In the final assessment, these uncertainties are real, and remain, despite the serious and sober verification work of the IAEA. The agency's initial conclusions may have exceeded the technical evidence. In any event, long-term monitoring has enhanced the technical evidence and reduced the levels of uncertainty, leading some to argue that the ambiguous situation has been remedied.[166] However, it is unlikely that we can fully know whether South Africa's declaration was correct and complete.[167]

The Predominance of Political Considerations

What caused the IAEA to be confident that South Africa did completely roll back its nuclear-weapon program if this conclusion was not fully supported by the technical evidence? It appears that the IAEA's assessment was based on the technical conclusion that South Africa's records were consistent with its initial declaration, which was both shaped by and enhanced by *political* conclusions— involving the regime change that ultimately ended apartheid rule. Absent the fundamental political changes set in motion by F. W. de Klerk, the IAEA's technical conclusions and ways that those conclusions were understood by the international community would likely have been different.

This is not to say that some political considerations should not be taken into account as part of the verification process. For example, there has been some interest in recent years in moving toward new modes of verification that could be ad hoc, tailored, and fully responsive to national and regional circumstances, including such factors as overall relations with the state, levels of cooperation, and the like.[168] While such approaches can be useful, they need to be pursued with caution, especially when technical evidence is limited and questionable, which in the South African case was owing to unobserved disarmament. The political considerations could therefore cause international verification organizations to draw conclusions that go far beyond what is supportable by the technical evidence. Moreover, political situations are subject to change, often dramatic ones. As suggested earlier, if South Africa's political evolution had happened differently, would we be at all comfortable with the country's apparent disarmament?

The Downside to Cooperation

Part of the IAEA's confidence also resulted from South Africa's cooperation with IAEA inspectors. Indeed, the IAEA repeatedly noted the high level of cooperation by the regime.[169] After all, South Africa had voluntarily joined the NPT; and South African officials claimed that they had voluntarily dismantled the country's nuclear-weapon and related programs and, later, that they had voluntarily disclosed the previous existence of the nuclear-weapon program.[170] These claims were taken as counterevidence to, and were apparently weighed more heavily than, previous instances of apparent and clear concealment and deception (including "apparent discrepancies," declarations that needed corrections, and the indisputable deception of inspectors at former nuclear weapon sites). Once it appeared that South Africa was complying, the bar was apparently lowered.

Cooperation is rightly valued in monitoring and verification efforts; however, apparent cooperation can also be a strategy designed to hinder monitoring and verification. This, for example, appears to be the strategy Libya may have followed after its WMD renunciation in 2003. As the 2011 revelations of the undeclared CW stockpile demonstrated, it turns out that Libya gave the *appearance* of full cooperation in some areas (such as its nuclear program and parts of its CW program), while actually concealing a CW stockpile.[171] In fact, there was little evidence at the time of concealment and deception. As in the case of South Africa, however, the belief that Libya was cooperating appeared to lead to a lowering of the bar for verification.

Applicability to Other Cases?

As noted in the introduction to this chapter, South African has often been held up as a model for disarmament, including for some of the most difficult cases in the last decades in Northeast Asia and the Middle East, and even for the recognized nuclear-weapon states to follow as they consider the prospects for global nuclear disarmament.

For example, when discussing the verification process in Iraq, Hans Blix, the former IAEA director-general and executive chairman of the United National Monitoring, Verification, and Inspection Commission (UNMOVIC), stated in 2003 that the South African case "is an example that I have invoked many times in the past, that our experience in the IAEA was that South Africa wanted to . . . create confidence that they did away with the nuclear weapons they had built, and they invited the IAEA to carry out the full inspection of that . . . . And they were setting an example, I think, for Iraq."[172]

The South African case has also been invoked as a model for other difficult cases, including Iran and North Korea. For example, with respect to the Iranian case, Thomas Pickering, former U.S. ambassador to the United Nations, stated, "I would be willing to adopt what I would call the South African model—a no-fault process. You tell the truth, and the whole truth, there are no consequences. If you don't tell the truth, there are all conceivable consequences. In part, it's a test of good faith; in part, it's a way to determine the answer; and in part, it's to take the burden of the guilt trip off of Iran, which in my view is not necessary if we are proceeding with a reasonable view to the future."[173] Similarly, with respect to North Korea, Cheon Seongwhun and Tatsujiro Suzuki wrote: "The hopeful course is to follow the peaceful resolution scenario, where the DPRK follows the South African model. The North Korean leadership would announce its intention to halt its nuclear weapon programs, deliver the relevant information to the IAEA, and accept full-scale inspections from the Agency."[174] Finally, in a study on building a WMD-free zone in the Middle East, Cserveny and others state that "[o]n signing the NPT, Israel should demonstrate its nuclear-weapon-free status in light of the experience of South Africa."[175]

Nevertheless, at the time that the IAEA verified South Africa's declarations, significant questions remained unanswered. Even though there has been some progress in answering some of these questions, ambiguity remains. This ambiguity poses a problem for attempts to apply the South African model to these other difficult cases. It may be that a politics that allowed for the resolution of these issues would be sufficient to temper the qualifications and uncertainties of verification. However, in hotly contested regions such as Northeast Asia and the Middle East, or with such challenging issues as global disarmament, it is very difficult to envision the South African model being applied without significant risks for security and stability.[176]

The evidence appears to be even more problematic when it comes to South Africa's CBW rollback. Not only was the rollback not externally verified, but, if the testimony by South African officials at the Truth and Reconciliation Commission was true, the rollback may not have even been verified internally, either. To be fair, most people advocating a South African model are thinking of the country's nuclear-weapon rollback, but when it comes to verification of CBW rollback, South Africa may best demonstrate what *not* to do.

Even if the South African verification *had* by itself provided a "high confidence" in the country's rollback, it would still be very difficult to use South Africa as a model for such difficult cases as North Korea and Iran. Given the clear attempts by these countries to conceal their WMD programs and to deceive international inspectors, they would not be believed if they later claimed that they had unilaterally dismantled their WMD programs.[177] Indeed, despite what Hans Blix argued at the time, this is exactly what Iraq claimed in the lead-up to Operation Iraqi Freedom in 2003, but these claims were not considered to be reliable evidence of disarmament and were insufficient to prevent the war.[178] Thus, it is highly unlikely that a verification process similar to that which occurred in South Africa would be considered sufficient in these cases. Christopher Ford makes a similar argument in the case of North Korea, though it could equally be applied to Iran and other proliferants as well:

> South African dismantlement is a very special case, and cannot—as a practical matter—be separated from the broader circumstances in which it occurred. . . . Given the DPRK track record of nuclear deception and concealment, however—and the presumed unwillingness of DPRK negotiators to agree to analogous circumstances of regime change as a means of increasing outsiders' verification confidence— . . . international partners would find it inadequate for weaponization-related dismantlement to be conducted by DPRK officials entirely on their own. Accordingly, weaponization V&E [verification and elimination] must be undertaken either by NPT Nuclear Weapon State officials themselves or by DPRK authorities under their supervision. Anything less, it is assumed, would not create adequate verification confidence.[179]

It is also unclear that the South African case would be a useful model for global disarmament. It has been argued that the "de jure" nuclear-weapon states—the United States, Russia, Great Britain, France, and China—could follow the South African model of verified rollback as a key first step in the pursuit of the goal of a nuclear-weapon-free world (NWFW). For example as Daryl Kimball, executive director of the Arms Control Association, wrote in July 2011, "Is a world free of nuclear weapons possible? Do states that have developed nuclear weapons have the vision and the courage to verifiably eliminate their arsenals? As South Africa has shown, some do. Others can."[180] However, there are a host of difficulties that could arise from the adoption of the South African model by the recognized NWSs, especially if it meant unilateral disarmament followed by verification efforts by the IAEA or some other verifying body. Because the recognized NWSs have had their nuclear-weapon programs for much longer than South Africa did, which raises questions of historical material and warhead production, and because their programs are likely more complex than South Africa's was, the verification difficulties would be much greater. As the CISAC study, cited above, argues, "[T]he difficulties experienced by the IAEA in verifying South Africa's declaration are likely to be much more difficult for the *de jure* nuclear-weapon states, making it much more difficult to conclude that their declarations are complete."[181]

Conclusions

Without a doubt, South Africa's elimination of its nuclear weapons and related nuclear-weapon infrastructure was an extremely positive step for nonproliferation. However, the South African rollback did introduce a great deal of ambiguity that affects its status as a model for disarmament.[182]

The South African case has had considerable appeal, perhaps, as Ambassador Pickering referenced, as a model of a "no fault" disarmament process. Because the technical and political issues involved in the verification of nuclear disarmament are so difficult, some arms control specialists have worked to identify alternative, and potentially easier, paths to nonproliferation and disarmament. If some proliferants chose to take South Africa's path, this would be a positive outcome. However, attempts to apply the South African case as a model for regional disarmament objectives in Northeast Asia and the Middle East, or for global disarmament objectives, have serious problems. The limited applicability of the South African model—in particular the limits and uncertainties of verification efforts in the aftermath of the dismantlement of weapons, the difficulties of obtaining a clear and full accounting of a country's fissile material production, and the resulting ambiguity—would be magnified in the cases of North Korea, the P-5 nuclear-weapon states, or possibly Iran.

The limits of this model remind us that it is imperative that we develop the tools for verifying disarmament that would be satisfying in the challenging cases listed above. Moving forward, monitoring and verification regimes need to develop new tools, or refine existing ones, to assist in verifying nuclear disarmament. These tools could include more effective use of satellite surveillance and environmental sampling, and a better utilization of existing verification authorities.

When the South African model was first discussed twenty years ago, the extent of noncompliance in the NPT regime and the expectations for broader disarmament appeared very different.[183] Today, the South African model has appeared to many observers as a solution for extremely difficult disarmament challenges. However, as arguments for its applicability have expanded, the model appears far more limited than was the case in the early 1990s. As a consequence, reliance on simple lessons developed decades ago, or even a misinterpretation of those lessons, could lead to misleading or incorrect conclusions. This, in turn, could have the unintended effect of weakening the regimes tasked with verifying WMD rollback or the prospect of disarmament.

3   Iraq

On September 6, 2007, Israeli jets bombed a mysterious facility known as al-Kibar, located in Syria about 100 miles from the Iraqi border. Although both Syrian and Israeli officials refused to comment on what this facility might be, it was widely suspected of being an undeclared nuclear facility. Suspicions about this facility grew in April 2008 when U.S. officials reported on intelligence information—and released photographs and video footage—purporting to demonstrate conclusively that this facility was an undeclared nuclear reactor being built with North Korean assistance.[1] Inspections by the International Atomic Energy Agency (IAEA) in June 2008 appeared to confirm these suspicions.[2]

And yet, at nearly the same time that these apparent revelations were occurring, the IAEA was considering a proposal to provide technical assistance and funding to assist Syria in developing a civilian nuclear program and in determining a site at which to build a nuclear reactor. U.S. officials sharply criticized the IAEA's initial decision to fund Syria's nuclear program at a time when the country was under suspicion of violating its nonproliferation commitments.[3] Mohammed ElBaradei, at that time director-general of the IAEA and corecipient (along with the IAEA) of the Nobel Peace Prize, rejected these criticisms by bringing up and applying apparent lessons from Iraq:

> There are claims against Syria: yes, we are looking at them. There were claims against Iraq, which proved to be bonkers, but only after a terrible war. So we have to be very careful when we talk about investigations. . . . All of you, even if you are not lawyers, know that people and countries are innocent until proven guilty. We continue to act on that basis.[4]

This is a remarkable statement. By setting the standard of "innocent until proven guilty," Dr. ElBaradei appeared to be returning to pre-1990s assumptions of the IAEA—assumptions that allowed countries such as Iraq to build extensive nuclear-weapon programs that flagrantly violated the NPT but were completely undetected by the IAEA. After the violations of the 1990s, it was clear not only that IAEA monitoring and verification capabilities needed to be strengthened but also that states needed to be held to a more stringent standard than an *assumption* of compliance unless clear, irrefutable evidence of weapons came to light.[5] By setting this standard, ElBaradei was in effect making the case for lowering the threshold for demonstrating compliance to such an extent that no state could ever be proven to be in noncompliance.

But what was equally striking in ElBaradei's statement is the manner in which he argued for providing the funding to Syria: "There were claims against Iraq, which proved to be bonkers, but only after a terrible war." Because, El-Baradei implied, the allegations against Iraq were so flagrantly wrong prior to the 2003 Iraq War, the IAEA was justified, *in this instance*, in giving Syria the benefit of the doubt.

ElBaradei's reference to Iraq reflected and played off the generally accepted view that the U.S. government misinterpreted, or even deliberately miscon-strued, the intelligence on Iraqi weapons of mass destruction (WMD) and that, in sharp contrast to the errors of the Bush administration, the international monitoring and verification regimes were correct. ElBaradei was by no means alone in this viewpoint. Although some scholars, as well as members of the Bush administration, questioned the effectiveness of such monitoring and veri-fication regimes prior to the 2003 war,[6] these regimes were largely vindicated in the eyes of the arms control community and the general public following the war. Numerous scholars and officials have argued that the inability to dis-cover WMD in Iraq after the 2003 invasion demonstrated that the monitoring and verification worked—the inspections correctly verified that Saddam had no WMD and deterred him from trying to achieve them.[7] As Hans Blix, the former head of the UN Monitoring Verification and Inspection Commission (UNMOVIC), later wrote:

> After the war, it is becoming clear that inspection and monitoring by the IAEA, UNMOVIC, and its predecessor UN Special Commission (UNSCOM), backed by military, political and economic pressure, had indeed worked for years, achieving Iraqi disarmament and deterring Saddam from rearming. . . . It has also become clear that national intelligence organizations and government hawks, but not the inspectors, had been wrong in their assessments.[8]

Similarly, Jessica Mathews of the Carnegie Endowment for International Peace, wrote in 2013 that the inspections in Iraq "were a striking international suc-cess. . . . In the lead-up to the [2003] war, while national intelligence services were getting the story wrong, UN inspectors knew pretty much what was there and where to look for it."[9]

This viewpoint has had larger implications on international nonproliferation efforts as well. The Iraq War colored IAEA reports on Iran. Despite evidence that surfaced after 2003 that Iran had been pursuing a clandestine nuclear program for nearly two decades, involving enrichment, reprocessing, other sensitive technologies, and extensive deception and denial, ElBaradei admitted in a 2010 interview with Jack Shenker of the *Guardian* that the IAEA reports while he was director-general were "framed to avoid war," largely because of Iraq.[10] The Iraqi experience also shaped responses to U.S., French, and British 2013 allegations that Syria had used chemical weapons (CW) against rebels. Russian president Vladimir Putin, for example, publicly compared U.S. allegations of Syrian CW use to those made by U.S. officials prior to the Iraq War.[11]

Given the damage that the Iraq WMD issue has done—not only to U.S. credibility, but, as the above examples suggest, also to international nonproliferation and disarmament efforts—it is clear that the Iraqi case is worth revisiting. Amid the controversies over Iraqi WMD, we see a tendency to overstate the capabilities of monitoring and verification regimes and the levels of confidence that these inspection processes can give the international community in verifying WMD rollback claims. Although we strongly support international inspections as an irreplaceable and critical nonproliferation instrument, we do not believe the inspectors were or could have been as certain of their conclusions as is now being suggested.

The questions about the monitoring and verification processes in Iraq were underscored by October 2014 revelations that about five thousand CW warheads, artillery shells, and aviation bombs had been discovered in Iraq between 2003 and 2014—in many instances long after formal inspections in the country had been completed.[12] Although these CW delivery vehicles were produced prior to the 1991 Gulf War and many were no longer militarily useful when they were discovered, some reportedly still contained "potent mustard agent or residual sarin."[13] The number of weapons significantly exceeded the numbers previously reported publicly and demonstrate that the inspections were not fully successful in identifying the full extent of Iraq's CW arsenal.

The Iraqi case can be important for thinking about current and future monitoring and verification regimes, but we argue that important lessons were overlooked—and even the *wrong* lessons were learned—about monitoring and verification from the Iraqi case, owing to the extreme politicization of the topic. As we will argue, misconstrued lessons from the Iraqi case have caused some prominent policy-makers and analysts not only to overstate the capabilities of monitoring and verification but, perhaps even more damaging, to introduce new standards for noncompliance that could undermine the effectiveness of these regimes.

The most important *real* lessons from the Iraqi case arise from Iraq's being one of the most revealing examples of a "coercive verification."[14] The verification efforts in Iraq, led by the UN Special Commission on Iraq (UNSCOM) and the IAEA, and later UNMOVIC and the IAEA, were largely carried out in an uncooperative environment, in which the Iraqi regime systematically attempted to conceal its extensive WMD programs and materials.[15] As much as anything, the experience in Iraq (prior to and after the 2003 war) demonstrates the limitations of the international monitoring and verification regimes in confirming declared rollback of WMD programs, especially in "coercive" verification environments.

Despite unprecedented access to facilities, scientists, documents, and materials—access that was only allowed owing to a defeat in war—substantial questions remained about the status of Iraq's WMD programs, both before and even after the 2003 war. The limitations include difficulties that are inherent to monitoring and verification processes themselves, involving such issues as measurement uncertainty, limited access to facilities, and incomplete reporting. However, the limitations are also political, including a lack of political unity within the UN Security Council, the international community, or the very organizations conducting inspections. Challenges in both of these areas can undermine the effectiveness of the regimes.

This chapter examines in detail the specific successes, failures, and lessons that can be learned from the WMD monitoring and verification regimes in Iraq before and after the 2003 war. These regimes included the inspection teams established by UNSCOM and the IAEA following the 1991 Gulf War; by UNMOVIC and the IAEA in the lead-up to the U.S-led Operation Iraqi Freedom (OIF) in 2002–3; and the inspections carried out by the Iraq Survey Group (ISG) following OIF. After examining the set of inspections that took place in Iraq, the chapter then examines the specific lessons that the Iraqi case holds for future monitoring and verification efforts and identifies what we can reasonably expect from such regimes.

Monitoring and Verification in Iraq: An Uncertain Record

The monitoring and verification process in Iraq can be broken up into three distinct periods: the inspections by UNSCOM and the IAEA following the first Gulf War (1991–98), those conducted by UNMOVIC and the IAEA prior to OIF (2002–3), and those following OIF (2003–4). Each of these periods reveals important lessons and will be discussed in turn.

UNSCOM and IAEA Verification, 1991–98

When it invaded Kuwait in August 1990, Iraq was believed to possess an extensive arsenal of chemical and biological weapons (CBW) and a well-established nuclear-weapon program.[16] Indeed, it was feared that Iraq, which had used WMD in the 1980s, might use its CBW against the U.S.-led, UN-mandated coalition that was formed to remove Iraqi forces from Kuwait.[17] After the conclusion of the Gulf War, the UN Security Council (UNSC) adopted Security Council Resolution (SCR) 687, which was a conditional cease-fire outlining the disarmament of Iraq. A central component of Resolution 687 was the dismantlement of Iraq's WMD and ballistic missiles with a range greater than 150 km.[18] The resolution further mandated the formation of a special commission (UNSCOM) to supervise the dismantlement of these programs; the IAEA would provide assistance in the nuclear area.[19]

It was originally estimated that the verification process would take a few months, particularly because it was assumed that the Iraq would cooperate fully with the process, providing full disclosure of its programs and allowing unimpeded access to its facilities.[20] Instead, it became increasingly clear that the regime had not, in fact, committed to the process. Within three months of the adoption of SCR 687, the Ba'athist regime began obstructing the work of UNSCOM and the IAEA, denying inspectors access to suspected facilities and presenting incomplete accounts of their clandestine weapon activities. This pattern of systematic obstruction and incomplete reporting would continue until UNSCOM inspectors were removed in 1998. Over the seven years that UNSCOM operated in Iraq, they experienced numerous armed standoffs with Iraqi security forces at suspected facilities, concealment of vital information relating to their WMD programs, and lying about clandestine programs by Iraqi officials.[21]

Neither UNSCOM nor the IAEA was originally designed to verify WMD rollback in the coercive verification environment that they encountered in Iraq.

Because the inspection teams had expected cooperation, they were initially unprepared for the invasive searches necessary to demonstrate noncompliance. Indeed, the Iraqi reluctance to disarm in effect reversed the orientation of the inspections. Originally, the inspection teams had been intended only to *confirm* disarmament; now, they had to prove that Saddam's regime had *not* disarmed. In his December 1997 letter to the United Nations, UNSCOM executive chairman Richard Butler reported that "Iraq would not itself volunteer any new information. It preferred a situation where it would verify the information held by the Commission."[22] As Graham Pearson notes, "[T]his arrangement completely inverted the relationship between the United Nations and Iraq and effectively put UNSCOM, not Iraq, in the dock!"[23]

POLITICIZATION OF THE INSPECTION PROCESS

Almost from the start, divisions within the UN Security Council began to politicize the inspection process. This politicization, correspondingly, began to undermine the reliability and credibility of inspections.[24] As a result of early noncompliance by Iraq, the Security Council did pass resolution 707, which stated that Iraq's opposition placed it in "material breach" of resolution 687, implying that the Security Council might use force against Iraq.[25] But it quickly became clear that the Security Council would not be likely to back up the resolution with force; indeed, Iraq interpreted the resolution itself as evidence of this fact. According to Charles Duelfer, who served as the deputy chairman of UNSCOM from 1993 to 2000, "[I]t thus became clear to Baghdad early on that the risk of noncompliance was limited."[26]

As a result, Iraq was emboldened to begin undermining the inspectors at nearly every step of the process. Inspectors were placed in the difficult situation of having to decide whether to report each particular instance of obstructionism to the UNSC. Because it was clear that the Security Council would not intervene except in the most clear, egregious cases, "Iraq learned that small offenses would not be punished."[27]

This politicization of the inspections did affect the inspectors' ability to continue to press key issues. For example, according to Duelfer, Iraqi officials informed UNSCOM director Rolf Ekeus in May 1995 that if UNSCOM gave a positive report on Iraq's chemical and missile programs, they would answer UNSCOM's remaining questions on biological weapons. Despite continuing concerns in these areas, Ekeus reportedly acquiesced: "Ekeus recognized that [Security] council support was weakening and took a decisive decision to straddle all the technical doubts about Iraqi compliance. His report skipped over some of UNSCOM experts' concerns in the missile and chemical areas."[28] Ultimately, Ekeus's report appeased neither Iraq nor the Security Council. Although Iraq did provide some information on its biological-weapon program, the information turned out to be highly misleading, as soon became apparent after the August 7, 1995, defection of Hussein Kamel, Saddam's son in law and the director of Iraq's WMD programs. Nor did Ekeus's decision ultimately end the French, Russian, and Chinese pressure to lift the sanctions. The divisions in the UNSC eased a bit after major Iraqi revelations following Kamel's defection showed clear evidence of Iraqi deception. But the pressures by France, Russia, and China to end the sanctions intensified again in 1997.

In the final years of UNSCOM's existence, the political divisions within the Security Council deepened significantly and contributed to the increasing difficulties of the inspection process. The Security Council managed to maintain a more or less unified position in the early years, with the 1990–91 war fresh in their minds, but by the late 1990s, the situation was fundamentally different. At key points where a strong, unified position would have been necessary, France, China, and Russia not only refused to support any threat of military action to force Iraqi compliance but also interpreted any slightly positive sign as an opportunity to remove the sanctions from Iraq altogether. Several top UNSCOM officials have pointed to these divisions within the Security Council as a key reason why the inspections regime ultimately collapsed.[29]

KEY BREAKTHROUGHS

Despite the challenges that UNSCOM encountered, it did manage over time to evolve and improve its ability to operate in a coercive verification environment. UNSCOM inspectors often refused to be intimidated when Iraqi military and guard forces threatened them or refused to allow them access to facilities. This increasingly confrontational approach employed by UNSCOM led to a number of very tense situations including armed standoffs outside of suspected facilities, explicit verbal and written threats to inspectors, and several instances in which shots were fired to intimidate weapons inspectors.[30] Nevertheless, this new approach, combined with the extended process of intrusive investigations, eventually began to pay off. In 1995, UNSCOM discovered evidence of a far more extensive biological-weapon program than had previously been believed to exist. International experts concluded from this evidence that Iraq had not reported a full-scale biological-weapon program and had not accounted for 17 to 22 tons of bacterial culture media. UNSCOM similarly concluded in May 1995 that Iraq had concealed significant parts of its chemical-weapon program.[31]

The increasing pressure that UNSCOM was able to apply also created tensions within the Iraq regime, as senior officials were caught lying to inspectors. These tensions are believed to have played a role in spurring Hussein Kamel's defection.[32] Kamel's defection led to another set of major revelations about Iraq's WMD programs. Just prior to the defection, the Iraqi regime had presented its third "full, final, and complete declaration" (FFCD) of its activities, but Iraq then quickly revised its statement, fearing that Kamel would reveal critical information on the Iraqi programs. Claiming that they had just "discovered" additional documents that Kamel had hidden without the Iraqi regime's knowledge, Iraq directed inspectors to a chicken farm purportedly owned by Kamel. Hidden on this farm were more than one hundred trunks and boxes containing 650,000 pages of materials relating to Iraq's WMD programs. These documents revealed a great deal that was previously unknown about the Iraqi programs, including the confirmed existence of a major biological-weapon program and production efforts of VX chemical weapons.[33]

The IAEA, however, then under the direction of Hans Blix, had somewhat more difficulty in adapting to the coercive verification environment in Iraq. Unlike UNSCOM's confrontational approach to Iraqi obstruction, the IAEA chose to follow a "policy of behavioral non-belligerence."[34] The disagreement between UNSCOM and the IAEA over the conduct of, and general approach to, inspections created significant tensions between the two organizations and, critics have argued, caused the IAEA not to press hard enough for information that the Iraqi regime continued to conceal.[35]

It does appear that IAEA's more congenial approach caused the agency to accept some of Iraq's misleading declarations too readily. From the start, UNSCOM inspectors viewed IAEA heads Hans Blix and Mohamed ElBaradei as "too quick and too willing to accept Iraqi protestations that there had never been a nuclear weapons program" and too willing to dismiss early evidence to the contrary.[36] Moreover, on August 2, 1995—only a few days before Hussein Kamel's defection and at a time that UNSCOM was uncovering extensive Iraqi concealment of CBW programs—the IAEA largely accepted the Iraqi regime's third FFCD of its nuclear weapon activities, supporting the conclusion that "the essential components of Iraq's past clandestine nuclear program have been identified and have been destroyed, removed, or rendered harmless and that the scope of the past programmes is well understood."[37] This conclusion was found to be premature when Kamel defected a few days after the IAEA submitted its report. Following Kamel's defection, the Iraqi regime turned over more than a half-million pages of documents, most of which reportedly concerned a crash program initiated just prior to the war to produce nuclear weapons by subverting safeguarded nuclear material.[38]

UNANSWERED QUESTIONS AND THE END OF UNSCOM

Over the seven years that UNSCOM inspectors were in Iraq, they conducted several thousand inspections at more than one thousand facilities, destroyed 38,500 munitions, 480,000 liters of chemical agents, and 1.8 million liters of precursor chemical agents.[39] They also made tremendous headway in dismantling Iraq's missile and nuclear-weapon infrastructure. Despite these tremendous successes, however, they did not resolve significant questions about key aspects of Iraq's WMD programs. The biggest questions remained about Iraqi chemical- and especially biological-weapon programs. These unresolved issues included the status of about 31,600 chemical munitions, 550 mustard gas bombs, and 4,000 tons of chemical precursors; the possibility that Iraq retained some missile propellants; Iraq's ability to produce VX agent; and extensive questions about Iraq's biological-weapon program.[40]

On the nuclear side, the IAEA reported that they believed they had largely dismantled the program, though they did emphasize some remaining questions. For example, Hans Blix reported in October 1997:

> I have . . . cautioned [the UN Security Council] that beyond questions which arise from our study of the coherent nuclear program in Iraq, from interrogations in Iraq, from talking to suppliers, etc., there are questions that are not prompting answers. There could still be components which we cannot see that they are missing, but which could have been there. There could have been some program or some activity outside of what we have termed the coherent technical pictures. . . . There will, in the case of Iraq as in the case of any other inspection, always remain an element of uncertainty.[41]

In April 1998 a panel of experts concluded that Iraq had met its obligations to provide information on its nuclear-weapon program, reporting that they had found no new evidence of an ongoing program. Despite this finding, however, the new IAEA director, Mohamed ElBaradei, underscored the impossibility of resolving the issue completely and therefore stressed the need for ongoing monitoring and verification in Iraq. On June 1, 1998, reacting to critics who were concerned about the agency's conclusions, ElBaradei wrote that Iraq's nuclear file remained open:

> [A]fter seven years of investigation and inspection . . . there are "no indications" that Iraq retains the material or practical capability to produce nuclear weapons, but it must be understood that "no indication" is not the same as "no existence." This is because no matter how comprehensive the inspection, any country-wide verification process, in Iraq or anywhere else, has a degree of uncertainty that aims to verify the absence of readily concealable objects such as small amounts of nuclear material or weapons components.[42]

As the inspections continued into 1997 and 1998, however, UNSCOM inspectors encountered increasing difficulty in answering the remaining questions, especially on Iraq's CBW programs. In the end, after continued politicization of the inspection process, increasing Iraqi obstruction, and significant opposition by some members of the UNSC to continued intrusive inspections, UNSCOM's executive director, Richard Butler, reported to the Security Council in December 1998 that because of a lack of Iraqi cooperation, UNSCOM was "not able to conduct the substantive disarmament work mandated to it by the Security Council and, thus, to give the Council the assurances it requires with respect to Iraq's prohibited weapons programmes."[43] Shortly after Butler gave this report, the United States and Great Britain called for the removal of UNSCOM inspectors from Iraq and began Operation Desert Fox, in which they bombed suspected Iraqi military facilities. At this point, it was clear that UNSCOM inspectors would no longer be welcome in Iraq. Shortly thereafter, UNSCOM was disbanded and a successor verification and inspection regime, UNMOVIC, was created to take its place. Despite UNMOVIC's creation on paper in December 1999, Iraq did not permit inspections again until November 2002.

UNMOVIC and IAEA Verification, 2002–3

THE CREATION OF UNMOVIC AND UNSCR 1441

Despite a recognized need for an organization to replace UNSCOM, there was a good deal of controversy over the initial creation of its successor, UNMOVIC. Critics argued that UN Resolution 1284, which created UNMOVIC in 2000, changed the orientation of the verification regime. According to the former UNSCOM executive chairman Rolf Ekeus, "Resolution 1284 gives the impression that the matter of past weapons, which was the focus of 687, is no longer as significant. The new resolution doesn't indicate that there are any existing weapons in Iraq. The emphasis is on monitoring, and by implication that gives the impression that the Security Council is no longer concerned with existing capabilities but more concerned about Iraq's intentions."[44]

There was also a controversy over who would lead the organization. The United States and Britain lobbied hard to select Ekeus to head the new organization but encountered strong opposition from France, Russia, and China. In the end, the UNSC settled on a compromise of Hans Blix.[45] Critics at the time reportedly raised concerns about this choice, arguing that Blix had not pushed hard enough when he had led the IAEA inspections of Iraq in the 1990s.[46]

Because Saddam had refused to let weapon inspectors back into Iraq after 1998, UNMOVIC's operational role was at first a bit unclear. But political pressure (and the threat of force) mainly from the United States and Britain soon allowed for inspectors to return to Iraq. On November 8, 2002, the UN Security Council adopted Resolution 1441, which declared Iraq to be in "material breach" of its obligations and gave Iraq a "final opportunity to comply with disarmament obligations." UNMOVIC and the IAEA were given far reaching authorities, including "immediate, unimpeded, unrestricted, and private access to all officials and other persons whom UNMOVIC and the IAEA may at their discretion interview." It also gave the inspectors the ability to "conduct interviews inside or outside of Iraq" and to "facilitate the travel of those interviewed and family members outside of Iraq." Furthermore, it required Iraq to provide a list of all personnel and facilities that were currently and formerly associated with Iraq's nuclear, chemical, biological, and ballistic missile programs.[47]

With the threat of war looming, Iraq agreed to the terms of Resolution 1441 and allowed inspectors back into the country. UNMOVIC and the IAEA subsequently conducted 750 inspections at 550 sites between November 25, 2002, and March 17, 2003.[48]

INSPECTION CHALLENGES AND MISSED OPPORTUNITIES

Even in the best of circumstances, it would have been very difficult for the inspectors to have produced conclusive results from their operations in Iraq. The inspectors faced a difficult position with the inspections they conducted in Iraq. At best, inspections can confirm that something does exist, that the destruction of specific items took place, or that a certain facility would not be able to produce certain items for some time. They cannot—as the inspectors were mandated to do—ever give complete confidence that proscribed programs do not exist, especially in a country as large as Iraq.[49]

This challenge was compounded by the fact that Iraq had twelve years of experience in playing "cat and mouse" games with inspectors, and that, despite years of sanctions, the regime nevertheless still retained plenty of resources that it could have devoted to concealing its weapon programs.[50] Moreover, the inspections themselves were conducted under severe time constraints and tremendous political pressures to produce conclusive results one way or the other. UNMOVIC was expected to answer definitively, in less than four months, questions that UNSCOM was not able to answer during seven years of operation in Iraq.

Critics of the UNMOVIC inspections also raised questions about the expertise of some of the inspectors. Indeed, almost none of the people from UNSCOM were used in the UNMOVIC inspections.[51] One reason for this was that the inspectors had to be UN officials, rather than experts provided for shorter stints by individual countries. It was believed that this would alleviate concerns that the inspectors were tools of their home countries, but an effect was that many experienced inspectors were unwilling to leave prestigious positions at home for temporary positions in the United Nations.[52]

In addition to these difficulties faced by the inspection process, the inspectors also missed key opportunities to gain information about Iraq's programs. One of the critical goals of the inspections was to obtain a clear picture of Iraqi programs by interviewing key scientists who had worked on Iraq's WMD programs. Throughout this inspection process, however, there was clear evidence of intimidation of these scientists, particularly because interviews generally took place with members of Iraq's National Monitoring Directorate (NMD) present. Unfortunately, neither UNMOVIC nor the IAEA took advantage of the right under UNSCR 1441 to interview scientists outside of Iraq, away from the pressure from the Iraqi regime. Although Iraqi officials grudgingly agreed to allow scientists to leave the country and provided a list of five hundred scientists in December 2002 to UNMOVIC,[53] Blix stated in his March 7 report, thirteen days before OIF began, that they were only then planning "to request such interviews shortly."[54] Moreover, in a directive originating from Blix, neither the Iraqi NMD minders nor the interviewed scientists were allowed to tape the interviews. Some scientists refused to be interviewed at all after UNMOVIC denied their requests to be allowed, for their own protection, to record their interviews. By the end of February 2003 (roughly three weeks before the war began), only three Iraqi scientists had reportedly agreed to be interviewed. In the end, only eleven scientists ever were reportedly interviewed at all.[55]

UNMOVIC AND IAEA REPORTS

Throughout UNMOVIC's inspections, most observers agreed at the time that "Iraq's compliance was superficial and oriented to facilitating the process of inspections, rather than on providing cooperation on substantive matters."[56] Hans Blix reported as much in his January 27, 2003, report to the Security Council, stating that Iraq had cooperated on process "fairly well," noting that "access has been provided to all sites we have wanted to inspect and with one exception it has been prompt." However, Blix said that Resolution 1441 required Iraqi cooperation to be "active," and he reported that Iraq had not assisted UNMOVIC in finding documents, answering unresolved disarmament issues in the areas of chemical and biological weapons, providing a list of all personnel who had participated in WMD and missile programs, or allowing UNMOVIC private access to scientists for interviews.[57]

Blix reported similar difficulties in his subsequent reports to the Security Council, on February 14 and March 7, again noting cooperation on process but less on substance, which "requires more than the opening of doors."[58] In his February report, Blix stated that on many outstanding "issues of substance," including anthrax, the nerve agent VX, and long-range missiles, Iraq had, in its December 7 declaration, "missed the opportunity to provide the fresh material and evidence needed to respond to the open questions. This is perhaps the most important problem we are facing. . . . Iraq itself must squarely tackle this task and avoid belittling the questions."[59] Blix did note that the Iraqi regime had turned over some documents pertaining to these issues just prior to his briefing, and although "no new evidence was provided in the papers," they "could be indicative of a more active attitude focusing on important open issues."[60]

In his final March 7 report, Blix reported that "after a period of somewhat reluctant cooperation, there has been an acceleration of initiatives from the Iraqi side since the end of January."[61] These initiatives included Iraqi assistance in excavating and beginning to take steps toward disposing of several R-400 bombs, admitting (after some resistance) that its Al-Samoud-2 missiles violated UNSC requirements and beginning disposal of them, and eventually turning over an expanded list of scientists for UNMOVIC to interview. But Blix did express "disappointment" over Iraq's not providing more documentary evidence about its proscribed programs, stating that "Iraq, with a highly developed administrative system, should be able to provide more documentary evidence about its proscribed weapons programmes. Only a few new such documents have come to light so far and been handed over since we began inspections."[62] Overall, Blix summarized the inspections by stating that "while the numerous initiatives, which are now taken by the Iraqi side with a view to resolving some long-standing open disarmament issues, can be seen as 'active,' or even 'proactive,' these initiatives 3–4 months into the new resolution cannot be said to constitute 'immediate' cooperation. Nor do they necessarily cover all areas of relevance."[63] UNMOVIC compiled a list of more than one hundred unresolved disarmament issues shortly before the end of their inspections. Most of these questions were never sufficiently resolved before the war.[64]

The IAEA reports were more positive, though they did initially raise some questions as well. For example, in his January 27, 2003, report to the UN Security Council, ElBaradei reported ongoing and as-yet inconclusive IAEA investigations in attempted aluminum tube imports (which later proved not to be for nuclear purposes) and missing high explosives, and a lack of "proactive" assistance by the Iraqi regime. He further reported that "little progress has been made in resolving the questions and concerns that remained as of 1998," and that "further verification activities will be necessary before the IAEA will be able to provide credible assurance that Iraq has no nuclear weapons programme."[65] And yet, despite these gaps in information and unresolved questions, ElBaradei seemed certain of the conclusions that the IAEA would find well before the inspection and verification process had been completed. He ended his report noting full confidence that the verification process would vindicate Iraq:

> [W]e have found no evidence that Iraq has revived its nuclear weapons programme since the elimination of the programme in the 1990s. However, our work is steadily progressing and should be allowed to run its natural course. With our verification system in place, barring exceptional circumstances, and provided there is sustained proactive cooperation by Iraq, we should be able within the next few months to provide credible assurance that Iraq has no nuclear weapons programme. These few months would be a valuable investment in peace because they could help us avoid war.[66]

It is not fully clear, however, why the IAEA would have had such confidence about what their conclusions would be, given that key investigations were still ongoing and given that, by their own admission, Iraq had not yet provided the necessary "proactive" assistance.

Although the IAEA report also expressed disappointment over some areas of Iraqi cooperation (such as providing a list of all scientists involved with Iraq's proscribed programs),[67] its later reports on January 27 and especially March 7 indicated Iraqi cooperation. Much of these last IAEA reports focused on investigating claims, mainly based on U.S. and British intelligence, about continued attempts by the Iraqi regime to acquire technology that may have assisted in a nuclear-weapon program, such as high-strength aluminum tubes, and a forged document reporting Iraqi attempts to acquire uranium from Niger. The IAEA reported that it had seen no evidence of procurement attempts relating to nuclear weapons, and that, in summary, "[W]e have to date found no evidence or plausible indication of the revival of a nuclear weapon program in Iraq."[68]

INCONCLUSIVE RESULTS?

As one can see, the IAEA and UNMOVIC reported somewhat mixed results, indicating unresolved questions in the chemical, biological, and missile areas but expressing confidence that Iraq had abandoned its nuclear program. In subsequent interviews, however, both ElBaradei and Blix did express doubts about whether they could verify that Iraq did not have active programs in these areas. As the heads of the two organizations that oversaw the inspections in Iraq from 2002 to 2003, these statements should be taken seriously. In a lengthy interview on August 29, 2003, with Tim Sebastian of the BBC News program *Hardtalk*, ElBaradei was asked by Sebastian: "Bottom line, there could be a nuclear weapons program in Iraq?" ElBaradei responded:

> Oh there could be, there could be, I'd be surprised if there were because in 1998 we believed that we eliminated Iraq's nuclear weapons program—they could have restarted it. . . . I would be very surprised if they were, if we were to discover that there was a nuclear weapons program restarted in Iraq. However if there were . . . what . . . I did not, I did not, certify that Iraq was clean when we left Iraq.[69]

Later in the same interview, when discussing apparent disagreements with British foreign secretary Jack Straw, ElBaradei stated that they "both agreed that the jury is still out" on Iraq's WMD programs, admitting that there may be not only chemical- and biological-weapon programs but also a nuclear-weapon program.[70] On his apparent disagreement with Straw over the possible existence of a nuclear-weapon program, ElBaradei said that "it's just a question of different perceptions of where we are coming from, of what information he gets, what information I get. *Again, I could be wrong, he could be right . . .*"[71] In the same vein, after receiving the Nobel Peace Prize in 2005, ElBaradei stated in an interview with the Associated Press Television News: "We had disagreement before the Iraq War—honest disagreement. We could have been wrong, they could have been right."[72]

Hans Blix, similarly, admitted that UNMOVIC was not certain that WMD programs—or even WMD *arsenals*—did not exist in Iraq when the 2003 war began. When asked, four months after Operation Iraq Freedom began, whether he was surprised that U.S. forces had not yet located weapons of mass destruction, he answered: "No, I would not say I am surprised, but nor would I say I would have been surprised if they had found something."[73] This is a formulation that Blix would repeat over the next several years. In a 2004 joint interview with ElBaradei, he stated: "[W]e could not say definitively that there aren't any weapons of mass destruction. . . . [T]here were things unaccounted for. It meant they could either exist or not exist. So we could not affirm that they weren't there, but we—at least we didn't fall into the trap that the U.S. and U.K. did in asserting that they existed."[74] Blix later wrote of his final March 7, 2003, report: "I did not answer the question whether or not Iraq had disarmed. I did not know."[75]

Later reports by UNMOVIC further underscored the unanswered questions that remain to this day. In a briefing accompanying UNMOVIC's final report before it was closed down on June 29, 2007, Acting Executive Chairman Demetrius Perricos warned that in the present security environment, the possibility that nonstate actors could obtain toxic chemical agents remaining in Iraq "is real." He noted that a "residue of uncertainty" remained about Iraq's chemical, biological, and missile programs because a number of issues remained unresolved. And while some of these issues "could have been clarified with some additional activities like sampling, interviews, check of documents in the possession of the ISG or even information from the coalition authorities . . . [s]ome issues would not have been resolved even with these measures. . . . Under the present circumstances the remaining outstanding issues cannot be resolved and therefore contribute to the residue of uncertainty."[76]

One therefore must wonder what confidence the international community would have about the status of Iraq's WMD programs if the 2003 war had not occurred. A great deal of the confidence that Iraq had abandoned the bulk of its WMD programs and stockpiles in the early 1990s came from the investigations carried out by the ISG after the initial military operations took place. Indeed, Perricos stated that, because UNMOVIC had not been allowed to enter into Iraq after OIF began, UNMOVIC's final report often relies heavily on the findings of the ISG.[77]

The Inspections of the Iraq Survey Group (2003–4)

Even while the major combat operations of OIF were still taking place, U.S. special operations teams were conducting inspections of suspected Iraqi facilities to search for WMD. The Iraq Survey Group was established in June 2003 by the United States, with British and Australian assistance, to help systematize and coordinate this search.[78] The first director of the ISG was David Kay, who led the group until he resigned in October 2003. He was replaced by Charles Duelfer, who led the ISG until it ended its search for Iraqi WMD in December 2004.[79]

Most of the available information on the ISG's findings is located in the interim report provided by David Kay in October 2003, and in the ISG's final report, which was presented on September 30, 2004, under the direction of Charles Duelfer. Although Kay and Duelfer present divergent theories about Iraq's WMD programs, one conclusion that they share is that Saddam never truly gave up his WMD aspirations.

In a report to Congress shortly before he resigned, Kay theorized that the WMD were not in Iraq, that they probably had not been there since shortly after the 1991 war, but *that Saddam had believed that WMD stockpiles existed.*[80] Duelfer suggested in the 2004 ISG report, as well as in subsequent interviews and a book, that although Saddam did not have any active WMD programs (and was presumably aware of that fact), he tried to retain the intellectual expertise for the programs and the ability to restart the WMD programs quickly once the sanctions regime against Iraq crumbled. In the meantime, Saddam would actively try to undermine sanctions regime—and had made significant progress in that endeavor—and would try to improve Iraq's capabilities for delivery vehicles, including missiles.[81]

THE REPORTED FINDINGS OF THE ISG

The headlines in the press reports on the ISG's findings declared that "the ISG found no stockpiles of weapons of mass destruction."[82] These headlines are correct, but the ISG's reports were a bit more nuanced.

Nuclear: David Kay reported in October 2003 that "the testimony we have obtained from Iraqi scientists and senior government officials should clear up any doubts about whether Saddam still wanted to obtain nuclear weapons. They have told ISG that Saddam Husayn remained firmly committed to acquiring nuclear weapons."[83] Charles Duelfer, similarly, reported to Congress in 2004 that "the ISG has developed information that suggests Iraqi interest in preserving and expanding the knowledge needed to design and develop nuclear weapons."[84] This information included:

> documents describing diagnostic techniques that are important for nuclear weapons experiments, such as flash x-ray radiography, laser velocimetry, and high-speed photography. Other documents found outside the laboratory described a high-voltage switch that can be used to detonate a nuclear weapon, laser detonation, nuclear fusion, radiation measurement, and radiation safety.[85]

The September 2004 Duelfer Report also indicates that the ISG found documents and equipment hidden in some scientists' homes that would have been useful in resuming uranium enrichment by centrifuge and electromagnetic isotope separation. Moreover, the report states that in the year before OIF, the Iraqi regime reportedly did undertake improvements to technology that could have been used in a renewed uranium enrichment program, including projects to acquire a magnet production line, carbon fiber filament winding equipment, and a new Department of Rotary Machinery. However, the Duelfer Report notes that they "uncovered no indication that Iraq had resumed fissile material or nuclear weapon research and development activities since 1991."[86]

Chemical and Biological. In his 2003 report to Congress, David Kay stated that the ISG discovered a clandestine network of laboratories and safe houses controlled by Iraqi intelligence and security services containing equipment that was suitable for chemical and biological research and "new research on BW-applicable agents, Brucella and Congo Crimean Hemorrhagic Fever (CCHF), and continuing work on ricin and aflatoxin."[87] Kay also reported that the ISG discovered a prison laboratory complex possibly used in human testing for biological-weapon agents. None of these activities had been reported to the United Nations by Iraq, and Kay reported evidence that explicit orders had been given to conceal these activities from UNMOVIC inspectors when they returned to Iraq in 2002. He further reported that Iraq had the infrastructure and talent to resume CBW production, and that "ISG teams have developed multiple sources that indicate that Iraq explored the possibility of CW production in recent years, possibly as late as 2003."[88]

Charles Duelfer reported in March 2004 that "Iraq was working up to March 2003 to construct new facilities for the production of chemicals. There were plans under the direction of a leading nuclear scientist/WMD program manager to construct plants capable of making a variety of chemicals and producing a year's supply of any chemical in a month. This was a crash program."[89] Although most of the chemicals specified in this program were conventional commercial chemicals, Duelfer noted that some of them were dual use, including one that "was used by Iraq before 1991 as a stabilizing agent for the nerve agent VX. Iraq had plans before OIF for large-scale production of this chemical."[90] The ISG did not uncover evidence that the regime had ever resumed actual production of chemical or biological weapons.

Missile. The ISG discovered an aggressive missile program that had been concealed from the international community. This program included advanced design work for liquid propellant missiles with ranges up to 1,000 kilometers and new work underway on solid propellant missiles. The ISG also confirmed that Iraq had conducted secret negotiations with North Korea between 1999 and 2002 to acquire North Korean technologies relating to 1,300-kilometer range ballistic missiles.[91]

QUESTIONS ABOUT THE DUELFER REPORT'S
CONCLUSIONS ON IRAQI INTENTIONS

As noted, the Duelfer Report concluded from this evidence that Saddam still desired to develop weapons of mass destruction, that the regime retained the capability to restart these programs once the sanctions regime was lifted, and that the Iraqi efforts were focused primarily on undermining the sanctions regime and on acquiring the delivery systems for these weapons. Moreover, although not fully reflected in the conclusions of the Duelfer Report, the report does catalog a variety of programs suggesting that the Iraqi regime was expanding its research in all areas of their proscribed programs—nuclear, chemical, biological, and missile—though, with the exception of missiles, at relatively low levels.

Other analysts have drawn different conclusions from the evidence presented in the Duelfer Report, speculating that Iraq may simply have been following a different production model for chemical and biological weapons than those taken by other states. As Graham Pearson argues, if the country views its WMD arsenals as offensive weapons to be used aggressively on the battlefield rather than as defensive weapons for deterrence, the country could produce, "deploy and use chemical and biological weapons *at the time of its choosing.*" With this approach, he notes, "there is no stockpile to unequivocally demonstrate non-compliance with the international prohibition regimes of the BTWC and CWC."[92] Former UNSCOM executive chairman Rolf Ekeus had presented a similar thesis about Iraq's WMD programs in 2003, arguing that because Iraqi chemical agents deteriorated rapidly owing to low-quality technology and laboratories, "[T]he Iraq policy after the Gulf War was to halt all production of warfare agents and to focus on design and engineering, with the purpose of activating production and shipping of warfare agents directly to the battlefield in the event of war. . . . Such work could be blended into ordinary civilian production facilities and activities."[93]

However one evaluates such questions about the ISG's assessment of the intended production model for Iraq's chemical and biological weapons, there are questions that can be raised about the evidence that the ISG examined and the methods it employed in its investigations.

METHODOLOGY, EVIDENCE, AND
OTHER ISSUES IN THE DUELFER REPORT

According to the Duelfer Report, the ISG inspected hundreds of facilities, examined a vast number of documents obtained from Iraqi security and intelligence facilities, and interviewed numerous Iraqi officials.[94] Yet both David Kay and the Duelfer Report also note a number of serious difficulties that the ISG encountered in its searches that raise significant questions about the level of confidence we can have in the ISG's findings. These difficulties include the following:

Looting of and Limited Access to Facilities. Although the ISG carried out numerous inspections of Iraqi facilities, both David Kay and the Duelfer Report admit that the ISG was nevertheless severely constrained in these inspections, not only because many sites were destroyed or looted but also because of the lack of security. For example, at the time that David Kay reported that he believed the WMD had been destroyed in the early 1990s, by Kay's own account the ISG had inspected only about 10 of the 130 known ammunition storage sites—some of which were the size of Manhattan—let alone any hidden or underground sites.[95] Many of these sites were severely looted by the time the ISG visited them. According to the Duelfer Report: "First, many sites had been reduced to rubble either by the war or subsequent looting. The coalition did not have the manpower to secure the various sites thought to be associated with WMD. Hence, as a military unit moved through an area, possible WMD sites might have been examined, but they were left soon after. Looters often destroyed the sites once they were abandoned."[96] Moreover, because the insurgency began targeting the ISG, they were unable to gain access to some sites or stay at some sites for long.[97]

Intimidation of Iraqis. The Duelfer Report indicates that the ISG obtained much of its information from Iraqi detainees. And yet, it also notes that detainees were extremely hesitant to talk frankly with the ISG, fearing retribution once they were released.[98] Indeed, as it was, a number of the Iraqis with experience with the nuclear-weapon program were reportedly assassinated in the early months following OIF.[99]

Organized Destruction of Documents and Material. In his 2003 congressional testimony, David Kay reported "[d]eliberate dispersal and destruction of material and documentation related to weapons programs [that] began pre-conflict and ran trans-to-post conflict."[100] George Tenet, at that time the U.S. director of central intelligence, summarized these difficulties in 2004: "We have been faced with the organized destruction of documentary and computer evidence in a wide range of offices, laboratories, and companies suspected of WMD work. The pattern of these efforts is one of deliberate rather than random acts."[101]

Unexamined Documents. The Duelfer Report notes that nine hundred workers translated and reviewed millions of documents related to Iraq's WMD. And yet there were literally millions of documents that were seized in Operation Iraqi Freedom that were not translated before the ISG submitted its final report.[102]

Unpursued Leads. After the release of the final report of the ISG, Duelfer admitted that there were leads relating to Iraq's WMD that had not been pursued.[103] Nevertheless, Duelfer reported in April 2005 that he had "a lot of confidence" in the ISG's findings, including the dismissal of the possibility that Iraq's WMD had been moved to Syria, because "someone would have told something to us about that."[104] And yet, just a month before, the *Addendums to the Comprehensive Report*, published by the ISG in March 2005, stated:

> There was evidence of a discussion of possible WMD collaboration initiated by a Syrian security officer, and ISG received information about a possible movement of material out of Iraq, including the possibility that WMD was involved. In the judgment of the working group, these reports were sufficiently credible to merit further investigation. ISG was unable to complete its investigation and is unable to rule out the possibility that WMD was evacuated to Syria before the war.[105]

The judgment of the ISG in the *Addendums* was that, while unlikely, they were unable to rule out this possibility. One month later, that conclusion surprisingly had become "a lot of confidence" that a transfer had *not* taken place.[106]

Additional reports surfaced suggesting that other leads were not pursued by the ISG. Some of these reports were from military and civilian personnel who worked with the ISG on the search for Iraq's WMD.[107] Obviously, it is not clear that any "smoking guns" would have been discovered if the ISG investigations had continued. But, given the leads that had not been pursued and documents that had not been examined, one has to wonder why the ISG was so willing to close the investigation on Iraq's WMD and why the Bush administration was so willing to allow the end of the investigation. Perhaps the Bush administration wanted, if possible, to put the issue behind them and focus public attention on other issues in the lead-up to the 2004 election.

Methodology. When speaking of the methodology it used, the Duelfer Report indicated that it tried to get inside Saddam's mind—to identify "what Saddam thought"—to characterize his "likely vision" of the future role of WMD in Iraq.[108] UNMOVIC raised questions about this method, however, noting that "[i]n many cases, especially regarding Iraq's intentions, the report does not include substantiating information to support the judgments and assumptions it contains."[109]

In summary, the strength of the Dueler Report's conclusions were affected by several factors, including security problems that prevented the experts from examining all the sites they needed to, the ISG's inability to check all leads and documents, and a methodology that raised questions. In the end, we may never have a complete picture of Iraq's WMD programs and capabilities, though recent revelations of CW in Iraq have provided a clearer picture than had existed. In any case, the ISG reports offer the most systematic assessment to date.

The 2014 CW Revelations, the al-Muthanna Chemical-Weapon Complex, and ISIL

The issue of WMD in Iraq again received media attention when, in June 2014, over the span of a few days, Sunni forces from the Islamic State in Iraq and the Levant (ISIL) captured a large swath of Iraqi territory. On June 19, reports surfaced that ISIL had captured the al-Muthanna chemical-weapon complex.[110] The facility was believed to be the center of Saddam Hussein's chemical-weapon program and was used to produce large amounts of chemical-weapon agents, including sarin and mustard gas.[111] According to the Duelfer Report: "The majority of the Al Muthanna complex was bombed during [Operation] Desert Storm, completely incapacitating Iraq's chemical weapon production capabilities, however, large stockpiles of chemical weapons and bulk agent survived."[112]

Following Operation Desert Storm, UNSCOM's Chemical Destruction Group oversaw destruction operations at the site. The majority of CW agents at the site, as well as those gathered from elsewhere in Iraq, were reportedly destroyed at the facility. However, the Duelfer Report did mention that some materials remained: "Stockpiles of chemical munitions are still stored there. The most dangerous ones have been declared to the UN and are sealed in bunkers. Although declared, the bunkers contents have yet to be confirmed."[113] The report also provided more detail on these bunkers:

> Two sealed cruciform bunkers containing the largest declared stockpile of chemical munitions, old bulk chemical agent, and hazardous material associated with the CW program remained. The surrounding area at the facility became a refuse area or junkyard for relics of Iraq's past CW program.[114]

After the al-Muthanna site was captured by ISIL, U.S. State Department officials downplayed the utility of these materials for weapon use. In a written statement, State Department spokeswoman Jen Psaki, said: "We remain concerned about the seizure of any military site by the ISIL. . . . We do not believe that the complex contains CW materials of military value and it would be very difficult, if not impossible, to safely move the materials."[115] Duelfer also wrote about the seizure of the site by ISIL on his personal blog:

> [S]ome of the precursor chemicals were too unstable to move safely to the incinerator and hydrolysis plant we operated from 1992–1994. So we placed barrels of this toxic waste and contaminated equipment in two huge bunkers on the facility, inventoried the contents and entombed them. The contents are dangerous, but not as weapons. . . . They were closer to toxic waste than weapons. . . . [T]he risk that the contents can somehow be used against others is minute. It is more akin to toxic waste than a weapons bunker.[116]

More troubling, however, were the October 2014 revelations in the *New York Times*, which reported that numerous chemical weapons were discovered at or around the Muthanna site, including large stockpiles that were found after the ISG completed its investigation of the site.[117] The *New York Times* reported: "By mid-2008, as incidents with mustard shells accumulated, ordnance disposal techs suspected one area had become a principal source of the weapons: Al Muthanna State Establishment. . . . Although incidents with chemical arms were scattered across Iraq, many were clustered near the ruined complex, which this June was overrun by the Islamic State."[118] In one incident, in July 2008, U.S. Marines were reportedly exposed to chemical agents after they examined "a freshly cut hole in a small bunker." According to one soldier reportedly involved with the incident, when they looked inside the bunker, they discovered "that there were just rounds everywhere."[119]

Although the CW discovered at that time were presumably destroyed, the incident does raise questions about how thorough the ISG investigation of Muthanna was in 2003–4 and what may still have remained at the site when it was captured by ISIL. On July 8, 2014, the Iraqi ambassador to the United Nations, Mohamed Ali Alhakim, reported to the United Nations that "about 2,500 corroded chemical rockets remained on the grounds, and that Iraqi officials had witnessed intruders looting equipment before militants shut down the surveillance cameras."[120]

In the same letter to the United Nations, Alhakim stated that ISIL had obtained nearly 40 kilograms of nuclear-related materials that had been stored at Mosul University, stating that "[t]errorist groups have seized control of nuclear material at the sites that came out of the control of the state."[121] Although Alhakim stated that these materials "can be used in manufacturing weapons of mass destruction," the risks may be overstated. Because the material reportedly consisted of natural or depleted uranium, it would be "useless for a terrorist group trying to make a nuclear bomb."[122] Moreover, because uranium is not very radioactive, it would also be of little use in a radiological dispersion device (RDD), or "dirty bomb."[123]

Lessons Learned

There are lessons to be drawn from the Iraqi case that will allow us to improve international efforts to monitor and verify nonproliferation activities. Unfortunately, lessons have been drawn that have the ability to erode the international nonproliferation regime's monitoring and verification efforts.

Misconstrued Lessons from the Iraqi Case

After the invasion of Iraq, statements by ElBaradei, Blix, and others led to conclusions that the inspections prior to 2003 had been largely, if not completely, successful, especially in the nuclear realm.[124] They also suggested that all remaining questions would have been resolved if the inspections had not been interrupted.[125] In retrospect, that is not so clear. Despite its extensive resources, it was clear that the United States would not sustain the kind of military pressure that had allowed for the intrusive inspections in the first place.[126] Moreover, as noted, UNMOVIC reports indicated that the Iraqi regime began cooperating more fully only in the last weeks before the final deadline. An extended deadline may have meant only a longer period of incomplete cooperation and a greater likelihood that political divisions in the international community could weaken the pressure on the Iraqi regime.

Ultimately, even if Iraq had been far more cooperative, there still would likely have been serious doubts about its full compliance with the UN disarmament mandate, barring fundamental and favorable political developments in Iraq that altered the risk calculus of the international community. As noted above, UNMOVIC admitted in its final report that while continued activities might have clarified some issues, others would not have been resolved even with these measures—and indeed remain unresolved today.[127] And the ISG report argued that not only were elements of a breakout capability being pursued, but that Saddam Hussein intended to break out at the first opportunity.

Perhaps even more important, the apparent lessons from Iraq led the IAEA in the aftermath of Iraq to promote new standards for noncompliance that weakened the international response to the actions of Iran and Syria for a number of years.[128] Since the election of the current IAEA director-general Yukiya Amano, the IAEA has been willing to take stronger positions on Syria and especially on Iran (though it still has never employed special inspections in these cases), but significant damage had already been done. The questions about Syria's nuclear program still remain, and Iran continued to develop its nuclear infrastructure for more than a decade after its covert facilities came to light before any significant progress was made in addressing its nuclear program.

The Real Lessons of Iraq

The lessons of the Iraq inspections reveal the importance of international inspections, as well as the limitations of monitoring and verification processes themselves. In the best cases, monitoring and verification can help resolve underlying questions about the status of WMD programs and help create confidence that a state is complying with its nonproliferation commitments or implementing pledges to roll back WMD programs. This is true for cooperative monitoring and verification regimes, where monitoring and verification, including onsite inspection, can provide valuable information that would not otherwise be obtained. It can also be true in cases where there is little or no cooperation on the part of an inspected state.

In Iraq, defeat in war, a decision to act decisively and quickly in the aftermath of the war, the UNSC-mandate and extraordinary powers given to UNSCOM and UNMOVIC, good intelligence until the late 1990s, long periods of P-5 consensus, and good fortune all combined to allow unprecedented access—access unlikely ever to be agreed by a state on a routine basis—and some measure of success. Despite Iraq's limited cooperation and other problems, UNSCOM and UNMOVIC were nevertheless able to discover a considerable amount about Iraq's WMD and ballistic missile programs. The conditions for such successes as were achieved in Iraq are clear; they have not been as apparent in other cases, including North Korea, Iran, Syria, and Myanmar. Given these cases, it is important to understand as well the limitations of monitoring and verification regimes as revealed by Iraq.

INHERENT LIMITATIONS TO MONITORING AND VERIFICATION

Some limits are inherent, the result of such factors as the geographical expanse of the area to be monitored; the limited range of instruments and technological measurement uncertainties; limits to access; uncertainties produced by poor, lost, distorted, or otherwise incomplete information; and uncertainties resulting from active efforts to conceal and deceive by the inspected party, including efforts to hide or destroy documents or evidence. As a result, there is considerable uncertainty or ambiguity surrounding any conclusions, which are very often "judgment calls," even in the best cases.

These inherent ambiguities and the judgments based on them can lead to problems. Disagreements among inspectors themselves, as well as among international organizations and states, can and do arise. Some of the early disagreements between UNSCOM and IAEA inspectors demonstrate this point. More destructive to the integrity of the monitoring and verification process, however, is the exploitation of ambiguities and imperfect judgments by the state inspected and its supporters within and outside international organizations such as the IAEA and the UN Security Council. In either case, inspections can unravel before their objectives are accomplished.

Even if the inherent limits of the process can be overcome in practice and disarmament occurs, it may not be demonstrated or even demonstrable. UNMOVIC's final report underscores the importance of external verification of the destruction of materials.[129] Iraqi claims to have destroyed some equipment and materials unilaterally may have turned out to have been true. But unless there is some sort of external verification of such actions, the state will never be able to prove to the international community what equipment and materials, and in what amounts, were destroyed. Nor should it: it is generally not enough simply to take a state's word that it has dismantled facilities or destroyed vital equipment and materials. Even in the best cases, where there is full access to a state's documents and materials after the fact, vital information would still be lost.

Although a problem in the nuclear arena, the cases of Iran, North Korea and Syria indicate that even if there is an attempt to deceive inspectors, nuclear activities may leave traces that demonstrate what a state has or has not done. Confirming or disproving claims in the chemical and biological arenas may be more difficult, as was the case in Iraq. This lesson, of course, will be particularly relevant to efforts to identify and eliminate any undeclared chemical weapons or CW-related facilities that may remain in Syria.

The difficulties in verifying CBW elimination are not only due to the greater technical difficulty of detecting the presence of chemical and biological agents, but also to issues associated with verification of the Chemical Weapons Convention and Biological Weapons Convention. Although the Organization for the Prohibition of Chemical Weapons (OPCW) does have significant verification authorities and has fully inspected declared chemical-weapon facilities, to date, it has paid comparatively little attention to dual-use facilities and has undertaken no challenge inspections. The Biological Weapons Convention has no verification mechanisms at all.[130]

THE CHALLENGES OF COERCIVE VERIFICATION

As suggested, the Iraqi case also demonstrates that the difficulties of monitoring and verification in unfriendly political environments exacerbate any intrinsic limits. The deception and denial efforts of Iraq were a constant problem for UNSCOM, UNMOVIC, and the ISG. This was especially the case with UNSCOM, where Iraqi obstructionism was the most evident and demonstrable, but as Blix's reports to the Security Council underscored, it was also the case with UNMOVIC. Even the ISG reported evidence of systematic destruction of WMD-related documents after OIF began and ongoing intimidation of scientists.[131] As a result, in all these cases, good fortune, or the prospect of force were often required for breakthroughs.

In this context, Iranian and Syrian delays in allowing the IAEA access to suspected nuclear sites, refusal to provide requested information and transparency measures, and moves to raze sites and to build over them have to be taken more seriously. This will also be an issue that inspectors should keep in mind in the CW rollback verification in Syria—especially now that the declared CW agents have been removed from the country and, presumably, inspectors have moved into more difficult stages of the verification process involving searches for concealed CW-related facilities, stockpiles, precursors, and documents.

THE IMPORTANCE OF POLITICAL CONSENSUS

Some limits are fundamentally political in nature. While political consensus was a critical factor in the successes achieved by Iraq inspections, the lack of political unity was responsible for key breakdowns in the process during the last year or so of UNSCOM and at other times. The Iraq case clearly shows how monitoring and verification efforts were repeatedly undercut by political constraints, undermining the legitimacy of inspection teams, and otherwise causing the conclusions drawn from the verification processes to be suspect. Furthermore, the findings, which were often ambiguous, were often and readily "politicized" by various parties to support political positions and arguments that were not and could not be sufficiently supported by the evidence gathered by the inspection teams. Political constraints on the selection of inspectors and disagreements over methods of inspections, among other issues, reflect this problem and worsened its impact.

In similar fashion, we learned all too well that action without the broad support of the international community and the P-5 is more difficult and controversial at best. For example, during UNSCOM's inspections, the Iraqi regime became increasingly obstructionist as it became clear that divisions within the Security Council had made threats of force less credible. In Iraq, and more broadly, as we have seen with respect to North Korea, Iran, Syria, and Myanmar in recent years, insufficient support for addressing noncompliance can undermine the effectiveness of monitoring and verification. As noted, the IAEA has not been using its most effective tool, special inspections, largely because of politics among the board of governors, and certain P-5 states have acted to prevent UN consideration of these cases, or if they were not successful, meaningful UN action.

These issues have been relevant to CBW noncompliance as well. Despite solid evidence of Syrian CW use during the ongoing civil war, the evidence was disputed by Russia. From the time that Syria agreed to accede to the CWC and eliminate its chemical arsenal, there has been little agreement on enforcement. As the Iraqi case demonstrates, when international organizations are unable to act effectively or when P-5 states protect their allies from sanctions or other consequences of noncompliance, the regime is weakened and the prospect of its collapse becomes a real concern.

THE ROLE OF FORCE AND THE THREAT OF FORCE

When the prospect of force is on the table, the political element can become even more central to the monitoring and verification equation. It is clear in the case of Iraq that the prospect of force was important, not only in getting inspections started, but also in the conduct and potential success of the inspections themselves. One must recall that the UNMOVIC inspections teams were only allowed to enter Iraq because of the presence of 150,000 troops on Iraq's borders. Moreover, as Blix reported, Iraq only began to provide more information in the final days before the deadline, when war was becoming imminent.[132] But by then it was too late. This lesson seemed to have had some impact on Libya's decision to disarm shortly after Saddam was overthrown.[133] While the prospect of force may have had an initial impact on Iranian and North Korean thinking at that time, in subsequent years their actions became bolder in part because continuing reverberations of the Iraq War made military action unlikely. However, it was clear that the U.S. threat of force following allegations of Syria's CW use, combined with a timely intervention by Russia, was instrumental in the regime's stated decision to eliminate its CW.

AMBIGUITY

In the case of Iraq, the inherent limits in monitoring and verification as well as Iraq's limited cooperation resulted in serious uncertainties, especially in the biological- and chemical-arms arenas. Would the remaining questions have been answered by extending the inspections? As noted above, ElBaradei and Blix have suggested that they probably would have. In reality, though, it is unlikely that all questions would have been answered if inspections had continued. Monitoring and verification of WMD are intrinsically difficult, especially if there is not cooperation by the inspected state. This reality is greater for chemical and biological weapons than nuclear, but holds for all WMD. It may not be possible to remove all uncertainty. In the case of North Korea, questions regarding it nuclear intentions were removed by its nuclear tests, but many states remain unconvinced about the nuclear-weapon intentions and capabilities of Iran, Syria, and Myanmar today. This complicates the possibility of undertaking effective monitoring and inspections and of drawing the appropriate conclusions.

Recognizing the need for the international community to address the unique monitoring and verification challenges of WMD rollback, especially in such difficult cases as Iran, North Korea, Syria, and Myanmar, some scholars and policy-makers have recommended creating a permanent body with a mandate and capabilities like those of UNMOVIC.[134] This possibility was never likely and became remarkably less so after UNMOVIC was formally disbanded in June 2007.[135]

It was clear that such an organization could remove some of the technical limits to monitoring and verification, as it did in Iraq. However, such an organization would not have solved the *political* problems that plagued UNSCOM and UNMOVIC, and it may have even hindered their resolution. The international community will have to confront each rollback challenge as it presents itself, and be mindful of the mixed experiences in Iraq. It may be possible to create ad hoc bodies in the future to address specific cases, such as the U.S.- and British-led verification teams in Libya. However, the fact that we have not seen efforts to create such organizations to address proliferation concerns in North Korea or Iran, or to assist the OPCW in verifying Syria's CW renunciation, is revealing. The Iraq overhang remains an obstacle of the creation of any body that even remotely resembles the UNSCOM or UNMOVIC experience. The post-Iraq record to date is not ideal and suggests limits to interest in repeating the UNSCOM/UNMOVIC experiment.

Conclusions

Monitoring and verification, including onsite inspections, will remain critical tools in the international community's ongoing nonproliferation efforts. They remain one of the most important means of determining the validity of claims made by states. International inspections provide capabilities, access, and legitimacy that national efforts cannot. But it is important to understand what these inspections can and cannot reliably do.

There is a widespread belief that the key lesson of Iraq was that international inspections had uncovered and eliminated the WMD programs. In this objective, the efforts of both UNSCOM and UNMOVIC were largely commendable. However, it is important not to overstate the capabilities of monitoring and verification regimes and the levels of confidence that these inspection processes can give the international community in verifying WMD rollback. There were problems in both organizations, many not entirely of their own making, and there were many remaining questions and uncertainties, especially in the chemical and biological arenas, in the work they were able to accomplish.

In reality, the monitoring and verification regime in Iraq was hampered by numerous difficulties that undermined its effectiveness. These difficulties include:

- widespread and systematic concealment of facilities;
- incomplete and misleading reporting;
- extensive concealment or destruction of critical documents relating to Iraqi WMD programs;
- delayed or denied access to facilities;
- divisions within the UNSC and even UNSCOM that undermined the enforcement of key UNSC provisions and weakened international support for the inspection process; and
- ambiguous results that were interpreted by various parties as evidence of cooperation and were used to create pressure to remove sanctions.

As a result of these and other difficulties, there was less certainty about the results of the inspections than was proclaimed, and the extension of the inspections would not have by itself addressed this uncertainty. Indeed, even the conclusions of the ISG, which were conducted after the Ba'athist regime was removed, are less certain than they are often portrayed and are open to some serious questions.

The lessons from Iraq will remain relevant to future proliferation efforts, including those in North Korea, Iran, Syria, and Myanmar. As we will argue in Chapter 6, in these and other difficult cases, the international community will be likely to face challenges in monitoring and verification efforts similar to those faced in Iraq. In fact, it may be even *more* difficult to obtain clear and widely accepted evidence of noncompliance than was possible in Iraq, since the extensive authorities and access that were granted to the IAEA and UNSCOM, and later the IAEA and UNMOVIC, were unique and the result of a defeat in war. None of the current difficult cases were defeated in war, and the ability to get IAEA or UN support for extraordinary measures has not been possible. Nor have the IAEA or OPCW been willing to use special or challenge inspections, respectively. In this context, it is therefore extremely troubling that essentially every one of the methods that Iraq used to conceal its proscribed programs in the list above has been employed by North Korea, Iran, Syria and to an extent, Myanmar. With the possible exception of Iran after the negotiation of the 2015 Joint Comprehensive Plan of Action, the outcome of which remains uncertain, we have, to date, not seen a consensus within the UNSC to apply consistent pressure on these countries to resolve the serious questions about their programs.

Because monitoring and verification will, and should, remain an essential element in international nonproliferation efforts, it is important that we retain a clear understanding of their capabilities. These issues, however, became increasingly politicized as a result of the war in Iraq. It is therefore all the more important that the international community carefully and objectively reassess the strengths and weaknesses of these monitoring and verification regimes. To the extent that analysis of these issues has been distorted by the controversies of the Iraq War, the interests of the future nonproliferation regime has been poorly served.

4   Libya

Beginning in late 2010, the revolutionary wave of protests and popular revolts of the "Arab Spring" spread across countries in the Middle East and North Africa, including Libya. Over the next several months, Libya was engulfed by a civil war between forces supporting Colonel Muammar Qadhafi and rebel forces reinforced by NATO air power. The rebel forces gradually gained momentum, eventually toppling the Qadhafi regime in August 2011. A few months later, in October 2011, Libya's new National Transitional Council announced that they had discovered an undeclared cache of chemical weapons (CW).[1] This discovery was later confirmed by the Organization for the Prohibition of Chemical Weapons (OPCW) to be an undeclared stockpile of mustard gas and associated artillery shells.[2]

This announcement was startling to many observers, since Libya had publicly renounced its weapons of mass destruction (WMD) programs in 2003 and had apparently dismantled its WMD stockpiles, related equipment, and delivery vehicles in the months that followed. Indeed, after Libya's 2003 declaration and the verified dismantlement of its declared programs, governmental officials, nonproliferation experts, and various international organizations across the globe roundly praised the Libyan regime for its cooperation. For example, in words that would come back to haunt him in 2011, British prime minister Tony Blair stated in March 2004 that Libya had provided "full and transparent cooperation" throughout the disarmament process.[3] U.S. president George W. Bush similarly stated in September 2004: "Libya was a threat. Libya's now peacefully dismantling its weapons programs. . . . [And] the world is better for it."[4]

Such statements were certainly not unusual. Libya's public renunciation of its WMD and long-range missile programs, and the subsequent removal of large amounts of these programs, had repeatedly been referred to as a positive "model" for nonproliferation: here was an instance in which a country had, more or less, voluntarily renounced its WMD programs—or at least was willing to renounce the programs without requiring the use of force.[5]

The descriptions of the Libyan case changed dramatically after the CW discovery. Shortly after Transitional Government's announcement, British prime minister David Cameron stated: "Although Gaddafi agreed to declare and dismantle all his weapons of mass destruction and although we made real progress diminishing the threat he posed, in the last few days we have learnt that the new Libyan authorities have found chemical weapons that were kept hidden from the world."[6] This discovery forces us to wonder whether the Libyan "model" really was as successful as initially described.

In reality, significant questions had already been raised in certain quarters about the verification and dismantlement of Libya's WMD programs as early as 2005. The 2005 bipartisan Commission on the Intelligence Capabilities of the United States Regarding Weapons of Mass Destruction (otherwise known as the Robb-Silberman Report) raised a number of questions about the Libyan case, reporting: "There is little doubt that significant questions remain about Libya's WMD programs."[7] The report stated that "it is clear that Libya has been considerably less forthcoming about the details of its chemical and biological weapons efforts than about its nuclear and missile programs." The report also cautioned that there is a growing concern in the intelligence community that "shifting priorities" and the belief that "Libya is done" may "leave collectors and analysts without the resources needed to track and monitor future change."[8] These suspicions were validated to some degree.

Despite the 2011 revelations, weapons inspectors dismantled large parts of the Libyan nuclear- and chemical-weapon programs in 2003–4—and the Libyan case may still provide positive lessons for monitoring and verification regimes tasked with confirming that countries had in fact rolled back their WMD programs. This chapter will examine the successes, challenges, and lessons that can be learned from the Libyan case of WMD renunciation and verification. As one model of cooperative verification, the Libyan case highlights not only the opportunities afforded by monitoring and verification regimes, but also some of the difficulties that any such regime will encounter.

On the "Libyan Model": Libya's Decision to Renounce WMD

Although Libya had broached the subject of renouncing its WMD programs several times over a period reaching back as far as 1992, Libyan officials reportedly approached British officials formally with a firm overture to abandon these programs in March 2003, when Operation Iraqi Freedom was imminent.[9] Over the next several months, U.S. and British officials attempted to convince Libyan officials to set a date for a technical meeting to discuss Libya's programs. In September 2003, they did manage to meet with Colonel Qadhafi, who agreed in principle to allow technical visits, but still no date for the technical visit was set.[10]

The tempo of negotiations increased dramatically, however, after the October 3, 2003, interdiction of the *BBC China*, a German-flagged vessel carrying over one thousand assembled gas centrifuges and components, on its way to Libya.[11] After the evidence was presented to Libya on October 7, a date for a technical visit was immediately set and a U.S./U.K. technical team made its first visit beginning on October 19.[12] In November 2003, Libyan officials were reportedly presented additional intelligence information about their nuclear program.[13] Only a few weeks later, following a period of intense negotiation, Libya announced the decision to renounce their weapons of mass destruction.[14]

This declaration was made on December 19, 2003, in a joint U.S.-British-Libyan statement and broadcast publicly. In this declaration, Libya agreed to "disclose and dismantle" all of its WMD programs and "immediately and unconditionally" allow weapons inspectors to verify the dismantlement process.[15] Over the next several months the verification teams removed highly sensitive stockpiles and equipment that were part of Libya's WMD and missile programs and conducted verifications "to better understand the extent of those programs, and the procurement work supporting them."[16]

The Force-Diplomacy Debate: A Model of Diplomatic Success?

Libya's public renunciation of its WMD and long-range missile programs, and the subsequent removal of large amounts of these programs are a clear nonproliferation success. For this reason, the Libyan case has often been held up as a nonproliferation "model," where the regime was willing to renounce and eliminate its WMD programs without the use of force.[17] Scholars have frequently contrasted the Libyan case with that of Iraq, which required the use of force and ultimately a regime change to accomplish the same goal. Robert Litwak, for example, argues that unlike in the Iraqi case, where the United States presented Saddam Hussein with a choice of regime change or war (with the result being war), in the Libyan case, the United States presented Libyan leadership with a choice between regime *behavioral* change or war—with a peaceful result.[18]

Others have presented the contrast between the Iraqi and Libyan models more starkly, often removing the prospect of force from the picture almost entirely. Some scholars have argued that the prospect of force played little or no role in Libya's decision, that Libya was well on its way to renouncing its WMD programs prior to the Iraq War, and that the main reason for its decision was to rejoin the international community.[19] For example, Joseph Cirincione has argued: "The world now has two very different models for how to eliminate a threatening nation's nuclear and missile capabilities. The Iraq model of regime change has been enormously costly, chaotic and uncertain. And the Libyan model of changing regime behavior has been efficient, effective, and almost cost free."[20]

These latter descriptions likely go too far in removing the prospect of force from the picture. Although it is likely that Libya did want to rejoin the international community (and have international sanctions removed), the fact that Libya was still acquiring parts for its program in October 2003 suggests that this is not a sufficient explanation. And, as International Atomic Energy Agency (IAEA) deputy director Herman Nackaerts pointed out: "Only when Libya was caught red handed as a result of intelligence, did it decide to renounce this programme."[21] Thus, the arguments by Cirincione and others that Libya would have renounced the program anyway, without the threat of force, seem unconvincing at best and politically motivated at worst.[22] There were likely several confluent factors that played a role in Libya's decision, but prominent among these factors was the prospect of force, as represented by the military operations in Iraq, after Libya was presented with clear evidence of undeclared procurement activities. As Bruce W. Jentleson has argued: "It was force *and* diplomacy, not force *or* diplomacy that turned Gadhafi around . . . a combination of steel and a willingness to deal."[23]

In retrospect, however, the 2011 discovery of the hidden CW stockpile may shed additional light on this debate. Proponents of the "diplomacy" side of this debate point to Qadhafi's previous offers to disarm as key pieces of evidence supporting their position. It now appears that those offers were insincere. It may be that Qadhafi did want to "rehabilitate" his reputation and obtain the removal of sanctions—while still retaining some WMD capabilities. But one could hardly say that this would have been a success for diplomacy. Given the timing of his 2003 offer (made only days before the onset of the Iraq war and apparently only in earnest after he was caught red-handed), Libya's continued nuclear acquisitions, and the CW stockpile that he managed to retain, it does appear that the prospect of force (and the lesson of Iraq) may ultimately have been what forced Qadhafi's hand. And yet, in light of the covert CW stockpile that was later discovered, it may be that *neither* side sufficiently won this debate. In the end, neither force *nor* diplomacy completely "turned Gadhafi around."[24]

Libya as a Model for Cooperative Verification

Whatever the reasons for Libya's decision to disarm, the Libyan case does present very important lessons as a model, however imperfect, of what one might call a "cooperative verification."[25] Despite the later discovery of the covert CW stockpile, the Libyan regime did provide significant cooperation following its 2003 renunciation, providing a great deal of information to inspectors, turning over equipment and materials, and identifying facilities as part of its WMD programs. In such an environment, verification efforts would appear to encounter comparatively few difficulties in verifying the rollback of WMD programs. This verification model can be sharply contrasted with a "coercive verification," such as the one that inspectors investigating Iraq's WMD programs faced after the 1991 Gulf War.[26] Those verification efforts, led by the UN Special Commission (UNSCOM) and the IAEA, and later the UN Monitoring Verification and Inspection Commission (UNMOVIC) and the IAEA, were carried out in a largely uncooperative environment, in which the Iraqi regime systematically attempted to conceal its extensive WMD programs and materials.[27]

Nevertheless, as outlined in the introduction of this book, questions and difficulties would arise even in an apparently "cooperative" verification scenario such as in Libya. These questions included such matters as how to assess "genuine" cooperation; whether we could be confident that all the information, equipment, and materials used in the programs were turned over; and what the requirements for long-term monitoring should be. These questions prove to be of utmost importance in the Libyan case, especially in light of the 2011 CW revelations. Without clear answers to these questions, the international community will be unable to verify with certainty that a country is fully disarming. Instead, as may have been the case with Libya, the apparent cooperation may be used to give the state cover for proscribed activities or covert stockpiles. Although the Libyan case is unique and may not be repeated, it offers important lessons for the international community as it attempts to address the most challenging cases of monitoring and verification in the future.

Verifying and Dismantling Libya's WMD
and Long-range Missile Programs

After Qadhafi's December 19 declaration, the verification and dismantlement process proceeded very quickly. Indeed, U.S.-led verification teams were already on the ground and receiving equipment by January 20, 2003, one month after Colonel Qadhafi's declaration.[28] As Robert Joseph emphasized, there were important reasons for moving this process forward so rapidly: "The U.S. and UK participants understood that speed was essential. A drawn-out process would have increased the prospects for press leaks. Moreover, once the first team was granted access to visit Libya, any delay in moving forward would decrease the pressure on the Libyan leadership, and could allow time for opposition to mobilize internally and within the region."[29]

Dr. Joseph indicates that the necessity for rapid progress meant that the U.S./ British team had to move forward before it had fully answered all of the critical questions about Libya's WMD and missile programs. Nevertheless, he argued, inspectors were confident enough with the declarations to proceed. "While a number of questions remained even after the return of the experts in December [2003]—including the precise nature of the North Korean connection to Libya's missile project, the extent of the work on nerve agents, and the possibility of hidden centrifuges—the intelligence assessment was that sufficient confidence existed to proceed to policy discussions and that these outstanding questions should not be an obstacle to moving forward."[30]

The verification and dismantlement process itself was carried out in three phases. Phase I reportedly focused on removing the most proliferation-sensitive materials and equipment from Libyan territory, including warhead designs, uranium hexafluoride (UF6), centrifuges, SCUD-C missiles, and related parts for these sensitive technologies.[31] Phase II, which began in mid-February 2004, involved the dismantling, removal, or destruction of any remaining components of Libya's WMD programs. This stage reportedly involved much larger quantities of equipment, including the destruction of more than three thousand chemical munitions and the removal of SCUD-C missiles and launchers, further dismantling of the centrifuge program, and an agreement to remove 16 kilograms of HEU. Phase III was "primarily a verification phase." According to Paula DeSutter, at that time the assistant secretary of state for verification and compliance, Phase III was the most difficult part of the process, since the inspection teams had to meet with large numbers of personnel and work to "determine whether Libya had truly eliminated its WMD programs." On September 22, 2004, DeSutter testified that these three phases were more or less complete.[32]

At Qadhafi's insistence, various international verifying organizations, especially the IAEA and the OPCW, were brought into the process as soon as was feasible to oversee significant aspects of the verification and dismantlement process. By rapidly bringing these organizations into the process, Libya helped maintain the image that it had undertaken the decision of its own free will and not as a result of coercion.[33]

What the Verification Process Revealed

Although there had long been concerns about Libya's WMD programs, most of the suspicions had been focused on Libya's suspected chemical-weapon program. However, the declarations by Libya in 2003–4 revealed a great deal about a range of WMD and missile programs. Perhaps most disturbingly, Libya revealed four undeclared nuclear sites previously unknown to inspections officials, including IAEA director Mohammad ElBaradei.[34] Overall, the declared WMD programs revealed greater capabilities in a number of areas than previously estimated in intelligence reports.

NUCLEAR-WEAPON PROGRAM

Libya's declarations revealed that the regime had acquired a great deal of the equipment and material necessary for producing nuclear weapons, including nearly all the material necessary for providing fuel for atomic bombs, along with bomb designs. Although initial statements by the IAEA downplayed the significance of the program, these statements were later revised in light of the evidence.[35]

Overall, the Libyan regime had managed to acquire the majority of pieces for a successful nuclear-weapon program, although there were some questions about the quality of Libya's workforce and not a lot was done on putting the pieces together. As stated by Sharon Squassoni, "Many observers over the years discounted Libya's nuclear weapons program because of its failure to procure key components and lack of indigenous resources and expertise. Yet, Libya's declarations revealed that A. Q. Khan seemed to have solved the procurement problem, if not the problem of expertise."[36] Indeed, as David Albright wrote in a detailed study of the A. Q. Khan smuggling network, "[T]he Khan network established an impressive transnational supply operation aimed at providing Libya with the ability to make nuclear weapons. IAEA and U.S. experts who have reviewed the evidence judge that the network would have succeeded if the network had not been exposed and Libya had continued to pursue its nuclear ambitions."[37]

What was uncovered was indeed substantial. For example, Libya had reportedly received a warhead design from the A. Q. Khan network, as did other countries (such as Iran) that had done business with Khan's network. According to some reports, this warhead design was based on an early, but operational, Chinese nuclear weapon that had been provided to Pakistan in the 1980s (before China entered the Nuclear Nonproliferation Treaty [NPT]).[38] Libya had also acquired a large amount of the necessary equipment and materials for uranium production from the A. Q. Khan network. The verification teams reportedly removed 1.8 metric tons of UF6 and more than 15 kilograms of fresh highly enriched uranium.[39] Libya had also received a modular uranium conversion facility that could produce uranium dioxide, UF4 or uranium metal.[40]

Perhaps even more troubling, Libya had also forged a deal with the A. Q. Khan network for a turn-key centrifuge-based enrichment facility, along with the capability to make centrifuges. In the terms of the deal, Libya would pay $100–200 million for the centrifuges, along with associated equipment and materials.[41] By the time the network was discovered, Libya had also received twenty preassembled P-1 gas centrifuges and the components for another two hundred.[42] By 2002, Libya had assembled an operational nine-centrifuge cascade and had partially completed installation of two additional cascades (one with nineteen centrifuges and another with sixty-four).[43] Libya also received two completed centrifuges of the more advanced P-2 design and thousands of additional P-2 parts.[44] Although Libya possessed only a small number of P-2 rotors, Tripoli "possessed the specialized equipment and materials for P2 motor production and was working on obtaining a domestic production capacity for UF6."[45] Libya had already tested some centrifuges and had placed orders for ten thousand additional centrifuges.[46]

Although, Albright notes, Libya was still about four years from starting the centrifuge plant when it ended its nuclear-weapon program, "the Libyan program appeared sized to produce at least four nuclear weapons per year. For a country like Libya, this production rate was enough to create a formidable, albeit small, nuclear arsenal."[47]

CHEMICAL WEAPONS

Libya had long been suspected of having a large-scale chemical-weapon program, and this program was mentioned repeatedly in unclassified intelligence estimates during the 1990s.[48] Libya's 2003 declaration revealed that its CW program was housed in three main facilities—those at Rabta, Sebha, and Tarhunah—which were previously declared to be petrochemical or water-delivery complexes.[49]

The country's declared chemical-weapon infrastructure consisted of 3,563 chemical bombs, a 23-metric-ton stockpile of mustard gas, small amounts of the nerve agents sarin and soman, and 1,300 metric tons of precursor agents.[50] (Interestingly, Libya's initial declaration had reported only 1,500 chemical bombs instead of 3,563. When asked why they did not declare the full amount, "the Libyans explained that they had not yet believed that Qadhafi would go through with the disarmament plan.")[51]

Although some of the biggest unresolved questions in the early stages of the verification process reportedly involved Libya's nerve-agent program, the Libyan regime did apparently have initial aspirations to develop a large-scale production capability for nerve agents, especially sarin and soman.[52] To that end, Libya's CW program included "equipment to begin a second production line for more advanced agents, as well as precursors that could be used to produce mustard and nerve agents."[53] Libya had reportedly imported "corrosion-resistant equipment for the planned production facility at Tarhunah, along with industrial quantities of the sarin precursor isopropyl alcohol and a few hundred gallons of the soman precursor pinacolyl alcohol."[54]

By September 2004, the OPCW had verified all declared CW stockpiles, destroyed the declared aerial bombs, negotiated plans for the destruction of the declared chemical-weapon stockpiles, and set in motion the conversion of the Rabta facility into a pharmaceutical plant.[55]

BIOLOGICAL-WEAPON ACTIVITIES

Throughout the 1990s and early 2000s, reported U.S. intelligence assessments as well as congressional reports alleged that Libya maintained a small-scale biological-weapon program. For example, a 2001 State Department report indicated that "evidence suggests Libya is seeking to acquire the capability to develop and produce Biological Weapons (BW) agents for offensive purposes."[56] A 2006 Department of Defense report noted that Libya's biological-weapon program was "in the early research and development stage."[57] And a 2003 CIA report indicated that "evidence suggested that Libya also sought dual-use capabilities that could be used to develop and produce biological agents."[58]

Despite these fears, the verification activities following Libya's 2003 declaration did not reveal an advanced BW program or any operable facility. Although

Paula DeSutter would later write that the United States visited "sites that had been part of Libya's biological-weapons program," analysts at the time reportedly agreed that, based on the evidence that they saw, Libya's agreed BW program would have been small scale.[59] However, an overall lack of substantive evidence either for or against a Libyan BW program made it impossible for the intelligence community to definitively confirm or deny its existence. According to the Robb-Silberman Report, Libya's "declarations have failed to shed light on Tripoli's plans and intentions for its biological program."[60] Carl Kropf, a spokesman for the Robb-Silberman Commission, indicated that there was a "discrepancy" between the information that Libya provided about its biological weapons efforts and U.S. intelligence reports, but he refused to elaborate because the information was classified.[61]

BALLISTIC MISSILES

In the December 19 agreement, Libya pledged to eliminate all ballistic missiles with ranges 300 kilometers or greater and payloads of 500 kilograms or greater. By September 22, 2004, the verification teams had removed Libya's five SCUD-C missiles, which had a range of 800 kilometers, and their launchers.

Libya had initially decided to convert its arsenal of 417 SCUD-B missiles with a 300-kilometer range in order to ensure their range was less than 300 kilometers with a payload of less than 500 kilograms.[62] Given questions about the technical feasibility of accomplishing this task, and difficulties in negotiating a monitoring arrangement to oversee the modifications, the United States eventually managed to convince Qadhafi to destroy all of Libya's SCUD-B missiles. This agreement faltered, however, when Libya struggled to find an acceptable replacement for the SCUD-Bs, and the regime still retained the SCUD-B missiles at the time of its collapse.[63]

INITIAL ASSESSMENTS OF LIBYA'S COOPERATION

Libya was praised for its clear cooperation in numerous areas throughout the verification and disarmament process. By late 2004, senior officials in the United States and Britain were declaring the process to be largely complete.[64] On September 22, 2004, in a testimony before Congress, Paula DeSutter stated: "Verification is not a science, and no verification determination can be absolutely certain. But what we can say, and what I am saying with regard to Libya, is that we have verified with *reasonable* certainty that Libya has eliminated, or has set in place the elimination of all its WMD and MTCR-class missile programs."[65]

The IAEA was somewhat more guarded in its final assessments of the Libyan verification and disarmament process, but also deemed the process a success. For example, in 2008 the director-general reported:

> Libya's past nuclear programme, from the mid-1980s until 2003, was aimed at the development of nuclear weapons. However, Libya has stated that it did not proceed with the design of nuclear weapons nor did it have complete fissile material production capabilities. The Agency did not find any indications of actual work related to nuclear weapons development. Given the fact that Libya's programme extended over two decades and was conducted to a great extent clandestinely, and in view of the corresponding lack of supporting documentation, there are some parts of Libya's past programme which the Agency has not been able to reconstruct fully. However, with the cooperation and transparent response shown by Libya, the Agency has been able to conclude that Libya's statements concerning its nuclear programme are not inconsistent with the Agency's findings.[66]

The IAEA report went on to conclude that the agency "will continue to implement safeguards in Libya as a routine matter and work to reach a conclusion about the absence of undeclared nuclear material and activities in Libya."[67]

Subsequent Disarmament Delays, 2004–11

During the initial months of the verification, inspection teams made rapid progress in dismantling large amounts of Libya's WMD programs. The majority of the equipment and materials were removed and a plan of action set in place for the destruction or removal of the remaining declared stockpiles and equipment. Over time, however, the timetables began to slip and Libya increasingly began to delay taking the final steps to disarm. U.S. officials were quick to repeat that Libya was a success story, but the disarmament process dragged out over the next seven years. Libyan officials, including Qadhafi, increasingly began expressing frustration that that they were not receiving sufficient benefits as a result of their WMD renunciation.[68]

In the subsequent years, Libya took a number of steps that suggested at least a partial change of heart and had the effect of delaying the disarmament process significantly.

• On June 14, 2007, Libya annulled its contract with the United States to work jointly to destroy its chemical-weapon stockpiles, including 23.6 metric tons of mustard gas and approximately 1,300 metric tons of precursor chemicals.[69] This decision was reportedly a "major factor" in Libya's missing repeated deadlines for the destruction of the agents. In 2009, in a request for a deadline extension, the Libyan government cited "strong but unspecified opposition to the destruction of the chemical agents."[70] It eventually teamed up with an Italian company to resume the CW destruction, but reportedly stalled the signing of contracts, possibly in efforts to extract further concessions in return for the destruction.[71] The destruction process finally resumed, but was again shut down after a reported malfunction of key equipment in February 2011. The regime was toppled before chemical destruction activities were resumed.

• Despite commitments to "sell its stockpile of 1,000 metric tons of natural uranium yellowcake ore," Libya retained the uranium stockpile until the regime was toppled.[72]

• In November 2009, when Libya was scheduled to ship the last 5.2 kilograms of its weapon-grade HEU to Russia, Libyan officials abruptly halted the shipment. Holding the materials on loading docks for several days, Saif al-Islam al-Qadhafi (Muammar al-Qadhafi's son) reportedly presented the U.S. State Department with a list of demands, including technical and military assistance and a significant sum of money. He expressed ongoing frustration with the bargain that Libya had struck with the United States and Great Britain and warned that "[s]lowly, slowly we are moving backward rather than forward." After a flurry of diplomatic exchanges, the material was finally removed to Russia on December 21, 2009.[73]

• As noted above, Libya also retained its arsenal of more than four hundred SCUD-B missiles, despite an initial commitment to destroy them. Although an August 2011 brief by the State Department indicated that the majority of these missiles were assessed not to be operational, the Qadhafi regime did reportedly fire several of the missiles at advancing rebel forces at the end of the regime.[74]

One has to wonder what the reasons for these multiple delays were. It is possible that the delays were the result of frustration, as Saif Qadhafi stated. However, some of the delays do appear to track with times that the apparent prospects of U.S. military operations in Iraq were at their most grim (and, therefore, any prospects of military operations against Libya appeared significantly more remote). In any case, a practical effect of the retention of chemical-weapon and uranium stockpiles was to maintain small-scale CW capabilities and the prospect for resuscitating other programs for years after the regime officially renounced WMD. These remaining CW stockpiles did create great concerns—both in the West and in Libya—that Qadhafi might use the known chemical weapons against the rebels fighting against the regime in 2011.

Remaining Stocks and Undeclared Facilities, 2011–14

Prior to the uprising that ultimately brought down the Qadhafi regime, Libya was believed to possess approximately 11.3 metric tons of mustard agent and 845 metric tons of chemical precursors, and a substantial cache of natural uranium.[75] According to the OPCW, "[T]he Qadhafi government succeeded in destroying 54% of its declared sulfur mustard and about 40% of the precursor chemicals before operations had to be suspended in February 2011 when the destruction facility malfunctioned."[76] OPCW inspectors left the country at that time and did not return until the following October, well after the Qadhafi regime had been overthrown.

Although many policy-makers and arms control experts expressed relief that a great deal of Libya's WMD materials had been removed prior to the revolt, many still raised concerns about a potential loss of centralized control over the remaining materials during the upheaval of the revolt and the subsequent transition.[77] For example, Representative Mike Rogers, chairman of the House Permanent Select Committee on Intelligence, argued that the United States had to help secure caches of Libyan military hardware, including missiles and chemical agents, to avoid their falling into terrorist hands.[78] General Carter Ham, chief of U.S. Africa Command, likewise indicated that there was "a very great concern about the security" of various chemical agents remaining in the country. "It's not weaponized—it's not easily weaponized, but nonetheless we want to make sure that the OPCW gets back in there and completes the destruction of the remaining materials."[79]

Much more troubling, however, was the National Transitional Council's October 2011 announcement of the discovery of the cache of suspected chemical-weapons agent and hundreds of associated artillery shells.[80] These shells were reportedly discovered at two sites in central Libya and had not been declared by the Qadhafi regime. Libya had previously declared only CW aerial bombs, which were destroyed in 2004. One senior U.S. official was quoted as saying: "'We are pretty sure we know' that the shells were custom-designed and produced by Iran for Libya." Another U.S. official was quoted as saying: "These were acquired over many years."[81]

The OPCW sent inspectors to investigate the newly discovered materials and artillery shells on January 17–19, 2012. On January 20, the OPCW released a brief stating that "the inspectors verified the declared chemical munitions, which consists of sulfur mustard agent that is not loaded into munitions."[82] Although the brief does not specify how much mustard agent was discovered,

OPCW spokesman Michael Luhan indicated that it was "a fraction of what was in the original declaration."[83]

The OPCW brief also referenced the artillery shells, stating that "at the same time, at the request of the Libyan authorities, the inspectors examined munitions, mainly artillery shells, which they determined are chemical munitions and hence declarable."[84] According to the terms of the agreement with the OPCW, Libya was obligated to declare the munitions. Contrary to prior reports, Luhan indicated that the shells were not currently usable because they were not loaded with chemical-weapons agents.[85]

These statements by the OPCW were revealing. Why, for example, did the OPCW not give any details on the amounts of chemical weapons or artillery shells that were verified? Luhan's statements appeared almost to be dismissing these findings as unimportant, since Libya had initially declared a much larger amount and since the artillery shells were apparently empty. But, put together, these undeclared chemical weapons and CW delivery vehicles in effect gave Libya a small but potentially viable hedge chemical-weapon arsenal—clearly something that should be considered a serious breach of Libya's international commitments.

On February 2, 2014, the last of Libya's chemical weapons were destroyed by a joint team composed of Libyans who had been trained for this task, along with support personnel from the United States, Germany, and Canada.[86] According to the U.S. assistant secretary of defense for nuclear, chemical, and biological defense programs, Andrew C. Weber, the destroyed weapons included "517 artillery shells filled with mustard gas, eight 250 kilogram bombs filled with mustard gas and 45 tubes filled with mustard gas."[87] Prior to their destruction, there were concerns that these weapons could fall into the hands of violent extremists.[88] Weber told reporters: "We ensure that they never fall in the hands of violent extremists, so we are preventing the potential for weapons of mass destruction terrorism." According to OPCW officials, the final destruction of the country's remaining Category 2 chemical precursors is expected to be completed by the end of 2016.[89]

The Libyan Case: An Assessment

The Libyan case reveals positive and negative aspects of verification and ongoing monitoring after a WMD and missile rollback. In late 2003, U.S. and British officials were able to respond quickly, negotiate effectively, and steer the trilateral agreement—in many cases, at least—to require the removal of equipment rather than allow for a drawn-out dismantlement process. The IAEA and OPCW worked effectively with British and U.S. officials to coordinate and lead dismantlement efforts.

However, the Libyan case also reveals a number of problems with both the international monitoring and verification regimes and those ad hoc groups that are brought together to verify and dismantle declared WMD programs in specific cases. Clearly these problems were driven home most powerfully by the 2011 discovery of the undeclared chemical-weapon arsenal and delivery vehicles. According to Donald A. Mahley, a former deputy assistant secretary of state who was the senior WMD representative in Libya, this incident showed that "we will have to think very seriously about finding inspectors with a different skill set, and about more intelligence-sharing, and about looking widely, not just at declared sites."[90] These comments are very revealing and point to lessons about monitoring and verification that extend beyond the Libyan case.

Even if an undeclared chemical-weapon stockpile had not been discovered in 2011, the verification process conducted in Libya encountered a host of difficulties and shortcomings that need to be examined. Indeed, as noted, serious questions had already been raised about the Libyan case in 2005 by the Robb-Silberman Report.[91] The following discussion addresses the difficulties that the Libyan case brings to light both within the international monitoring and verification organizations such as the IAEA and OPCW and within ad hoc groups.

Shortcomings in the Work of the IAEA, OPCW, and other International Organizations

The Libyan case provides a litany of shortcomings with the international community's set of verification mechanisms. Libya's WMD programs consisted of numerous undeclared facilities and most of the components necessary for a viable nuclear program, acquired without the knowledge of the international community. As IAEA deputy director Herman Nackaerts candidly stated in 2011: "Only when Libya was caught red handed as a result of intelligence, did it decide to renounce this programme . . . . The Agency missed the indicators and played no role in the detection of Libya's clandestine programme."[92] Granted, in 2003, Libya had acceded to neither the Additional Protocol (AP) nor the Chemical Weapons Convention (CWC), so some established authorities for monitoring and verification were not available to the international organizations at the time. But even if Libya *had* acceded to these agreements, there were significant shortcomings—both inherent to monitoring and verification and in the implementation of these agreements—that would have made it difficult for the organizations to have discovered Libya's illicit programs, barring third-party information or a run of dramatic good luck.

As we will see, Libya was able to exploit various structural limitations in international monitoring to develop a significant WMD program. And while some of these structural limitations have been strengthened via various agreements such as the Additional Protocol, which gave increased authorities to the IAEA, some of these structural improvements have been impaired by implementation issues—including ineffective or incomplete use of both old and new authorities, technological limitations, and funding constraints.

STRUCTURAL LIMITATIONS TO MONITORING AND VERIFICATION

As noted previously, monitoring and verification regimes encounter various structural limitations that are inherent to the monitoring and verification processes themselves. These limitations include the geographical expanse of the area to be monitored; limited access to facilities; uncertainties produced by poor, lost, distorted, or otherwise incomplete information; and uncertainties resulting from active efforts to conceal and deceive by the inspected party. As a result, there is considerable uncertainty or ambiguity surrounding any conclusions, which are very often "judgment calls," even in the best cases.[93]

It should be noted that international verifying bodies such as the IAEA and OPCW have been effective in monitoring declared facilities. However, they have much greater difficulties in detecting covert facilities and stockpiles, in part because of the inherent difficulties of this task and in part because states can exploit the limitations of monitoring and verification. This certainly was the case with Libya. As Wyn Bowen put it, the IAEA "had been stung by the nuclear revelations that came out of Libya as they demonstrated the wholesale failure of the agency's safeguards."[94] Robert Joseph states this issue more starkly, arguing that the Libyan case demonstrates that "illicit activities by a state willing to cheat on its NPT and IAEA safeguard obligations are not likely to be detected by the international monitoring practices in place."[95] While these statements may judge the IAEA too harshly overall, they are certainly applicable to the IAEA's ability to detect undeclared facilities before the introduction of the AP.

Some of the structural problems with IAEA oversight have been subsequently improved by the AP, which expands the authorities of the IAEA to conduct routine inspections at both declared and undeclared buildings at declared nuclear sites, conduct wide-area environmental sampling, and utilize technological monitoring capabilities (including via satellites). However, significant inherent or structural limitations to IAEA authorities remain. These include limits based on the authorities themselves—for example, limited off-site access far short of "anytime, anyplace" that is often put forward; by their implementation, including integration and residual cultural issues; by technological gaps, such as wide-area environmental sampling; and by cost issues.

The Libyan case demonstrates similar structural limitations within CBW monitoring and verification regimes as well. As we have seen, significant questions remain about Libya's pre-2003 BW program, but at a minimum Libya could have maintained a small-scale BW research and development (R&D) program without detection—despite being a member of the Biological Weapons Convention (BWC) since 1982. Because there are no verification measures associated with this treaty, other countries would potentially be able to conceal BW programs in similar ways.[96] The verification mechanisms for the CWC are significantly stronger but have not been implemented optimally during the lifetime of the convention. Moreover, inherent difficulties remain in confirming or disproving claims in both the chemical and biological arenas, in part because of the technical difficulty of detecting the presence of chemical and biological agents, which is greater than that of detecting nuclear materials. This holds true both for both the BWC and the CWC. Despite the latter's stronger verification authorities, these authorities have not been fully implemented. As a result, countries will potentially have the ability to conceal illicit CBW activities or stockpiles, as Libya did with chemical weapons prior to and after 2003.

Finally, the Libyan case highlights a new and nearly unprecedented threat to nonproliferation regimes: the emergence of nonstate smuggling rings. As Wyn Bowen has argued, "[R]evelations about the A. Q. Khan network's activities vis-à-vis Libya have also generated significant concerns about the true nature and scale of the nuclear black market."[97] Herman Nackaerts voiced similar concerns, arguing that the Libyan case "highlighted the emergence of a new non-State threat—that is, covert nuclear technology supply networks—the most notable example of which was that operated by A. Q. Khan." The Libyan case among others, Nackaerts continues, serves "to illustrate the ever-evolving nature of the IAEA's operating environment, and help[s] to underscore the importance of the Agency better preparing itself for the future and of improving both the effectiveness and the efficiency of the safeguards system."[98]

PROBLEMS WITH IMPLEMENTATION

As discussed above, some of the greatest shortcomings with the monitoring and verification regimes in Libya occurred before 2003, when Libya acceded to the AP and the CWC. After 2003, some of the structural difficulties with monitoring and verification in Libya were to some degree improved. But this by no means implies that all of the difficulties were resolved. There were significant shortcomings in the implementation of these agreements, weakening the monitoring and verification regimes in Libya (and elsewhere). This would have made it difficult for the regimes to discover illicit stockpiles and weapons.

The most significant of these problems is that neither the IAEA nor the CWC is utilizing the most stringent verification tool it has: the authority to employ "special" or "challenge" inspections. The IAEA is empowered by both INFCIRC-66 and INFCIRC-153 to carry out special inspections at suspected facilities in those countries bound by the agreements. Although these authorities are in fact much *stronger* than the new authorities granted by the AP, the IAEA has never effectively exercised this right.[99] Similarly, the CWC gives the OPCW the authority to conduct challenge inspections, which are even more invasive than the special inspections of the IAEA. Under the CWC's challenge inspection procedure, parties to the CWC "have committed themselves to the principle of 'any time, anywhere' inspections with no right of refusal."[100] Despite these significant authorities, the OPCW has to date never undertaken a challenge inspection.[101] By not utilizing all the verification tools at their disposal, the IAEA and OPCW are actually making it more difficult to uncover clandestine programs. Indeed, we have to recall that it took the overthrow of the Qadhafi regime for the undeclared stockpile of chemical weapons to come to light—even after the OPCW had full authorities in Libya.

The hesitation of these agencies to utilize their full authorities is in some respects very understandable. Their member states are concerned about costs, reciprocity (other states retaliating in various ways when a state levels charges against them), revealing their intelligence sources and methods, and other issues.[102] However, as the Libyan and other recent cases of noncompliance suggest, there is a need to work to reduce these barriers. As Herman Nackaerts has argued, the IAEA has interpreted its authorities, especially special inspections, too narrowly, and that the IAEA should be less wary of deploying this verification tool. He further noted that other authorities may also be underutilized.[103]

Shortcomings in the Ad Hoc Disarmament Efforts, 2003–4

The Libyan case also yields important lessons about ad hoc efforts to verify declared WMD rollback in specific cases. In particular, it highlights a number of questions about the levels of confidence that these processes can give the international community in verifying WMD rollback claims. As noted above, some of these questions were already highlighted in the 2005 Robb-Silberman Report, and these and other questions about the U.S.-led verification in Libya have become are all the more important in light of the 2011 CW revelations.[104]

PROBLEMS WITH THE PROCESS

Robert Joseph's first-hand account of the verification and dismantlement processes underscores several important constraints that faced U.S. and British diplomats. First, and perhaps most important, it is clear that Qadhafi's serious decision to disarm was made fairly rapidly. Although the Qadhafi regime floated the idea in March of 2003, the majority of the diplomatic advances were made between October 7 and December 19—and the actual dismantlement process began soon after that.[105]

At most, U.S. officials would have had only a few weeks to prepare for this major undertaking. That would have left very little time to gather a sufficient team of technical experts who knew what to look for, which sites should be visited, what technologies are the most vital, and what equipment they needed to bring with them to make the verifications the most effective. Indeed, some of the limited time leading up to the verification activities was consumed resolving basic implementation issues—for example, there was no basic diplomatic process to build upon or passports for various personnel to enter Libya.[106] Furthermore, as Robert Joseph emphasizes, even once the verification teams were on the ground in Libya, they needed to move very quickly to ensure that they were able to remove key equipment before the mercurial Qadhafi changed his mind, before opposing forces within the Libyan regime gained momentum, or before word leaked about the negotiations.[107]

All of this makes sense from a political or strategic standpoint, but clearly it has the potential to undermine the verification process itself. Indeed, as Dr. Joseph emphasizes, U.S. teams were forced to move forward before they had fully answered questions about Libya's missile project, its work with nerve agents, the possibility of hidden centrifuges—or in retrospect, the possibility of hidden chemical-weapon stockpiles. If this process had taken place with North Korea, which has a far more expansive and complex program, it would have been a disaster.

THE EASING OF STANDARDS

During the efforts to verify Libyan disarmament, there was an easing of standards in both the ad hoc group and the international organizations, which were confident about Libya's apparently "full and transparent cooperation." There are likely several reasons for this overconfidence. First, Libya *appeared* to be cooperating. Unlike in Iraq, Libyan officials revealed previously undisclosed sites, turned over substantial equipment and stockpiles, and allowed inspectors access to multiple facilities. Once it appeared that that Libya was complying, the bar was apparently lowered. This may reflect an interest in moving toward new modes of verification that could be ad hoc, tailored, and fully responsive to national and regional circumstances, including such factors as overall relations with the state, levels of cooperation, and so forth.[108] The tendency to lower the standards for compliance was exposed both in the ad hoc U.S./British effort and in the international organizations tasked with monitoring Libya's programs after 2003. One should recall, for example, the IAEA director-general's statement in 2008 that, despite the fact that "there are some parts of Libya's past programme which the Agency has not been able to reconstruct fully," the agency was largely satisfied because of "the cooperation and transparent response shown by Libya."[109]

A second reason why the ad hoc group was confident that Libya was not concealing anything was the apparent lack of development of the programs, at least on the nuclear side. Because much of the equipment and material was still in boxes, inspectors concluded that Libya did not have a sophisticated program to hide.

A possible third reason why the ad hoc group was willing to accept Libya's declarations at face value was that there was a fear that if U.S. diplomats applied too much pressure on Libya they would undercut Libya's cooperation before the job was finished.

None of these reasons justified the easing of standards that took place, and the consequences of what was done were significant. As noted above, the Robb-Silberman Report stated: "It is clear that Libya has been considerably less forthcoming about the details of its chemical and biological weapons than about its nuclear and missile programs." We now know that some of those concerns were justified. But we may not even have a complete picture of Libya's nuclear and missile programs, because it is not clear that the ad hoc teams conducted a sufficiently thorough or sustained verification process.

Lessons

The Libyan case is more complex than it appeared, and offers lessons that may be useful in addressing future cases of noncompliance.

The Limits of International Monitoring and Verification

As noted above, there are intrinsic limits to international monitoring and verification. Faced with these limits, the IAEA and OPCW have not optimally utilized the authorities they possess, including systematic use of inspections of undeclared buildings at declared nuclear sites or dual-use chemical facilities, detection technologies such as wide-area environmental sampling (WAES) or satellites, or the use of special or challenge inspections.

It may be argued that Libya's most egregious violations of the NPT and safeguards commitments with the IAEA were carried out before Libya bound itself to the AP in 2003, and are therefore irrelevant to today's world. That is not the case. Safeguards have been significantly improved by the additional authorities provided under the AP, even though some of those authorities are not being implemented effectively. However, some of the states of greatest proliferation concern are currently not bound by the AP—or in some cases by the NPT itself. North Korea withdrew from the NPT, Syria and Myanmar have not ratified the AP, and Iran is "provisionally" applying the AP.[110] In those cases where the AP is not being applied, the IAEA will have access to only limited information and its ability to detect illicit facilities and activities will be sharply constrained.[111] The lessons from Libya's pre-2003 activities will thus continue to provide important insights about safeguards for the foreseeable future.

This does not diminish the role of safeguards or other efforts at monitoring and verification. The mission of inspection agencies is very difficult, especially the need to detect undeclared WMD programs and stockpiles even in countries that are determined to conceal them. As the Robb-Silberman Report suggests, the intelligence community will be expected to detect such covert activities, but the intelligence community's capabilities will be limited if inspection agencies are not doing all they can to put "boots on the ground." The ability of inspection agencies to do so is constrained by limited authorities, unused authorities, and poor intelligence. There is also increasingly a mistrust among intelligence agencies, states, and international organizations.

The international community must be aware of these limits, work to improve the political, cultural, and technological means to minimize them, and tailor responses to noncompliance with full knowledge of those limits.

The Problems with Cooperation

Cooperation is rightly valued in monitoring and verification efforts; however, apparent cooperation can also be a strategy that is designed to hinder monitoring and verification. The strategy that Libya appeared to follow was to give the appearance of full cooperation in some areas (such as its nuclear program and parts of its chemical-weapon program) but to conceal stockpiles or programs in other areas. Thus, the most troubling implication from the 2011 CW discovery is that the Libyan regime actually may not have completely changed course in the first place, despite appearances.

Given the stakes, the appearance of cooperation is not a sufficient criterion of compliance unless it is *truly* borne out through a thorough verification.[112] In fact, one might wonder whether undisputable evidence of serious noncompliance in the past might make the verification bar *higher* than for normal cases—regardless of whether the country later appeared to be cooperating. Such cases of noncompliance should require a higher demand for transparency, more intensive ad hoc verification, and ongoing and sustained monitoring. If, as was the case in Libya, the country's officials demand that an international organization conduct the verification, the authorities granted to that organization in these instances should exceed normal authorities.

The Need for Long-term Monitoring

Given the potential for revival of WMD programs or retention of covert stockpiles and facilities, there need to be mechanisms to implement more intrusive, long-term monitoring to provide greater assurance that a given country did not have an ulterior motive for renouncing its proscribed weapons. This holds true for Libya and other apparent cases of rollback. And yet, the various ad hoc groups and verification regimes do not appear to have mechanisms for stringent long-term monitoring after noncompliance has been discovered.

Indeed, at the time, there appears to have been little recognition of the need for mechanisms that went beyond normal, or routine, monitoring in Libya. In fact, as the Robb-Silberman Report warned in 2005, attention appeared to be moving away from Libya as a potential proliferator:

> There is growing concern within the Intelligence Community that thinking "Libya is done" may leave collectors and analysts without the resources needed to track and monitor future change. Competing priorities have reduced focus on Libya since the 2003 declarations, and Libya may again become a low priority for collectors. Some analysts say they have already begun to feel the effects of the shift in priorities.[113]

A similar perception that "Libya is done" may have affected the behavior of the international verification organizations as well. Clearly, they did not seem to have taken steps to provide for long-term monitoring and verification sufficient to ensure that noncompliance had been addressed and that it did not recur.

In part, these are cultural problems, implementation problems, and are related to the structural problems with monitoring and verification organizations previously discussed. One is reminded of the statement by Donald Mahley in this context—that "we will have to think very seriously about finding inspectors with a different skill set, and about more intelligence-sharing, and about looking widely, not just at declared sites."[114] Mahley's criticism may be a bit unfair to the ad hoc group that led the disarmament process in Libya, since the U.S.-led group did bring in many of the right technical experts to work on the dismantlement.[115] However, Mahley correctly highlights serious deficiencies with long-term monitoring, including a lack of information-sharing and an incomplete use of inspections of undeclared buildings and facilities.

The Potential Consequences of Failure

As we have seen, there were significant concerns over a potential loss of control over Libya's WMD technologies and materials during the uprising and after the regime change. These concerns remained in 2014, following the events in Benghazi, where Al Qaeda–affiliated groups were able to infiltrate into Libya and carry out a successful attack on a U.S. diplomatic post. This attack raised serious concerns about the ability of the new Libyan government to control the stockpiles of chemical agents that remained in the country awaiting destruction.[116] These risks played a significant role in spurring the final push in 2014 to destroy country's remaining chemical agents and delivery vehicles,[117] and risks could arise in other countries during similar circumstances.

Given that long-term regime stability for most, if not all, of the "difficult cases"—such as Iran, North Korea, and Syria—is not ensured, similar concerns may surface in these countries as well. At the time of this writing, it is still possible that the Assad regime in Syria may be toppled, though the regime has recently gained ground against the rebels.[118] The recent removal of Syria's declared CW agents has reduced the severity of these risks, but there could still be risks if the regime has retained a covert CW stockpile. In the event that regimes such as Iran or North Korea encountered significant domestic upheavals (possibilities that are remote for the present, but are possible over the longer term), similar dangers could arise in those countries as well. Needless to say, the risks of loss of central control over weapon stockpiles, equipment, and related technologies would be much worse if these states never adopted the Libyan course of turning over the majority of their WMD programs. But even if they did, there could still be concerns over stolen or lost WMD materials, as we saw in Libya after the end of the Qadhafi regime. The United States, NATO, the UN Security Council, and international verification entities such as the IAEA and OPCW need to be prepared to act—rapidly—to secure suspected WMD facilities, stockpiles, and munitions depots should these sorts of crises come about.

Conclusions

The Libyan case offers important lessons for the international community as it attempts to address the most challenging cases of monitoring and verification, such as North Korea, Iran, and Syria. With the possible exception of Syria's CW rollback, the international community has yet to convince these counties to abandon their suspected WMD programs and submit to a verified elimination of those programs. But this objective remains the stated policy of the Obama administration and other key states.[119] The Libyan case is therefore a very important case to examine in this context not only because it likely represents one of the best scenarios we could hope for in such "difficult cases" but also because it helps us identify the pitfalls and challenges associated with verifying and monitoring WMD and missile rollback—and in some cases shows us what *not* to do—even in the most optimistic cases.

The Libyan case reveals the most basic difficulty with monitoring and verification regimes: even in what one might consider the best case scenario, it is very hard to detect undeclared WMD programs and stockpiles in countries that are determined to conceal them. Despite Libya's apparently unprecedented cooperation—including a voluntary renunciation of WMD, revelations of previously undeclared facilities, and delivery of substantial amounts of equipment and materials—it was still able to conceal a small stockpile of chemical weapons. Similar concerns are currently being raised in relation to Syria's elimination of its chemical-weapon stockpile.[120]

Beyond the intrinsic limits of monitoring and verification, the Libyan case yields a perhaps surprising result. Despite Libya's cooperation and the nonproliferation successes that were achieved, there may have been clear instances in which the *cooperation actually undercut effective monitoring and verification*— both by lowering the threshold for acceptable compliance and by providing cover for the undeclared CW facilities and stockpiles.

Given the hidden stockpile of chemical weapons and CW artillery shells that came to light after the Arab Spring, ad hoc verification groups and international monitoring organizations need to take more seriously the possibility that a voluntary rollback may not be sincere, even if the state appears to be cooperating. After all, the same people ruled Libya before and after the December 19 renunciation, and—despite what some scholars have argued—appeared to move rapidly to renounce their WMD programs only after it was clear their efforts to acquire nuclear weapons technologies via the A. Q. Khan network had been discovered.[121] The Libyan case suggests, therefore, that in future cases, both ad hoc disarmament teams and international inspectors should be more suspicious of such apparent sudden and complete changes of heart.

In retrospect, the international community, especially the United States, Great Britain, and the IAEA, did an incomplete job of verification of Libya's programs. There were also few provisions for rigorous, long-term monitoring to ensure that these programs were not restarted later. As Robert Joseph has indicated, there were clear and justifiable reasons for moving forward with the dismantlement and removal of equipment and materials from Libyan territory even before all the questions were completely answered about Libya's WMD programs. In principle, verification isn't perfect, and political judgments (such as the need to move rapidly to undercut Libya's domestic opposition) will need to be considered. But even if the decision is made to move forward, there still is a need to have an *ongoing* process to verify that the political judgments are sound.

Specifically, once the most sensitive equipment and technologies were successfully removed, the ad hoc U.S.- and British-led group should have insisted on a more sustained and rigorous verification process. It is indeed perplexing why U.S. officials were in such an apparent rush to give Libya a clean "bill of health." One possible reason is that the Bush administration may have determined that it needed a clear nonproliferation success at a time when the Iraq War controversies were simmering. A drawn out verification process, while better serving long-term nonproliferation and disarmament goals, does not produce clear political victories in the short term.

It was not inevitable that the monitoring and verification processes would leave so many questions and capabilities uncovered in the Libyan case. Nor is it certain, however, even if a more systematic verification process had taken place, that Libya's covert CW stockpile would have been detected—or that the international community would be able to detect similar covert programs in other cases of WMD rollback. But the long-term dangers of ineffective inspection and verification regimes cannot be overstated. International security depends, in part, upon organizations summoning the political courage to make difficult decisions. Leveraging the IAEA's and OPCW's existing authorities to advance nonproliferation efforts represents a good start.

5   Verifying Global Disarmament

There have been long-standing interests in and hopes for global nuclear disarmament among many governments, nongovernmental organizations (NGOs), and individuals across the globe. Beginning in 2007, this disarmament movement gained significant credibility when luminaries like George Schultz, Henry Kissinger, William Perry, and Sam Nunn called for a world without nuclear weapons. With their appeal, serious hopes for nuclear disarmament moved from the political fringe to the mainstream, and expectations grew.[1]

U.S. president Barack Obama furthered these expectations when in Prague on April 5, 2009, he spoke of "America's commitment to seek the peace and security of a world without nuclear weapons."[2] He recognized that this objective "will not be reached quickly—perhaps not in my lifetime. It will take patience and persistence. But now we, too, must ignore the voices who tell us that the world cannot change."[3] The 2010 Nuclear Posture Review (NPR) report outlined the administration's approach to promoting the agenda put forward by President Obama for reducing nuclear dangers and pursuing the goal of a world without nuclear weapons while maintaining, as long as nuclear weapons remain, a safe, secure, and effective arsenal, both to deter potential adversaries and to assure U.S. allies and other security partners that they can count on America's security commitments.[4]

Reflecting the belief that the prospects for a world without nuclear weapons would depend on political, military, and technical conditions, the NPR called for a national program to address these conditions, including a monitoring and verification research and development (R&D) program to meet future challenges arising from the administration's nonproliferation, arms control, and disarmament agenda. In the NPR, the administration also committed to implementing existing nuclear arms control treaties such as New START, and negotiating follow-on arms reduction treaties; negotiating and eventually ratifying the Comprehensive Test Ban Treaty (CTBT) and a fissile material cutoff treaty (FMCT); enhancing nuclear safeguards to prevent additional proliferation threats; and encouraging Russian and Chinese stability and transparency.[5] These were seen by the administration as concrete steps leading toward the vision of a world without nuclear weapons.

These initiatives were praised by many individuals and organizations across the globe. Organizations such as the Nonaligned Movement praised President Obama for taking the lead in working to achieve the goals outlined in Article VI of the Nuclear Nonproliferation Treaty (NPT), in which the recognized nuclear-weapon states (NWSs)—the United States, Russia, Great Britain, France, and China—committed to undertake "good faith negotiations" with the goal of nuclear disarmament.[6] The hopes for global nuclear disarmament that were encapsulated in President Obama's Prague Speech, along with his appearing at the time to represent a sharp break from the policies of his predecessor, were likely the main reasons why Obama was awarded a Nobel Peace Prize in 2009.[7] For the first time in decades—perhaps more than at any time since nuclear weapons were first used in 1945—it seemed to many that it was not simply a fantasy to imagine putting the nuclear genie back in the bottle.

However, in subsequent years, the excitement began to diminish. Although President Obama reaffirmed the disarmament goals outlined in Prague and the NPR in Berlin in 2013,[8] this agenda became stalemated following the New START treaty, and the prospects for disarmament became clouded by questions and difficulties, including what precisely "disarmament" meant and a clearer sense of the political constraints on achieving that goal.[9] The prospects for disarmament hinge upon the willingness of current nuclear-weapon states, as well as the de facto nuclear powers and proliferating states, to take serious steps toward disarmament as well, and it was not clear that this would happen. While all of the NPT-recognized nuclear states have expressed interest in disarmament, some states have taken serious steps to reduce their arsenals while others have not been willing to take concrete steps toward disarmament. Russia has reduced its strategic arms in tandem with the United States but reportedly views its nuclear arsenal as an important counterbalance to the conventional capabilities and emerging missile defense systems of the United States. France, which has significantly reduced its arsenal, is hesitant to go further and believes its power and status depend on its nuclear weapons. China's nuclear-weapon modernization program has raised questions about the role of nuclear weapons in its future. Other, de facto, nuclear states, which have not signed the

NPT, never made any commitments to make progress toward disarmament. And the ongoing nuclear programs of proliferant states appeared to be moving the world in the wrong direction—toward greater proliferation instead of disarmament. Overall, the four statesmen, President Obama, and others did create the mood that real progress on disarmament could be achieved, but the enthusiasm has waned as progress on those next steps has become increasingly difficult to imagine.[10]

Owing to these political constraints, the most realistic scenarios for progress in the foreseeable future would be additional cuts in nuclear forces, possibly leading to a nondeployment commitment among nuclear states. But the biggest, most challenging technical issues relating to disarmament have not been seriously addressed yet, even if the political stalemates were to be resolved. Some of the problems are understood, and many of the most challenging will involve verification.

This chapter examines what the prospects and challenges are for developing a verification regime to confirm movement toward, and achievement of, global nuclear disarmament. The limits on verification that are examined in the other case studies in this book are relevant to the challenges of verifying disarmament, but there are new challenges that are unique to global disarmament as well. Realizing this agenda will require the development of technologies, procedures, and systems for monitoring and verification of warhead declarations and dismantlement, fissile material stockpiles and disposition, and the detection of clandestine stockpiles and facilities. It will also require the development of additional verification tools for international safeguards and for other international treaties. Each of these steps involves significant hurdles that will need to be overcome if we are to achieve the ultimate objective of a nuclear-weapon-free world.

The Challenges of Verification

Verification of a follow-on to New START would likely have to address warheads and possibly components along with delivery capabilities. Deeper cuts and disarmament would need to address all of these elements along with nuclear weapon testing, nuclear material and weapon production facilities, virtual capabilities from old weapon and existing energy programs, and undeclared capabilities. Verification of the disarmament process itself would also be faced with unprecedented new requirements. This section will address some of the key verification challenges—including those relating to confirming warhead declarations, warhead dismantlement, fissile material stockpiles, and fissile material disposition, as well as the challenge of detecting covert facilities. Moreover, it points to similar challenges in the chemical- and biological-weapon arenas that would need to be overcome as part of an effort to achieve nuclear disarmament, as well as weapons of mass destruction (WMD) disarmament as a whole.

Warhead Transparency/Verification

The verification of nuclear warheads and components, as well as their storage, dismantlement, or elimination, is widely recognized as the most daunting verification challenge we can identify today. It is often assumed that the difficult and complex task of verifying warheads and their dismantlement would occur later rather than sooner on the path to zero; however, the U.S. position on the follow-on to New START raises these issues in the context of further arms reductions. It would, in principle, require intrusive warhead verification and transparency, which raises the questions of whether this can be done effectively and whether it will be acceptable to the Russians and eventually other NWSs.

Even before the conclusion of New START and the discussion of a follow-on treaty, some observers held that warhead transparency was needed early in the process. In what they describe as the "standard model" for verification of disarmament, Perkovich and Acton argue that "first would be detailed declarations of nuclear possessions: where, what, how many, and so forth." Such declarations, they argue, are necessary for obtaining a detailed "baseline" declaration that specifies the "location, deployment, and possibly the history of each warhead."[11]

However, this "standard model" seriously oversimplifies this element of the verification process. It is not clear when information on warhead numbers and locations would be forthcoming from the nuclear states, but it is unlikely that it would come all at once, or early in the process. Rather, such declarations would be more likely to occur at the end of the process as dismantlement occurs and numbers become smaller. In any case, to date, most of the NWSs have been very reluctant to increase transparency about their arsenals. Of the nuclear-weapon states, only the United States has provided a declaration of its total number of deployed strategic warheads, as well as the total number of nuclear weapons in its stockpile.[12] (It has not revealed all the U.S. storage locations, however, presumably owing to concerns about security and survivability.) Great Britain and France have declared that their arsenals would be capped at 225 and 300 warheads, respectively, but the other states have been less forthcoming.[13] The situation is the same for fissile material production.

Although some transparency measures have been implemented as part of U.S.-Russia arms control treaties, including START, SORT, and New START, the main emphasis of these treaties has been on delivery vehicles instead of warheads. As Steve Fetter notes:

> The Russian–US nuclear arms control treaties focus mainly on limiting or eliminating nuclear delivery vehicles and their launchers; they do not impose direct controls on nuclear warheads. The focus on delivery vehicles and launchers is understandable because they are much easier to count and far more difficult to hide than warheads or materials.[14]

New START verification draws largely from the provisions of old START, and focuses on delivery systems with some attention to accounting for deployed warheads. In the U.S. view, verification of a follow-on to New START could have to address deployed and nondeployed, strategic and nonstrategic, warheads, along with continuing attention to delivery systems. This could, in principle, require intrusive warhead verification and transparency, which raises the questions of whether this can be done effectively and whether it will be acceptable to the Russians. Because of these uncertainties, there have been proposals to avoid the daunting challenges of warhead verification at this stage of the process.

On the basis of the U.S. position, there have been proposals for a total ceiling of warheads, perhaps 3,000 to 3,500, including deployed and nondeployed, strategic and nonstrategic warheads. For at least the strategic deployed warheads, there would be a subceiling of perhaps 1,000 warheads. Verification would be based on the warheads, but would not involve elaborate schemes to identify and track them. Rather, these proposals would rely on procedures in New START for verifying deployed warheads that are limited but could be adequate at the levels proposed. It is recognized that there will be even more limited capabilities for addressing nondeployed and nonstrategic warheads, involving perhaps declarations, centralized storage, and some transparency measures. This would result in a two-tiered system. While such limited verification may be deemed acceptable at the next phase of reductions, deeper reductions and the goal of "zero" will require different, more far reaching measures.

Thus, despite the U.S.-Russian experience in providing declarations about their strategic arsenals and in negotiating certain verification strategies for arms reduction treaties, declarations on warheads would be largely unchartered territory—as would the creation of a verification regime to confirm the accuracy of such declarations. It would likely be even more difficult to obtain such declarations from countries with smaller arsenals, such as China, India, and Pakistan. Full disclosure of their arsenal size and location could raise some concerns about security (sufficiently protecting them from terrorist attacks) and survivability (vulnerability to a first strike). For example, although China is not being asked to take steps that could threaten its security, it is nevertheless using this issue to avoid nearly all transparency about its nuclear-weapon program. Although China's arsenal has historically been estimated to be fairly small compared with those possessed by the United States and Russia, there are a number of recent estimates which suggest that the arsenal could be significantly larger than long thought.[15] The large range represented in these estimates would be very hard to verify. Obtaining and confirming baseline declarations from India and Pakistan would be difficult as well. Although analysts like David Albright have done an excellent job over the years estimating potential arsenal sizes of India and Pakistan based on the likely fissile material production rates at their facilities, such estimates include significant margins of error.[16]

Thus, the kind of "baselines" that Perkovich and Acton envision would not be the first steps. They would instead likely be developed and refined over time and, however they are made, would be difficult to verify. They would also need to be closely connected with the baselining of fissile material production, in order to obtain estimates on the number of nuclear weapons the state could have credibly produced.

THE PROBLEM OF CONCEALMENT

One of the biggest, and most immediate, challenges for a verification regime would be to confirm that NWSs did not conceal some portion of their nuclear arsenals. As Perkovich and Acton acknowledge, "The question arises of why states would go to the trouble of trying to defeat a verification system when they could simply fail to declare hidden warheads. Retaining warheads would be easier and cheaper, and there would be much less risk of being caught."[17]

The problem of concealment would be minimized if verifying entities could maintain a "chain of custody" over the weapon from deployment to dismantlement. As Perkovich and Acton note: "[I]deally, verification of deployed warheads would start at their deployment sites, so that a chain of custody could be established for as much of the disarmament process as possible."[18] However, both the United States and Russia now have significant nondeployed strategic and tactical nuclear stockpiles, making it very difficult to establish a solid chain of custody.

There are also public uncertainties in the size and locations of U.S. and Russian tactical nuclear arsenals, but the estimations of the Russian arsenal vary widely. In the early 1990s, both the United States and Russia declared that they would remove large numbers of tactical nuclear weapons from deployment and destroy many of these weapons as part of the Presidential Nuclear Initiatives (PNIs).[19] But since the PNIs were not carried out in the context of a treaty, there was no verification to confirm that each side carried out its declaration. The United States has been reasonably open and forthcoming on its actions to implement the PNIs. Russia has not.[20]

Moreover, as the United States and Russia—as a result of recent arms control agreements (especially the 2002 Strategic Offensive Reduction Treaty and the 2010 New START)—are increasingly transitioning large numbers of deployed strategic weapons to nondeployed, stored weapons maintained as a hedge or awaiting dismantlement, the ability to track the chain of command is disappearing. It is estimated that less than one-third of the U.S. arsenal is now deployed; Russia, as well, is believed to have a large nondeployed stockpile, though it is not clear exactly how large it is. For deployed systems, maintaining a chain of command would therefore be useful, but this approach would not be available for most of the nuclear weapons now possessed by the United States and Russia. In the future, the situation is likely to worsen in this regard.

As a result, there would need to be a verification system in place capable of detecting clandestine stockpiles of strategic weapons, tactical nuclear weapons, and other components that could be used in reconstituting a nuclear-weapon program. Such a verification system is today technically beyond our grasp. If the technical challenges underlying its creation could be addressed, such a system would be extensive, intrusive, costly, and extremely difficult to implement. As Christopher Ford argues:

> The ability of any imaginable verification regime to search for hidden nuclear warheads or material outside a country's "declared stockpile" slated for elimination would likely be quite limited—both as a matter of technology (e.g., the data-quality and access provided by sensors or other information resources, and the accuracy of materials accountancy) and with regard to procedural tools (e.g., the intrusiveness of any inspection rights and the availability of personnel and resources with which to implement what authorities exist).[21]

Dismantlement Transparency/Verification

The considerable research and development done in the United States and elsewhere on warhead and dismantlement transparency/verification since the early 1990s reveals the enormity of the problems and the challenges of developing effective capabilities to verify very small arsenals, let alone "zero," however defined.

The United States has focused on developing attribute measurement systems to determine whether an item is like, or consistent with, a nuclear weapon (for example, mass, isotopic ratios, and so forth), and information barrier systems to prevent direct inspector or third-party access to these measurements. However, both systems have serious technical challenges, including the need to address authentication, transparency, and other issues.

There has also been considerable work on verification schemes that follow an item through the dismantlement process. They are limited, especially by the uncertainties concerning the item at the point of entry, wherever that may be; by the possibility of illicit activities that may occur during the process; and by potentially overwhelming costs.

On the basis of such considerations, presumably, Patricia Lewis notes that although most NWSs are familiar with warhead dismantlement, which is necessary for maintenance of their own arsenals, "verification of this stage would be quite a departure."[22] The challenges include the sensitivity of information, the problem of defining and measuring the attributes of a nuclear weapon, and the difficulties of tracking weapons and components through the dismantlement process.

THE SENSITIVITY OF INFORMATION

An immediate challenge a verification regime would encounter is how to verify the dismantlement of warheads without revealing sensitive information about those warheads. Not surprisingly, NWSs reportedly keep information on their warhead designs highly classified.[23] Not only would this information reveal a great deal about the military capabilities of the NWSs, but in most cases it would be against the laws of the states possessing that information. Moreover, release of this information by a NWS would potentially be a violation of Article I of the NPT. If available to a nonnuclear-weapon state (NNWS), this information could create serious proliferation risks by showing proliferating countries how to design advanced nuclear weapons.

A verification system would therefore need to be designed to verify dismantlement without revealing this sensitive information. The difficulty, however, is that security concerns will be present in almost every aspect of the dismantlement process—from the basic design of warheads, to their shape, to the amount and isotopic makeup of the fissile materials, to the features of the nonnuclear components. So the verification regime faces a basic dilemma: the stakes of verification are high for all parties, but it is unlikely that verification will be undertaken by all parties equally. The NWSs will likely be unwilling and unable, under law and policy, to fully share information among themselves and with NNWSs, but the NNWSs may not trust the NWSs to dismantle the warheads themselves. Verification by an international organization or other third-party could in principle address the NNWSs' concerns; however, it would potentially reveal classified information and create proliferation risks that are the reason why the NWSs have limited information in the first place.

CHALLENGES IN DETERMINING WHAT IS A NUCLEAR WEAPON

For the verification process to be successful, it is essential that verification teams be confident that the items they are starting with actually *are* nuclear weapons. But obtaining a simple definition of what constitutes a nuclear weapon without revealing sensitive information is difficult. If inspectors could measure the warhead directly—including mass, design, isometrics, and so forth—there would not be any issue. However, they cannot measure warheads in this way because of the sensitivities involved.

In an attempt to help address these definitional and sensitivity challenges, the United States has focused on developing attribution measurement systems to determine whether an item is like, or consistent with, a nuclear weapon (for example, containing a certain mass, isotopic ratios, and the like) and information barrier systems to prevent direct inspector or third party access to these measurements. The United States proposed "that a warhead could, in principle, be measured by six different attribute measures to confirm declarations, including: presence of plutonium, plutonium isotopic ratio, plutonium mass, plutonium age, presence of oxide, and symmetry of plutonium."[24]

As Patricia Lewis notes, however, "[M]uch work remains to be done on this technically tricky aspect of the verification chain."[25] This is certainly the case. For starters, the attribute method would introduce significant uncertainties into the verification process—even if the disarming states and third parties were to identify clear, well-defined, and measurable attributes for a nuclear weapon.

Even in the best case, all verification teams could say is that the item they are assessing is *like*, or consistent with, a nuclear weapon. Even the information that would potentially be revealed would be classified or sensitive and would have to be filtered through an information barrier or other means of protection. An inspector might, for example, see only a green or red light indicating whether or not the item matched the attributes. Moreover, there would be the potential for significant disagreements over what attributes should be considered fundamental to a nuclear weapon. Indeed, the attribute method was explored in detail in the late 1990s during the Trilateral Initiative (discussed below), but the United States and Russia could not agree on the attributes to be measured.

Another verification approach that has been explored is the template method. In this type of verification, a system would be designed to obtain something like a standard image of the item (whether it be an x-ray, a radioactive assay, or the like). That image template would then be compared with specific images of what comes out of a declared weapon during dismantlement.[26] As with the attribute measurement system, given the information that would potentially be revealed, inspectors would not be able to view the images, which require an information barrier or other means of protection.

As a consequence, despite important differences with the attribute verification method, the template method would potentially run into similar challenges. A template is, after all, only a template: as such, an item could potentially match the template—thereby receiving a "green light"—without actually being a weapon. Also, given the information contained in the template, there would potentially be more information available if the systems were breached.

Overall, the difficulties with both the attribute measurement system and template method may prevent a verification system from ensuring that the item brought into the verification system is a weapon, is fully consistent with being a weapon, or has a "weapon origin." If so, that could raise questions about whether one is genuinely addressing warheads and their dismantlement directly, and may put a premium on focusing on weapon-usable material that may or may not have been removed from a weapon. Such an approach has its own issues, and does not address the problems of past production uncertainties and of detecting clandestine activities.

PROSPECTS FOR INFORMATION BARRIERS?

Because the attribute measurement and template methods both would risk revealing sensitive design information, both would require that an information barrier be set in place to protect the information from inspecting teams or third-party observers. This information barrier would, in effect, hide or reduce data to only a yes/no evaluation.

Although some analysts have viewed the attribute measurement/information barrier concept as a potential way to resolve the issue of sensitive information, information barriers would create serious challenges for verification.[27] The following are some of the issues that still need to be worked through:

False Positives/False Negatives. A "false positive" would occur when the verification technology incorrectly identifies the item as possessing the attributes of a warhead when in reality it does not. Depending on the frequency of false positives and what the actual dismantlement process is after items are identified as warheads, a state could potentially declare that it was dismantling warheads when it actually was not. And, of course, because the item had been incorrectly classified as a warhead, other parties would not be aware that this was occurring. Moreover, if other parties were suspicious that false positives were occurring, they would have little ability to challenge the other state or look at the declared item because of the classification of the information that necessitated the information barrier. Participants and third parties would thus need to have sufficient confidence that the technologies were indeed able to detect "negatives" correctly with very small margins of error.

"False negatives" could be even more difficult to address. A false negative would occur when the technology incorrectly identified an item as not possessing the characteristics of a warhead when it actually did. If an item received a "red light" by the attribute measurement technology, it is not clear what inspectors could do, because the information barrier would prevent them from looking at the item to confirm one way or the other. In the end, they would not be able to accept the item. That would not necessarily be a problem initially if the disarming states had large arsenals, but the issue would gain in importance as arsenal sizes became smaller.

In fact, there are many potential scenarios that could cause serious disruption. What if there were initially large numbers of items rejected? What if an item initially received a "green light" but was rechecked a few months later and received a "red light"? Again, verification teams could not look at the actual items to determine what the issues were.

All of these scenarios are plausible—and indeed, the potential for false positives/negatives is reportedly one of the reasons why the United States, Russia, and the International Atomic Energy Agency (IAEA) failed to come to an

agreement about the attribute measurement/information barrier system during the Trilateral Initiative in the late 1990s.[28] At the very least, for this verification strategy to be successful, alternate systems would have to be designed to
measure questionable containers. It is not clear, however, what those alternative
systems would be.

Creating Uncertainties in Fissile Material Stockpiles. Even if these technical challenges are resolved, attribute measurement systems would create additional verification difficulties, including introducing uncertainties in fissile
material estimates. Because the specific amount of nuclear material contained
in the warhead is classified, one of the ways to address this issue is to establish a
"threshold" amount of fissile material for the item to be considered a warhead.
For example, the attribute measurement system would define a warhead as an
item that contained at least "x" amount of highly enriched uranium (HEU) or
plutonium (or other fissile material).

The problem with this approach, however, is that attribute verification
would create serious and potentially insurmountable problems for establishing
baseline estimates for fissile material stockpiles. By design, these measurement
systems introduce uncertainties in fissile material estimates, potentially creating opportunities for diversion. As Perkovich and Acton acknowledge:

> Even if acceptable attributes could somehow be chosen, attribute verification
> cannot provide assurance that none of the fissile material from a nuclear weap-
> on had not been diverted. It is often overlooked that authenticating a warhead
> using the attribute method is not equivalent to verifying that no material has
> been removed from a warhead.[29]

Indeed, because the uncertainty is an inherent design feature of the information barrier system, these uncertainties in fissile material stocks, which may not
be resolvable, may never be reduced—and will be compounding over time as
more warheads are disassembled.

Maintaining Adequate Information Security. Finally, new security challenges
have arisen in recent years that could make the NWSs less confident that information barriers will be able to protect their sensitive information. For example, when information barriers were first explored, we did not have the same
kind of cyber security challenges that we have today. There are questions about
whether the information can be secure in ways that were envisioned in the
mid-1990s—especially if the verification is being overseen by an independent
verification organization or other third party, rather than a state's intelligence
agency (which could be the case).

WARHEAD AND COMPONENT TRACKING

There has also been considerable work on verification schemes that follow an item through the dismantlement process. In the late 1990s, in preparation for possible START III reductions (which covered warheads and may have required their verified destruction), the Los Alamos National Laboratory developed a potential system to track nuclear-weapon and nuclear-component containers during the dismantlement process. This system, named the Integrated Facility Monitoring System (IFMS), could potentially assist in providing evidence that the warheads had actually been dismantled. The basic idea of the IFMS was that it

> is a limited chain-of-custody system that can monitor nuclear warhead containers from the point at which the nuclear warheads are authenticated as treaty-limited items, through stops at various dismantlement bays, all the way to some final onsite storage of the nuclear weapons components. The IFMS is intended to provide confidence that treaty activities are taking place as declared, while protecting sensitive and classified information.[30]

Similarly, Los Alamos developed systems for detecting unauthorized movement of warheads or components from storage sites and the like. This technology, known as the Magazine Transparency System, "detects unauthorized movement of weapon containers from storage, and maintains magazine inventory. It is installed in magazines or storage areas containing nuclear warheads or components."[31]

Although these and similar systems hold some promise for verification of warhead dismantlement, their potential is limited. It is technically possible to follow a container through a dismantlement system, but the primary challenges include the uncertainties concerning the item at the point of entry, wherever that may be, by the possibility of illicit activities that may occur during the process, and by potentially overwhelming costs. For example, even though inspectors can track a container through the dismantlement process, the primary question is what exactly is inside the container. Given the sensitivity of information and the possible use of information barriers, inspectors will, at best, know that they contain something that is "like" a nuclear weapon. If a country introduces something other than a warhead, the verification process can be undermined.

Lessons from the Trilateral Initiative, Mayak, and U.S.-Russian Plutonium Disposition. Some scholars have argued that efforts to create a verification system for warhead dismantlement could build upon the work that the United

States and Russia have already done in the context of the Trilateral Initiative, as well as other cooperative initiatives such the joint plutonium disposition. For example, Thomas E. Shea argues:

> Those seeking to design a system for verifying the dismantlement of nuclear weapons do not have to start from a blank slate. They can benefit a great deal from building on the experience of the Trilateral Initiative. This was a six-year (1996–2002) effort to develop a verification system under which Russia and the United States could submit classified forms of weapons-origin fissile material to International Atomic Energy Agency (IAEA) verification and monitoring in a [*sic*] irreversible manner and for an indefinite period of time.[32]

Despite this and other positive assessments, the accomplishments of the Trilateral Initiative and similar U.S.-Russia cooperative dismantlement initiatives have been seriously oversold. In fact, the lessons from these initiatives should not be viewed as particularly positive. Instead, the Trilateral Initiative highlighted the serious and fundamental technical challenges, as well as the significant disagreements, between the United States and Russia on how to proceed with a verification strategy.

In the Trilateral Initiative, the United States, Russia, and the IAEA explored the potential application of an attribute measurement/information barrier system to verify excess defense material. In the end, however, the negotiations were concluded but the approach developed under the initiative was never implemented, in part because of outstanding technical issues and in part because the United States and Russia viewed this problem through very different lenses. They had very different views about what attributes should be used to verify warheads entering the system—and, as noted above, were ultimately unable to agree on the attributes to be measured. The differing classification systems in place in the United States and Russia also complicated the achievement of the objectives of the Trilateral Initiative.

The fundamental disagreements between the United States and Russia over warhead dismantlement verification were underscored in the negotiation (and subsequent deadlock) over the warhead dismantlement facility at the Russian nuclear site of Mayak. In 1992, the United States designated an initial $15 million of Cooperative Threat Reduction funds to assist Russia in designing a facility to store nuclear materials from dismantled weapons.[33] This funding was subsequently expanded to help Russia build the storage facility.[34] At the insistence of Congress, however, it was required that a verification system be put into place to confirm that the fissile material stored at Mayak was in fact drawn from dismantled nuclear weapons. The United States and Russia explored implementing an attribute verification system similar to what was developed in the Trilateral Initiative. After ten years, huge delays, and enormous cost over-runs—ultimately costing more than $400 million—the facility was finally completed in 2002. However, the negotiations over the verification system eventually broke down when Russian officials insisted on reshaping all plutonium before shipping it to Mayak—effectively eliminating the ability to confirm that the plutonium had come from dismantled weapons.[35] In the end, no monitoring and verification system was put into place at the facility.

The experiences of the Trilateral Initiative and Mayak facility also raise questions about whether other states and third-party observers would agree over the relevant criteria, even if the United States and Russia were to come to agreement on verification mechanisms.[36] As Christopher Ford notes:

> Today's various nuclear weapons possessors may each have different ideas of what constitutes sensitive information, and it still is far from certain at this point what the rest of the international community would consider data sufficient to give them confidence in the reality of claimed dismantlements and protect the process against sophisticated "spoofing" scenarios.[37]

It remains to be seen whether a viable verification system can be designed that can protect sensitive information while simultaneously satisfying the international community's demands for credible proof of disarmament.

Similar verification challenges will also inevitably be encountered as steps are taken to implement the U.S.-Russia plutonium disposition agreement. During the Clinton administration, the United States and Russia committed to eliminate 34 metric tons of excess weapon-grade plutonium each. This agreement resulted in the Plutonium Management and Disposition Agreement (PMDA), which was signed in 2000. The subsequent administrations of George W. Bush and Barack Obama each renewed the U.S. commitments, and the PMDA was finalized in 2010.[38] Under this agreement, both the United States and Russia would each convert the excess plutonium by turning it into mixed-oxide (MOX) fuel and burning it in domestic reactors. The United States was to build a MOX fuel fabrication facility at Savannah River, and Russia was to build a similar fuel fabrication facility.[39] This initiative was dealt significant blows, however, after the Obama administration called for deep funding cuts to the MOX fuel fabrication facility in 2014 and Russia later announced the freezing of the program in 2016.[40]

There are still ongoing trilateral negotiations among the United States, Russia, and the IAEA to explore how this agreement could be implemented and verified. However, the U.S.-Russian PMDA does not provide for monitoring storage until the material has been processed into unclassified form. This would mean that it would likely be decades until the materials were placed under safeguards, even if the program were to continue. In this context, the parties have not worked out how to monitor classified/sensitive materials, although, as noted, the Trilateral Initiative made some progress in that area before it ended.

It can be hoped that verification lessons from this and other past efforts will be taken into account. More R&D is needed to enhance current approaches under development and to develop new options. Many held that technical cooperation was desirable and that collaboration on authentication information barrier technologies would be especially valuable. In this context, however, Russian concerns about safeguards are also reflected in their lack of enthusiasm about any verification/transparency efforts involving classified information.

LESSONS FROM THE UK-NORWAY INITIATIVE?

Beginning in 2007, the United Kingdom and Norway conducted a set of exercises "designed to elucidate the technical and procedural issues surrounding managed access of inspectors into highly sensitive facilities."[41] In the exercises, an imaginary NWS, "Torland," worked with an imaginary NNWS, "Luvania," to verify dismantlement of its ten remaining nuclear weapons.

Many scholars have praised the results from this initiative as substantively furthering the ability to verify warheads.[42] In reality, however, the UK-Norway Initiative was mainly interesting because it explored how the NNWSs could be brought into the verification process. Its value was clear, but primarily *political*. If we get to that stage, the NNWSs as well as the NWSs (and other verification bodies, such as the IAEA, if it is involved) should be reasonably satisfied that the nuclear states gave up their weapons. This would be a valuable political step. However, the UK-Norway Initiative also raised fundamental technical and operational difficulties that will complicate verification. It also did not get to the heart of exercising or testing the issues involved with protecting sensitive information. And to the extent that it addressed the more fundamental issues, it highlighted the seriousness of the challenges.

For example, during the 2008 and 2009 exercises, the imaginary NNWS was to verify the dismantlement of one of the NWS's weapons. In particular, the key objective of the exercise was to establish confidence in Torland's declaration and "to demonstrate, to the satisfaction of both Parties, a chain of custody through the dismantlement process."[43] Although the official report on the 2008 and 2009 exercises was generally quite positive, it does note that "during 2008/2009 both teams were instructed that the process was collaborative."[44] This would likely not be a realistic scenario. As Christopher Ford wrote of the early sets of these exercises: "Despite disarmament advocates' eagerness to cite the Anglo-Norwegian effort as proof that dismantlement verification will be possible, the project seems to have assumed complete good faith on both sides. Deception scenarios were apparently neglected, which hardly seems wise in assessing the verifiability of disarmament by a potential adversary."[45]

Perhaps recognizing the validity of such criticisms, in 2010 the assumptions of the exercise were changed to make the verification scenario more confrontational (and thus likely more realistic), emphasizing national security and proliferation concerns much more than previous exercises. The more confrontational scenario changed the results of the exercise significantly. In its formal summary of the 2010 exercises, the UK-Norway Initiative reported that while the inspecting party did reportedly meet its goals, it did so "with a low level of confidence in the outputs of the visit."[46]

Despite the mixed results of the UK-Norway Initiative so far, these exercises are potentially very useful for working through important verification challenges that will need to be addressed if disarmament were to occur. But it is too soon to be confident that these and other initiatives *will* resolve the significant technical as well as political verification challenges.

SUMMARY: ASSESSING THE CHALLENGES
OF WARHEAD DISMANTLEMENT

All of the above problems derive from tensions between the secrecy of nuclear-weapon information and the transparency needed for verification. Some problems are increasing as weapons are moving from deployed status to increasingly consolidated storage (which can affect the value of chain of custody procedures for verification). They are also affected by limits on access, by different classification systems among states, and by other issues.

In short, a great deal of research has been done on potential verification systems for warhead dismantlement, but the technical solutions remain preliminary and have been oversold. This overselling can be seen in the numerous studies that refer very positively to the accomplishments of the Trilateral Initiative or the UK-Norway Initiative, or to the potential successes of information barriers or controlled access, without sufficiently addressing the questions and obstacles that remain, the low levels of confidence that resulted from the exercises, or how much research remains to be done.[47]

Ultimately, the current state of research cannot yet determine whether these strategies, including the attribute measurement/information barrier approach, will be adequate. Most advocates of the "Global Zero" and other disarmament initiatives do not recognize that verification difficulties associated with warhead dismantlement could be a show-stopper.

Given these serious problems, some have advocated lowering classification restrictions in order to facilitate verification. Doing so, however, would create serious difficulties and risks. Because the information is proliferation sensitive, it could provide essential information to proliferating states or terrorist groups, and it would also almost certainly strengthen the latent capabilities of the NWSs. The release of information would be unlikely to change the capabilities of states like the United States and Russia fundamentally, but it could potentially change other states' capabilities significantly.

In addition to the serious international security implications resulting from a further breaking down of barriers to proliferation, as noted, releasing classified information would violate treaty obligations as well.[48] Under Articles I and II of the NPT, the NWS are obligated "not to transfer to any recipient whatsoever nuclear weapons or explosive devices or control over such weapons or explosive devices directly or indirectly; and not in any way to assist, encourage, or induce any non-nuclear-weapon State to manufacture or otherwise acquire nuclear weapons."[49] This passage "is widely interpreted as meaning that any information obtained about the design or manufacture of a weapon in the course of verifying treaty compliance may not be transmitted to any other party," and many states "interpret it as meaning that the verification process must not reveal any such information to the verifier."[50]

Material, Warhead, and Delivery Vehicle Production Baselines/Verification

A first step toward dealing with fissile material would be the conclusion of an FMCT. However, negotiations in the Conference on Disarmament (CD) are stalemated, and there are contentious issues even if negotiations were to begin.[51] The sensitivities and costs of verifying an FMCT, among other issues, pose challenges for applying safeguards or similar verification measures, especially at bulk handling facilities in the NWSs, which were not designed for safeguards.

Under an FMCT, the need to increase capabilities for detecting undeclared facilities and activities is a fundamental verification challenge. The approach advocated by the United States, which focuses on enrichment and reprocessing, makes sense for the NWSs at this time, given resource and other issues, but that verification scope may have to be expanded and requirements changed over time. The issue of protecting classified/sensitive information is especially difficult for nonroutine or challenge inspections. Moreover, an FMCT would likely not directly cover current fissile material holdings or establish a verification system to confirm any declarations of these holdings, although these issues are still in contention. If an FMCT is concluded, and if the disarmament process advances, significant challenges would need to be addressed in obtaining and verifying declarations on stockpiles of fissile material.

OBTAINING ACCURATE FISSILE MATERIAL INVENTORIES

With the exceptions of the United States and Great Britain, no other nuclear-weapon state has released information on its military fissile material inventory.[52] This reluctance is understandable, given that capabilities and potential nuclear stockpile size could be estimated from such declarations. As such, states with large fissile material stockpiles or with stockpiles deemed adequate for their weapons needs would be more likely to reveal this information.[53] But even if other countries were ultimately to make such declarations, verification would be extremely challenging.

Even under the best circumstances, when countries have the best of intentions, there are tremendous difficulties associated with fissile material inventories. There are measurement uncertainties that are compounded over time, and the issue of "material unaccounted for" (MUF) is significant. U.S. and British estimates released in the 2000s reveal significant amounts of MUF. Perhaps more important, as Alexander Glaser states: "The bulk of today's global fissile material inventory was produced decades ago, and typically with a sense of urgency that did not prioritize accurate recordkeeping. This makes determining the completeness of a declaration a difficult task, even for the declaring state."[54]

This difficulty has proven to be the case with the production information released by the United States and Great Britain. The documents include significant uncertainties in the estimates. However, the records kept by the United States and Britain are likely to be among the most accurate of the nuclear-weapon states.

At the other extreme, it is not clear that Russia would have much certainty at all in its fissile material production history. Numerous reports in the 1990s documented the serious difficulties that Russia encountered in maintaining and upgrading its nuclear material controls. One of the serious problems was that Russia had not established a sufficient nuclear material accounting system to measure and track the fissile materials it had produced. And what accounting system it did have tracked only the financial value of the fissile materials (rather than mass)—a measure that fluctuates over time. Moreover, given the penalties that facilities could incur if they did not meet production timetables, many reportedly kept some spare materials hidden away in case they came up short during some production campaigns.[55]

As it became clear how serious the problems were with Russia's material accounting and control systems, the United States initiated the Cooperative Threat Reduction and the Material Protection, Control, and Accounting (MPC&A) programs in the early 1990s to help Russia improve these controls. Nearly two decades later, those programs have made substantial progress in addressing the problems and are ending. However, to this day it appears that Russia does not have the ability to make a "baseline" declaration of its full fissile material stockpile. As Matthew Bunn et. al, note:

> Most [Russian] facilities, for example, have never measured the contents of the thousands of canisters of nuclear material built up over decades, many of which use easily defeated wax or lead seals. No one knows whether the material in some of those canisters may have been stolen long ago. For today's processing operations, facilities keep accurate nuclear material accounts, but the statistical analyses of the accounting records necessary to detect ongoing thefts of small amounts of material at a time are still not required (and mostly not done) in Russia.[56]

Although Bunn and others emphasize the risk of thefts of Russian fissile materials, this issue has clear implications for disarmament as well. If Russia still does not have an accurate accounting of its fissile materials—after two decades and many billions of U.S. dollars dedicated to improving Russian MPC&A—it would be extremely difficult to obtain fissile material baselines, establish verification systems, or detect concealment of materials by the Russian government.

Similar though smaller-scale difficulties could be encountered by other nuclear-weapon states, including China, India, and Pakistan. Most evidence suggests that their systems of accounting and control of nuclear materials historically were based on similar designs to those of the Russians—relying more on the presence of security personnel than on sophisticated measurement technologies. This may be especially the case at their nuclear weapons facilities, which were not designed with IAEA safeguards and monitoring standards in mind.[57]

DOCTORING RECORDS

Thus far, this discussion of the challenges of verifying fissile material stockpiles has focused on challenges that will arise even when countries are doing their best to achieve transparency. Significantly greater challenges are associated with detecting intentionally inaccurate, or doctored, reports.

Although Alexander Glaser argues that nuclear states might have little incentive to present false information in their initial declarations about their fissile material stockpiles, because "a state would neither be committing itself to subsequent increases in transparency nor accepting constraints on its nuclear arsenal," it is not clear that this is the case.[58] If one assumes that pressures for disarmament may rise—and that this information could ultimately be used against the state if the disarmament initiatives were to gain traction—there could be plenty of incentives for states to deceive.

And such deception could be relatively easy to achieve. As Perkovich and Acton note, in many cases the only evidence about a state's fissile material production is contained in the state's own records. It therefore might be possible for that state to doctor those records to conceal undeclared fissile material stockpiles.[59] Moreover, they note, the transition to computerized records over the last few decades would make doctoring records "easier and less time consuming."[60]

NUCLEAR ARCHEOLOGY

Despite these difficulties, there may be some opportunities that derive from the use of what has come to be known as "nuclear archeology."[61] The role of nuclear archeology may be critical to the effort of establishing fissile material production baselines needed if further cuts—or even zero, however defined— were to be possible. This application of nuclear archeology is not a panacea, but it must be pursued to reduce uncertainties to the extent possible. It is unlikely that there will be agreements on nuclear archeology at present, but it is important to keep open the option to do so in the future by:

• collecting samples from decommissioned reactors, production facilities, and perhaps tailings, and placing them under IAEA seal in the host state;
• preserving records, declarations, and the like; and

• conducting oral histories for those involved with key decisions, production, facilities, and so forth.

The IAEA has significant expertise in completing initial inventories for every NNWS under the NPT, as well as INFCIRC/153, and INFCIRC/540 safeguards.[62] It has also done similar work in South Africa and elsewhere. Whether or not the IAEA had this role, in practice, verification teams could use several potential methods to verify how facilities were used and even produce rough estimates of how much fissile material was produced at given facilities.

For example, studies conducted at the Pacific Northwest National Laboratory have demonstrated that "the amount of plutonium produced at such reactors can be reconstructed using nuclear-archeology techniques to analyse the trace isotopes that accumulate in graphite during reactor use."[63] Significant research has been done on this method, and it is estimated that the expected error for the total plutonium produced at a given graphite reactor is about 5 percent.[64] Despite the accuracy of this method, however, for some countries that have maintained active plutonium production programs for decades, a 5 percent uncertainty could allow for a substantial plutonium stockpile to be concealed.

The technologies currently available for conducting nuclear archeology at other types of fissile material production facilities are significantly less effective. As Perkovich and Acton note, "[F]orensic techniques relating to heavy-water reactors (which account for 11 of the world's 24 plutonium-production reactors) and enrichment plants (which account for the majority of past fissile-material production) are much less accurate."[65] As Glaser notes, "[N]o obvious evidence is left behind in the processing equipment used at enrichment plants."[66] Nevertheless, he argues that "some nuclear archeology might be possible by taking measurements of depleted uranium tails (waste byproducts of enrichment), which are often kept for decades in storage cylinders at enrichment plants."[67]

Despite these shortcomings, nuclear forensic methods do hold some promise for verification activities. But these techniques will significantly increase the cost of verification activities. For example, as noted in Chapter 2, despite an "apparent discrepancy" between South Africa's declared HEU stockpile and the production capacity of its Y-Plant (believed to be the country's sole HEU production facility), the IAEA decided not to conduct more accurate measurements of the depleted uranium tails owing to their "considerable expense."[68]

Material Disposition Transparency/Verification

As Perkovich and Acton note, "[A] disarmament treaty would probably require all states to dispose of all fissile material from dismantled weapons."[69] A verification method would therefore need to be designed to ensure both that the fissile materials in question originated from dismantled weapons and additional verification methods to confirm that the nuclear states actually destroy the materials that they have declared.

The actual disposition process for HEU is relatively straightforward, involving a "blend-down" of the HEU by mixing it with uranium of lower enrichment to produce (LEU). There is no similar method for plutonium disposition. One proposed method for plutonium disposition would involve immobilizing it (one proposed method is to encase it in glass, possibly after mixing it with other radioactive materials) and burying it in a geologic repository. This method, as Perkovich and Acton note, is "unproven,"[70] and there are risks that it could create proliferation risks by creating plutonium "mines" that could be targeted for theft by proliferating states or terrorists. The other proposed method for disposing of plutonium is burning it as MOX fuel in a reactor (the method that the United States and Russia explored for disposing of their declared excess plutonium, discussed above).[71]

There are several significant monitoring and verification challenges associated with fissile material disposition as well. First, there are the difficulties of confirming that the fissile material was removed from warheads. These difficulties have been discussed above, and the process of confirming that the fissile material originated from warheads is especially daunting, as demonstrated by the impasse in negotiations over a verification system at the Mayak disposition site.

Part of the difficulty in verifying fissile material disposition arises from the need to protect sensitive information that could be revealed by detailed measurements of the fissile materials as well. "Nuclear weapon states have traditionally been reluctant to reveal the isotopics or other properties of their weapons plutonium and HEU; these isotopics would reveal insights into their production strategies."[72] There would presumably need to be some verification system to ensure that the materials are indeed HEU and plutonium (as opposed to LEU or other radioactive materials), perhaps combined with an information barrier to prevent the isotopics from being revealed. The technological challenges to such a system have been noted.

A further challenge arises from verifying both the amounts of fissile materials being disposed of and the numbers of warheads. Doing so would reveal the amount of HEU or plutonium in each warhead, which is classified information. As Ford notes:

> To the extent that the masses of plutonium or uranium per warhead constitute sensitive information—which is certainly true in the United States—a verification system might face a dilemma: it could verify that a certain quantity of material had been presented and disposed of, *or* it could verify that a certain number of warheads-worth of such material had been processed, but it would be very hard to do *both* of these things at the same time, because permitting observers to derive mass-per-warhead numbers would itself compromise sensitive information.[73]

The facility itself would need to be designed to control access into and out of the facility and be designed with key measurement points for material moving through the facility, and be fitted with portal monitors at the facility's entrances and exits to detect attempted diversion of the material before it is destroyed. This piece might be the easiest to accomplish, because it is comparable to, and might utilize, technologies and techniques from standard State System of Accounting and Control, aspects of IAEA safeguards, and the material and control (MC&A) accounting systems designed and implemented through the U.S.-Russia MPC&A program.[74]

The IAEA could have some "verification" role in the fissile material disposition, but given the sensitivities associated with fissile materials, it is not clear that it would be a major one. At present, for example, Russia has been reluctant to place its excess defense materials under IAEA safeguards.[75] It is possible that the IAEA could be involved with utilizing remote sensing technologies to detect access to storage containers for fissile materials prior to processing, and to ensure that no unauthorized radioactive material was removed from facilities. It could also potentially monitor geologic repositories for storing plutonium (if such a method proves technically feasible, and if it is chosen over, or in conjunction with, the MOX fuel alternative). For the IAEA to play a greater role in these areas, steps would need to be taken to ensure that sensitive information is protected and to garner the support of NWSs, which, so far, have shown limited interest in IAEA involvement with excess fissile material disposition.[76]

Detecting Clandestine Facilities, Materials, or Weaponization

If nuclear states possess undeclared or clandestine facilities, they could have already produced warheads or fissile materials that could be retained as part of an undeclared stockpile. Covert facilities could also potentially allow countries to continue producing nuclear weapons or materials without detection.

The current tools to identify and assess covert facilities remain limited. As Ford notes: "It is quite easy to squirrel away nuclear weapons, and not much harder to conceal small-scale production infrastructure. Nuclear material can be shielded and hidden handily; current technology can detect it only when within mere feet or inches."[77] Many facilities that could produce significant quantities of nuclear materials, such as gas centrifuges for uranium enrichment, are difficult to detect with current technologies. Some of the primary technologies that could potentially be used to detect covert facilities are satellite surveillance and wide-area environmental sampling (WAES), but these methods have been underdeveloped and underutilized.

In addition, the growing presence of clandestine supply networks, including nonstate networks, complicates the problem of assessing whether a state might have a covert program, or of preventing it from initiating one. In a 2011 address, Herman Nackaerts stated: "We are also now seeing that the more sensitive chokepoints in the nuclear fuel cycle—particularly, enrichment and reprocessing, and even those relating to potential weaponization—are more widely available to more States. In a number of instances, clandestine supply networks have already offered their services to States intent on developing nuclear weapons."[78]

Probably the best known of these smuggling networks was spearheaded by Pakistani nuclear scientist Abdul Qadeer (A. Q.) Khan, and which reportedly provided extensive enrichment technologies and warhead designs to Iran, North Korea, Libya, and possibly others.[79] But other smuggling networks have come to light in recent years as well. For example:

• In March 2011, Malaysian authorities announced the seizure of two containers of dual-use material en route from China to the Middle East. Dating back to the days of the A. Q. Khan smuggling network, Malaysia had "served as a significant manufacturing base and trans-shipment point for the nuclear black market. Although it was hoped that new Malaysian export laws had curtailed smuggling activities, the 2011 seizure prompted Malaysia's home minister "to concede that the country is 'likely [still] being used as a transit point . . . for WMD.'"[80]

• On July 13, 2012, Parviz Khaki, an Iranian national, was arrested for allegedly attempting to purchase "large quantities of dual-use equipment and raw materials for Iran's gas centrifuge program" from U.S. companies.[81]

• On October 24, 2012, the U.S. Department of Justice announced the arrest (and guilty plea) of Susan Yip for working to ship U.S.-made dual use equipment to Iran. Yip reportedly placed 599 orders with sixty-three U.S. companies and multiple orders from other companies, "obtaining over 105,000 parts valued at some $2,630,000 and making more than 1,250 transactions."[82]

• On May 6, 2013, the U.S. Department of Justice announced the arrest of a Taiwanese father and son on charges of conspiring to send U.S. machines relevant to production of advanced weapons to Taiwan. It is reportedly believed that the machines were ultimately intended for North Korea.[83]

• On June 25, 2015, Kunlin Hsieh of Taiwan pled guilty to conspiring to violate U.S. export control laws and trans-shipment of dual-use military equipment, including missile guidance systems, secure tactical radio communications, and military radar networks, from the United States to Iran.[84]

These and other incidents of nuclear smuggling raise concerns about the ability to detect efforts by states to acquire materials for clandestine nuclear programs. For obvious reasons, these smuggling networks have focused primarily on providing materials to proliferating states such as Iran and North Korea. However, if other states, including those that claimed to have disarmed, were to begin to seek to develop or enhance clandestine nuclear-weapon programs, we could see an unprecedented expansion of such networks in the future.

LIMITS TO CURRENT INTERNATIONAL VERIFICATION MEASURES

One potential verification tool that could be used to detect clandestine facilities would be onsite inspections. However, a number of issues would need to be addressed before they would be effective.

Even in the best cases, it is very difficult for inspection teams to detect covert stockpiles or facilities. But the prospects for such detection are worsened by both structural limitations and problems with implementation of the authorities given to current monitoring agencies. Currently, the primary organization able to carry out onsite inspections at nuclear sites is the IAEA. The agency's safeguards system is being transformed, and there are a host of critical continuing and emerging challenges confronting the agency and its safeguards system, including the prospect of new technologies and fuel cycles in the context of nuclear power growth; the agency's continuing role in addressing noncompliance; and possible new or expanding roles for the agency in the areas of safety and security, weaponization, rollback operations, and arms control and disarmament.

There is a need to enhance efficiencies and to better address requirements that are not optimized, including:

- the time, cost, and limited capacity to analyze environmental samples;
- in-line nondestructive assay (NDA), or the measurement of material under safeguards without destroying it, to monitor and verify the flows, enrichment levels, and so forth, at enrichment plants;
- monitoring holdup, waste containers, and the like at reprocessing plants; and
- the development and deployment of novel technologies for long-range, wide-area detection of undeclared facilities.

Beyond current challenges, there are future proliferation challenges we can anticipate, including:

- large, increasingly complex new facilities, with high material throughputs;
- difficult-to-measure materials; and
- harsh environments with high dose rates and temperatures.

Historically, the IAEA was authorized to carry out routine inspections only at declared nuclear facilities, which would have severely constrained any ability to detect covert facilities or materials. It was also authorized to carry out "special inspections" at declared or undeclared facilities if it found the state's declarations inadequate, but it has only rarely utilized that authority.

The IAEA's authorities were strengthened by the Additional Protocol (AP), which authorized the IAEA to inspect any building at a declared nuclear site and to utilize such verification technologies as satellite surveillance and wide-area environmental sampling. If the IAEA were tasked with carrying out onsite inspections to confirm disarmament, these enhanced authorities could assist it in detecting covert facilities in those states that have ratified the AP. But they are far from sufficient. As we have noted in the other chapters of this book, even the enhanced inspection authorities granted by the AP are far from "anytime, anyplace." Moreover, to date, the IAEA has not made use of its full set of authorities.[85]

Given the ongoing structural limits to the IAEA's authorities to carry out routine inspections—even with the enhanced authorities provided to it by the Additional Protocol—combined with its reluctance to utilize special inspections, it may be that an additional follow-on to the Additional Protocol will be necessary.[86] This might especially be the case if the global disarmament initiative were to make further substantive progress.

As numbers approached zero, and once they were to reach zero, the IAEA in the view of many would have a major role in verifying disarmament. The experience and capabilities of the IAEA, along with the provision of its statute that allows it to take on verification roles requested by member states, argue for a greater role in arms control and disarmament. Among the possibilities put forward are the following:

- fissile material cut-off treaty verification;
- monitoring excess defense materials;
- nuclear archaeology (production baselines);
- confirming warhead declarations; and
- monitoring warhead dismantlement.

Even if the IAEA's role were limited to the universal application of safeguards, there would be a real need for change. The requirements for safeguards would likely increase as the challenges of finding concealed stockpiles of nuclear weapons and fissile materials grow. The necessary intrusiveness of inspections would increase, along with required tools.

Addressing safeguards challenges—both anticipated and unanticipated— will require a defense-in-depth approach that includes:

- state-of-the-art instrumentation and methodologies for materials measurement, accounting and tracking, including sensor platform integration;
- enhanced containment and surveillance, including portal and area radiation monitoring, and measures to assure the absence of materials or radiation signals;
- integration of access denial and transparency elements of physical protection and safeguards; and
- integration of traditional process monitoring with nontraditional indicators, such as detection of radiation signals where they should not be, questionable movement of equipment and people, and so forth.

To support such an approach, it is necessary to build upon the U.S. Next Generation Safeguards Initiative (NGSI) and other programs to develop a flexible and adaptive technology base for advanced safeguards; a new generation of inspectors and analysts; and to modernize the agency's safeguards infrastructure.[87] A technology R&D program should investigate next-generation technologies to determine the best near-term detection, measurement, and forensic technologies, along with analytic tools and methods for development. It should also explore such issues as:

- integrated facility design to enable advanced safeguards and eliminate/minimize diversion pathways;
- more robust integration of safety and security with safeguards in the design process (for example, safeguards by design) and throughout operational life cycles; and
- intrinsic transparency in facility operations and safeguards implementation.

In this context, there is a need to utilize systems analysis to evaluate design trade-offs between facility operations, safeguards effectiveness, and cost, as well as to assess the effectiveness of an integrated safeguards system as a whole.

However, even if the IAEA's authorities for routine inspections were to be strengthened, or if it were to start carrying out special inspections, there would be yet other difficulties that would complicate efforts to verify disarmament. Highly intrusive inspections would potentially reveal state secrets, including those relating to conventional military capabilities. Furthermore, as Perkovich and Acton note, "[T]he host state is only required to give such access as is consistent with any 'constitutional obligations it may have to proprietary rights or searches and seizures' and national-security concerns. Such managed access would probably impair the effectiveness of inspections to detect secret stockpiles of nuclear weapons or materials."[88] In this context, the reported role of states' national technical means would continue to be valuable for the effective implementation of safeguards, but would likely remain both limited (because of sensitivities and other issues) and contentious in this context.[89]

The Problem of Latency

Deeper cuts and disarmament highlight the issue of irreversibility, which complicates verification and presents a serious technical challenge. In the past, irreversibility has largely been seen as increasing the time and cost involved in the reconstitution of weapons, ideally so that it is no less than what would have been required to produce a new weapon. While this may have been acceptable at the high levels of weapons in the past, and may be acceptable at current force levels, it becomes far more questionable as numbers further decline. Yet nuclear weapons cannot be disinvented, and nuclear latency will to some degree continue to exist in a nuclear-free world, allowing disarmament, in principle, to be reversed.

As noted, nuclear latency can be viewed as the possession of most or all of the technologies, facilities, materials, expertise (including tacit knowledge), resources, and other capabilities necessary for the development of nuclear weapons, without full operational weaponization. It derives from the dual-use nature of the atom. The issue also has to be seen historically—involving the full range of capability possessed by aspiring, existing, and former nuclear-weapon states, and the possible diffusion of nuclear-weapon-relevant information via a number of outlets, including nonstate nuclear supply networks, the Internet, and others. In this context, nuclear latency poses an over-the-horizon strategic technological threat that could result in strategic surprise. Neither the Nonproliferation Treaty nor the other nonproliferation and arms control treaties reached so far directly address latency, and the concept is not fully encompassed and has not fully been explored in the policy debates over nuclear-weapon proliferation or the treaties, institutions, and norms designed to address these threats through nuclear nonproliferation, arms control, and disarmament.

Latency is a reality for NWSs and many NNWSs today. Latency has already provided some level of virtual nuclear-weapon capabilities as a result of spreading nuclear-energy technologies and programs. Nuclear capabilities are now widespread and will increase with nuclear-power programs, especially those that involve direct-use nuclear materials such as plutonium and HEU. States' weaponization, delivery, and support capabilities are also critical and provide an indicator of intent, albeit one with low visibility and high ambiguity.

In practice, latent capabilities will exist in a nuclear-weapon-free world. Shut down nuclear-weapon programs can be reconstituted; civil nuclear programs can be used, or misused, to make weapons by states and possibly even nonstate actors. Given this view, nuclear latency is a concern today and would remain a concern even if nuclear disarmament were achieved.

In the disarmament arena, the implicit or explicit assumption of many observers is that virtual capabilities enable disarmament, and nuclear-weapon states can choose whether or not to rely on these capabilities as a hedge against disarmament.[90] In practice, these capabilities could in an agreement be merely recognized, sanctioned and preserved, or proscribed and dismantled to the extent possible.

If virtual capabilities (without forces in being) are to serve as a hedge—albeit one of uncertain value—this would require, among other things, human capital and facilities that cannot be just mothballed and will need to be exercised. This may appear threatening, and raises questions about crisis stability at the least. The acceptance of such a strategy by NNWSs and NGOs is by no means certain. It has been criticized by some abolitionists. It would also potentially produce an unstable worldwide situation in which states with latent nuclear capabilities could rush to rearm during crises.[91]

The Need for Additional Verification Tools

There will be other verification challenges in a world of deeper cuts and disarmament, some of which we are already facing.

There will need to be a fully operational verification regime for a CTBT, where the implementation of onsite inspections remains an issue. As numbers are reduced, improved monitoring for low-yield tests and supercritical experiments will be essential for effective verification, as will transparency at declared or shut down test sites where some activities are likely to continue.[92]

There is new attention to the challenges of monitoring an FMCT as a result of the sensitivities of some of the materials and facilities that would presumably be under its scope. There are issues with the use of IAEA safeguards to verify a CTBT, including the challenges of whether and under what conditions the use of environmental sampling will be permitted, and the difficulty and costs of retrofitting old facilities for safeguards implementation. Managed access, or the conduct of inspections designed to avoid the release of classified, sensitive, or proprietary information, will also be a difficult and complex issue.

At some point, if the reductions process is progressing, uncertainties about past nuclear materials production will have to be addressed. They will not be fully reconciled, or even reconcilable. However, these uncertainties will have to be significantly reduced, using declarations, transparency, new techniques in nuclear archeology, and other means.

Past weapon production uncertainties, along with existing or mothballed production capacity, will have to be addressed. To the extent production capabilities will be important in dismantling weapons, there will be some interest in ensuring that the redirection of dismantlement to production or other illicit activities is not occurring, and the existing asymmetries in capacity between the United States and Russia (and other nuclear-weapon states) are likely to present negotiating difficulties. Production capacity that derives from civil nuclear activities will also need to be addressed.

IAEA safeguards will need to continue to evolve to meet current and future challenges, and to take advantage of new technologies and approaches. Addressing safeguards challenges—both anticipated and unanticipated—will require a defense-in-depth approach. It is necessary to develop a flexible and adaptive technology base for advanced safeguards and a new generation of inspectors and analysts, and to modernize the agency's safeguards infrastructure. Specific needs include inexpensive and effective wide-area environmental monitoring and novel detection technologies and techniques to meet the challenges of material accountancy in bulk handling facilities and for the detection of undeclared facilities and activities. Proliferation resistance measures that enhance the effectiveness and efficiency of safeguards ("safeguardability" or safeguards-by-design) will increase in importance as nuclear energy expands. Along with better use of existing authorities, particularly special inspections, new authorities and capabilities may be required.

Other verification challenges will also be encountered. For example, transparency and verification of nuclear and dual-use exports will also have to be addressed, and there will be a need to make other nonproliferation measures in the nuclear as well as biological and chemical arenas more watertight and transparent. Additional verification challenges include those for WMD delivery systems. Delivery vehicles and testing may no longer be the focus of strategic reductions as numbers are further reduced, but they will have to be even more carefully addressed, including clandestine production and storage, dual-use systems, unconventional delivery, and other issues.

Conclusions: Meeting Future Challenges

Although many pieces of the puzzle are in place or are understood, we do not today know how to verify very low numbers or zero. Nor do we fully know what the completed puzzle would look like—that is, what the path to the goal of disarmament would involve in terms of specific provisions for specific treaties, agreements, and other steps over time. The verification requirements may be more rigorous in the context of deeper cuts as well as disarmament, although the political-military conditions that could make this level of progress possible would presumably affect verification requirements at some time and to some degree.

Recognizing the significant verification challenges, some scholars have argued that it might not be necessary to achieve "perfect" verification—as if there were such a thing—in order for disarmament to proceed. The disarmament process itself, they argue, combined with less stringent (but still "robust") verification, could build enough trust for nuclear states to be confident that other states are adhering to their commitments. For example, Perkovich and Acton argue that "verification is a means to an end, not an end in itself. The end is compliance, and enforcement mechanisms too must exist for compliance to be promoted.... Imperfections in any verification system could potentially be offset by more robust enforcement mechanisms."[93] However, there are fundamental problems with this argument. Enforcement must depend upon detection of noncompliance. Without adequate verification that has the prospect of such detection, there can be little hope of effective enforcement. As Patricia Lewis points out, "Coming to agreement in such environments when the evidence is overwhelming is hard enough; when the evidence has differing interpretations, decision making is fraught and enforcement is patchy—as every potential violator knows."[94]

If the verification process is not stringent enough to detect cheating, then it is not clear how "indications of cheating" would necessarily ever come to light. As suggested by a classic Prisoners' Dilemma scenario, even if a nuclear state were otherwise inclined to keep its disarmament commitments, if the state knows that other states could cheat without detection—thereby achieving significant military advantages—it would be unlikely to trust the intentions of the others—or to adhere to its own disarmament commitments.

Efforts to dismiss the very real verification challenges—or to lower verification standards in order to achieve the appearance of meeting disarmament goals—thus seem misguided. If the goals outlined in President Obama's Prague and Berlin speeches and elsewhere are to be achieved, scholars and policymakers must acknowledge the essential role that effective verification must play in disarmament. As Patricia Lewis correctly argues, "The only worthwhile scenario to consider in designing a verification plan is that of complete elimination in the end—however difficult that might be to achieve and however long it may take."[95] In this context, Perkovich and Acton argue that verification difficulties could diminish as confidence in the verification process builds over time. They state that "if, as zero is approached, robust verification finds no unresolvable indications of possible cheating and states become convinced that each truly intends to fulfill the agreement, they may no longer require such stringent verification."[96] To an extent, that is true, but unless the confidence is based on effective verification, the confidence would be misplaced, creating opportunities for concealment and deception.

We need to develop the verification tools and systems approaches that could allow us to meet the complex set of challenges and the uncertainties of ne-gotiations (bilateral, multilateral, and international). There is a critical need for multiple options to address sensitive areas where classified or proliferation-sensitive information may come into play along with other challenges.

At a time when, despite some rhetoric, the trend line has been toward less-er attention to verification—because of current force levels and the changing post–Cold War U.S.-Russian relationship—there is a real opportunity to ex-plore verification options. Any realistic time frame for disarmament should allow considerable scope to invest resources at the national and international levels to undertake research, development, and demonstrations in an effort to address the anticipated (and perhaps unanticipated) verification challenges of disarmament now and for the next decade at least. This will require:

- prioritizing verification challenges,
- understanding gaps in monitoring and verification technologies and ap-proaches,
- developing plans for R&D in an effort to address these gaps and other monitoring and verification challenges, and
- ensuring the necessary human and material resources.

The national R&D program called for by the NPR, the UK-Norway collabora-tion, the P-5 process that has emerged in the last several years, and other initia-tives has the potential to drive international R&D efforts that can address these issues. Ultimately, verification requirements and their prescribed effectiveness will be decided politically; however, the role of technology is critical, especially at this time. It may be possible to create effective monitoring and verification options that do not yet exist, to build trust and confidence among the coop-erating states (and also NGOs), to enable agreements on today's agenda to be realized, and possibly to underwrite the long-term goal of progress toward disarmament.

6   Applying Lessons to the "Difficult Cases": North Korea, Iran, Syria

> Unfortunately, experience has shown that the safeguards system has not been as effective as it should be, nor has it been implemented as efficiently as it could be. Despite the adoption of measures to strengthen the system over the years, events in a number of countries have demonstrated systemic deficiencies. In most of these cases, safeguards were implemented successfully at declared facilities, while *undeclared* nuclear activities took place unnoticed by the Agency. . . . We don't have to look any further than the problem cases that have been reported to the Board [of] Governors, such as Iran, Syria, and the DPRK, each of which involved a lack of cooperation by the State.
>
> —Herman Nackaerts, International Atomic Energy Agency (IAEA) Deputy Director-General[1]

Monitoring and verification are among the most important tools for nations' and international organizations' efforts to stop the spread of weapons of mass destruction and work toward verifiable rollback of weapon programs in critical regions of the world. However, these regimes face unprecedented challenges, as demonstrated by the cases of Iran, North Korea, Syria, and possibly Myanmar.

The years 2013 to 2016 highlighted a number of nonproliferation challenges. In the case of North Korea, Pyongyang conducted its third, fourth, and fifth nuclear tests, pushed forward with fissile material production, and threatened war against the United States and South Korea. In the cases of Syria and Iran, potential steps forward were offset by significant questions, frustrating delays, and uncertain outcomes. Syria, faced with possible U.S. military action in response to its use of chemical weapons, dismantled its declared stockpile of chemical-weapon (CW) agents and delivery vehicles. However, at the time of this writing, vital infrastructure still remains in the country—including CW production plants that could allow for a reconstitution of the arsenal—and significant questions remain about whether Syria's initial declaration was accurate.[2]

And Iran, in return for an easing of an increasingly intrusive sanctions regime, first agreed in 2013 to freeze temporarily certain parts of its nuclear program and to blend down half of its stockpile of 20 percent enriched uranium. In 2015, Iran agreed to the terms of the Joint Comprehensive Plan of Action (JCPOA), which temporarily scaled back significant parts of its nuclear program. Neither the 2013 Interim Agreement nor the JCPOA set back the program as much as many advocates desired, and it remains to be seen whether the longer-term agreement will in practice fully resolve many of the concerns over its nuclear program.

In this chapter we examine the difficult cases of North Korea, Iran, Syria, and Myanmar, exploring the various methods that these countries have used to conceal proscribed activities and facilities, delay or obstruct monitoring and verification activities, and ultimately to allow these programs to push forward with their weapons of mass destruction (WMD) programs. The chapter then applies the lessons learned from the other cases in the book to assess both the challenges and opportunities for monitoring and verification in these cases.

The Difficult Cases of North Korea, Iran, Syria, and Myanmar

With the troubled histories and uncertain futures of the nuclear and other WMD programs of these states in mind, the cases of North Korea, Iran, Syria, and possibly Myanmar pose unique challenges for monitoring and verification. As Herman Nackaerts emphasizes in the passage above, not only have these countries historically been unwilling to cooperate with international verification entities, but they have all attempted to obstruct verification efforts in the past. The first part of this chapter provides brief descriptions of the suspected WMD programs in each of these countries and outlines the verification challenges associated with each case.

North Korea

Consider first the case of North Korea. North Korea had long been suspected of possessing clandestine WMD programs, but information on those programs has always been difficult to obtain owing to the extreme isolation and secrecy of the regime. Verification efforts have focused exclusively on the regime's nuclear program and date back to the early 1990s, when the IAEA first began conducting inspections of North Korea's nuclear sites in efforts to verify Pyongyang's declarations about the program.

NORTH KOREA'S NUCLEAR PROGRAM

North Korea acceded to the Nuclear Nonproliferation Treaty (NPT) on April 18, 1985, but did not complete negotiation of a safeguards agreement until April 19, 1992, after the United States declared that it would withdraw its nuclear weapons from South Korea as part of a global nuclear withdrawal. Initial inspections of North Korea's nuclear facilities to verify the accuracy of Pyongyang's declarations about the status of its nuclear programs began the following May.

IAEA Inspections and the 1993–94 Crisis. The IAEA conducted six inspections of North Korea's nuclear facilities in 1992 and 1993. A great number of these inspections focused on North Korea's plutonium separation facilities. North Korea had declared that it had performed a one-time removal of 90 grams of plutonium from several "damaged" fuel rods in 1989, but chemical analysis of samples of this plutonium by the IAEA found that North Korea had extracted plutonium on four separate occasions beginning in 1989.[3]

The IAEA's findings sparked a crisis, beginning with the IAEA's request in February 1993 to perform a special inspection of two suspected waste sites, in accordance with the procedures provided for in North Korea's Safeguards Agreement.[4] North Korea refused to grant access to these sites and announced on March 12 that it was exercising its right to withdraw from the NPT, which would take place in ninety days (in accordance with NPT stipulations). Although Pyongyang subsequently agreed to suspend its withdrawal from the NPT on the eighty-ninth day after it made its announcement, it continued to constrain IAEA inspections of its facilities for the next nine months. In December 1993, IAEA director Hans Blix announced that the IAEA was unable to provide any assurance that North Korea was not diverting plutonium into a nuclear-weapon program.[5]

This crisis reached its peak in May 1994, when Pyongyang announced that it would remove the fuel rods from its 5MW reactor, potentially providing enough plutonium for several nuclear weapons. The United States responded to these events by circulating a proposal to the UN Security Council to impose a new round of sanctions on North Korea. The United States was also reportedly considering a military strike to destroy North Korean nuclear facilities.[6]

In efforts to ease these tensions, former U.S. president Jimmy Carter met with North Korean president Kim Il Sung on June 16–17, 1994.[7] This meeting led to the 1994 Agreed Framework, which successfully eased the crisis for the time being.

The 1994 Agreed Framework. The core of the Agreed Framework was a deal whereby the United States would provide a package of nuclear, energy, economic, and diplomatic benefits to North Korea in return for Pyongyang's freezing the operations and infrastructure development of its nuclear program. North Korea would freeze the operation of graphite-moderated reactors and related facilities (including a large fuel fabrication facility and small-scale reprocessing plant), halt the construction of several additional reactors and a major plutonium reprocessing facility, and allow the IAEA to verify these measures.[8] North Korea also agreed to "consistently take steps to implement" the 1992 Joint North-South Declaration on the Denuclearization of the Korean Peninsula, which states that "South and North Korea shall not possess nuclear reprocessing and uranium enrichment facilities."[9]

The United States, along with Japan, South Korea, and other countries, agreed to provide two light-water reactors to compensate for the loss of the power output of the graphite-moderated reactors and established the Korean Peninsula Energy Development Organization (KEDO) to oversee construction of the reactors. Prior to the completion of the light-water reactors, the United States had agreed to provide heavy oil to North Korea. Between 1996 and 2002 the United States provided about 500,000 metric tons of heavy oil per year.[10] However, North Korea was accused of violating this agreement in October 2002, sparking a serious nuclear crisis that has lasted well over a decade.

The Current Crisis (2002–16). The current crisis over North Korea's nuclear program erupted in 2002 after U.S. officials accused North Korea of pursuing a covert uranium enrichment program. North Korean officials reportedly initially admitted that they possessed such a program, but then subsequently denied it. As a result of these apparent revelations, KEDO halted construction of the light-water reactors and ended oil shipments to the regime in December 2002. Pyongyang responded in January 2003 by declaring that it was no longer bound by the NPT. As the crisis worsened in 2003, North Korea ejected IAEA officials and restarted plutonium production, which had been on hold since 1994.

After several frustrating years of unsuccessful negotiations and a nuclear test in 2006, there was a surprising breakthrough in 2007 when North Korea reportedly agreed to give up its nuclear-weapon program and participate in a verifiable destruction of its nuclear-weapon facilities.[11] Pyongyang subsequently disabled several facilities as part of this agreement. However, the tentative agreement did not address the suspected enrichment program that had sparked the crisis in the first place. Moreover, what progress had been made stalled again when Pyongyang insisted on controlling the terms of the verification mechanisms and refused to allow intrusive inspections, thereby ensuring that verification would be inadequate and incomplete.[12] In the end, the talks again broke down and were followed by a resumption of plutonium reprocessing, a second nuclear-weapon test, and a string of missile tests in 2009.[13] On June 14, 2009, North Korea announced that it was pushing forward with uranium enrichment and a few months later stated that it was in fact in the "final stages" of this program—the very program it had spent seven years denying it had.[14]

In November 2010, former Los Alamos National Laboratory director Siegfried Hecker visited North Korea and was shown what appeared to be two thousand "advanced centrifuges, apparently fully operational."[15] Although he was told that construction of the enrichment facility had begun in April 2009, he reported that this was "not credible . . . given the requirements for specialty materials and components, as well as the difficulty of making the centrifuge cascades work smoothly." Hecker described the particular facility he was shown as likely intended for a civilian program, but that it could be configured for a military one. He also reported that it is "highly likely that a parallel covert facility capable of HEU [highly enriched uranium] production exists elsewhere in the country."[16]

After the death of North Korean leader Kim Jong Il and the succession of his son Kim Jong Un to power in December 2011, relations between the Stalinist state and the West steadily worsened. Although the regime initially agreed in February 2012 to suspend nuclear tests and uranium enrichment and to allow international inspectors to verify and monitor its activities at its main reactor in Yongbyon, all in exchange for increased U.S. aid, this apparent breakthrough turned out to be short-lived. In April 2012, the regime resumed ballistic missile testing, and in May 2012 satellite imagery had detected resumed construction at Yongbyon. Over the next several years, the regime continued to escalate tensions by testing a third nuclear weapon in February 2013, nullifying the 1953 truce between North and South Korea, announcing that it would utilize all of its nuclear facilities (including its uranium enrichment facilities and the reactors that had been mothballed or under construction) toward nuclear-weapon production, directly threatening war with South Korea and the United States, and conducting a fourth nuclear weapon test in January 2016 and a fifth the following December.[17] IAEA inspectors have been banned from the country for the majority of this period, from 2002 onward, with the exception of a brief period from late June 2007 to April 2009 (and IAEA inspectors reported that were denied access to Yongbyon beginning in October 2008).[18]

CBW PROGRAMS

As we have seen throughout this book, obtaining accurate assessments of chemical- and biological-weapon (CBW) programs and stockpiles is quite difficult, owing to the comparative ease by which a country could conceal CBW facilities and the dual-use nature of the related technology and materials. As Elisa Harris correctly notes, these challenges are even more acute in North Korea, since it is one of the most politically, economically, and diplomatically isolated countries in the world.[19] Also, it has never signed the Chemical Weapons Convention (CWC), so the Organization for the Prohibition of Chemical Weapons (OPCW), which monitors compliance with the CWC, does not have the ability to conduct verification activities in the country. It has signed the Biological Weapons Convention (BWC), but as we have indicated elsewhere, the BWC does not contain any verification requirements. Nevertheless, various intelligence agencies have made some estimates of North Korea's CBW program and stockpile.

It is believed that North Korea began experimenting with chemical-weapon programs in the late 1960s, expanding those programs significantly in the late 1980s. North Korea is believed to possess somewhere between 2,500 and 5,000 metric tons of chemical agents. Some reports have indicated that the DPRK has the capability of producing all traditional varieties of chemical weapons, including blister, blood, choking, and nerve agents, though some reports indicate that the regime's chemical industry is aging.[20] In 2001 testimony before the Senate Armed Services Committee, however, General Thomas A. Schwartz, the commander of U.S. forces in Korea, suggested that North Korea is self-sufficient only in first-generation CW agents, which would exclude most nerve agents.[21] More recent estimates of the regime's CW agents have provided less detail. For example, in a 2011 report, the Office of the Director of National Intelligence (DNI) stated: "We assess that North Korea has had a longstanding CW program. We judge Pyongyang possesses a stockpile of agents."[22]

Most unclassified intelligence estimates and reports agree that North Korea also likely possesses a dedicated biological-weapon program, including the capability to produce and possibly weaponize BW agents. For example, in his 2002 Senate testimony, General Schwartz stated that "North Korea has the capability to develop, produce and weaponize biological warfare agents."[23] More recent reports have again provided less detail about North Korea's programs. The 2011 DNI report mentioned above states that "North Korea has a biotechnology infrastructure that could support the production of various BW agents. We judge that North Korea possesses a conventional munitions production infrastructure that could be used to weaponize BW agents."[24]

CHALLENGES FOR MONITORING AND VERIFICATION

North Korea is clearly a difficult case for monitoring and verification, especially given that inspectors have not had access to North Korea for most of the last decade. It clearly possesses nuclear weapons and will be unlikely to give them up anytime soon. Indeed, for the foreseeable future, North Korea will likely continue to expand its arsenal. Some of the primary concerns over North Korea's nuclear-weapon program are not only that it will continue operating its functioning nuclear facilities (especially its 5MW reactor), but that it will complete the construction of the larger nuclear reactors and separation facilities that had previously been mothballed. Moreover, because North Korea may have clandestine facilities (especially for uranium enrichment), it may be able to build its nuclear arsenal faster than international organizations, intelligence agencies, and national security analysts realize. Not only do these weapons present a threat to the region (and increasingly, as it continues to make advances on its ballistic missiles, the world), but the materials and weapons that North Korea develops could be used for export.

Verification and Potential Rollback. Even if North Korea could be induced to give up its nuclear weapons willingly (likely through some combination of economic and humanitarian aid, along with security guarantees), its existing arsenal and related infrastructure would provide the regime with latent capabilities. Given the existing shortcomings of international monitoring and verification regimes—both structural and self-imposed—it would be very difficult to detect clandestine nuclear-weapon or fissile material stockpiles, let alone latent programs that enabled the regime to retain the knowledge and ability to restart those programs at a later date. The same challenges would hold true for North Korea's CBW programs, especially if the regime did not sign the CWC. The potential for latent WMD underscores the need for long-term monitoring in the (unlikely) event of WMD rollback.

Prospects for Long-term Regime Survival. For nearly two decades, scholars and pundits have been predicting North Korea's imminent demise. In fact, for many, the ongoing surprise is that, contrary to these ongoing predictions, the regime has not yet collapsed. It is fairly clear that the current system is not sustainable over the long term.[25] Although predictions of the collapse of the North Korean regime have proven to be overstated, the continuous strain of feeding the masses, fending off generational pressures, struggling with corruption, and maintaining absolute control of information, all while keeping the military and ruling elite satisfied, may be too much for the system to handle indefinitely.[26] However, this prospective future may not be reassuring. The regime may well be able to survive and to pose a grave danger to the Korean Peninsula, the northeast Asian region, and the global nonproliferation regime for the foreseeable future.

While the regime may eventually collapse regardless of international pressure, North Korea's recent actions may also begin to solidify international opinion on the need for stronger stances against the regime. At the very least, the regime's main providers of international assistance—the United States, China, South Korea, and Japan—may be less willing to support the ailing regime, making the regime's survival even less certain.

A collapse of the regime could create very significant risks of "loose" nuclear weapons or materials that could fall into the wrong hands. If rapid and concrete steps were not taken to dismantle the weapons and related infrastructure, a regime collapse could also create questions about whether the regime that took its place were inheriting a nuclear arsenal, nuclear-weapon infrastructure, or latent capabilities. Similar transitions in the past (such as in the former Soviet republics or in South Africa) raised related questions about nuclear inheritance and nuclear latency. Some of these cases were handled more successfully than others.[27]

Iran

For more than thirty years, Iran followed a similar path of deception, denial, and concealment of key elements of its nuclear program—which many suspect to be part of a nuclear-weapon program—as well as its suspected CBW programs.[28] Although Iran has recently taken steps to scale back parts of its nuclear program and provide greater assurance to the international community that it is not using its substantial nuclear infrastructure for military purposes, a number of questions remain about its prior activities and latent capabilities, as well as how it will behave in the future. Regardless of what Iran's ultimate intentions for its nuclear program might be, it is clear that for many years Iran followed many of the steps that both North Korea and Iraq took to conceal their nuclear-weapon programs. Less is known about Iran's possible CBW programs, in part because these programs are easier to conceal and, especially for biological programs, there are fewer mechanisms for obtaining information on suspected programs.

NUCLEAR

Iran had long been suspected of pursuing a clandestine nuclear program, but these suspicions increased significantly in 2002 when an Iranian opposition group helped bring to light the existence of an undeclared uranium enrichment facility at Natanz and an undeclared heavy water production site (and plans for a heavy water nuclear reactor) at Arak.

In the subsequent years, IAEA inspections revealed nearly two decades of clandestine nuclear activities involving uranium enrichment and plutonium separation. During this period, Iran provided incomplete and inaccurate reports to the IAEA, refused to provide access to suspected nuclear weapons facilities, and appears to have gone to great lengths to conceal its activities—including in some instances destroying buildings, removing vegetation, and paving over surrounding areas at suspected sites in apparent efforts to destroy evidence.[29]

Through this entire period, Iran claimed that its nuclear activities were exclusively peaceful in nature, but in 2011 the IAEA reported new evidence of "possible military dimensions to Iran's nuclear programme" that included research "related to the development of a nuclear payload for a missile" and other work related to warhead development and triggering mechanisms.[30] In its 2012 and 2013 reports, the IAEA reiterated these concerns and stated that it had received additional information to support these suspicions.[31]

While these events were occurring, there were intermittent efforts to negotiate with Iran on its program, originally by the E.U.-3 (Great Britain, Germany, and France), which secured a brief suspension of Iranian enrichment from 2003 to 2005, and eventually led to the P5+1 (United States, Russia, Great Britain, France, China, and Germany) negotiations that resulted in agreements to scale back aspects of Iran's program.

The following discussion describes the various facilities and alleged programs that have raised suspicions in the international community about Iran's ultimate intentions about its nuclear program. It then discusses the evolution of international negotiations over Iran's program, including the 2013 Interim Agreement and 2015 JCPOA, and the long-term prospects for Iran's nuclear program.

Iranian Nuclear and Military Facilities. Iran has numerous facilities located throughout the country that are believed to be contributing to its nuclear capabilities. In addition to the light-water reactor at Bushehr, which is generally not discussed in detail in the debate over Iran's nuclear program,[32] many of Iran's facilities are suspected of having been directly related to the country's nuclear-weapon program. Below are some of the known facilities that have raised the biggest questions about Iran's capabilities and intentions. None of these sites were originally declared by Iran, and they came to light only through third-party information:

• *Natanz.* In August 2002 an Iranian opposition group, the National Council of Resistance to Iran, disclosed information on two possible Iranian nuclear sites, including a facility located near Natanz, a town 200 miles south of Tehran. Open-source satellite imagery subsequently revealed several facilities at the site, large underground structures, and a vehicle tunnel leading to the structures.[33] An IAEA inspection of the site in February 2003 revealed a completed pilot-scale enrichment facility and a much larger underground enrichment facility under construction.[34]

In the subsequent decade, Iran continued to make progress at this site, adding thousands of both IR-1 and more advanced IR-2 centrifuges. As of June 2014, Iran had installed 15,420 IR-1 centrifuges at the Natanz underground Fuel Enrichment Plant (FEP), 9,166 of which were fully operational and producing 3.5 percent enriched U.[35] It had also installed 1,008 more advanced IR-2 centrifuges at this site, but the operation of those centrifuges was reportedly frozen in accordance with the Interim Agreement.[36] Iran also installed 328 IR-1 and 326 IR-2 centrifuges at the Pilot Fuel Enrichment Facility (PFEP). Until January 2014, the IR-1 centrifuges at the PFEP were used to enrich uranium to 20 percent.[37] As will be discussed below, Iran committed to remove a number of these centrifuges from operation as part of the JCPOA.

• *Arak.* The 2002 announcement by the National Council of Resistance to Iran also indicated that another clandestine nuclear site might be located near Arak, Iran. Satellite imagery and a subsequent inspection by the IAEA in February 2003 confirmed that the Arak facility was to be a construction site for a heavy water plant.[38] At the time of the IAEA's inspection, Iran also disclosed that it planned to build a heavy-water reactor at the Arak site.

In the subsequent years, Iran completed the heavy water production plant (HWPP) and largely completed construction of the heavy water reactor (known as the IR-40 reactor), in violation of UN Security Council resolutions.[39] In its May 2013 report, the IAEA estimated that the reactor would become operational in mid-2014, though at the time of this writing, construction at the site has been temporarily halted by the 2013 Interim Agreement and the JCPOA (discussed below).

Iran has stated that this reactor will be used for the production of medical isotopes rather than electricity.[40] Because these medical isotopes could be produced at the Tehran Research reactor or purchased internationally, this reactor was widely viewed as commercially unnecessary and a potential separate, plutonium-based path to nuclear weapons in addition to uranium enrichment.[41] As discussed below, the terms of the JCPOA modify significantly the size and operation of this reactor with a view to reducing the risks associated with plutonium production at this reactor.

• *Fordow.* The monitoring and verification challenges in Iran were illustrated even further on September 25, 2009, when the leaders of the United States, France, and Great Britain announced that Iran was building a small, covert uranium enrichment site near the city of Qom. The announcement and subsequent press briefings indicated that Western intelligence agencies believed that the design and configuration of this "very heavily protected, very heavily disguised" facility to be "inconsistent with a peaceful program."[42] Iran's construction of this site was widely criticized as violating its safeguards agreement with the IAEA because the agreement obligated Iran to declare its intention to build a nuclear site prior to initiating construction.[43] In the years since the 2009 revelations about the site, Iran installed four cascades of 174 IR-1 centrifuges (totaling 696) and used them to produce uranium enriched to 20 percent U-235.[44] After January 21, 2014, these centrifuges were used to produce 3.5 percent U-235. Under the terms of the JCPOA, the centrifuges at Fordow will not be used to enrich uranium for a period of fifteen years.

• *Parchin.* This military site has long been suspected of being used for high explosives testing related to the development of nuclear weapons.[45] Although a containment vessel was reportedly first introduced into the site in 2000, the building believed to contain the vessel was reportedly identified to the IAEA only in March 2011. Upon its discovery, the IAEA repeatedly requested access to the Parchin site but was not allowed access to the building for years.[46] Moreover, as pressure for Iran to allow access to the site increased, Iran apparently took steps to sanitize the site.

In its February 2013 report, the IAEA reported that satellite imagery detected "virtually no activity" at or near the building housing the containment vessel from February 2005 through January 2012. After the agency's first request for access to this location, however, "satellite imagery shows that extensive activities and resultant changes have taken place at this site." These activities include dismantlement of parts of buildings; "construction of one small building at the same place where a building of similar size had previously been demolished"; and "spreading, leveling and compacting of another layer of material over a large area."[47]

In its May 2013 report, the IAEA indicated that "Iran has conducted further spreading, leveling, and compacting of material over most of the site, a significant proportion of which it has also asphalted."[48] These activities would significantly and detrimentally impact the ability of the IAEA to conduct effective environmental sampling at the site. As the Institute for Science and International Security (ISIS) reports, by taking these steps at the site, "Iran may seek to further erode the IAEA's ability to determine whether nuclear weapons development work happened at this site, as IAEA evidence supports."[49]

In the aftermath of the Joint Comprehensive Plan of Action, the IAEA was eventually allowed to evaluate environmental samples at the site, but they were not permitted to collect the samples themselves. After the environmental samples were taken, IAEA director-general Yukiya Amano was subsequently given access to the building believed to contain the high-explosive vessels. Amano reported that there was no equipment in the building, but he did note that the site had recently been renovated and he reiterated that the actions Iran had apparently taken since 2012 to sanitize the site "undermines the Agency's ability to conduct effective verification there."[50]

In its December 2, 2015, report on the outstanding issues relating to Iran's nuclear program, the IAEA did note that the environmental samples taken at Parchin had detected the presence of man-made uranium particles at the site. This finding raised further speculation that the site had been part of a nuclear-weapon program.[51] As Olli Heinonen notes, "Such a small number of particles with this elemental composition and morphology is insufficient to definitively connect the location with nuclear activities, but the IAEA concluded that the information available does not support Iran's statements on the building's purpose."[52]

Possible Nuclear Weaponization Activities. As noted in the introduction to this book, the IAEA presented an annex to its standard 2011 report outlining "possible military dimensions" to Iran's nuclear work. As William H. Tobey argues: "[T]he November 2011 report raised allegations of work that can only be explained as part of a nuclear weapons development program, including efforts pertinent to the development of an HEU [highly enriched uranium] implosion device."[53] Tobey notes that the suspicious activities identified in the 2011 report include:

• a secret "green salt" project to "provide a source of uranium suitable for use in an undisclosed enrichment program";

• procurement activities for equipment "useful for triggering and firing detonators";

• a "large scale experiment in 2003 to initiate a high explosive charge in the form of a hemispherical shell";

• information "that Iran has manufactured simulated nuclear explosive components using high density materials such as tungsten";

• construction of a chamber to conduct hydrodynamic experiments to test conventional explosives applicable to a nuclear weapon;

• "modeling of spherical geometries, consisting of components of the core of an HEU nuclear device subjected to shock compression, for their neutronic behavior at high density, and a determination of the subsequent nuclear explosive yield"; and

• a project consisting of "a structured and comprehensive program of engineering studies to examine how to integrate a new spherical payload into the existing payload chamber which would be mounted in the re-entry vehicle of the Shahab 3 missile."[54]

Iran flatly rejected the IAEA's allegations as "counterfeit,"[55] but for many years continued to refuse to give the IAEA access to the Parchin site, where some of these activities are believed to have taken place. In its November 2012 report the IAEA elaborated on some of this information, stating: "The information indicates that, prior to the end of 2003 the activities took place under a structured programme; that some continued after 2003; and that some may still be ongoing." In its November 2013 report, the IAEA reiterated that it had received more information since November 2011 "which further corroborates the analysis contained in that Annex."[56]

The IAEA compiled a list of questions about the possible military dimensions (PMDs) of Iran's program that needed to be answered. The IAEA reportedly "received responses from Iran on only one of the dozen technologies on his list, and those answers have prompted more questions."[57] The JCPOA calls for Iran to take steps, in conjunctions with the IAEA, to resolve these questions. Specifically, the JCPOA commits Iran to implementing a "Roadmap for Clarification of Past and Present Outstanding Issues," which is a separate agreement signed by Iran and the IAEA dedicated to clarifying the outstanding issues relating to alleged past weaponization.[58] The JCPOA does not specify what steps these are, but it does specify that all steps in the roadmap must be taken before sanctions are lifted. This obligation was completed when the agency issued its report on the PMDs in December 2015.[59]

Negotiations over Iran's Program (2003–13). After the National Council of Resistance to Iran revealed the existence of Natanz and Arak in August 2002, the IAEA requested access to those sites. Although the IAEA was granted access only months later, in February 2003, it did confirm that the two sites contained undeclared nuclear activities. The IAEA reported that Iran had "failed to meet its obligations under its Safeguards Agreement with respect to the reporting of nuclear material, the subsequent processing and use of that material and the declaration of facilities where the material was stored and processed," but the agency stopped short of declaring Iran in material breach of its safeguards agreement or the NPT.[60]

In February 2003, an additional suspected nuclear site, the Kalaye electrical establishment in Tehran, was reported by the Iranian opposition group.[61] Although Iran reportedly claimed that this site was a watch factory, the regime rapidly took steps to sanitize the site after it came to light, removing equipment and reconstructing the interior of the building.[62] As Gregory Giles notes: "Despite these deception efforts, the IAEA confirmed that nuclear material had been present at the site, a safeguards violation that forced Iran to divulge more details about its secret enrichment activities."[63]

As tensions worsened over its nuclear program, and perhaps spurred by the toppling of the Iraqi regime, Iran indicated a willingness to engage in negotiations with European leaders in fall 2003. On October 21, 2003, after two days of intense negotiation with the foreign ministers of Great Britain, France, and Germany (which came to be called the E.U.-3), Iran acceded to many of the IAEA's demands. As part of this apparent breakthrough, Iran agreed to sign the Additional Protocol (which it subsequently did in December 2003), temporarily suspend its uranium enrichment, and provide the IAEA with all the information it requested about the enrichment program.

For a time Iran allowed unprecedented access to its facilities, going beyond the terms of the Additional Protocol despite not having ratified it yet. Before long, however, Iran began to delay the ratification of the Additional Protocol (AP), refuse to provide information requested by the IAEA, and otherwise obstruct IAEA verification efforts. Relations further deteriorated in June 2004 after Iran demolished the Lavisan-Shian complex before allowing the IAEA access to it.[64] Although Iran later admitted that the site had been used for "nuclear defence" research, the IAEA was unable to detect any undeclared nuclear material, presumably owing to Iran's sanitizing activities.[65]

In August 2005, Iran resumed enrichment of uranium and effectively walked away from the ongoing talks with the E.U.-3. In response, the IAEA board of governors adopted a resolution finding Iran in "non-compliance" with its safeguards agreement. The resolution set the stage for the board to refer the Iranian nuclear issue to the UN Security Council but did not specify what circumstances would trigger such a referral.[66]

In response to Iran's actions, the Security Council approved several rounds of sanctions over the years. Beginning in 2006, the UN Security Council passed a resolution (UNSC resolution 1737) preventing any transfers of technology or expertise that could assist in its nuclear program, including uranium production and enrichment, or in ballistic missile development. Subsequent resolutions in 2007 and 2008 "blocked nonhumanitarian financial assistance to Iran and mandated states to inspect cargo suspected of containing prohibited materials." An additional 2010 resolution "tightened the international sanctions regime . . . . It adopted the U.S. approach, linking Iran's oil profits and its banking/financial sector, including its central bank, to proliferation efforts, therefore subjecting them to international sanction."[67]

Although sanctions by the European Union initially lagged behind those of the United States, these sanctions were strengthened significantly, especially beginning in 2010. The E.U. effectively brought its sanctions in line with U.S. sanctions "by blocking European institutions from transacting with Iranian banks, including its central bank, and restricting trade and investment with the country's energy and transport sectors, among others."[68]

By 2013 the combined effects of the sanctions by the United States, the UNSC, and the E.U. began taking their toll on the Iranian economy. According to a report by the Congressional Research Service, Iran's crude oil imports fell from about 2.5 million barrels per day in 2011 to about 1.1 million barrels per day in 2013, and Iran's economy shrank about 5 percent in 2013.[69] These sanctions are believed to have played a significant role in Iran's renewed willingness to negotiate over its nuclear program, setting the stage for the negotiations that led to 2013 Interim Agreement.

Iran and the 2013 Interim Agreement. Diplomatic efforts yielded little sustained progress in resolving international concerns or in scaling back Iran's nuclear program for a decade after the programs first came to light. However, on November 24, 2013, the Obama administration announced that the P5+1 and Iran had successfully negotiated an interim agreement over Iran's disputed nuclear program. Described as an historic deal by many, this agreement froze certain aspects of Iran's nuclear program in exchange for an easing of sanctions on the regime for a period of six months (though the agreement was subsequently extended twice because a more permanent agreement had not been successfully negotiated).[70] Although the two sides later disagreed over some of the actual details of the Interim Agreement, the following are the general terms of agreement.[71]

• *Blend-down or Convert 20 Percent Enriched Uranium.* Iran would convert half of its 20 percent enriched stockpile of uranium to uranium oxide (UO2) and blend down the other half to 5 percent or less.

• *Temporarily Freeze Uranium Enrichment above 5 Percent Uranium-235.* For a period of six months, Iran would not enrich uranium over 5 percent or increase its stockpile of uranium hexafluoride enriched to 5 percent uranium-235. Any newly enriched 5 percent U-235 would be converted to uranium dioxide, which cannot be further enriched while in the oxide form. (This step would be taken once Tehran completed a conversion facility, which was currently under construction at that time.)[72]

• *Leave Some Centrifuges at Enrichment Facilities Temporarily Inoperable.* Iran agreed to leave roughly half of the centrifuges at the Natanz enrichment facility inoperable and roughly three-fourths of the centrifuges at Fordow inoperable for the duration of the interim period (initially six months, but subsequently extended until June 30, 2015). The agreement also required Iran to refrain from feeding UF6 into installed centrifuges that were not yet enriching uranium and to replace damaged centrifuges only with centrifuges "of the same type."[73] The agreement commits Iran not to construct any new enrichment facilities during this period.

• *Freeze Some Activities at the Arak Facility.* The Interim Agreement required Iran to submit an updated Design Information Questionnaire (DIQ) for the heavy-water reactor under construction at Arak. It further required Iran to refrain from commissioning the reactor, transferring fuel or heavy water to the reactor site, or installing remaining reactor components for the duration of the interim period. (However, Iran would presumably be permitted to prepare components for installation.)[74]

The Interim Agreement also allowed for daily inspections by the IAEA at Iran's uranium enrichment sites at Natanz and Fordow, as well as the heavy-water production plant and the heavy-water reactor under construction at Arak. This is fairly unprecedented access, expanding the IAEA's routine verification authorities at these sites. The agreement also called for P5+1 and Iran to "take steps" to negotiate a more permanent safeguards agreement with the IAEA for Arak.

After several delays, the Interim Agreement went into effect on January 20, 2014.[75] By mid-April 2014 the IAEA declared that Iran had met the terms of several key elements of the agreement, including the blend-down of half of its stockpile of 20 percent enriched uranium.[76] However, with the initiation of the Interim Agreement, the deadline of July 20, 2014, was set for achievement of a more permanent agreement. This and subsequent deadlines passed without the conclusion of a longer-term agreement, which was finally announced on July 14, 2015.[77]

Although the Interim Agreement did achieve some important steps, especially relating to the blend-down of 20 percent enriched uranium, it was a temporary agreement and it left a number of steps incomplete. For example:

• *The agreement eliminated only part of Iran's enriched uranium stockpile and did not freeze additional enrichment.* While the agreement did call for a blend-down of half of Iran's stockpile of 20 percent enriched uranium, it did not require the elimination of any of Iran's stockpiles of uranium enriched to 5 percent. Moreover, although agreement did call for the remaining half of the 20 percent enriched uranium to be converted to UO_2 and any new uranium enriched to 5 percent to be converted to UO_2, UO_2 can be converted back to UF_6 through a fairly straightforward chemical process and the uranium enrichment can resume where it left off.[78]

• *It did not require dismantlement of any enrichment facilities, centrifuges, or the Arak reactor; nor did it forbid research on more advanced centrifuges.*

• *The agreement was silent on the weaponization efforts and missile programs identified in IAEA reports.*

• *The agreement did not include any additional IAEA authorities to search for clandestine facilities.*

The Interim Agreement thus left open a number of issues that needed to be settled in a final agreement between the P5+1 and Iran. Although Iran did reportedly blend down half of its stockpile of 20 percent enriched uranium and was adhering to the temporary cap on enrichment above 5 percent, the Interim Agreement really did not freeze Iran's enrichment activities, prevent the regime from installing equipment (such as advanced centrifuges), or forbid preparing equipment for installation at the Arak site. Nor did the agreement strengthen IAEA verification authorities in ways that would increase the likelihood of detecting clandestine facilities or require inspections of suspected weaponization sites such as Parchin. Ultimately, the Institute for Science and International Security estimated that the agreement set back Iran's breakout capability by about one month.[79]

Even with the successful negotiation of the JCPOA (discussed below), there remains considerable ambiguity about Iran's nuclear program. It has a latent capacity that can be limited but not eliminated by a formal agreement. This latency, combined with the inherent challenges of verification and various organizational or institutional difficulties, suggests that some degree of ambiguity about Iran's program will necessarily remain.

The 2015 Joint Comprehensive Plan of Action. Although the Obama administration originally stated that the United States would not be satisfied unless Iran's nuclear program was eliminated, as the negotiations unfolded it became clear that this would be unlikely to occur.[80] The Obama administration's position shifted to preventing Iran from developing nuclear weapons themselves, rather than preventing the weapon capability that its nuclear program could provide. As the details of the JCPOA began to take shape, Obama officials stated that the purpose of the agreement would be not to eliminate the program altogether or to eliminate fissile material production, but to increase the breakout time (that is, the time needed to produce a bomb) to one year instead of the current several months—possibly enabling the international community to detect noncompliance and respond to it. With this revised goal as the target, the JCPOA put in place the following stipulations, in return for sanctions relief:

- *Enriched Uranium Stockpile Cap.* For fifteen years, Iran commits to maintaining a stockpile of no more than 300 kilograms of uranium enriched to 3.67 percent uranium-235 in hexafluoride or other chemical forms. (This does not include uranium that has already been fabricated for fuel, including the 20 percent enriched U for the Tehran Research Reactor). In addition, nearly 12 tons of excess LEU will be blended down to natural uranium or sold in exchange for natural uranium. In a related provision, Iran commits not to produce or acquire uranium or plutonium metals, or conduct research on or work with such metals for fifteen years.

- *Limitations on Centrifuges and Uranium Enrichment.* For a period of ten years, Iran must remove about two-thirds of its centrifuges, leaving about 5,060

IR-1 centrifuges at Natanz and about 1,040 IR-1 at Fordow. For ten years the IR-1 centrifuges at Natanz will continue to produce low-enriched U (enriched to 3.67 percent U-235). At Fordow, about one-third of the remaining 1,000 IR-1 centrifuges will be used to produce isotopes (that is, not uranium). No uranium enrichment or fissile material production is permitted at Fordow for fifteen years.

• *Advanced Centrifuge Research and Development (R&D).* Iran must dismantle, initially, existing cascades of IR-2 centrifuges but is permitted to commence small-scale R&D on more advanced (IR-6 and IR-8) centrifuges "from one and a half years before the end of year 10."[81] None of the test activities can accumulate enriched uranium for ten years.

• *Plutonium Production and the Arak Reactor.* Iran must convert Arak to a lower power 20MW heavy water research reactor and use low-enriched fuel instead of natural U, in order to reduce the amount of plutonium produced in the spent fuel and in their view prevent production of "weapons-grade" plutonium. All spent fuel is to be shipped out of Iran for the lifetime of the reactor. Iran commits not to build any additional heavy water research reactors for fifteen years and ship out any surplus heavy water not used at Arak for the same period. Iran commits not to conduct R&D on reprocessing or build a reprocessing plant for fifteen years. Iran states that after that it does not "intend" to build a reprocessing plant.

• *Resolving Questions about Possible Military Dimensions.* As noted, under the JCPOA Iran was obligated to work with the IAEA to clarify the outstanding issues relating to alleged past weaponization activities. The IAEA submitted a report in December 2015 providing a "final assessment" of these suspected activities. The report indicated that there were "ambiguities" in the information provided by Iran in August 2015 and that the agency had worked with Iran over the preceding months in efforts to resolve these issues. In the end, a number of issues remained unresolved. For example, the IAEA noted that "explosive bridgewire (EBW) detonators developed by Iran have characteristics relevant to a nuclear explosive device," though it did note that such detonators did have civilian or conventional military applications as well. It reported that Iran did not provide additional requested information on "activities relating to scientifically monitored explosive research capabilities." The agency assessed that Iran had "conducted computer modelling of a nuclear explosive device prior to 2004 and between 2005 and 2009," despite Iranian denials that such work ever took place. Regarding the suspected weaponization work at Parchin, the agency reported that "the information available to the Agency, including the results of the analysis of the samples and the satellite images, does not support Iran's statements on the purpose of the building," and that the "extensive activities undertaken by Iran since February 2012 at the particular location of interest to the Agency seriously undermined the Agency's ability to conduct effective verification." Nevertheless, despite these and other remaining questions, the IAEA ultimately reported "no credible indications of activities in Iran relevant to the development of a nuclear explosive device after 2009." This was viewed as sufficient to proceed with the implementation of the JCPOA.[82]

• *Enhanced Monitoring and Verification.* There are mechanisms to *enhance* the normal IAEA authorities, including the Additional Protocol. For twenty-five years, the IAEA will monitor natural uranium ore produced or acquired from any source (these monitoring mechanisms are not specified). For fifteen years "or longer," the IAEA will be allowed to use "modern technologies" to monitor activities at declared facilities. For fifteen years the IAEA will be permitted continuous monitoring to verify that stored centrifuges and infrastructure at Natanz remain in storage (and are used only to replace failed or damaged centrifuges). For fifteen years the IAEA will be permitted daily access as requested to all relevant buildings at Natanz. For twenty years the IAEA will implement continuous monitoring of all locations and specialized equipment (for example, those used for centrifuge motors and bellows). (This does not include equipment for nonnuclear technologies such as ballistic missiles.)

• *Challenge Inspections.* For ten years the JCPOA establishes a mechanism for authorizing IAEA challenge inspections of any facility in Iran if the IAEA has concerns regarding undeclared nuclear materials or activities, or activities inconsistent with the JCPOA. These include any facility in Iran, including military facilities, within the following stipulations. Upon the IAEA's request for access to a suspected facility, Iran and the IAEA have fourteen days to make these arrangements or find alternative means of alleviating the IAEA's concerns. If that fails, the issue is referred to the Joint Commission (made up of the United States, United Kingdom, France, Germany, Russia, China, Iran, and the E.U.), which has seven days to decide on appropriate action by consensus, or by a vote of five or more of the eight members. Iran then has three days to implement the Joint Commission's decision. As specified in the JCPOA, failure to comply would trigger reimposition of international sanctions.[83]

• *Sanctions Relief.* According to the JCPOA, once the IAEA confirms that Iran has met its nuclear commitments, all of the UN sanctions, most of the U.S.

and E.U. sanctions on the nuclear industry, and E.U. sanctions on Iran's oil and financial sectors will be lifted.

UN Security Council Resolution 2231 sets the stage for the nullification of six previous Security Council resolutions that placed restrictions on the Iranian nuclear industry, financial sectors, and oil and natural gas exports. It does maintain restrictions on exports relating to conventional weapons for five years and ballistic missiles for eight years (or unless the IAEA comes to a broader conclusion sooner).[84]

U.S. sanctions relief includes the primary economic sanctions on Iran's financial and energy sectors, once Iran has completed key nuclear steps. The United States commits to end its "efforts to reduce Iran's crude oil sales," and will release approximately $115 billion in frozen oil revenue. The United States also commits to remove requirements for secondary sanctions on companies and individuals doing business with proscribed entities in Iran. This secondary sanctions regime was an essential element in leveraging European entities to maintain sanctions on Iran.[85] After eight years, the United States will "seek such legislative action as may be appropriate to terminate" most sanctions directly related to nuclear proliferation.[86]

The sanctions that would be removed by the European Union include restrictions on Iran's financial and energy industries, including sanctions on shipping, construction, gold, and precious metals, and the oil embargo that was imposed in 2012.[87] As soon as the JCPOA was announced, many countries in the E.U. reportedly began lining up to negotiate contracts with Iran in a host of industries, including construction, rail, oil, and natural gas.[88]

The JCPOA does contain provisions for "snapping back" economic sanctions if the deal were to fail. If any members of the Joint Commission have doubts about whether the terms of the JCPOA are being met, there is a thirty-five-day process to resolve the dispute. If the issue is not resolved in the thirty-five days, any member of the Joint Commission can refer the issue to the UNSC. The UNSC must vote to *continue* the sanctions relief. If the UNSC does not pass a resolution within thirty days, the UNSC sanctions will snap back into place.[89]

There may be some limitations on this "snapback" mechanism, however. First, it is unclear to what extent *all* sanctions will automatically be reinstated, or only the UN Security Council resolutions. Although the UNSC resolutions, especially Resolution 1929, do tie sanctions to Iran's critical oil industry, it is unclear whether all sanctions (especially those employed by the E.U.) would snap back into place. The JCPOA states that this snapback mechanism would "not apply with retroactive effect to contracts signed between any party and Iran or Iranian individuals and entities prior to the date of application."[90] There are differing views on whether this clause means that contracts negotiated prior to the application of the snapback clause will be "grandfathered" in, or whether existing contracts would be terminated once the clause is invoked, and it is not clear how this issue will be resolved.[91]

Basic Challenges of the JCPOA. The JCPOA does make positive steps in reducing Iran's stockpile of enriched uranium, scaling back the number of operating centrifuges at Natanz, limiting the number and purpose of the centrifuges at Fordow, and setting in place strengthened monitoring and verification mechanisms—all of which increase the difficulties of using uranium as a source material for a nuclear weapon, or at least increase the likelihood of detection if Iran were to attempt to do so. Furthermore, the conversion of the Arak reactor, the restrictions on the type of fuel, the requirements for the removal of spent fuel, and the fifteen-year ban on reprocessing facilities and R&D all create barriers for use of plutonium as a source of material for nuclear weapons. These developments are positive, but they do not constitute "blocking paths" to the bomb—especially the clandestine path. In fact, there are a number of significant challenges that remain or are not fully addressed by the JCPOA. These challenges include the following:

• *The Future of the Agreement Will Depend on Implementation.* A great deal will depend on whether Iran is satisfied with the arrangement over the next fifteen years or whether it decides to cheat on key elements of this deal. Aside from the intrinsic limits to monitoring and verification (see the next section), the level of implementation of the Iran deal will be crucial to its success.

In the past, the IAEA has proved to be unwilling to use all of its authorities, including special inspections, to address potential noncompliance—including in the case of Iran. It remains to be seen whether they will be willing to utilize their full authorities, including the mechanisms for challenge inspections that are established by the JCPOA. So far, the evidence appears to be mixed, given that the IAEA has treated Iran as a typical state in the safeguards agreements it has negotiated with Iran following the JCPOA, rather than a state with a proven record of noncompliance and thus requiring more stringent monitoring and verification mechanisms.

But even if the IAEA proves willing to utilize the full authorities established by the JCPOA and is willing to press Iran to provide full transparency and demonstrate that they are complying fully with the agreement, it remains to be seen whether the various parties—including in the Joint Commission and the UNSC—provide sufficient support to the IAEA. We have already had the situation in which the Iran case has been politicized—the previous IAEA director-general, Mohamed ElBaradei, was criticized as being too pro-Iran; the current director-general, Yukiya Amano, has been criticized as too anti-Iran.[92] Will being at the center of compliance disputes affect the legitimacy of the agency, or otherwise affect its ability to carry out its mission?

In instances of noncompliance, it remains to be seen what steps the IAEA and international community will be willing to take to enforce the agreement or punish the noncompliance, and how those steps may be viewed by the international community. In the end, a great deal will hinge on whether or not the great powers and the international community effectively demand Iranian compliance, take potential noncompliance seriously, and provide full support of the IAEA in pursuing its mission.

• *Challenges with Monitoring and Verification.* The JCPOA does require Iran to "provisionally apply the Additional Protocol to its Comprehensive Safeguards Agreement" until Transition Day, set for October 20, 2023, at which time Iran will "seek . . . the ratification of the Additional Protocol."[93] Despite the ambiguities of this language regarding ratification, the ratification of the AP is an important part of the case that proponents have made in favor of the deal. For example, in the speech in which he announced the deal, President Obama stated: "Because of this deal, inspectors will also be able to access any suspicious location. Put simply, the organization responsible for the inspections, the IAEA, will have access where necessary, when necessary. That arrangement is permanent."[94] While the authorities granted to the IAEA through the AP would presumably be permanent, as noted elsewhere in this book, AP is an important but limited tool, and would not be sufficient for ensuring that clandestine facilities are not in place.[95]

Proponents of the deal have therefore likely engaged in oversell of the monitoring and verification mechanisms of this deal, especially as they relate to clandestine activities. The White House factsheet on the Iran deal stated with astonishing confidence: "Basically, from the minute materials that could be used for a weapon comes out of the ground to the minute it is shipped out of the country, the IAEA will have eyes on it and anywhere Iran could try and take it."[96]

This clearly overstates the confidence that the IAEA, or even the IAEA supplemented with third-party information, could have about a country's activities.

There are also significant questions about the mechanisms for challenge inspections established by the JCPOA. As noted, there are mechanisms for the IAEA to call for challenge inspections, but there are potential practical difficulties that may come into play. If the IAEA has concerns regarding undeclared nuclear materials or activities, it can request access to suspected sites. However, the process for providing the IAEA access to a suspected site could require up to twenty-four days and a vote of five of eight of the members of the Joint Commission.[97] While the twenty-four-day timeline may not allow sufficient time for Iran to conceal large-scale experiments with nuclear materials or enrichment activities, it could permit Iran to conceal evidence related to R&D activities with nonnuclear components associated with triggering or weaponization, or smaller-scale programs with nuclear materials. As Olli Heinonen has argued: "Much of this equipment is very easy to move. So you can take it out over the night . . . [A]nd then there is this dispute settlement time which is 24 days—you will use that to sanitize the place, make new floors, new tiles on the wall, paint the ceiling and take out the ventilation." Depending on the facility, the twenty-four-day timeline could enable Iran to conceal important evidence, or at least prevent inspectors from uncovering a proverbial "smoking gun," which could allow Iran or other members of the Joint Commission to dispute the evidence.[98]

Moreover, there are also questions about whether the mechanisms and make-up of the Joint Commission would provide sufficient support to the IAEA. The mechanisms of the Joint Commission allow members of the Joint Commission to question IAEA proposals on inspections. What remains unclear is whether this will occur in practice and whether it will undermine the agency. Voting within the Joint Commission is intentionally stacked in favor of the West, and it is assumed that a vote of five of the eight members would require the E.U. voting in support of the IAEA (with the United States, the United Kingdom, France, Germany, and the E.U. voting against Iran, Russia, and China). But this presupposes that the E.U. would be able to come to a unified position, which is far from certain given differing interests and possibly differing interpretations of evidence. Moreover, the sitting members of the E.U. on the Joint Commission might individually vote the other way as a result of commercial or other interests. Would these outcomes be more likely if inspections do not produce a smoking gun? Would a smoking gun even be recognized?

• *Resolving the PMDs and "Subsidiary Arrangements."* As noted above, the JCPOA references a "roadmap" negotiated between Iran and the IAEA to resolve the remaining questions about the "possible military dimensions" of Iran's program that came to light in 2011. It was initially unclear how the IAEA would be resolving the questions on the PMDs—in particular, what the verification measures would be, or how they would be carried out. However, soon after the deal was announced, two U.S. senators reported that they had learned that the verification measures were outlined in two confidential agreements between Iran and the IAEA.[99] These revelations sparked renewed criticism of the Iran deal, along with demands that the specifics of these "side deals" be made public.

Some critics have argued that these subsidiary arrangements may be contrary to U.S. law, since *The Iran Nuclear Agreement Review Act,* which was passed by Congress and signed into law by the president, states that the president shall transmit to the appropriate congressional committees and leadership "all related materials and annexes."[100] Regardless of the specific legality of these subsidiary arrangements for U.S. law, the IAEA is treating the measures for resolving the PMDs of Iran's nuclear program as a bilateral (and therefore confidential) arrangement, as would occur under a standard safeguards agreement. Because these measures themselves play a critical role in the implementation of a multilateral agreement, this approach has raised questions about transparency and the credibility of the verification process.

Despite repeated calls from many observers for the details of these subsidiary arrangements to be made public, the IAEA has refused to do so, citing the integrity of its system of bilateral safeguards arrangements. The controversies over these subsidiary arrangements intensified after the Associated Press published what it claimed was the draft of one of them.[101] The text of this document indicated that the IAEA would not be allowed to take environmental samples at the site, but instead would rely on Iran to take the samples. Although some analysts initially questioned the authenticity of the document published by the Associated Press,[102] the reported arrangements between Iran and the IAEA for environmental sampling at Parchin appear to have been borne out. In a September 24 speech relating the environmental sampling procedures and a subsequent visit to the Parchin site, IAEA director-general Yukiya Amano confirmed that the environmental sampling had been undertaken by Iranian officials rather than the IAEA.[103]

IAEA officials have defended this procedure, stating that it was a fairly common bilateral arrangement between the IAEA and states. Deputy IAEA director-general Tero Varjoranta stated that "there have been more than 40 instances of letting a country being inspected use their own nationals to do the sampling and that the process is only a small part of a rigid regimen established by the agency to make sure there is no cheating."[104] It is not clear why Iran's demonstrable track record of deceiving the IAEA would be treated in the same manner as these other states. As Heinonen has indicated, he "knows of no other case where a country under investigation for possibly trying to make nuclear weapons was permitted to use its own personnel to collect environmental samples as part of the investigation."[105] A report by the Institute for Science and International Security summarizes the difficulties with this procedure:

> It is difficult to have confidence in any sampling result if the IAEA is unable to fully investigate the suspect location and adjacent site and then decide how best to conduct environmental sampling or other verification activities in order to defeat any Iranian attempts to hide uranium or other evidence. The taking of samples by Iran, while a clever idea allowing it to stick to the fiction of never allowing inspectors to have access to sensitive military sites, also undermines the IAEA's credibility. It risks missing an important chance to determine what occurred at Parchin, part of the important overall investigation the IAEA is conducting into the possible military dimensions issue before U.N. and national sanctions on Iran can be removed.[106]

Amano did indicate that he had subsequently been given access to the building after the sampling work had been completed, but he reported that "inside the building, we saw indications of recent renovation work. There was no equipment in the building." In other words, if there had been high explosive test chambers located in this building, as the IAEA suspected, they had already been removed. Amano reiterated in this speech that "the extensive work that has been conducted at the location since early 2012 undermines the Agency's ability to conduct effective verification there."[107]

The December 2015 IAEA report made clear that a number of issues related to PMDs remained unresolved, despite the fact that their resolution is central to verification. Without fully understanding the PMDs, it is not possible to establish clear baselines or to determine what steps remain for Iran if it were to decide to produce nuclear weapons. It will also be difficult for the IAEA to draw a "broader conclusion" on Iran should it otherwise be in a position to do so.[108]

Despite the clear necessity of establishing such baselines, some administration officials have denied that more extensive steps are necessary for understanding Iran's PMDs. We have, they argue, in effect already established such a baseline. As John Kerry has stated, "We know what they did. We have no doubt. We have absolute knowledge with respect to the certain military activities they were engaged in."[109] In response to this statement, intelligence officials have pointed out that intelligence rarely, if ever, can achieve "absolute knowledge,"[110] and it is striking how many of the people who are defending our ability to know everything about Iran's program have forgotten that they criticized the U.S. intelligence shortcomings in Iraq.

Aside from questions about the quality of intelligence that will be available at any given time, it is perhaps more important to recognize that the verification process needs to be open and transparent to the greatest extent possible— at the very least to help convince members of the Joint Commission and the international community about Iran's compliance. Moreover, the verification activities at Parchin raise questions about the credibility of the process and also potentially set precedents for other verification activities at other facilities. As Albright and others argue:

> This approach also creates dangerous precedents, whether or not uranium is found. . . . It sets a precedent for limiting IAEA sample taking and possibly access to other sites at Parchin or additional military facilities this fall as the IAEA seeks to resolve its concerns about Iran's alleged work on nuclear weapons. What happens if a new issue arises and the IAEA again needs access to a site within the Parchin Military Complex? Would the same type of agreement apply here as well? Iran could also try to insist on the same type of sampling and one-time access arrangement at the other sites associated with the IAEA's investigation of past military nuclear activities. . . . After Implementation Day of the JCPOA, Iran could also use this Parchin precedent to demand a similar approach to environmental sampling if the IAEA requests access to a suspect military site.[111]

• *Sanctions.* As noted, the JCPOA sets in place mechanisms for sanctions relief. The stipulations relating to sanctions have also been significantly criticized, and there are still some remaining questions both about how the sanctions will be removed and how they might be reinstated in cases of noncompliance.

How sanctions would be removed—and which sanctions would be removed— has been a contentious issue since April 2015, when Obama administration officials stated that the sanctions would be phased out over time and Iranian officials stated that they would be removed all at once. Even after the deal was announced, this topic was still unclear. When he introduced the deal on July 14, President

Obama argued: "This relief will be phased in. Iran must complete key nuclear steps before it begins to receive new sanctions relief. And over the course of the next decade, Iran must abide by the deal before additional sanctions are lifted, including five years for restrictions related to arms, and eight years for restrictions related to ballistic missiles."[112] However, this conclusion has been disputed—by Iran and by some members of the European Union—at least for the sanctions on Iran's critical financial and energy sectors.[113]

There have also been questions about the "snapback" mechanisms for sanctions, should Iran be found in violation of the JCPOA, or should the IAEA be unable to answer questions that arise about aspects of Iran's program. Although the JCPOA does contain mechanisms for reinstating the sanctions, as Lorber and Feaver have argued, there are enormous practical and political consequences for doing so that could prevent the sanctions from ever being put back into place:

> Such a dramatic course of action could be hugely unpopular with our allies and likely would jeopardize the implementation and enforcement of any reinstated sanctions. It is worth emphasizing: an effective sanctions regime consists of a legal basis, the institutional capacity to implement the sanctions, and the political will to carry it through. This course of action provides for only the first.[114]

Would President Obama, or the next U.S. president, be willing to hamstring Western corporations that will have invested billions in reestablishing oil and other major contracts in Iran? Would our allies actually comply? That is far from clear.

Another difficulty with the mechanisms for reinstituting sanctions is that there is essentially only one punishment for violations—snapping back all of the sanctions that were removed by the JCPOA, an action that would simultaneously release Iran from any of its commitments that were established by the agreement as well. With this as the only penalty for noncompliance, the United States and any other member of the Joint Commission would likely be hesitant to scrap the entire deal over small violations, even if there were a series of them. As Matthew Levitt has pointed out, "Iran is sure to cheat on the deal—a point administration officials concede—but it will take only small steps over the line at a time. The snap-back mechanism is poorly suited to deal with small violations because when the only sentence available is capital punishment, only capital crimes will be prosecuted."[115] Step by step, Iran could undermine the effectiveness of the monitoring and verification regime established by the JCPOA with a fair degree of confidence that it would not be significantly punished for doing so.

Finally, as noted earlier, there remain questions about whether the JCPOA "grandfathers" in contracts that had been negotiated prior to the invocation of the "snapback" mechanism. Paragraph 37 of the JCPOA states that the snapback mechanism would "not apply with retroactive effect to contracts signed between any party and Iran or Iranian individuals and entities prior to the date of application."[116] As noted, it remains to be seen how the clause is interpreted should the snapback mechanisms be initiated.[117]

• *Are All Pathways to the Bomb Truly "Blocked"?* As noted, the Obama administration and other proponents of the deal have stated repeatedly that the JCPOA "blocks" the four potential pathways to the bomb, including potential enrichment at Natanz, potential enrichment at Fordow, plutonium production at Arak, and use of clandestine facilities and activities. However, while rhetorically simple, the basic image of "blocking pathways" is not the most fitting image to use, and it is in fact rather misleading. What we are actually discussing are the probabilities of detection of noncompliance along all the potential pathways to the bomb, and it is not possible to have 100 percent certainty about whether a system will detect noncompliance—let alone that a given pathway is "blocked." Moreover, there are a number of potential ways that Iran could proceed along the path to the bomb, despite the provisions of the JCPOA.

One potential way that Iran could acquire nuclear-related equipment and materials would be to import them. That has been a common path for many states seeking to develop WMD programs, and Iran is no exception. Over the years, Iran has established an extensive procurement network, "hid[ing] its nuclear purchases behind a web of front companies, banks, and international middlemen that stretches from the United States and Germany to South Korea and China."[118] Tehran has also benefited from smuggling networks, including the A. Q. Khan network, from which Iran is believed to have received much of its centrifuge infrastructure, and others based out of such places as China and South Africa.[119]

For these reasons, the JCPOA calls for the establishment of a "procurement channel," by which the Joint Commission would review and decide on proposals by states seeking to trade with Iran in materials whose "end-use will be for Iran's nuclear program . . . or other non-nuclear civilian end use."[120] These provisions were reinforced by UN Security Council Resolution 2231, stipulating that "all states are legally required to seek prior approval from the UN Security

Council, on a case-by-case basis, to transfer or sell 'directly or indirectly' to Iran 'all items, materials, equipment, goods, and technology' contained in the Nuclear Suppliers Group (NSG) Trigger List of nuclear items and its list of nuclear related dual-use items."[121] The JCPOA and the UNSC resolution establish a "Procurement Working Group" that will oversee the approval of exports to Iran.[122] Through this procurement channel, the JCPOA thus attempts to shut down Iran's smuggling networks.

This is a positive development, but it is not clear how well it will fare in practice, and how well it will fare against various smuggling networks. As Albright and Stricker point out: "[M]any aspects of the Procurement Channel were left unsettled during the negotiations. During the next several months, the E3+3 will need to establish a range of capabilities and procedures to implement this channel."[123] Samore and others also argue that "on paper, the Procurement Channel is a powerful tool," but they raise questions about whether Iran might be able to circumvent the Procurement Channel without detection, given the scale of global commerce; ongoing opportunities for utilizing private dealers and middlemen; and the sheer scope of the Procurement Working Group's task, since it involves both nuclear- and nonnuclear-related items.[124] A number of questions will therefore need to be addressed for this system to work optimally: Will dual-use technology useful for nuclear weapons get through this procurement channel? How far removed will the imported technologies need to be from nuclear end use? What are the mechanisms to ensure that the procurement procedures outlined in the JCPOA are the only avenue for imports?

It is possible that all of these challenges will be addressed effectively and that this procurement system will work. But there are also some significant risks that it will be ineffectively implemented or intentionally misused. The Institute for Science and International Security, which tracks illicit procurement and smuggling networks closely, has indicated that:

> ISIS has already been receiving reports that Iranian companies or agents are accelerating efforts to seek U.S. defense companies' equipment, falsely arguing that sanctions are ending and companies can freely sell these goods to Iran. They are apparently seeking opportunities to exploit the current confusion over the implementation of the JCPOA and the new United Nations Security Council Resolution 2231 on Iran. . . . Entities in Iran may also seek to circumvent the JCPOA's provision regarding using an oversight channel to procure goods with dual nuclear and civilian uses.[125]

In addition, there are other potential ways that Iran could exploit the various "pathways" to develop a nuclear weapon, should it choose to do so. As noted, one of the biggest challenges is detecting whether Iran may already have developed, or may decide to develop, clandestine facilities or stockpiles. The administration has pointed to the Additional Protocol, along with the enhanced monitoring and verification mechanisms introduced by the JCPOA (including mechanisms for challenge inspections) as a solid way to detect clandestine facilities or materials. As noted, however, there are potential limitations associated with both the AP and the IAEA's new challenge inspection authorities that may affect both implementation and the likelihood that a facility would be detected.

In the end, even if the AP and challenge inspection mechanisms were utilized thoroughly and effectively, and the IAEA received consistent and broad support from the international community, there still would remain a basic difficulty—one cannot inspect an undeclared nuclear facility if one does not know it exists. The potential existence of undeclared facilities will necessarily remain, and it will therefore be impossible to say with confidence that all pathways are indeed "blocked." Similar questions could be raised about undeclared stockpiles of fissile materials. If Iran possesses an undeclared and undetected enrichment facility, it could move toward a nuclear weapon without detection at any point. Moreover, it is also possible that Iran has enriched a greater amount of uranium than it has declared, either at a covert site, or at a declared site (though this latter possibility became much more difficult after the Interim Agreement, and then the JCPOA, were implemented). As we saw in Chapter 5, for one to be certain that a country does not possess a covert fissile material stockpile, one would need to know, or reconstruct, the entire production history at every nuclear site in the country. This level of knowledge would be at best very difficult to obtain.

Finally, the specific additional restrictions in the JCPOA on the Natanz and Fordow sites will be removed in ten to fifteen years. After that, many of the roadblocks will be lifted and the pathways will be subject to IAEA safeguards and other nonproliferation measures (such as export controls), which offer a level of effectiveness far more limited than the expiring provisions.

• *At Best, Iran Remains a Latent Nuclear Power.* It is already a latent nuclear power and not even the entire removal of the nuclear infrastructure would eliminate that reality. However, the JCPOA reinforces Iranian latency.

While Iran will be required to remove about two-thirds of its centrifuges from operation, including its more advanced IR-2 centrifuges, it is permitted to keep 5,060 IR-1 centrifuges operational and enriching uranium at Natanz, and 1,000 centrifuges operational at Fordow (though they cannot be used to enrich uranium). Iran will thus not only be able to retain a substantial enrichment infrastructure, but it can also maintain an operational expertise in uranium enrichment.

The agreement does not require Iran to destroy a single IR-1 or IR-2 centrifuge. Instead, Iran is permitted to store the disconnected centrifuges at the same facility in which they were previously operating. Iran would potentially be able to reconnect the centrifuges at a later date, particularly once the fifteen-year period ends.

Furthermore, Iran is permitted to engage in R&D on more advanced IR-6 and IR-8 centrifuges, provided that they do not accumulate a stockpile of uranium. According to Iranian officials, the IR-8 centrifuge "was 16 times more capable than the current generation IR-1 centrifuge."[126] In an analysis of Iranian officials' statements about the IR-8 centrifuge, David Albright concludes that "the IR-8 centrifuge is likely far less capable than implied by a literal reading of Iranian statements about enrichment outputs. Nevertheless, its size—both longer than the IR-1 and wider than the IR-2m centrifuge—would imply a capacity far in excess of the IR-1 centrifuge, at least theoretically."[127] Although it may take some years before Iran is able to use these advanced centrifuges for industrial-scale uranium production, they may be able to perfect them by the time the restrictions established by the JCPOA expire.

Iran's latent capabilities for plutonium production, while still present, will be reduced significantly by the JCPOA, since the core of the reactor will be removed (and its holes plugged with concrete), the reactor will be reconfigured from 40 megawatts-thermal (MWt) to 20 MWt, and low-enriched uranium instead of natural uranium will be used as its fuel. These modifications in the design and operation of the reactor, if fully implemented, have been estimated to result in a production of around 1 kilogram of plutonium per year instead of 6 to 8 kilograms per year.[128] Moreover, low-enriched uranium would be used as fuel for the reactor, with the goal of making the plutonium "somewhat more difficult to weaponize."[129] In the end, Iran would retain a capability of producing plutonium (both at the Bushehr reactor and at Arak), though given the technical challenges and the difficulty of concealing its activities, it might opt instead to build another reactor, either overtly (after fifteen years) or covertly, instead of utilizing Arak.[130]

As noted in the introduction to this book, President Obama himself highlighted the potential difficulties that could arise from Iran's latent capabilities in future years, especially in the area of uranium production, as the restrictions on stockpile size and centrifuges, as well as the enhanced monitoring and verification mechanisms, are phased out: "[A] more relevant fear would be that in year 13, 14, 15 they have advanced centrifuges that enrich uranium fairly rapidly, and at that point breakout times would have shrunk almost down to zero." Citing Obama's statements, Bob Menendez stated the significance of this issue: if President Obama's statement "is true, then it seems to me that—in essence—this deal does nothing more than kick today's problem down the road for ten-fifteen years, and, at the same time, undermines the arguments and evidence we'll need, because of the dual-use nature of their program, to convince the Security Council and the international community to take action."[131]

In the fact that the JCPOA leaves an extensive nuclear infrastructure intact, thereby reinforcing its latent nuclear capability, there are troubling analogies to the 1994 Agreed Framework in North Korea. Because the Agreed Framework did not eliminate North Korea's nuclear infrastructure, requiring only a mothballing of its key nuclear site at Yongbyon, Pyongyang was able to resuscitate its nuclear-weapon program after it was confronted with evidence in that it was cheating on the Agreed Framework by developing uranium enrichment capabilities. John Kerry has argued that the Iran deal is different, and superior, to the Agreed Framework because it includes the requirement for Iran to sign the Additional Protocol, which in itself was "an outgrowth of the failure of the North Korea experience."[132] This overstates the strength of the Additional Protocol, but, more important, it does not at all address the fundamental problem of latency.

As suggested, the true test of the JCPOA will be seen in its implementation. Proponents are confident that it will be implemented effectively, while critics have remained very skeptical. It may be too early to tell with certainty which side will prove to be correct, but a number of questions definitely remain: Will the full set of provisions outlined in the JCPOA, including stringent monitoring and verification mechanisms and eventual AP ratification by Iran, be fully implemented? Will potential roadblocks be sufficiently addressed? Will military sites be visited? Will the IAEA be sufficiently forceful in resolving concerns? Will the Joint Commission be willing to support the IAEA? These and many other questions remain unanswered so far. It is unfortunate that this topic has become so politicized, given the stakes that are involved.

CBW

The information on Iran's CBW programs is much more limited. Although Iran ratified the BWC in 1973 and the CWC in 1997, it is believed that Iran began developing its offensive chemical- and biological-weapon programs during the Iran-Iraq War, which lasted from 1980 to 1988.[133] Iran is believed to have used CW during this war, though less extensively and less effectively than did Iraq.

Iranian Chemical Weapons. Although Iran is suspected of having a well-developed CW program, unclassified intelligence reports and briefings have provided varied estimates of Iran's exact CW capabilities. For example, a 2003 unclassified report by the director of Central Intelligence stated that Iran "may have already stockpiled blister, blood, choking, and possibly nerve agents—and the bombs and artillery shells to deliver them—which it had previously manufactured."[134] However, a 2011 report by the U.S. director of National Intelligence was more tentative, stating that "Iran maintains the capability to produce chemical warfare (CW) agents and conducts research that may have offensive applications. Tehran continues to seek dual-use technologies that could advance its capacity to produce CW agents. We judge that Iran is capable of weaponizing CW agents in a variety of delivery systems."[135] There are also open-source reports detailing Iranian assistance to Syria's chemical-weapon program.[136] According to these reports, Iran provided "the construction designs and equipment to annually produce tens of hundreds of tons of precursors for VX, sarin, and mustard [gas]."[137]

Overall, there has been a limited amount of open-source information on Iran's chemical weapons, in part because, unlike the IAEA on nuclear issues, the OPCW "has published very little information on Iran's industry declarations and chemical-defense activities."[138] Nor is it clear how extensively the OPCW has conducted those inspections to which it is entitled, including routine inspections of declared Iranian chemical facilities. Moreover, the OPCW has not conducted challenge inspections in Iran or any other state because it has not been requested to do so.

Iranian Biological Weapons. There is even less reliable information about Iran's suspected biological-weapon programs, especially because the BWC lacks any provisions for conducting verification activities.[139] Unclassified U.S. intelligence reports and background briefings repeatedly alleged a dedicated Iranian biological-weapon program throughout the 1980s and 1990s, including reports of BW research facilities established in the mid-1980s at the Iranian Pasteur Institute and Vira Laboratory.[140] For example, an unclassified CIA briefing in

1996 stated: "Currently, the program is in its research and development stages, but we believe that Iran holds some stocks of BW agents and weapons."[141]

However, in more recent years, the reports have become less definitive. The 2011 report by the director of national intelligence stated that "Iran probably has the capability to produce some biological warfare . . . agents for offensive purposes, if it made the decision to do so. We assess that Iran has previously conducted offensive [biological warfare] agent research and development. Iran continues to expand its biotechnology infrastructure and seek dual-use technologies that could be used for [biological warfare].[142] As noted, there are currently few prospects for verifying Iranian claims about its lack of a biological-weapon program because the BWC contains no verification provisions.

CHALLENGES FOR MONITORING AND VERIFICATION

Over the years, Iran engaged in a clear pattern of denial and deception with respect to its nuclear, biological, and chemical programs—including a reluctance to provide information, concealing of facilities, denying IAEA access to facilities, and even direct violations of UNSC resolutions. In fact, they took very bold measures such as destroying buildings or paving over large areas at both the Lavizan-Shian facility and the Parchin facility in apparent efforts to destroy evidence. These activities raised serious questions about Iran's intentions and created enormous challenges for monitoring and verification regimes. As a result, organizations such as the IAEA have had difficulty detecting proscribed activities or confirming the peaceful purpose of these programs.

The monitoring and verification challenges were compounded by Iran's long refusal to ratify the Additional Protocol, an issue which has not been fully resolved in the JCPOA. Although the AP has sometimes been oversold as a solution to the IAEA's monitoring and verification authorities—in part because it still seriously limits inspections outside of declared nuclear facilities—it nevertheless would be an important addition to the IAEA's available monitoring and verification tools.[143]

Breakout Capability. Iran's breakout capability was a key element of the negotiations over its nuclear program, a key objective of JCPOA, and it remains an issue. By September 2014, Iran had produced a total of 12,772 kilograms of 3.5 percent low-enriched uranium and 448 kilograms of 20 percent U-235. Estimates at the time were that if Iran were to "sprint to the bomb," it could enrich enough uranium for a nuclear weapon in about one month.[144]

Under the terms of the 2013 Interim Agreement, the regime ceased production of 20 percent enriched uranium on January 20, 2014, blended down half of its 20 percent stockpile of LEU, and converted the other half to uranium oxide. However, Iran still retained a "large total stock of near 20 percent LEU, enough if reconverted into hexafluoride form and further enriched for a nuclear weapon."[145] Thus, the Interim Agreement did reduce Iran's breakout capability, but not by as much as some proponents claim. Even with the requirements established by the Interim Agreement, the Institute for Science and International Security (ISIS) estimated at the time that "[i]f Iran used all of its installed centrifuges, the time it would need to produce a weapon would expand to at least 1.9 to 2.2 months, up from at least one month to 1.6 months."[146] This estimate conformed with other estimates that placed Iran's breakout timetable under the Interim Agreement at about two months.[147]

As noted, one of the stated goals of the Obama administration in the negotiations over the JCPOA (especially later in the negotiation process) was to increase Iran's breakout times to about a year. Although members of the administration and many nonproliferation experts have argued that the JCPOA achieves this goal, some critics have raised questions about the set of assumptions that went into the twelve-month estimates for the breakout times.[148] Others have argued that Iran would be able to shorten its breakout times considerably—and thus reduce its potential breakout timeline to significantly below twelve months—if it were able redeploy its already manufactured IR-2 centrifuges relatively quickly.[149]

Regardless of the debate over the precise breakout times established during the first ten to fifteen years of the JCPOA, Iran's breakout times will continue to be a major issue over time. As President Obama has underscored, once the various restrictions on Iran's nuclear program are removed, "the breakout times would have shrunk almost down to zero."[150]

Possible Clandestine Facilities and Activities. Of course, these estimates are based on the currently known facilities. It is quite possible that Iran possesses undeclared and undetected facilities—both for uranium enrichment and weaponization activities. This was a concern in the JCPOA. Some U.S. officials have stated that this problem has been resolved by the JCPOA, and that all pathways, including clandestine facilities, have been blocked. Their optimism was based especially on Iran's commitment to ratify the AP and the requirements on Iran's imports. However, as has been discussed, these issues are not so clear.

No Special Inspections. Despite numerous and egregious instances of Iranian deception of inspectors and concealing of evidence, including at Lavizan-

Shian and Parchin, the IAEA has not, to date, called for special inspections in Iran. Indeed, for the first several years of this crisis, then-IAEA director-general Mohammed ElBaradei clearly went to great lengths to downplay the significance of Iran's violations, as he all but admitted later.[151] Although the IAEA reporting has become much more critical of Iran under the current director-general, Yukiya Amano, the organization still has yet to call for special inspections. This step is long overdue. However, at such sites as Parchin, which have never been sufficiently inspected, it may be too late. Given the difficulties with the challenge inspections in the JCPOA, it seems like a real opportunity was lost when the agreement did not call for the use of special inspections.

Prospects for Regime Survival. Because Iran is currently relatively stable, the proliferation concerns—and monitoring and verification challenges—outlined above will likely continue for the near- and mid-term. However, it is not impossible that regime-threatening protests may bring down the regime, as they have almost done in the past. The ongoing disputes between the dissatisfied reformists who seek popular sovereignty within a more open society and the unelected conservatives who desperately cling to their power under the current system have created substantial sociopolitical instability.[152] The younger generations in Iran identify little with the Islamic revolution, which took place well before they were born. Instead, they see ongoing political corruption and economic stagnation rather than the blessings promised by the Islamic revolution.[153] Even as far back as 2003, CIA director George Tenet speculated on the potential for this instability to erupt into a popular uprising, stating, "[W]e take the prospect of sudden, regime threatening unrest seriously and continue to watch events in Iran with that in mind. For now, our bottom line analysis is that the Iranian regime is secure, but increasingly fragile."[154]

Iran has experienced numerous protests and violent clashes between reformers supporters of the mullahs—including in 1999 and significant protests in 2002 and 2003.[155] However, the largest protests by far erupted on June 13, 2009, after widespread suspicions that the Iranian regime had fixed the re-election of President Mahmoud Ahmadinejad over the more reform-minded candidate, Mir Hussein Mousavi. In what came to be called the "Green Revolution," reformists' frustration over the election, compounded by thirty years of suppression, boiled over into the largest antiregime protests since the 1979 revolution.[156]

In the end, these protests were crushed by the regime through a series of violent crackdowns, and Iran descended into an uneasy calm for the next several years. The June 2013 election of proclaimed moderate Hassan Rouhani may have had the effect of appeasing reformers for the time being—while likely not changing anything fundamentally in the regime. But the basic political, economic, and demographic trends in Iran have not changed, which suggest that the conditions for a domestically led regime change may remain as well.

Syria

As a recent report by the International Institute for Strategic Studies notes, Syria "ranks with Iraq under Saddam Hussein and Libya under Muammar Gaddafi as the most ambitious Arab state in terms of its WMD acquisitions."[157] The Syrian regime managed to "overcome resource scarcity and other structural constraints to build a significant chemical-weapon arsenal, develop missile capabilities and, to the surprise of many, build a nuclear reactor."[158]

Over the last several years, issues relating Syria's chemical weapons—including Syria's alleged domestic use of these weapons against rebel groups, threats of U.S. military intervention to punish the regime for its CW attacks, and then Syria's renunciation of CW—have understandably been the primary WMD-related issues in Syria emphasized by the international community. Without a doubt, these issues are important. It should be remembered, however, that prior to reports of Syria's CW use in 2012 and 2013, the international community was primarily concerned with Syria's alleged nuclear-weapon program, especially following the alleged Israeli bombing of the al-Kibar site in 2007, and Syria's unwillingness to cooperate with the IAEA to answer key questions about this program.[159] This section will therefore address the monitoring and verification challenges associated with all of Syria's WMD programs, including its nuclear program, its chemical-weapon program and subsequent CW renunciation, and the possibilities of a biological-weapon program, as well as the prospects for future monitoring and verification in Syria.

NUCLEAR

Syria engaged in extensive concealment mechanisms both before and after the Israeli bombing of the al-Kibar facility, and more recently, at several additional suspected sites.[160]

Al-Kibar (Diar Alzour). Prior to the Israeli bombing of al-Kibar, Syria utilized multiple methods of concealing the alleged nuclear reactor site, including employing minimal security at the site, burying power cables to the facility, and camouflaging the entire building within a façade to make it look like a Byzantine fortress.[161] After the Israeli bombing, Syria bulldozed the site and built a larger building over the site presumably in an attempt to conceal all evidence.[162] Despite these activities, the IAEA discovered man-made (or anthropogenic) uranium at the site, but Syrian officials subsequently refused to let inspectors return to al-Kibar, and have also refused to allow the IAEA access to three other facilities to which the agency has requested access.

In its 2011 report, the IAEA stated that "based on all the information available to the Agency and its technical evaluation of that information, the Agency assesses that it is very likely that the building destroyed at the Diar Alzour site was a nuclear reactor which should have been declared to the Agency."[163] To date, Syrian officials have refused to answer any additional questions about their suspect activities at the al-Kibar site or allow additional access to the site.

Other Suspected Sites. In 2008, the IAEA reported that member states had provided information on three additional sites that were "functionally related" to the al-Kibar reactor.[164] These sites were subsequently identified as being located near Masyaf, Iskandariyah, and Marj as Sultan.[165] The IAEA reported that it had requested access to these three sites. Satellite imagery detected significant activity at these sites shortly after the IAEA's request, including "landscaping activities and the removal of large containers."[166] Upon analysis of satellite imagery, ISIS reported that the activity at the Marj as Sultan site "may represent an effort to lay down a new concrete or asphalt foundation around the building." ISIS further reported that "a senior official close to the IAEA said that Syria was seen in imagery laying down slabs at these sites. Laying down a new foundation could be an attempt to defeat the environmental sampling that IAEA inspectors would likely carry out to see if uranium was present in the event of a visit to these suspected sites."[167]

In June 2009, the IAEA also reported that it had discovered additional man-made uranium particles in routine samples of hot cells at the Miniature Neutron Source Reactor (MNSR) in Damascus that had not been included in Syria's declarations to the IAEA.[168] As David Albright and Paul Brannan report: "[T]hese findings raise questions of whether Syria had taken natural uranium intended for a reactor at the [Al-Kibar] site and used a portion of it to perform cold-testing of reprocessing on a small scale at the hot cell facility."[169] According to the IAEA, Syria explained that these particles had "originated from previously unreported activities performed at MNSR related to the preparation of ten grams of uranyl nitrate using yellowcake produced at Homs" (which was a site approved by the United Nations and IAEA in 2007). The IAEA did report in

2011 that it was provided with additional information on the site and allowed access to both Homs and MNSR. Based on this additional information, the IAEA concluded that Syria's statements concerning the origin of the man-made uranium particles "were not inconsistent with the Agency's findings," and that "the matter will be addressed in the routine implementation of safeguards."[170]

No Special Inspections. Given the lack of Syrian cooperation in providing additional information and IAEA access to the al-Kibar site or the three functionally related sites, numerous nonproliferation policy-makers and scholars began calling for the IAEA to request a special inspection of these sites.[171] To date, the IAEA has not done so, despite reporting a continued lack of progress in resolving these issues.

On May 26, 2011, Syria did reportedly state that the IAEA would be allowed access to the site, but set specific conditions on the visit, which the IAEA reported to be unacceptable. As a result, the IAEA board of governors adopted a resolution finding that "Syria's undeclared construction of a nuclear reactor at Diar Alzour and failure to provide design information for the facility constituted noncompliance by Syria with its obligations under its NPT Safeguards Agreement."[172] The issue was then referred to the UN Security Council.

Implications of the Ongoing Civil War. Given the ongoing civil war in Syria, it seems unlikely that the regime will be engaging in new nuclear-weapon initiatives for the foreseeable future. Indeed, it remains possible that the Assad regime will ultimately topple—although this prospect has become less likely in recent months. If the regime were eventually to collapse, the most direct proliferation risks arising from a covert nuclear-weapon program would be eliminated (while potentially creating others, such as "loose" nuclear equipment and materials).

SYRIAN CHEMICAL WEAPONS AND CW DISARMAMENT

Although estimates of Syria's CW stockpile size, deployment method, and locations have varied somewhat, the country was estimated to possess as much as 1,000 tons of mustard agents, sarin nerve agents, and possibly VX nerve agents. Syria was also believed to possess numerous delivery vehicles for CW, including various SCUD variations and SS-21 short-range ballistic missiles, as well as batteries of BM-21 mobile rocket launchers.[173] For years, Syria's CW stockpile was highlighted in various open-source intelligence briefings, but overall it received less attention than Syria's suspected nuclear-weapon activities.[174]

In 2012 and 2013, however, Syria's CW arsenal became the focus of international attention, after it became the first country to use chemical weapons offensively since Saddam Hussein's use of chemical weapons against the Kurds in 1988.[175] Syria was accused of using chemical weapons against rebels fighting against the Assad regime—especially in an alleged large chemical-weapon attack outside of Damascus said to have killed as many as 1,429 people—that ultimately led to the acceptance of a Russian proposal for Syria to dismantle and verifiably destroy its stockpile of chemical agents.

Although the regime reportedly turned over the last of its declared CW agents in June 2014, at the time of this writing it remains to be seen whether the Syrian regime will fully and completely eliminate the remaining CW infrastructure, resolve the reported "discrepancies" in its initial declaration, and work to address ongoing questions about clandestine stockpiles and facilities.

Ongoing allegations of continued Syrian use of chemical weapons raise further questions about the regime's seriousness in acceding to the Chemical Weapons Convention. Throughout 2014 and 2015, numerous allegations were made by senior government officials and the OPCW, citing "credible evidence" that Syria was using chlorine gas in multiple attacks against opposition groups and civilians.[176] Although chlorine was not included in the list of agents to be eliminated, its use in an attack is illegal under the CWC.

However the Syrian case unfolds, it will inevitably be affected by the limits on monitoring and verification, and it will likely encounter many challenges similar to those encountered in the cases of Iraq and Libya. The Syrian case also highlights the risks of weakened command and control of WMD during domestic instability and the potential role that force or threatened force may play in disarmament.

Verifying Syrian Chemical Weapon Use, 2012–13. From the beginning of the Syrian civil war in late 2011, there were significant concerns that the Assad regime would use CW against the rebels. In apparent efforts to deter this use, on August 20, 2012, U.S. president Barack Obama stated that the United States considered Syrian use of CW to be a "red line."[177] A few months later, after allegations of CW use by the Syrian government began surfacing, the British, French, and U.S. governments began investigating the available evidence. It turned out to be more difficult—and more controversial—to confirm the use than many observers had originally thought. Confirming CW use will remain relevant to the Syrian case, especially given the reports of the regime's ongoing use of chlorine gas against rebel groups.[178] It also ties into lessons from Iraq.

Efforts to confirm alleged CW use encounter difficulties similar to those encountered by monitoring and verification activities intended to identify covert WMD activities, stockpiles, or facilities. For example, the Syrian government was unwilling to allow inspection teams inside Syria to examine physical evidence at the sites of alleged CW use.[179] Inspection teams also faced the challenge of ruling out alternative explanations, such as CW use by rebel forces instead of the government. They also encountered problems of inconclusive results, which suggest the likelihood of use, but do not constitute a "smoking gun." These problems also led to challenges of political disagreements over the evidence, similar to those encountered by the UN Special Commission (UNSCOM) and the UN Monitoring Verification and Inspection Commission (UNMOVIC) in Iraq from the mid-1990s to the 2003 invasion and its aftermath.

Unlike the UNSCOM/UNMOVIC experience, the United States followed the lead of Great Britain and France on this issue, but all three governments did ultimately confirm by June 2013 that the Syrian government had likely used chemical weapons. Because UN or third-party inspectors have not been given access into Syria, "Western governments have relied on physical evidence smuggled out of the country by rebels or intelligence operatives."[180] Despite these limits, U.S. officials claimed that the evidence was significant. According to deputy national security advisor Benjamin J. Rhodes, the U.S. intelligence assessment "includes reporting regarding Syrian officials planning and executing regime chemical weapons attacks; reporting that includes descriptions of the time, location and means of attack; and descriptions of physiological symptoms that are consistent with exposure to a chemical weapons agent."[181] Nevertheless, the lack of absolutely definitive evidence—or a smoking gun—opened the door for Russia and other states to dispute the evidence.[182] Russia's position was widely viewed as driven more by political motivations than analysis of the evidence, but it was sufficient to prevent action on the issue.

The use of chemical weapons in the Damascus suburbs on August 21, 2013, changed the international perspective on Syria's chemical-weapon use. Investigations by the United States, France, Great Britain, and the United Nations confirmed a large CW attack. Although the UN investigation did not indicate who was responsible for carrying out the attack, UN secretary-general Ban Ki Moon described the attack as "the most significant confirmed use of chemical weapons against civilians since Saddam Hussein used them in Halabja in 1988—and the worst use of weapons of mass destruction in the 21st century."[183] Other investigations, including those undertaken by the United States and France, suggested that the attack had been carried out by the Assad regime.[184] Russia, however, continued to maintain that the attack was carried out by rebels.[185]

The 2013 Decision to Renounce CW. In the aftermath of the CW attack on August 21, 2013, President Obama and members of the Obama administration began making the case for a U.S.-led military strike to punish Syria for its egregious use of CW. Although President Obama had already set Syrian CW use as a red line, and members of the Obama administration had argued that congressional approval was unnecessary for U.S. military intervention, the Obama administration ultimately decided to present the issue to Congress for approval. Although the prospect of a military strike faced considerable congressional opposition, before Congress had the opportunity to vote on the issue, Russian president Vladimir Putin presented a plan to avoid military intervention if Syria dismantled its CW stockpile. That proposal was accepted by both Syria and the United States.

Although recognized by many as a potentially important opportunity for nonproliferation efforts, this plan was initially met with a good deal of skepticism. For example, as former British ambassador Charles Crawford wrote at the time:

> Chemical weapons are relatively easy to make and store (and fire), but much harder to dismantle safely. The chemicals themselves are fiendishly dangerous and need to be destroyed with specialist equipment without creating environmental hazards. Plus the explosive part of the delivery shell needs careful handling. Destroying CW stocks is therefore a complex and expensive operation, even under calm conditions. . . . There is no precedent for attempting anything like this in a country wracked by civil war. It just can't happen. No Syrian chemical weapons will be destroyed or "handed over" quickly.[186]

Despite some justification for such skepticism, Syria did take some important steps toward CW disarmament. Syria acceded to the Chemical Weapons Convention on September 14, 2013 (which became effective October 14).[187] The UN Security Council also passed resolution 2118 on September 27, which called for the "expeditious destruction" of Syria's CW and for a "stringent verification" of this process by the OPCW.[188] The UNSC resolution also stated that failure to disarm would be grounds for imposing measures under Chapter 7 of the UN charter, which would need to be negotiated but could include sanctions or the use of force.

On October 24, Syria submitted its initial declaration to the OPCW delineating its CW stockpile and identifying twenty-three chemical weapon production and mixing sites.[189] The dismantlement of Syria's CW facilities and the destruction of its CW agents would be overseen by the OPCW. The destruction of the chemical agents was to be undertaken aboard U.S. ships.[190] On October 31, the OPCW declared that Syria had disabled its declared CW production facilities and mixing and filling equipment.[191] The OPCW further declared on December 6, 2013, that it had "verified the destruction of all of Syria's unfilled munitions."[192] Despite several delays in the delivery timelines, on June 23, 2014, the OPCW reported that all of Syria's declared chemicals weapons had been removed, and the final destruction of the most deadly declared agents was confirmed at the end of August 2014.[193]

Verifying Syria's CW Destruction, 2013–14. The removal of Syria's declared chemical weapons and CW agents is an important and positive step. Nevertheless, a number of significant questions remain. These include the following possibilities:

• *Incomplete Reporting.* Numerous governmental and OPCW officials have raised serious questions about whether Syria's initial report gave a full account of its CW facilities and stockpiles.[194] In his announcement about the CW removal, Ahmet Üzümcü, director-general of the OPCW, stated: "We cannot say for sure it has no more chemical weapons. All we can do is work on the basis of verifying a country's declarations of what they have. I would not make any speculation to possible remaining assets, substances, [or] chemical weapons."[195] These questions have been underscored repeatedly by U.S., E.U., and OPCW officials and remain unanswered three years after Syria's initial declaration.[196] In a March 28, 2016 letter to the UN Security Council, Üzümcü reported that the OPCW Technical Secretariat "is unable at present to verify that the declaration and related submissions of the Syrian Arab Republic are accurate and complete."[197]

Not only do there appear to be discrepancies between the number of CW facilities declared by Syria and the number of CW facilities estimated by U.S. intelligence agencies, but there are also some questions about the declared CW stockpile itself.[198] U.S. intelligence had reportedly estimated that Syria had forty-five chemical-arms sites, which does not appear to match Syria's statement that it had twenty-three sites with forty-one facilities. In September 2013, when a U.S. attack looked imminent, there were reports that the Syrian regime had dispersed its CW agents to as many as fifty sites around the country.[199]

Moreover, according to a report in the London *Sunday Times*, Syria's declaration did not include any filled CW munitions.[200] This seems hard to believe, given the regime's repeated use of CW during 2012 and 2013.

The questions about Syria's declarations have raised concerns about whether Syria plans to retain clandestine stockpiles and facilities. In this context, it would be wise to keep the example of Libya in mind. Although the Qadhafi regime renounced its WMD programs in 2003 and ostensibly worked with inspection teams to dismantle those programs, a covert stockpile of chemical agents and associated delivery systems was discovered after the regime was toppled in 2011.

• *Possible Resuscitation of the CW Programs.* As early as October 2013, Syria tried to convince international officials to spare twelve structurally intact chemical-weapon production sites so they could be converted into civilian chemical facilities.[201] U.S. further alleged in May 2014 that Syria was attempting to use its remaining chemical stockpile as leverage to retain those sites.[202] These efforts reportedly caused a number of specialists to be concerned that Syria was trying to retain a latent capacity to restart its CW program down the road.[203]

Despite Syria's efforts to retain these facilities, the first two facilities were reportedly destroyed in February and March 2015.[204] At the time of this writing, the OPCW had reported that all but three of Syria's declared facilities had been destroyed, but cited security concerns that had prevented the destruction of the remaining facilities.[205] Until these sites are all destroyed (and any other undeclared facilities discovered and dismantled), Syria will potentially have the capability of resuscitating its CW stockpiles. As time goes on, pressure for a complete destruction of Syria's remaining CW infrastructure may ease, though the reports of ongoing CW attacks may bolster the elimination efforts.

• *Ongoing Instability and the Impact on Monitoring and Verification.* The ongoing civil war in Syria did affect the inspection process and the timetable for CW destruction. Throughout 2013 and the first half of 2014, the security situation caused significant delays in the timetable for Syria's deliveries of CW for destruction—raising questions not only about whether the regime would meet the June 30 deadline but also about whether Syria was using the security situation as an excuse to delay the disarmament process.[206]

The security situation also created significant difficulties for the verification process. For example, OPCW inspectors reportedly could not visit two of Syria's declared sites in 2013, owing to security concerns. The Syrian regime stated in October 2013 that the sites had subsequently been abandoned and that all materials and equipment had been removed. This, of course, meant that inspectors had to trust the Assad regime that everything had been removed and destroyed.[207] These difficulties parallel some of the difficulties encountered in 2003–4 by monitoring and verification teams in Iraq. As noted in Chapter 3, although the Iraq Survey Group (ISG) reportedly did not find any WMD stockpiles, it stated that the security environment had severely hindered its operations and had raised questions about the completeness of its findings.[208] Similar challenges have been encountered in Syria, though it is questionable whether the OPCW has attempted to discover clandestine facilities to the degree that UNSCOM did in Iraq.

• *Will the Verification Be Rigorous Enough?* Historically, the OPCW has been quite good at inspecting declared former CW sites in a number of countries. But they have demonstrated less interest in carrying out routine inspections at dual-use facilities. And, to date, they have never employed their strongest verification tool: challenge inspections, by which they can carry out short-notice inspections—anytime, anyplace—at suspected facilities. Will they be willing to carry out challenge inspections in Syria, if need be, especially now that the declared materials were reportedly removed? There are some reasons to question this so far.[209]

Despite the UNSC's call for a "stringent verification" of the destruction of Syria's CW stockpile by the OPCW, we have seen troubling signs that the OPCW may not take steps to ensure that such a "stringent verification" occurs. For example, the OPCW declared on December 6, 2013, that it had "verified the destruction of all of Syria's unfilled munitions."[210] If, however, the reports are accurate that no filled munitions were declared, one wonders whether the OPCW received Syria's declaration with sufficient skepticism, especially given the background and history of Syria's CW use to date. Moreover, as noted above, the OPCW declared on October 31, 2013, that Syria had disabled its declared CW production facilities and mixing and filling equipment, despite not being able to inspect two facilities because of the unstable security environment.[211] Although Syria stated that all materials had been removed from the two sites and that the sites were now abandoned, it is unclear how the OPCW would have been able to confirm that all related equipment and materials had been destroyed.[212]

Now that the declared CW agents have been removed from Syria, the pressure for carrying out rigorous verification procedures—including a search for possible clandestine stockpiles and facilities—may ease, and countries like Russia may push to end the verification process prematurely.

• *Enforcement.* It also remains to be seen whether enforcement of Syria's disarmament will become an issue. Certainly, the regime's willingness to turn over the last of its declared chemical agents is a propitious sign. However, given Syria's track record—including denying that it even possessed a CW program until mid-September 2013, its alleged ongoing use of chlorine gas, and its continued denial that it possessed a nuclear-weapon program—the international community should be prepared for a lack of true cooperation from Syria.

There are a number of other possible challenges to ensuring enforcement. If the verification standards set by the OPCW and others were insufficiently rigorous, the issue of noncompliance would never really come up.[213] Or, if there were to be a set of troubling signs, but no decisive evidence, Syria's allies on the UN Security Council and elsewhere would presumably attempt to block enforcement.[214]

Finally, as radicals gain ground over moderates among the rebels—and especially after the gains made by the Islamic State in Iraq and the Levant (ISIL) in both Syria and Iraq—the Assad regime may come to be seen as the only viable alternative in the civil war.[215] If so, one wonders whether the United States and the international community would still be willing to take action against Syria if the Assad regime turns out not to be serious about a thorough verification of Syria's CW rollback.

The Implications of Ongoing Chlorine Gas Attacks. Ongoing allegations of continued Syrian use of chemical weapons raise further questions about the regime's declarations and its seriousness about dismantling its CW stockpiles. On May 14, 2014, French foreign minister Laurent Fabius charged Syria with carrying out at least fourteen chemical strikes since October 2013. According to Fabius, these allegations are reportedly based on evidence from "credible witnesses," and may also involve the use of toxic chlorine gas.[216] U.S. secretary of state John Kerry appeared to support the French allegations, stating that unconfirmed "raw data" suggests Syria had launched more than a dozen new chemical attacks.[217]

In September 2014, the OPCW reported the results of a fact-finding mission appointed by the OPCW director-general to examine the alleged use of chlorine gas in Syria. The mission allegedly reported "information constituting 'compelling confirmation' that a toxic chemical was used 'systematically and repeatedly' as a weapon in villages in northern Syria earlier this year."[218] U.S. secretary of state John Kerry reportedly stated of the report that it "cites witness accounts indicating helicopters were used in the attacks—a capability the opposition lacks. . . . This strongly points to Syrian regime culpability."[219]

The allegations of Syrian chemical-weapon use continued into 2015, prompting the UN Security Council to condemn the use of chemical weapons in Syria in March 2015.[220] Although the United States has repeatedly alleged that Syria is responsible for the attacks—citing, for example, that only the Syrian regime has the helicopters necessary for dropping the barrel bombs that are used to deliver the chlorine gas—the UN Security Council has yet to attribute responsibility to any group for the CW use. As a report by the *New York Times* wryly put it: "[W]ith Russia, the Syrian government's most powerful ally, wielding a veto, there was no Council agreement to assign blame."[221]

On July 9, 2015, the United States put forward a UNSC resolution calling for an investigation into who is responsible for the attacks. U.S. ambassador Samantha Power stated that "given the frequent allegations of chlorine attacks in Syria, and the absence of any international body to identify the perpetrators of chemical weapons attacks, it is critical that the U.N. Security Council find consensus and set up an independent investigative mechanism."[222]

Chlorine was not included in the list of agents that Syria would be required to turn over and destroyed, but use of chlorine gas is banned by the CWC. The Assad regime's alleged use of chlorine gas does raise significant questions about whether Syria was acting in good faith when it acceded to the CWC in 2013. If the regime, in the end, has no qualms about violating the CWC, there is little reason for confidence that it would not be willing to violate the CWC by either retaining CW stockpiles or production capacity, or working to re-establish a CW stockpile at the first opportunity if it can be successful.

Regime Instability and "Loose" CW. The Syrian civil war also generated significant concern about the regime's ability to maintain centralized control over its CW arsenal—both prior to and after its CW renunciation. Initial assessments were that Syria had likely maintained control of its CW by ensuring that facilities were adequately protected and possibly by consolidating CW stockpiles.[223] As the civil war dragged on, however, many analysts raised concerns that the ongoing domestic upheaval could cause the Syrian regime to lose central control over the weapons—owing to defections of local commanders, facility or stockpile turnover in the course of battle, or a total collapse of the regime—resulting in the chemical weapons falling into the hands of local commanders or, even more troubling, radical Islamist groups such as Al Qaeda or its affiliates.[224]

The removal of Syria's declared CW from the country reduces these concerns significantly. Nevertheless, if the regime's declaration is incomplete and the regime is concealing clandestine CW stockpile or facilities, some risks remain. As has long been noted in the literature on survivability and command-and-control, the very methods that a state could use to conceal WMD stockpiles or ensure that these stockpiles would survive a military strike—such as dispersing its stockpile to numerous locations—can also dramatically increase the difficulties of maintaining centralized control over its WMD.[225]

CHALLENGES FOR MONITORING AND VERIFICATION REGIMES

In addition to the new issues that have arisen over Syria's renunciation of chemical weapons, the Syrian case also demonstrates significant difficulties in verifying the status of suspected nuclear-weapon programs. As has often been the situation in the cases we have studied, some of the monitoring and verification challenges have been structural, but some were self-imposed by international verification organizations. The Syrian case, so far, also demonstrates important lessons that will need to be recognized and incorporated in future monitoring and verification efforts.

Very Little International Inspection. Because Syria has not ratified the Additional Protocol and did not formally accede to the CWC until September 2014, the Syrian case largely reminds us of the international verification system during the 1980s and early 1990s. As such, it also demonstrates the shortcomings of the pre-AP and pre-CWC system, which allowed such countries as Iraq, Libya, and South Africa to develop significant WMD programs without detection. Unfortunately, we have not entirely moved past the pre-AP/pre-CWC system. In fact, none of the difficult cases discussed in this chapter have ratified both the AP and CWC, and the IAEA and OPCW will continue to have limited access to these states for routine inspections.[226]

Moreover, it is not entirely clear that Syria's nuclear activities would have been detected even if it had ratified the AP. As we have noted, the AP grants unrestricted "complementary access" to the IAEA at undeclared buildings *only at declared nuclear sites*—and none of the suspected nuclear facilities in Syria were declared. Moreover, even though the AP gives the IAEA the authority to conduct wide-area environmental sampling and utilize satellite surveillance, these methods are not being fully utilized. Thus, it is not clear that the IAEA on its own would have been able to discover these sites, even if Syria had been bound by the AP.

Relevant Information Was Provided by Third Parties. Prior to Syria's 2013 declaration about its chemical-weapon facilities and stockpiles, nearly all of the relevant information on Syria's nuclear and CW facilities had come from third-party intelligence.[227] This includes not only the information on al-Kibar, but as the IAEA makes clear in its reports, also the information on the three additional suspect facilities near Masyaf, Iskandariyah, and Marj as Sultan. The limited international inspections that occurred in Syria thus provided little information on what was really occurring there. Given the challenges and limits to formal inspection activities, it is clear that future monitoring and verification regimes will need to continue to utilize, and possibly to expand, information provided by third parties.

The IAEA Was Unwilling to Call for Special Inspections. Finally, the Syrian case is troubling, not only because of Syria's apparently flagrant violations of international nonproliferation norms and agreements, but also because—in spite of mounting evidence of these violations, ongoing obstructionism by Syria, *and* increasing calls for stronger action by international experts—the IAEA never opted to call for special inspections in Syria. It could be argued that special inspections were irrelevant in this case, because the IAEA board of governors still found the regime in noncompliance and referred the issue to the UN Security Council. This is misleading, however, because there was significant disagreement within the board—indeed, the resolution reportedly was passed by only an extremely narrow margin, with a number of states abstaining.[228] The lack of more conclusive evidence that might have been provided by a special inspection (or the clear red flag caused by Syria's refusal to grant such an inspection), along with the disagreements within the board of governors arising from the lack of more conclusive evidence, create conditions in which Syria is more readily protected by certain UNSC states.

The Role of Preventive Strikes? The issue of preventive war to eliminate potential WMD programs before a state has the ability to develop or use WMD has long been a controversial one—and one that has become even more controversial after the 2003 war in Iraq. The reported 2007 Israeli strike on al-Kibar will likely be an important case in this debate. As with the Israeli strike on the Osirak reactor in 1981, both proponents and opponents of military force will present their case.

The reported Israeli strike undoubtedly set Syria's nuclear program back on its heels, but the full significance of this strike still remains to be seen—and will likely continue to be debated long after the civil war is over. Defenders of preventive strikes have argued that the Israeli strike kept Syria from obtaining nuclear weapons prior to the civil war, thereby changing dramatically the events on the ground during the civil war; reduced or eliminated risks of "loose nukes" scenarios in Syria; and possibly prevented Syria from obtaining nuclear weapons indefinitely.[229] Opponents of preventive strikes will likely argue that it was impossible to have predicted in 2007 that the Arab Spring would sweep across the Middle East in late 2010, engulfing the Syrian regime as well. Nor, they may argue, is it entirely clear that the al-Kibar reactor would necessarily have been operational in time to produce sufficient plutonium for a bomb by late 2011, when the civil war started. Finally, opponents could add, because it is far from clear, at the time of this writing, that the Assad regime will be toppled, the regime could still eventually resuscitate its nuclear program.

As is often the case in such debates, the arguments are overstated and probably misleading. In similar fashion, the debate over the U.S. threat of force in Syria's CW disarmament shows the same problems. Although the threat of force by the United States certainly played a role in pushing events forward, realistically, "the credibility of the president's threat evaporated when it became clear that Congress would not authorize the use of force and the administration would not act absent that approval."[230] The Russian proposal came at a time when the Obama administration had few remaining alternatives—even if Syria's CW renunciation was a preferred outcome for the administration.

Myanmar

Myanmar, or Burma, is a signatory to the NPT and has negotiated a Comprehensive Safeguards Agreement with the IAEA. Although it signed the Additional Protocol in 2013, at the time of this writing it has yet to ratify it. It did ratify the BWC in December 2014 and the CWC in January 2015.[231] There is currently little solid evidence of CW and BW programs that existed in Myanmar, though there were ongoing accusations of a CW program by opposition groups and, more recently, more serious allegations of a clandestine CW facility.[232]

There have been disturbing reports of a secret, though rudimentary, nuclear-weapon program possibly undertaken with North Korean assistance. In June 2010, a documentary and report based on information provided by a defector from the Myanmar army alleged that Myanmar had acquired dual-use technologies that could be used in a nuclear program. Former IAEA inspector Robert Kelly, who coauthored the report, claimed that this new technology "is only for nuclear weapons and not civilian use or nuclear power."[233] Described as a "nuclear wannabe," Myanmar was suspected of being in the early stages of a nuclear program. The IAEA repeatedly requested additional information and access to multiple sites but, until recently, had been largely ignored by Myanmar's government.[234]

However, the isolated regime began taking steps toward joining the international community when it installed a civilian government in April 2011 and then released more than 650 political prisoners between May 2011 and mid-January 2012. The regime held national elections in November 2015, resulting in the landslide election of Aung San Suu Kyi's National League for Democracy (NLD) and effectively ending fifty years of military rule. These significant political reforms caused the international community to begin taking steps toward easing the substantial economic sanctions regime that had been in place for decades, though it remains unclear how fundamental or lasting the political transformation will be. Although the NLD won enough votes in Myanmar's parliament to select the next president and control the majority of the country's laws, it cannot change the country's constitution or select the leadership within many of the country's key bureaucracies. Only the military has that authority.[235]

Myanmar's political reforms also had the effect of easing international pressure for the regime to come clean about its nuclear program as well. In what has widely been viewed as a positive move, Myanmar agreed to sign the Additional Protocol on November 19, 2012, coinciding with the arrival of U.S. president Barack Obama in the country.[236] At the time of this writing, however, negotiations over ratification of the AP are reportedly still ongoing.

Ratification of the AP would certainly be a positive step in assuaging international suspicions about Myanmar's nuclear program, but it would not in itself be sufficient. Beyond the AP, there may be the need for more detail on its program and for significant inspections of suspected sites. Moreover, as advocated in a report by the Institute for Science and International Security, Myanmar could take additional steps to end suspicions by ending its close military ties with North Korea. The regime has yet to do so. In fact, on July 2, 2013, the Obama administration announced that it was imposing sanctions against Lieutenant General Thein Htay, the head of the Directorate of Defense Industries, because he "has disregarded international requirements to stop purchasing military goods from North Korea."[237] It remains unclear whether such bureaucracies will retain a degree of autonomy, despite the recent shift in control of the parliament and presidency.

The regime will also need to resolve any remaining questions about allegations of a possible CW site that was under construction—despite the regime's repeated statements in late 2013 and early 2014 that it was preparing to ratify the CWC.[238] Local reports of the possible CW facility began receiving international attention in January 2014, when the government of Myanmar arrested reporters and confiscated all copies of an issue of a weekly journal alleging that Myanmar was constructing a secret CW facility in the country's Pauk Township. In May 2014, Jeffrey Lewis and Catherine Dill published a set of reports examining these allegations and analyzing satellite images of the site.[239] Lewis and Dill reported that the site appears to be a high-value military site that includes an extensive high-security perimeter, underground tunneling, barracks-style housing, and helicopter pads.[240] Although they acknowledge that it is impossible to determine that it is a CW site from satellite imagery, the design features suggest it is not a typical military site. Also, they maintain, the regime's actions have been extremely suspicious. As Lewis argued in 2014: "I cannot imagine a country acting more suspicious than [Myanmar] in the last few months."[241]

Now that Myanmar has ratified the CWC, the OPCW should have the opportunity to inspect the suspected CW site and answer any remaining questions about the purpose of the facility. To date, it is unclear what steps have been taken to this end. It is also important to maintain pressure for Myanmar to ratify the AP and facilitate IAEA inspections of any suspect nuclear sites. The recent and positive political changes may create precisely the opportunities to do so.

Applying the Lessons from South Africa, Libya, Iraq, and Disarmament

It is striking how many similar techniques North Korea, Iran, and Syria used to conceal all or part of their WMD programs. Moreover, once suspicions about their programs came to light, they used similar techniques for denying that these were in fact WMD programs, covering their tracks and concealing evidence, and delaying or denying inspectors access to suspected sites.

Despite the recent progress with Iran, it remains important to think through potential monitoring and verification scenarios, which include the following possibilities:

• "Rollback," or the elimination of existing WMD arsenals and WMD production capabilities resulting from either regime change or a negotiated renunciation. This is obviously the hoped-for scenario with North Korea (though this remains unlikely for the foreseeable future) and, more promisingly (though still incomplete), with Syria's CW and CW-related facilities.

• "Nuclear restraint," or a possible scaling back of WMD production capabilities, combined with stringent verification to detect WMD activities (a hoped-for scenario with Iran after the JCPOA).

• Ongoing obstructionism. Unfortunately, this remains the most likely scenario for the time being, especially in the cases of North Korea's WMD programs; Syria's suspected nuclear program (and possibly even its CW program); and Iran's WMD programs, despite the JCPOA.

These issues are examined below. In the discussion, we draw on the lessons that we have seen in the other chapters of this book—South Africa, Iraq, Libya, and the challenges associated with verifying global disarmament.

"Rollback" of WMD Arsenals

As noted, "rollback" relates to the dismantlement of WMD arsenals, along with related stockpiles of CBW agents or fissile materials, as well as supporting production and R&D facilities. Although we have seen rollback by a number of other states in different circumstances, with the possible exception of Syria's CW, the likelihood of WMD rollback by the remaining difficult cases has been small. However, this does not mean that success is impossible in these countries. There are two primary scenarios for possible rollback of their WMD programs. The first scenario would involve the collapse of the regime, either from internal, domestic causes or external forces, including economic sanctions and warfare; the second would involve a voluntary renunciation of WMD, most likely arising from negotiation, diplomacy, or external pressure. We will discuss each of these rollback scenarios in turn.

POTENTIAL REGIME CHANGES

There have long been hopes that regime change in North Korea, Iran, and Syria would provide opportunities for rollback in these countries, either by political change or a governmental collapse and a replacement with a more moderate regime that is willing to renounce WMD. At the time of this writing, however, the prospects for rollback in any of these countries is not high. Even in the case of Syria, which remains consumed by a civil war, the likelihood that the regime will be toppled has diminished significantly in recent months. The

Assad regime has made significant progress against the rebels, with significant assistance from Iran, Hezbollah, and more recently, Russia.[242]

While the prospects of regime collapse in North Korea and even Iran appear less likely in the near to mid term, these regimes are far from healthy. If a regime collapse were to occur in one or more of these difficult cases, it would create opportunities for eliminating nuclear and other WMD-related programs, but it would also create a host of challenges that would need to be addressed rapidly.

Prospects of Loss of Central Control. If any one of the difficult cases, including North Korea, Iran, or Syria, were to experience a change of regime, caused by political collapse or by internal or external force, its controls over its nuclear and CBW materials could collapse as well. This would be true of any country possessing WMD, but it might be particularly true of these proliferating states, given the basic design of the security systems that these countries are believed to employ. All three of these countries are believed to use what are often referred to as the "3 G's"—guards, gates, and guns—to maintain security at their nuclear and other WMD-related facilities.[243] This type of system can operate effectively when a country is stable. However, as the case of Russia clearly demonstrated following the collapse of the Soviet Union, this type of security system is particularly fragile during political, social, or economic upheavals.[244]

Moreover, as we have seen, these countries have all employed various "denial and deception" techniques to conceal their weapons and weapon-related materials—and to prevent their being eliminated in a military strike. These techniques can include dispersing production and storage facilities; avoiding tell-tell signs such as security fences, extensive guard forces around a facility, and so forth. While these can be effective methods of concealing clandestine WMD programs, they can also reduce a country's ability to track and protect weapons and related materials—especially if central government controls or military discipline were to weaken.[245]

Thus, a change of regime can potentially weaken fundamentally a state's security systems, creating extreme risks that its WMD and related materials could fall into the wrong hands. This was a major source of concern with Syria, prior to the removal of its CW agents, and this is one reason why the removal of the declared CW was beneficial. Such scenarios could create nearly insurmountable problems for any organization attempting to track and secure these materials. For example, in the widespread looting following the toppling of Saddam Hussein, tremendous numbers of documents and other artifacts were lost. There was also significant evidence of intentional destruction of material.

Similar scenarios would be possible in the event of a regime collapse in North Korea, Iran, and Syria. Not only might citizens, long oppressed by the ruling elite, feel justified in grabbing all that they can to make up for the years of exploitation, but former regime officials may fear international punishment or reprisals if their illicit activities were to come to light.

Controlling and Eliminating Stockpiles and Facilities. Given these risks, the United States and its allies—ideally, working with and under the mandate of the United Nations—will need to work quickly to reestablish stability and facilitate a transition to a new government. The United States and others will also need to take steps to ensure that WMD stockpiles, facilities, and related documents and infrastructure, are secure.

If necessary, the United States and others may need to send forces into the country in order to secure or seize the known WMD material and facilities. According to some reports, the United States is developing plans for precisely such scenarios. For example, in February 2013 the U.S. reportedly conducted wargames to determine "how many American troops would be needed to go in and secure North Korea's nuclear arsenal if Kim's regime collapsed" as a result of either civil unrest or an internal or external challenge to his power.[246] There have been accounts of U.S. military preparations for similar scenarios in Syria and Iran as well.[247]

Conducting a Thorough Search for Hidden Stockpiles and Facilities. If a change of regime were to occur, the United States and either ad hoc or established verification entities would also need to take significant steps to identify hidden WMD stockpiles and facilities. It is widely suspected that all of these difficult cases may have clandestine facilities that are unknown to the IAEA, the OPCW, or third-party intelligence agencies. As a result, it will be very important to work to identify clandestine facilities as rapidly as possible—in order to prevent materials at those facilities from falling into the wrong hands, and to ensure that new regimes do not inherit stockpiles or significant latent capabilities (though some latency will likely be inevitable). Indeed, as demonstrated by the discovery of the covert CW stock in Libya, these materials and facilities may surface months after the regime has collapsed. But of course, the sooner they are identified and secured, the better.

As the experience of the ISG after the toppling of the Iraqi regime shows, it is not always easy to discover these facilities. In this process, it would be important to secure documents and materials at known sites and to identify and question former officials working in the WMD programs in order to obtain evidence on where clandestine sites might be located.

VOLUNTARY OR NEGOTIATED ROLLBACK

Over the last decades, we have heard countless times that North Korea had committed, in theory, to renouncing its WMD programs, along with other apparent breakthroughs in negotiations with either Iran or Syria. Given the failure to realize these expectations, many observers had come to be very skeptical that yet another round of negotiations would produce any real success, especially relating to the rollback of actual WMD arsenals. However, we have seen some potential progress with the removal of Syria's declared CW and its commitment to dismantle its CW facilities, and the negotiations that led to the JCPOA with Iran.

Although the prospects of a diplomatic breakthrough leading to WMD rollback do not appear likely anytime soon in North Korea, and the situation in Iran remains unclear as the JCPOA is implemented, the experiences in South Africa and Libya, and more recently in Syria, have demonstrated that circumstances can change quickly, leading to a willingness to disarm. In these instances, especially in Libya, the international community was unprepared to respond optimally. While this proved not to be overly debilitating in the Libyan case, owing to the limited nature of the Libya's program, it would have been disastrous if a similar scenario were to play out in North Korea or Iran. The international community would therefore be well served to prepare for such prospects ahead of time.

The lessons drawn from past experiences of verification of rollback would be extremely useful for future scenarios. As one policy-maker put it: "Libya was practice for Syria, which is practice for North Korea."[248] Based on the lessons learned from the other cases in this book, this section will examine the primary opportunities and challenges that monitoring and verification regimes will face in such cases of negotiated rollback.

What Would Be Necessary for Confidence? As the other cases in this book have demonstrated, it is not enough simply to trust a state to disarm—*especially* a state that has a demonstrated and extensive track record of lying to the international community, deceiving (or at least obstructing) international inspectors, and otherwise flouting international norms or commitments as it pursued its WMD programs. As we saw in the cases of South Africa, Iraq, and Libya, every one of these countries claimed to have disarmed—but in every one of the cases, there were remaining, unanswered questions about whether the disarmament was completely and thoroughly carried out.

Iraqi claims that it had unilaterally destroyed CBW stockpiles, for example, were not held to be credible by most observers at the time of the 2003 war. South Africa and Libya also claimed to have renounced their WMD programs—and were more generally believed by the international community—but it turns out that both countries concealed important information from inspectors and may have retained stockpiles or important WMD capabilities. In the case of Libya, we know that it retained a covert CW stockpile. In the case of South Africa, we know that it initially concealed the existence of its nuclear-weapon program, as well as important sites (such as its test shafts) from inspectors—and, in retrospect, may have retained additional latent capabilities beyond those provided by its knowledge, civil program, and HEU stockpile. Similar questions would be raised by a declared rollback by other proliferating states, and may currently be the case with Syria.

Lessons from Global Disarmament Efforts. Chapter 5 of this book gives us some indication of what would be necessary for monitoring and verification regimes to confirm the declared rollback with any confidence. As in the case of global disarmament, the monitoring and verification challenges would be substantial.

In fact, especially in proliferant states in which the programs have been extensive, with numerous covert facilities under development for many years, the verification difficulties would be almost as significant as with global disarmament. The difficulties include:

• Verifying warhead identification and dismantlement.
• Protecting sensitive information (so that it cannot be used by other proliferators).
• Tracking warhead components during dismantlement.
• Obtaining accurate fissile material inventories and eliminating the possibilities of doctoring records. This would likely include the extensive use of nuclear archeology.
• Material disposition verification.
• Detecting covert facilities.

Beyond these significant challenges in these areas—which are magnified by the fact that we currently lack the full range of technical and political tools necessary to address them—there are a few acute challenges that should be noted. Even if the disarming country were operating in good faith, it would be very hard to determine the fissile material production history with any accuracy. It would therefore be extremely difficult or even impossible to rule out that the country had produced an undeclared stockpile of fissile materials, nuclear weapons, or CBW. Moreover, and relatedly, even in the most optimistic circumstances, it will be nearly certain that these countries will retain some degree of WMD latency, which could allow the country to reconstitute its program at a later date.

Careful Oversight of Dismantlement. One of the primary lessons from the South African and Libyan cases is that any disarmament steps must be carefully overseen by a formal monitoring and verification organization or an ad hoc group designed for this precise purpose. In the case of South Africa, the biggest questions about the country's disarmament arose from the fact that it conducted the disarmament unilaterally. As we saw, the substantial efforts undertaken by the IAEA provided probably the best levels of confidence that were possible under the circumstances. However, in such instances, so much vital information is irrevocably lost that it becomes nearly impossible to verify a complete WMD rollback with certainty. If possible, the international community needs to make sure that verification and disarmament teams are present and oversee each step of the dismantlement process from the start.

Moreover, as the Libyan case clearly demonstrates, it is not even enough to have international verification teams participate in the disarmament process. These teams need to ensure that each step is taken carefully and is fully implemented. As we saw in the Libyan case, there were advantages in moving quickly—for example, to make sure that sensitive equipment is removed—but verification teams must be aware of the pitfalls as well.

Beware of Cooperation. Another one of the primary lessons from the Libyan case, and possibly from the South African case as well, is that apparent cooperation can potentially be a cover for noncompliance. In the Libyan case, once the country appeared to be cooperating, the bar for verification of compliance was apparently lowered. Even in the South African case, clear evidence of cooperation in certain areas—including voluntary entrance into the NPT, dismantlement of its nuclear program, and a later apparent full disclosure of the program (though only after March 1993)—appeared to have shaped the technical conclusions, which on their own terms were not as conclusive as was argued at the time. These could be precedents that haunt us in the future. As Herman Nackaerts has argued: "The more a State cooperates and 'goes the extra mile' the less likely it will be for us to need to undertake routine, in field verification activities: contrariwise, the less a State cooperates, the greater the likelihood that it will receive more attention from the Agency, and from the international community as a whole."[249] Nackaerts is more or less correct, but with sharp qualifications. Because apparent cooperation can actually be a method of concealment, it is not, in itself, sufficient for confidence. This holds true for any state that has a past record of not cooperating. Thus, if a declared rollback were to occur, the international community should commend the disarming state, but it should remain skeptical that the cooperation is entirely sincere until a thorough verification occurs.

The Need for Long-term Monitoring. Given the significant questions that will necessarily be raised by any declaration of rollback, along with latent WMD capabilities that the state will inevitably possess, there is a clear need for long-term monitoring to answer any ongoing questions about the state's intentions, continue searching for clandestine facilities, and attempt to detect a reconstitution of the state's WMD programs. Although ratification of the AP and CWC would presumably be part of a disarmament agreement if any of the difficult cases were to renounce their WMD programs, the long-term monitoring would nevertheless need to be more intrusive than the authorities granted by the AP and CWC. After all, in most instances of a voluntary or negotiated rollback, the same rulers will remain in power who had previously flaunted their nonproliferation commitments. Monitoring and verification regimes would be well served to be skeptical of fundamental policy shifts unless they are carefully verified over the long term.

International monitoring and verification entities will also need to utilize national technical means (NTM) and other third-party information as part of, or as a supplement to, the long-term monitoring. Even with strengthened authorities given through a rigorous long-term monitoring agreement, organizations such as the IAEA and OPCW will require additional tools and authorities. Such measures, combined with a negotiated long-term monitoring agreement, would significantly strengthen the abilities of the IAEA and OPCW to detect illicit activities. Nevertheless, these organizations will have difficulty in detecting covert WMD-related activities unless they know where to look. The evidence provided by NTM and other third parties will remain essential for drawing IAEA and OPCW attention to activities and facilities that may require further investigation.

Restraining Iranian WMD Programs

Even though the P5+1 may have considered rollback as a goal in Iran—and the United States certainly did earlier in the negotiations—the JCPOA is based not rolling back but restraining the Iranian program. As noted, there are some issues that will affect how well this objective can be obtained, and the implementation of the agreement will be critical in this regard. Even in the best case of implementation, nuclear latency, long-term monitoring, and enforcement, as well as the potential existence of other WMD programs will still remain.

LATENCY AND THE NEED FOR LONG-TERM MONITORING

As long as Iran retains the capability to produce fissile materials, it will necessarily retain one of the most important elements of nuclear-weapon latency.[250] The JCPOA reduced key elements of the Iranian program, but it has not affected Iranian latency in any significant way in the mid- to long-term. Moreover, depending on how extensive its alleged weaponization research and development activities were, Iran may have significant latent capabilities and breakout capabilities for the foreseeable future. Despite the JCPOA, there remains a need for extensive and intrusive long-term monitoring to detect Iranian efforts to develop its latent capabilities for as long as Iran retains a latent capability. While the long-term NPT and other obligations that Iran has undertaken will be valuable in this context, the scheduled end to many of the JCPOA's verification and monitoring measures, which are not tied to Iranian behavior, appears to represent a lost opportunity.

QUESTIONS ABOUT ENFORCEMENT

In the event that Iranian noncompliance is detected, it is questionable whether the international community will be able to respond sufficiently. The enforcement of the JCPOA primarily depends on how well the Joint Commission is implemented. This, in turn, will be affected by whether or not the interests and commitments of all the parties, particularly the P-5, can be maintained.

CBW FACILITIES

Finally, even if an agreement were reached that provided for Iranian restraint on its nuclear program, questions would still remain about the regime's CBW program. Although Iran's nuclear program is justifiably the highest priority, the international community should not forget about the regime's other WMD programs.

Conclusions

Although the United States and the international community made potential positive steps in the cases of Iran and Syria, there are reasons to expect full or partial obstructionism to continue in all the difficult cases. This will remain true in the case of Iran, even if the JCPOA is successfully implemented. As noted, nearly every one of the tactics employed by North Korea, Iran, Syria, and possibly Myanmar, was also employed by Iraq to conceal its nuclear and other WMD programs. This is perhaps not surprising. It is likely that these proliferating states looked closely at the political crisis unfolding in Iraq to determine what methods worked for Iraq, and which did not. Indeed, because these countries were clearly pushing forward with their programs during the 1990s and early 2000s—when UNSCOM and UNMOVIC were carrying out their activities—they would have been mightily foolish if they were not watching the events in Iraq closely. To the extent that future monitoring and verification of suspected WMD programs in these and other difficult cases will continue to encounter denial, deception, and concealment methods similar to those employed by Iraq, the Iraqi case will continue to yield important lessons.

This is not to say that the monitoring and verification challenges will be identical to those of the Iraqi case, of course. The extent of these challenges depends on both the extent and complexity of a state's WMD programs, as well as the authorities granted to the verifying organization. The North Korean program, for example, has progressed much further than Iraq's did because they appear to have successfully developed (and tested) a nuclear weapon and developed a more complete fuel cycle. Iran, as well, has successfully developed a much more advanced enrichment capability than Iraq's. Syria and Myanmar, on the other hand, have much smaller and less complex nuclear programs than Iraq's.

An additional factor to keep in mind is that the IAEA and OPCW currently have fewer authorities to carry out verification activities in these difficult cases than UNSCOM and the IAEA had in Iraq. Because UNSCOM's and the IAEA's authorities in Iraq were established after a war, and their verification activities were explicitly part of the terms of the cease-fire, their authorities were much greater than any other monitoring and verification organization in history. (Indeed, it is highly unlikely that *any* country would voluntarily agree to such intrusive inspections, let alone countries that may have something to hide.) Despite their authorities, Iraq was nevertheless able to undermine much of their work throughout the 1990s, and even after they returned to Iraq in 2002. In contrast, as we have seen, none of the current difficult cases have yet ratified the AP (though Iran and Myanmar have both signed it, and Iran has committed to apply it "provisionally" and "seek" ratification in 2023), and North Korea has not ratified the CWC.[251] As a result, some of the monitoring and verification challenges in the current cases may be significantly *greater* than those experienced in Iraq.

Given these limitations, monitoring and verification organizations will need to utilize their existing authorities more effectively if they are to achieve greater success in these cases. In each of the difficult cases the IAEA had ample cause to call for a special inspection yet attempted it only once, unsuccessfully, in North Korea in the early 1990s. Nor has the OPCW attempted a challenge inspection, widespread suspicions of CBW programs in all four countries. Because special and challenge inspections are the most intrusive sets of inspections available to these organizations, they should not be afraid of using them. If these inspections were semiregularly employed, the taboo on using them would ease.

In addition, international monitoring and verification entities will need to continue utilizing third-party information, including NTM, to support and supplement the activities of the IAEA and others. Barring any major diplomatic breakthroughs, with few exceptions these difficult cases will likely continue refusing to ratify the AP or sign the CWC. While these agreements are far from addressing all of the limitations of monitoring and verification, they do strengthen the authorities of the IAEA and OPCW considerably. Although controversial, especially after the 2003 war in Iraq, NTM have proved to be absolutely vital for monitoring and verification activities. It is the case, notably, that the IAEA did discover North Korea's misinformation on plutonium separation. However, one must recall that third-party information—rather than the IAEA—brought to light every one of the covert facilities so far discovered in Iran, Syria, or Myanmar.[252] The IAEA also failed to discover the massive covert nuclear-weapon program in Iraq prior to 1991. Moreover, the OPCW failed to detect the covert stockpile of chemical agents and related delivery vehicles in Libya—even after Libya had ratified the CWC. Given the important role that NTM and other third-party information have played in detecting covert WMD facilities—especially in countries that have not ratified the AP or CWC—they must remain an essential part of monitoring and verification activities in the future.

Finally, if past and ongoing events give us an idea of what to expect in the future, we will likely continue to encounter difficulties in obtaining political support from such countries as Russia and China. The ongoing obstructionism from these proliferating states, combined with Russian and Chinese opposition in the UNSC and elsewhere to international action, will pose significant challenges for monitoring and verification regimes. As we argue in the final chapter of this book, Western states and those allies who are dedicated to nonproliferation efforts may need to explore coalitions and regimes outside of the United Nations if they want to achieve ongoing success in North Korea, Iran, and Syria, as well as other difficult cases.

Conclusion: Strengthening Monitoring and Verification Regimes

As the case studies considered above suggest, the inherent challenges of verification, the decisions that are made on what to verify, and difficulties within existing mechanisms for verification all suggest that we are entering a new realm of greater ambiguity. This ambiguity will be amplified by latency that derives from rolled back weapon programs and dual-use activities involving weapons of mass destruction (WMD). Moreover, while ambiguity can be reduced, it cannot be eliminated, and its reduction depends greatly on understanding both the strengths and limits of monitoring and verification technologies and extant regimes, and of taking required steps to strengthen those regimes.

Unprecedented Monitoring and Verification Challenges

In the last twenty years, monitoring and verification regimes have encountered severe and unprecedented challenges. As noted in Chapter 1 of this book, a series of revelations of clandestine nuclear-weapon programs came to light during the 1990s that challenged the entire monitoring and verification system that had been established by the Nuclear Nonproliferation Treaty (NPT) and the International Atomic Energy Agency (IAEA). These revelations included:

• An extensive nuclear-weapon program in Iraq discovered in the aftermath of Operation Desert Storm. This program was developed largely through clandestine facilities that were not detected and could not be detected by the existing IAEA safeguards system.

• South Africa's development (and then subsequent destruction of) an operational nuclear-weapon arsenal without detection by the IAEA.

• North Korea's steps in establishing a nuclear-weapon program, developed in large part by diversion of materials from operational nuclear facilities.

At roughly the same time, concerns about the production and use of chemical and biological weapons (CBW) also grew significantly. Interest in a Chemical Weapons Convention grew in the late 1980s as a result of chemical-weapon (CW) use during the Iran-Iraq War. Moreover, after the collapse of the Soviet Union, it became clear that the Soviets had concealed a massive and extremely advanced biological-weapon program.[1] Revelations about extensive clandestine CBW programs in Iraq also came to light after the 1991 Operation Desert Storm and throughout the 1990s as the UN Special Commission (UNSCOM) attempted to verify Iraqi disarmament. And, finally, there were growing concerns about emerging CBW in such countries as Syria, Libya, Iran, Egypt, North Korea, and even such nuclear-weapon powers as China. These chemical- and especially the biological-weapon programs were often viewed as the "poor man's nukes"—although they most likely could not provide the same destructive power as nuclear weapons, they were less expensive and easier to produce, and could potentially be delivered quite readily via missiles and bombers but also by more unconventional methods such as crop dusters or by terrorists.

As a result, the international community worked to create new treaties and verification mechanisms—and to strengthen existing ones—to address these emerging WMD threats. Negotiations on the Chemical Weapons Convention (CWC) were completed and the treaty was opened for signature in 1993.[2] There were also efforts to strengthen the verification mechanisms of the Biological Weapons Convention. In September 1994, the member states of the BWC established the Ad Hoc Group, which began exploring the prospect of onsite inspections to monitor compliance.[3]

There were also efforts to fundamentally reshape the authorities and capabilities of the IAEA to strengthen and shore up the difficulties that had come to light. As is widely recognized in the scholarly literature, the main shortcoming of the international monitoring and verification system at the time was that it was oriented toward confirming declarations by states, rather than detecting diversion or identifying clandestine facilities that could be used to produce fissile materials or weapons without detection.[4] The Additional Protocol (AP) was designed to strengthen the IAEA's authorities in order to address the problems of diversion and clandestine facilities. As we have seen, however, it has subsequently become clear that AP may not be sufficient to prevent a dedicated proliferator from avoiding detection, but at the time there were high hopes that the AP would solve many of the monitoring and verification difficulties that came to light in the 1990s.

Indeed, in the late 1990s the picture was widely viewed as comparatively optimistic. In 1997 or early 1998, one would have had a very different impression of the WMD proliferation threat, and of the future prospects of the various nonproliferation regimes. At that time, the worst fears about the breakup of the Soviet Union—and the prospect of four nuclear-weapon states emerging from the ashes—were not realized. An unprecedented problem had been managed via unprecedented efforts to deal with "loose nukes," the "brain drain," and so on. The list of proliferation's "usual suspects" was decreasing—Argentina, Brazil, and South Africa gave up nuclear programs or weapons. The Nonproliferation Treaty was extended indefinitely in 1995. Efforts to strengthen IAEA safeguards resulted in the Additional Protocol, which was designed to fix the problems that Iraq's illicit program revealed, and North Korea's reaffirmed, in the early 1990s. The CWC had come into force on April 29, 1997, and in July 1997, the Ad Hoc Group began negotiations on a compliance protocol to supplement the BWC, though there remained significant national disagreements on this prospect.[5] Other positive trends at this time could also be noted. Serious problems remained, including NPT holdout states and a few states pursuing nuclear arms despite their nonproliferation obligations, but to many these problems appeared manageable.

However, the picture since then has not been nearly as positive. Not only did negotiations on strengthening the BWC fail in 2001 (owing in part to U.S. objections), but a series of revelations since 2002 compounded ongoing proliferation concerns and brought to light new monitoring and verification challenges. These challenges were unprecedented and included the following:

• *Iran.* The discovery of the large enrichment facility at Natanz as well as other clandestine nuclear and missile activities revealed two decades of Iran's noncompliance with its international obligations. Furthermore, Iran's utilization of "loopholes" within the NPT allowing states to develop complete fuel cycles created very real prospects that Iran, and possibly other states, could develop much of the infrastructure for a nuclear-weapon program while justifying it as a civilian program.

• *North Korea.* North Korea's nuclear tests and its diplomatic brinkmanship highlight the dangers of its long-standing nuclear and missile programs and missile exports. Furthermore, the 2002 revelations of a clandestine North Korean enrichment program—followed by an apparent North Korean confirmation in 2010 of an advanced uranium enrichment program—have raised extreme concerns that North Korea has developed a second pathway to the bomb.

• *Syria.* Following the 2007 Israeli bombing of the suspected Syrian reactor under construction at al-Kibar and an ongoing lack of cooperation by the Syrian government to answer questions about the building and several other sites, the IAEA found Syria to be in noncompliance with its safeguards obligations. The IAEA concluded that site was likely a nuclear reactor and documented Syrian efforts to sanitize the site and others in the country to prevent the IAEA from conducting a thorough investigation.[6]

In addition to these state-level proliferation concerns, new types of challenges have also been emerging, including:

• *New Technologies, Production Methods, and Acquisition Paths for CBW.* Recent advances in production technologies for chemical and biological agents pose new and particularly difficult challenges for CW verification regimes (there are no formal verification mechanisms for biological weapons [BW]). Recent advances include new production techniques; new agents (that may not be banned by the CWC or BWC); and the development of small, multipurpose facilities that are easy to conceal and can produce CBW agents in short runs, mixed in with legitimate agents. The dual-use nature of CBW agents, along with globalization, has also provided a number of acquisition paths for equipment and material that could aid CBW programs. As a result, monitoring and verification may have trouble keeping pace with technology, tracking CBW-related imports, and detecting clandestine facilities.[7]

• *Nuclear Smuggling.* We have seen a growing presence of clandestine non-state supply networks that have enabled proliferating states to develop or supplement clandestine programs. As Herman Nackaerts noted in 2011: "In a number of instances, clandestine supply networks have already offered their services to States intent on developing nuclear weapons."[8] In addition to the extensive smuggling network established by A. Q. Khan, there is evidence that nuclear smuggling networks still exist and have been utilized by such states as North Korea and Iran.[9] It remains troubling that the IAEA's initial response to the revelations that Libya had received substantial assistance from the A. Q. Khan network, including weapons designs and enrichment technologies, was to downplay the significance of the assistance.

• *Growing Cooperation among Proliferating States.* The growing reality of cooperation among rogue states is especially troubling. The nuclear and missile cooperation among North Korea, Pakistan, Iran, and Syria has been examined in the open literature.[10] The question is whether that cooperation was limited to these or a few other states or foreshadows an increasingly deadly future. Clearly, there are a growing number of states that now possess or are developing nuclear- and missile-related technological capabilities and expertise. Will these capabilities be shared, and under what if any constraints? How will these activities be detected and prevented? Will they wind up in black markets?

In recent years, nuclear risks have returned to the fore, though CBW remain a concern. The revelations of the clandestine activities in North Korea, Libya, Iran, and Syria led IAEA deputy director Herman Nackaerts to conclude: "We have not detected, let alone deterred, the clandestine activities of any of these States. This leads me to conclude that the way we have implemented safeguards in the past did not work."[11] Although Nackaerts noted that some of the programs in these "difficult cases" were initiated before the Additional Protocol was negotiated, of these countries, at the time, only Libya had acceded to the AP. Moreover, Nackaerts argues:

> It is worth noting that all of these cases involved only relatively small quantities of nuclear material, or material that had previously been exempted and on which the Agency, in effect, lost interest. I believe that there is a strong case to conclude that our risk model—that is almost exclusively based on declared nuclear material quantities and facility types—did not, and still does not, work either.[12]

Furthermore, as we have seen in the cases studied in this book, in many of the instances when monitoring and verification have been utilized, their effectiveness has been undermined in numerous ways, including divergent and at times politicized interpretations of evidence of noncompliance, incomplete utilization of verification authorities, the application of uneven standards for compliance, and problems with enforcement.

Nor have the prospects for total nuclear disarmament materialized to the degree hoped for, despite the initial excitement generated by President Obama's 2009 Prague speech.[13] Not only did Obama's initiative receive a cool reception from the other recognized and de facto nuclear powers, but upon examination, the prospect of global nuclear abolition would encounter serious monitoring and verification challenges.[14] For this initiative to be successful, the international community would need to resolve an array of difficulties relating to accurate warhead counts; warhead dismantlement sensitivities; uncertainties in fissile material stockpiles; production histories of fissile material enrichment and reprocessing facilities; the potential for concealment of warheads, fissile materials, or facilities; and the problem of latency. It is not clear that the technical capacity yet exists to verify global nuclear disarmament with any certainty—or even what such a monitoring and verification regime would look like. These challenges not only demonstrate the difficulty of verifying disarmament by the existing nuclear powers, but they also demonstrate the difficulties of verifying rollback by states with well-developed nuclear infrastructures such as North Korea and Iran.

Finally, and more recently, the events in Syria and Iran in 2013–15 presented additional and substantial opportunities and challenges for monitoring and verification. The removal of Syria's declared chemical weapons in June 2014 and the negotiation of the 2015 Joint Comprehensive Plan of Action (JCPOA) with Iran were seen as positive steps for international nonproliferation efforts, but it is too soon to determine whether they will be fully successful. In the case of Syria, almost all the attention focused on whether Syria would turn over all of its declared CW stockpile; there was comparatively little attention on whether its declarations were accurate in the first place. There has also been very little recent attention paid to the regime's suspicious nuclear activities and its refusal to answer the IAEA's questions about a possible nuclear-weapon program. In the case of Iran, the monitoring and verification system put in place by the JCPOA introduced greater transparency, but it still remains to be seen how effectively it will be implemented.

Learning—or Relearning—the Important Lessons

The cases of monitoring and verification examined in this book all offer important lessons. However, it is essential that the correct lessons be learned from these cases. In some instances, the most important lessons have not been sufficiently learned, while in others, counterproductive lessons have.

For example, South Africa and Libya have often been taken to be unambiguous success stories and models of voluntary, peaceful, and verifiable disarmament. One must recall the numerous references to South Africa by Hans Blix, Thomas Pickering, and others, as a model for verified disarmament that could be followed in Northeast Asia, the Middle East, or even the current nuclear-weapon states, or Joseph Cirincione's statement that, in contrast to the case of Iraq, "[T]he Libyan model of changing regime behavior has been efficient, effective, and almost cost free."[15]

Similarly, in the aftermath of the 2003 war in Iraq and the controversies over the fact that WMD were not reported to have been found after the regime was toppled, the case of Iraq was often seen as a clear vindication of international monitoring and verification efforts (as opposed to state-led efforts), leading various international organizations and arms control scholars at times to overstate the capabilities of monitoring and verification.[16] There were also instances in which the seriousness of apparent noncompliance was downplayed in order to avoid conditions that could potentially lead to war.[17] More recently, in the cases of Syrian CW disarmament or the agreement on Iran's nuclear program, Obama administration officials, along with many journalists and policy analysts, have seen these agreements as clear successes in the administration's foreign policy.

Overall, the cases examined in this book demonstrate that such optimistic assessments are often overstated. Although these cases demonstrate the essential role of monitoring and verification for international nonproliferation efforts, they also demonstrate sharp limits to monitoring and verification capabilities. Even in the most optimistic cases, ambiguities will remain. The important lessons underscored in these cases include:

Inherent Limitations to Monitoring and Verification

Even in the most optimistic scenarios—involving apparently voluntary disarmament or negotiated rollback and a thorough verification processes—it may be impossible to verify the disarmament with certainty. Although the most positive cases examined in this study, those of South Africa and Libya, were clear success stories, there nevertheless were significant questions that remained after the dismantlement and verification processes took place. Because South Africa dismantled its nuclear weapons and nuclear-weapon infrastructure prior to verification by the IAEA, it is not possible to know for certain if all materials and equipment were destroyed. However, the IAEA's inspections and analyses have been able to reduce the uncertainty significantly. And in the case of Libya, even after an extensive verification and dismantlement process spearheaded by the United States, Great Britain, the IAEA, and the Organization for the Prohibition of Chemical Weapons (OPCW), the regime was subsequently discovered to have retained a covert stockpile of chemical agents and delivery vehicles. But even if the stockpile had not been discovered, it was unclear whether the verification process was thorough enough to justify the confident assessments of Libya's WMD dismantlement.

Moreover, because at best monitoring and verification will rarely produce a "smoking gun" demonstrating noncompliance beyond a shadow of a doubt, these findings will necessarily be open to interpretation. Inconclusive evidence can allow certain states to raise doubts about findings suggesting clandestine activities or other noncompliance. For example, despite repeated evidence presented by UNSCOM suggesting a lack of Iraqi cooperation during the inspections throughout the 1990s, Russia, China, and France interpreted any slightly positive sign as an opportunity to oppose the potential use of force or increase pressure to remove the sanctions from Iraq altogether. Similarly, in the investigations of Syria's alleged chemical weapons use in 2013, the lack of absolutely definitive evidence—or a smoking gun—opened the door for Russia and other states to dispute the evidence.

There May Be Even Greater Inherent Difficulties in Verifying CBW Activities

Although nuclear, biological, and chemical technologies are all dual-use in nature, there are a wider range of civilian applications for materials and technologies that could assist in chemical and biological weapons. As a result, the challenges of tracking imports and transfers of CBW-related materials may be even greater than in the nuclear realm. Moreover, it is also easier to hide CBW facilities than nuclear ones (though it is more possible to hide centrifuge enrichment facilities than gaseous diffusion plants because they take up less space, require less electricity, and can have less distinctive features).

Problems with Implementation of Monitoring and Verification Authorities

Many of the difficulties with monitoring and verification identified in the cases in this book arose from historical problems. In some cases, the programs were started before the negotiation of the AP, or before a particular country joined the CWC. International monitoring and verification organizations thus potentially have more tools at their disposal than in the past. Nevertheless, as we have noted, countries such as Iran, Syria, North Korea, and Myanmar have not ratified the AP, or in some instances, the CWC, so the IAEA and OPCW will still have limited authorities in those countries. (Although Iran has committed to apply the AP "provisionally" as part of the requirements of the JCPOA, it will "seek" formal ratification of the AP in 2023.) As also noted, because the AP does not authorize the IAEA to employ routine inspections "anytime, anyplace," its use in identifying undeclared facilities is real, but more limited than is often understood.

Moreover, as we have seen, the IAEA and OPCW are not sufficiently utilizing all of the tools at their disposal. Although the AP authorizes the IAEA to utilize satellite surveillance and wide-area environmental sampling (WAES), satellite technologies are probably not being used optimally and, in the case of WAES, the technologies are underdeveloped and are generally not available to the agency. And, although the OPCW has the authority to inspect dual-use facilities, it has rarely exercised these authorities.[18] Most notably, however, the IAEA and OPCW have not employed "special" or "challenge" inspections—even in cases in which they would be particularly justified, such as in Syria and Iran.

Resource Constraints

In a speech in October 2014, IAEA director-general Yukiya Amano emphasized the dual challenges of an expanding mission and ongoing resource constraints for the IAEA, stating:

> The number of nuclear facilities coming under IAEA safeguards continues to grow steadily—by 12 percent in the past five years alone. So does the amount of nuclear material to be safeguarded. It has risen by around 14 percent in that period. IAEA resources are limited, demand from Member States for our services continues to grow and our budget is being squeezed. That means that we must constantly find ways of working more effectively and more efficiently in all of our activities, including safeguards.[19]

The IAEA's resource issues can be complicated in the future by expanding missions in nuclear safety, security, and possibly arms control.

The OPCW is underfunded as well. In a strategic plan for 2013–15, the OPCW reported similar resource constraints to those identified by Director-General Amano, and it recommended a similar need to "manage this reality by becoming more efficient in its day-to-day operations within the available appropriations."[20]

Although it is less clear what strategies the OPCW had in mind, Amano did indicate some steps that the IAEA was undertaking to improve efficiency:

> We have developed important new instruments, such as the additional protocol, as I mentioned. We also make increasing use of modern technology such as remote monitoring and satellite imagery. Safeguards implementation continues to evolve, including through what we call the State-level approach. This involves considering a State's nuclear activities and related technical capabilities as a

whole, rather than focusing only on individual facilities. This helps us to keep the frequency and intensity of routine inspections for States to the minimum level necessary to draw credible safeguards conclusions.[21]

The increasing organizational responsibilities and ongoing budget constraints pose real difficulties for international monitoring and verification organizations, and it is clear that these organizations will need to find ways to improve efficiencies. The challenge, however, is improving efficiency without undermining their capabilities. In this context, the IAEA has stated that its responsibilities under the JCPOA will require significant additional funding.[22]

The IAEA must ensure that efficiency measures do not undercut effectiveness, including the transition to the "State-level approach." In the same vein, there is a need to ensure that remote monitoring or other such measures do not inordinately reduce the role of onsite inspections, which remain a vital part of the IAEA's contribution to nonproliferation monitoring and verification. Moreover, while the Additional Protocol does give the IAEA the authority to utilize WAES and satellite imagery, both of these techniques remain underutilized. Given the inherent costs of the application of current technologies in both areas, their increased use would further exacerbate resource constraints.

Transparency and Regime Type

As noted in Chapter 1, in many ways, we appear to be moving toward a globalization of transparency, owing to the potentially transformative effects of commercial surveillance technologies and the rise of social media. Within this changing context, transparency is certain to become more significant for arms control and nonproliferation processes. In this sphere, we can expect transparency initiatives to have one or more of the following goals:

• to foster more formal arms control by breaking down barriers and obstacles;

• to avoid more formal arms control measures and verification procedures, especially in areas in which the items/activities to be controlled were not readily dealt with by traditional verification approaches; and

• to reduce costs, difficulties and intrusiveness of monitoring compliance.[23]

However, the transitions toward global transparency are not uniform among states, owing to historical, cultural, political, and other factors. The differences between democratic and authoritarian, or otherwise closed, regimes are especially important. Although there can be legitimate grounds for nontransparency and legitimate limits to transparency, authoritarian regimes remain more "opaque" than democratic regimes despite the global opening that we have witnessed. Perhaps more important, reflecting the limits to their transparency and in an effort to remain closed, these regimes may be more likely to use denial and deception techniques to weaken, undermine, or circumvent monitoring and verification regimes.[24] This denial and deception can be particularly effective because, in general, such regimes often are able to avoid internal checks on their power, limit the flow of information inside and out of their countries, and stifle domestic opposition that could bring such programs to light.[25]

"Cooperation" Can Be Deceiving

Another important lesson is that the appearance of cooperation can potentially provide cover for noncompliance. As demonstrated in the case of Libya, and apparently to a lesser extent South Africa, there can be a temptation to lower the standards for compliance when a country appears to be cooperating. As we have argued, especially in those countries that have a past record of noncompliance (such as North Korea, Iran, and Syria), apparent cooperation should not be viewed as a sufficient reason to lower verification standards or to assume that a country is entirely serious about rollback. Rather, the past record of noncompliance should, if anything, be grounds for a *higher* verification standard. Cooperation should be commended, but the international community would be well served if it maintained a healthy skepticism and rigorous verification standards, along with a long-term monitoring regime to provide confidence that an apparent change of heart is sincere. Of equal importance, noncooperation with monitoring and verification activities of any kind should be viewed as noncompliance with the attendant obligations.

Problems with Enforcement

One of the most serious challenges to monitoring and verification arises from the problem of enforcement. Historically, countries such as Russia and China have worked to undermine enforcement in cases of noncompliance and noncooperation. In the case of Iraq, the monitoring and verification process in the 1990s was undermined when it became clear that Russia and China would oppose the use of force when Iraq did not cooperate with inspectors. More recently, they have utilized their veto power to prevent strong UN Security Council resolutions calling for sanctions (let alone force) against North Korea, Iran, and Syria. Similarly, when the Obama administration drew a "red line" at CW use by Syria, then subsequently backed away from the possible use of force, the administration it made clear that the United States would no longer consider force to be a serious option if Syria did not cooperate.

As long as there are few prospects for significant enforcement to punish noncompliance through harsh sanctions or, if necessary, force, proliferating states will not be deterred from developing WMD—and states that would otherwise not have considered developing WMD arsenals may revisit their options, either by hedging (developing the capability to develop WMD rapidly if they choose to) or by developing WMD arsenals to counter potential threats. As Mitchell Reiss has emphasized, an ongoing lack of enforcement will have consequences for the nonproliferation regimes as a whole: "Without a sea change in the way the international community conducts its nonproliferation policies, a traditional disincentive to WMD acquisition—fear of penalties and retribution—will continue to wither, and with it the international nonproliferation regimes."[26]

Ambiguity

From measurement uncertainties, to active concealment and deception efforts, to questions about deliberate as opposed to accidental violations, to political judgments in verification, monitoring and verification will always have a degree of ambiguity surrounding them. The verification and compliance process is deeply affected by ambiguity. This ambiguity can be reduced but not eliminated through the use of advanced technologies and novel techniques. There are various technical, political, and budgetary limits that will curb the real application of technologies to monitoring and verification problems in the future. From governmental and perhaps public perspectives, there are potentially significant tradeoffs between cost and other objectives. In any event, it is critical that ambiguity be fully understood and factored into all monitoring and verification calculations.

Latency

Ambiguity is heightened by latency, which is inherent in civil nuclear, biological, and chemical programs. Latency is even more of an issue in cases of rollback. States that gave up WMD programs will necessarily possess latent capabilities—whether it is retained equipment and materials, or simply technical knowledge. Future monitoring and verification regimes will therefore need to address latency in order to detect, if possible, any efforts to reconstitute WMD programs. This will be a huge challenge for future monitoring and verification regimes. In the event of rollback—whether it is undertaken by proliferating states or, eventually, by the current nuclear-weapon states—it would be necessary to negotiate an agreement for long-term monitoring, either by one of the international monitoring and verification organizations (such as the IAEA or OPCW) or by an ad hoc organization created for the purpose.

Steps toward Strengthening Monitoring and Verification

Based on these lessons, there are a clear set of technical and political challenges that need to be addressed if we are to be able to meet future monitoring and verification challenges.

Addressing Cultural and Procedural Constraints

In the short term, the major players in international nonproliferation efforts, including countries such as the United States and Great Britain and organizations like the IAEA and OPCW, need to work more effectively together to improve technological sharing, perform joint exercises, and the like, to strengthen their abilities to monitor and disarm states in cases of declared rollback.

In the longer term, the international community needs to work together to change various cultural and technical constraints that have limited the effectiveness of monitoring and verification regimes. In this context, for example, it is quite troubling that that the IAEA and the OPCW initially displayed similar inclinations to downplay the seriousness of Libya's violations when the nuclear program came to light in 2003 and the undeclared chemical-weapon stockpile came to light in 2011. The IAEA and OPCW also need to make full use of the current authorities and technologies that they already have. For starters, this means a more effective use of "complementary access" of undeclared and dual-use facilities and especially a cultural shift that allows for a greater use of special or challenge inspections. As has been previously argued, the longer that these mechanisms are not utilized, the more difficult it will be to start using them. This, of course, would also require that states and international monitoring organizations make better use of information-sharing in order to combine and better utilize national technical means and the direct information that is acquired on the ground by the monitoring organizations.

Improving Technical Capabilities for Monitoring and Verification

States can also work together with international verifying bodies to develop and implement technologies that can improve monitoring and verification and thus enable the IAEA and OPCW to carry out their authorities more effectively.

To this end, the United States, the European Union, and other members of the international community should devote significant additional resources to research and development (R&D) to improve monitoring capabilities. Although monitoring capabilities have evolved significantly over time, insufficient resources have been devoted toward R&D in the last two decades. Indeed, a comprehensive study by the American Physical Society (APS) concluded that U.S. R&D efforts on safeguards were seriously underfunded, and that "[t]he current Safeguards program largely implements or transfers technologies that are the result of R&D carried out 10–20 years ago."[27]

In an effort to address some of the concerns raised by APS, the Department of Energy's National Nuclear Security Administration established the Next Generation Safeguards Initiative (NGSI) "to develop the policies, concepts, technologies, expertise, and international safeguards structure necessary to strengthen and sustain the international safeguards system as it evolves to meet new challenges."[28] One of the main pillars of this program was to develop and implement a strategic plan for safeguards R&D to make the implementation of safeguards at declared facilities "more efficient and effective by incorporating advances in automation, measurement, and information technology."[29]

Similarly, the Defense Science Board recently conducted a study to "examine a broad range of questions concerning the capability of the Department of Defense, the Department of Energy, and the Intelligence Community to support future monitoring and verification of nuclear nonproliferation and arms control treaties."[30] The study identified an array of new technological and political challenges that complicate and significantly increase the difficulty of monitoring and verification. The board concluded:

> The challenges of controlling and stabilizing the nuclear future, and the difficulty of monitoring global nuclear activities in that future, mean that the nation must plan for a long period of building both the political and technical groundwork for the next major steps in formal treaties or agreements, as well as for addressing proliferation more broadly where cooperation is unlikely for the foreseeable future.[31]

Because of the importance of U.S. leadership as well as its contributions to the development of the IAEA safeguards system and other arms control monitoring and verifications technologies, R&D efforts in the United States and in cooperation with foreign partners have global ramifications.[32] Particular emphasis needs to be placed on developing and expanding capabilities for detecting undeclared WMD facilities.[33] In addition to exploring novel technologies with this goal in mind, it will be important to better utilize two tools in the Additional Protocol.

As noted above, the Additional Protocol gives the IAEA the authority to utilize WAES and satellite imagery, but neither of these tools has been optimally utilized. Although these WAES techniques were used in the inspections in Iraq, they have not been utilized in traditional safeguards monitoring owing to costs and other factors. Similarly, recent technical advances in satellite resolution and multispectrum imagery have improved the capabilities for detecting important changes at facilities, including construction activities, heat signatures, and chemicals that have been introduced into the atmosphere. By more effectively implementing these capabilities, verifying entities will improve their abilities to detect clandestine facilities.[34]

In this context, commercial satellite surveillance may be particularly useful in verifying compliance. Such publicly available methods could in principle improve consensus-building in the international community about suspect WMD programs, because they could allow states to build a case based on unclassified information that may be less open to questioning or suspicions of doctoring intelligence.[35] However, the use of commercial satellites for verification and monitoring could also have some drawbacks. It could complicate the work of the IAEA and the verification and compliance process. For example, given the widespread availability of the Internet, combined with a lack of technical knowledge among the general populace, misleading interpretations of commercial satellite imagery could be used to spread misinformation about suspected WMD programs and to make accusations against states that are in compliance.[36]

In addition to R&D for monitoring and verification, there has been an effort in the Obama administration to increase opportunities for monitoring and verification in the context the Prague agenda. For example, the 2010 Nuclear Posture Review (NPR) called for a national program that included a monitoring and verification R&D program to meet future challenges.[37] In the years following the publication of the NPR, verification R&D has continued at a relatively high level, but the vision embodied in the NPR initiative has not been realized to date. Building on the NPR's proposal, on December 4, 2014, Rose Gottemoeller, U.S. undersecretary of state for arms control and international security, announced a new international verification initiative in which the United States proposed "to work with both nuclear weapon states and non-nuclear weapons states to better understand the technical problems of verifying nuclear disarmament, and to develop solutions."[38]

As we have argued in Chapter 5, "nuclear archeology" may also play an essential role in verifying rollback and disarmament—including in such cases as the current nuclear-weapon states and other states possessing nuclear weapons, as well as the difficult cases of North Korea and Iran.[39] There may be similar techniques in the CBW areas as well. These techniques could be helpful in obtaining an idea of the fissile material, chemical, or biological agent production capacities of WMD-related facilities, which in turn could give verifying organizations some idea of whether a declaration of a given WMD stockpile is roughly accurate and thus whether a state might be hiding an undeclared stockpile. Despite the potential utility of these techniques, they may be limited by the available information on given sites, the costs involved, the accuracy of these techniques, and (especially in the possibility of global nuclear renunciation) whether verifying organizations would be granted sufficient access to the sites.[40]

Relatedly, various states and international organizations are developing "nuclear forensics" methods to aid in international nonproliferation efforts. In the event of a discovery or the use of a nuclear weapon or fissile materials, nuclear forensics could help identify the state of origin of the materials used in the weapon. These techniques have received increasing attention post-9/11, as the threat of nuclear terrorism has been taken more seriously. They could also provide some evidence as to where materials or equipment may have originated, in the event that a country provided assistance to another country's WMD programs. There may be potential applications of nuclear forensic methodologies in other areas as well.[41]

A Greater Utilization of Third-party Information

In the aftermath of the 2003 Iraq War, there has been a reluctance to rely on third-party information, especially national technical means (NTM). This reluctance is understandable. Nevertheless, we must recall that vital information was provided by third parties, including via NTM, in nearly every one of the cases studied in this book. This has been particularly the case, most recently, with the "difficult" cases of North Korea, Iran, and Syria. It is clear that international monitoring and verification entities will need to continue utilizing NTM and other third-party information to supplement their activities, both in ongoing negotiations with the difficult cases, but also as part of any long-term monitoring regime should breakthroughs occur.

Multinational Efforts, Technologies, and Additional Agreements to Close Loopholes and Reduce Opportunities for Proliferation

There has been renewed interest in a number of old ideas on how to address proliferation, including proliferation resistance, and multinational approaches such as fuel banks and front- and back-end fuel-cycle services. Technological advances may make these approaches more feasible than in the past. In addition, there may be a need to negotiate an agreement that will add onto existing authorities provided by the AP. Finally, new initiatives in BW may offer a means of alleviating verification difficulties.

PROLIFERATION RESISTANCE

In the nuclear area, there have been an array of new technologies (including the concept of safeguards by design) and new multinational approaches (including multinational and multilateral ownership of nuclear reactors, enrichment facilities, and other proliferation-sensitive facilities and technologies) that could provide potential methods for preventing nuclear proliferation.[42]

FUEL BANKS AND OTHER MULTINATIONAL APPROACHES

There have been a series of proposals to reduce or eliminate the need for independent state production of nuclear fuel. These options include assuring supplies of nuclear fuel, establishing nuclear fuel banks, and providing for multinational control over enrichment and reprocessing facilities.[43]

ADDITIONAL AUTHORITIES BEYOND THE ADDITIONAL PROTOCOL?

As has been noted, there is a need to make the AP the standard for nonproliferation and export control. Although progress has been made in increasing the number of states that have brought the AP into force, this process remains incomplete—most notably in such cases as North Korea and Syria. In those cases in which the AP has not been ratified, "the Agency is not is a position to fulfill its obligation to confirm that all nuclear material is in peaceful activities and that there are no undeclared nuclear material and activities in these countries."[44]

Nevertheless, as we have also argued, the AP addresses the "Tuwaitha problem" (where Iraq had multiple undeclared buildings in which nuclear-weapon activities were taking place at the declared site) by providing for "complementary access" at undeclared buildings at declared nuclear sites. It also provides, but with more difficult and burdensome requirements, for complimentary access beyond declared sites. Thus, the AP does strengthen the IAEA's authorities in important ways, but these authorities fall far short of the "anytime, anyplace" standard often cited, especially outside of declared sites.[45] Because the strengthened authorities provided by the AP may not be sufficient for allowing the IAEA to discover undeclared facilities and activities, there is a need to begin exploring new IAEA authorities beyond the AP.[46]

NEW INITIATIVES IN BW

Finally, in the area of biological weapons, there is an effort to address the intrinsic difficulties of verification by focusing on industry's self-policing, industry best practices in biosecurity, and industry-government partnerships in the biosecurity arena. The potential benefit of this approach is to ensure that industry understands the issues and acts as a responsible stakeholder in addressing them. It will be possible to address, at least in part, the threat by empowering industry and utilizing industry's knowledge, capacity, and self-interest in controlling and tracking materials.[47]

Some analysts have recently argued that there are a new set of technologies that might make BW verification more feasible than in the past. However, while that is true, it also remains the case that biological production technologies have also advanced, making it more difficult to address BW verification challenges. It is therefore necessary to revisit the BW verification issue on the basis of new challenges and new technical opportunities while continuing to undertake R&D into the most promising technologies to determine whether they could provide effective results at a reasonable cost. In the end, new BW verification technologies are not likely to be decisive, so for the foreseeable future, the international community should continue pursuing BW confidence-building measures and incorporating industry into BW nonproliferation initiatives in tandem with the verification R&D.

Latency and the Need for Long-term Monitoring

As noted, the problem of latency will present challenges to monitoring verification regimes in any instance of rollback of an existing WMD program, whether it is undertaken by a proliferating state or existing nuclear power. Given the potential for latent WMD programs—including retention of stockpiles, equipment, and facilities that could enable state to resuscitate their WMD programs—there need to be mechanisms to implement more intrusive, long-term monitoring to provide greater assurance that a given country did not have an ulterior motive for renouncing its proscribed weapons. It will thus be necessary for a rigorous long-term monitoring regime to accompany any verification of the rollback.[48] This long-term monitoring regime would need to extend beyond the routine authorities of the IAEA or OPCW. And yet, the various ad hoc groups and verification regimes frequently do not have mechanisms for stringent long-term monitoring after noncompliance has been discovered. Where such mechanisms do not exist or may not be adequate to the situation, there is a strong need to need to develop them, if possible prior to the need for their implementation. Moreover, even with strengthened authorities provided by a long-term monitoring agreement, ad hoc groups and organizations such as the IAEA and OPCW will still need to work with states to detect covert facilities and other illicit activities.

Tackling the Problem of Enforcement

The appropriate set of effective and credible monitoring and verification tools are an important part of a global response to proliferation threats, as well as to efforts to reduce nuclear arms. To the extent that these tools are seen as inadequate or biased, however, they will not help, and may hinder consensus.

The technical and procedural steps outlined above could enhance international monitoring and verification regimes and thereby help consolidate a global consensus should apparent violations occur. However, all the technical and procedural fixes in the world would not begin to address the problem of noncompliance with WMD nonproliferation regimes or arms reductions agreements if the international community is not willing to take action—enforcing international law and punishing violators. Given the serious and longstanding disagreements over enforcement within the UN Security Council, it is unlikely that the United Nations will take strong steps to address noncompliance in the foreseeable future. While enforcement should continue to be pursued in the Security Council, as well as within the board of governors of the IAEA and OPCW, until better procedures can be put into place, enforcement is most likely to be achieved through the actions of individual states and coalitions. Such initiatives have produced positive results. For example, most evidence suggests that economic sanctions against Iran by the United States and especially the more recent sanctions by the European Union played a significant role in Iran's decision to negotiate with the P5+1, which resulted in the Interim Agreement and set the stage for the JCPOA.[49] Although the easing of the sanctions as a result of the JCPOA may make it difficult to ratchet up the sanctions on Iran again, despite provisions in the agreement related to "snapback," it does appear that such steps could play a role in future enforcement arrangements. For these reasons, it may be necessary to explore coalitions and regimes outside of the United Nations.

Conclusion: Future Challenges

Even if the steps outlined above are taken, questions will likely remain in *all* cases of WMD rollback. Not only will it be impossible to resolve all questions about potential covert stockpiles or clandestine facilities, but even if certain states were to engage in a verified rollback of WMD programs, the states will necessarily retain at least some degree of latency. In this sense, a certain amount of ambiguity will be unavoidable in cases of rollback.

Unfortunately, the uncertainties with monitoring and verification may be especially prevalent moving forward. The cases that have challenged us in recent years may pale in comparison with the challenges that may arise in the future—including North Korea, Iran, and the prospect for global disarmament. In the difficult cases of Syria, Iran, and North Korea, it is reasonable to expect ongoing efforts to conceal programs and stockpiles, and otherwise disrupt inspection processes. That remains true of Iran, even after the negotiation of the 2015 Joint Comprehensive Plan of Action.

Despite these unavoidable and ongoing challenges, monitoring and verification will remain an essential part of international nonproliferation efforts, and the long-term dangers of ineffective monitoring and verification regimes cannot be overstated. International security depends, in part, upon organizations summoning the political courage to make difficult decisions. These steps to change the cultural and technical constraints, improve cooperation, and more effectively leverage the IAEA's and OPCW's existing authorities to advance nonproliferation efforts would represent a good start.

Reference Matter

Notes

Introduction

1. Paul Kerr, "The IAEA's Report on Iran: An Analysis," *Arms Control Today*, Vol. 33, No. 10 (December 2003), http://www.armscontrol.org/act/2003_12/IAEAreport; Paul K. Kerr, "Iran's Nuclear Program: Status," CRS Report to Congress, Congressional Research Service, November 20, 2008, http://www.fas.org/sgp/crs/nuke/RL34544.pdf.

2. Report by the Director General, "Implementation of the NPT Safeguards Agreement and Relevant Provisions of Security Council Resolutions in the Islamic Republic of Iran," International Atomic Energy Agency, GOV/2011/65, November 8, 2011, p. 7, http://www.iaea.org/sites/default/files/gov2011-65.pdf.

3. Gary Samore et al., *The Iran Nuclear Deal: A Definitive Guide*, Belfer Center for Science and International Affairs, August 2015, p. 22, http://belfercenter.ksg.harvard.edu /files/IranDealDefinitiveGuide.pdf.

4. Joint Comprehensive Plan of Action, July 14, 2015, par. 14, http://www.eeas.europa .eu/statements-eeas/docs/iran_agreement/iran_joint-comprehensive-plan-of-action_ en.pdf.

5. According to the JCPOA, Iran will "provisionally apply the Additional Protocol to its Comprehensive Safeguards Agreement" and proceed with ratification of the AP on "Transition Day," which will occur eight years after Adoption Day, or upon "the date on which the Director General of the IAEA submits a report stating that the IAEA has reached the Broader Conclusion that all nuclear material in Iran remains in peaceful activities, whichever is earlier." (See JCPOA, paragraphs 13, 34.iv; Annex I, Section L; and Annex V, paragraph 15.10.)

6. Joint Comprehensive Plan of Action, Annex I, paragraphs 75–78.

7. Barack Obama, interviewed in "Obama: Iran Will Face Longer 'Breakout Time,' though Not Indefinitely," National Public Radio, August 11, 2015, http://www.npr.org/ sections/parallels/2015/08/11/431652556/obama-iran-will-face-longer-breakout-time -though-not-indefinitely; The White House, "The Iran Nuclear Deal: What You Need to Know," Fact Sheet, n.d., p. 5, https://www.whitehouse.gov/sites/default/files/docs/jcpoa _what_you_need_to_know.pdf.

8. Rebecca Kaplan, "Energy Secretary: Iran Deal Blocks Pathways to Bomb," CBS News, April 5, 2015, http://www.cbsnews.com/news/energy-secretary-iran-deal-blocks-all-pathways-to-a-bomb.

9. The White House, "The Historic Deal That Will Prevent Iran from Acquiring a Nuclear Weapon," Fact Sheet, n.d., https://www.whitehouse.gov/issues/foreign-policy/iran-deal.

10. Ibid.

11. See, for example, The White House, "The Iran Nuclear Deal."

12. Susan Rice, "Press Briefing by Press Secretary Josh Earnest," The White House, Office of the Press Secretary, July 22, 2015, https://www.whitehouse.gov/the-press-office/2015/07/22/press-briefing-press-secretary-josh-earnest-7222015.

13. Josh Earnest, "Press Briefing by Press Secretary Josh Earnest," The White House, Office of the Press Secretary, July 22, 2015, https://www.whitehouse.gov/the-press-office/2015/07/22/press-briefing-press-secretary-josh-earnest-7222015; Tom Carper, "Why I Support the Iran Nuclear Deal," *Delaware Online*, August 28, 2015, http://www.delawareonline.com/story/opinion/contributors/2015/08/28/support-iran-nuclear-deal/71282174; Kristina Wong, "Boxer Announces Support for Iran Deal," *Hill*, August 4, 2014, http://thehill.com/policy/defense/250206-boxer-announces-support-for-iran-deal.

14. Alan J. Kuperman, "The Deal's Fatal Flaw," *New York Times*, June 23, 2015, http://www.nytimes.com/2015/06/23/opinion/the-iran-deals-fatal-flaw.html.

15. David Albright, Houston Wood, and Andrea Stricker, "Breakout Timelines Under the Joint Comprehensive Plan of Action," ISIS Report, Institute for Science and International Security, August 18, 2015, p. 1, http://www.isis-online.org/uploads/isis-reports/documents/Iranian_Breakout_Timelines_and_Issues_18Aug2015_final.pdf.

16. White House, "The Iran Nuclear Deal," p. 6.

17. Michael Rubin, "Enough with the Iran Deal 'Most Intrusive Inspections' Canard," *Commentary*, August 10, 2015, https://www.commentarymagazine.com/foreign-policy/middle-east/iran/iran-inspections-canard.

18. David E. Sanger and Michael R. Gordon, "Future Risks of an Iran Nuclear Deal," *New York Times*, August 23, 2015, http://www.nytimes.com/2015/08/24/world/middleeast/in-pushing-for-the-iran-nuclear-deal-obamas-rationale-shows-flaws.html.

19. Barack Obama, cited in "Transcript: President Obama's Full NPR Interview on Iran Nuclear Deal," National Public Radio, April 7, 2015, www.npr.org/2015/04/07/397933577/transcript-president-obamas-full-npr-interview-on-iran-nuclear-deal.

20. Albright, Wood, and Stricker, "Breakout Timelines Under the Joint Comprehensive Plan of Action," p. 1.

21. See, for example, the comments of Secretary of Energy Ernest Moniz, quoted in Tim Devaney, "Obama Aide: 'Virtually Impossible' for Iran to Hide Nuclear Activity," *Hill*, July 19, 2015, http://thehill.com/policy/international/248444-energy-secretary-virtually-impossible-for-iran-to-hide-nuclear-activity.

22. Michael R. Gordon, "Verification Process in Iran Deal Is Questioned by Some Experts," *New York Times*, July 22, 2015, www.nytimes.com/2015/07/23/world/middleeast/provision-in-iran-accord-is-challenged-by-some-nuclear-experts.html.

23. Yukiya Amano, "IAEA Director General's Remarks to the Press on Visit to Iran," International Atomic Energy Agency, September 21, 2015, https://www.iaea.org/news center/statements/iaea-director-generals-remarks-press-visit-iran.

24. Olli Heinonen, interviewed in Raphael Ahren, "Parchin Inspection Plan Won't Work, IAEA's Credibility on the Line, Says Ex-Deputy," *Times of Israel*, September 4, 2015, www.timesofisrael.com/parchin-inspection-plan-flawed-iaeas-credibility-on-the -line-says-ex-deputy.

25. Samore et al., *The Iran Nuclear Deal*, p. 58. For a more detailed description of the sanctions relief outlined in the JCPOA, see Chapter 6 of this volume.

26. Joint Comprehensive Plan of Action, par. 36–37.

27. Menendez Delivers Remarks on Iran Nuclear Deal at Seton Hall University's School of Diplomacy and International Relations," Press Release, August 18, 2015, www .menendez.senate.gov/news-and-events/press/menendez-deliversremarks-on-iran-nu clear-deal-at-seton-hall-universitys-school-of-diplomacy-and-international-relations.

28. Parisa Hafezi and Louis Charbonneau, "Iran Demands End to U.N. Missile Sanctions, West Refuses," Reuters, July 6, 2015, http://uk.reuters.com/article/2015/07/06/uk-iran-nuclear-idUKKCN0PF0HE20150706; Gordon Lubold and Felicia Schwartz, "Critics of Iran Nuclear Deal Target Arms," *Wall Street Journal*, July 19, 2015, www.wsj .com/articles/critics-of-iran-nuclear-deal-target-armslifting-restrictions-1437348535.

29. Hafezi and Charbonneau, "Iran Demands End to U.N. Missile Sanctions.

30. CBS News, "U.S. Suggests Iran Ballistic Missile Test Might Be U.N. Violation," October 13, 2015, www.cbsnews.com/news/us-suggests-iran-ballistic-missile-test-might -be-un-violation. UNSC Resolution 2231 calls on Iran "not to undertake any activity re- lated to ballistic missiles designed to be capable of delivering nuclear weapons, including launches using such ballistic missile technology." See UN Security Council, "Resolution 2231," S/RES/2231 (2015), July 20, 2015, www.un.org/en/sc/inc/pages/pdf/pow/RES2231E .pdf.

31. Ben Brumfield, "It's 'Adoption Day'—Launch Time for the Iran Nuclear Deal," *CNN*, October 19, 2015, www.cnn.com/2015/10/18/middleeast/iran-nuclear-deal-adoption -day.

32. See David Albright and Corey Hinderstein, "Verifiable, Cooperative Dismantle- ment of the DPRK's Nuclear Weapons Program," Paper presented at the Institute for Nu- clear Materials Management (INMM) Annual Meeting, Orlando, Florida, June 15, 2004, www.isis-online.org/publications/dprk/dprk_cooperative_dismantlement.html; Ron Cle- minson, "International Verification of WMD Proliferation: Applying UNMOVIC's Lega- cy," *Journal of Military and Strategic Studies*, Vol. 9, No. 3 (Spring 2006/7), www.jmss.org/ jmss/index.php/jmss/article/view/104; Trevor Findlay, "Preserving UNMOVIC: The insti-

tutional Possibilities," *Disarmament Diplomacy*, No. 76 (March/April 2004), www.acronym
.org.uk/dd/dd76/76tf.htm; Paula DeSutter, Assistant Secretary of State for Verification and
Compliance, quoted in "U.S. Points to Libya as Disarmament Model," *Arms Control Today*,
Vol. 34, No. 3 (April 2004), p. 29, www.armscontrol.org/act/2004_04/DeSutter.asp; Paul
Kerr, "Libya's Disarmament: A Model for U.S. Policy?" *Arms Control Today*, Vol. 34, No.
5 (June 2004), pp. 36–38, www.armscontrol.org/act/2004_06/News Analysis.asp; Jessica
Tuchman Mathews, "The Lost Opportunity in Iraq," *Washington Post*, December 26, 2011,
http://carnegieendowment.org/2011/12/26/lost-opportunity-in -iraq/8pik.

33.   See John Hart and Vitali Fedchenko, "Inspection and Verification Regimes," in Nathan E. Busch and Daniel H. Joyner, *Combating Weapons of Mass Destruction: The Future of
International Nonproliferation Policy* (Athens: University of Georgia Press, 2009), p. 104.

34.   Despite the highly politicized nature of these issues, there is little question that
the Iraqi regime attempted to conceal parts of its WMD materials and programs well
into the late 1990s, if not later. See, for example, Richard Butler, *The Greatest Threat: Iraq,
Weapons of Mass Destruction, and the Growing Crisis of Global Security* (New York: PublicAffairs, 2000); and Tim Trevan, *Saddam's Secrets: The Hunt for Iraq's Hidden Weapons*
(London: HarperCollins Publishers, 1999). See also the numerous UNSCOM reports,
documented at "United Nations Special Commission," United Nations website, www
.un.org/depts/unscom/unscmdoc.htm, accessed August 8, 2013.

35.   On "denial and deception," see Roy Godson and James Wirtz, eds., *Strategic Denial and Deception: The Twenty-First Century Challenge* (New Brunswick, NJ: Transaction Publishers, 2002); David A. Kay, "Denial and Deception Practices of WMD Proliferators: Iraq and Beyond," *Washington Quarterly*, Vol. 18, No. 1 (Winter 1995), pp. 85–105;
Nathan Busch, "Risks of Nuclear Terror: Vulnerabilities of Thefts and Sabotage at Nuclear Weapons Facilities," *Contemporary Security Policy*, Vol. 23, No. 3 (December 2002),
pp. 19–60. On other obstacles to effective verification, see Hart and Fedchenko, "Inspection and Verification Regimes," pp. 95–117; and Ephraim Asculai, *Verification Revisited:
The Nuclear Case* (Washington, DC: Institute for Science and International Security
Press, 2002), pp. 7–11.

36.   The classical discussion of this problem is Fred Charles Iklé, "After Detection—
What?" *Foreign Affairs*, Vol. 39 (January 1961), pp. 208–20.

37.   On "denial and deception," see Godson and Wirtz, *Strategic Denial and Deception*; Busch, "Risks of Nuclear Terror," pp. 19–60. On other of these obstacles to effective
verification, see Hart and Fedchenko, "Inspection and Verification Regimes," pp. 109–12;
Asculai, *Verification Revisited*, pp. 51–68.

38.   David Albright, "South Africa's Nuclear Weapons Program," Lecture given at
the Massachusetts Institute of Technology, March 14, 2001, http://web.mit.edu/ssp/semi
nars/wed_archives01spring/albright.htm.

39.   Mitchell Reiss, *Bridled Ambition: Why Countries Constrain Their Nuclear Capabilities* (Baltimore, MD: Johns Hopkins University Press, 1995), pp. 24–27; Olli Heinonen,

"Verifying the Dismantlement of South Africa's Nuclear Weapons Program," in Henry Sokolski, ed., *Nuclear Weapons Materials Gone Missing: What Does History Teach?* (Arlington, VA: Nonproliferation Policy Education Center, March 2014), pp. 88–99, http://npolicy.org/books/2014muf/Nuclear%20Weapons%20Materials%20Gone%20Missing.pdf; Jodi Lieberman, "Dismantling the South African Nuclear Weapons Program: Lessons Learned and Questions Unresolved," in Henry Sokolski, ed., *Nuclear Weapons Materials Gone Missing: What Does History Teach?* (Arlington, VA: Nonproliferation Policy Education Center, March 2014), p. 85, http://npolicy.org/books/2014muf/Nuclear%20Weapons%20Materials%20Gone%20Missing.pdf.

40. Jeffrey M. Bale, "South Africa's Project Coast: 'Death Squads,' Covert State-Sponsored Poisonings, and the Dangers of CBW Proliferation," *Democracy and Security*, Vol. 2, No. 1 (January 2006), p. 46.

41. UN Monitoring Verification and Inspection Commission, "Unresolved Disarmament Issues: Iraq's Proscribed Weapons Programs," UNMOVIC Working Document, March 6, 2003, www.un.org/Depts/unmovic/documents/UNMOVIC%20UDI%20Working%20Document %206%20March%202003.pdf.

42. Jessica Tuchman Mathews, "What Happened in Iraq? The Success Story of United Nations Inspections," Keynote Speech to the International Peace Academy, March 5, 2004, http://carnegieendowment.org/2004/03/10/wmd-and-united-nations/2f99, accessed August 8, 2013.

43. Commission on the Intelligence Capabilities of the United States Regarding Weapons of Mass Destruction, Report to the President of the United States (also known as the Robb-Silberman Report), Government Printing Office, March 31, 2005, p. 263, www.gpo.gov/fdsys/pkg/GPO-WMD/pdf/GPO-WMD.pdfp. 262.

44. Ibid., p. 263.

45. Remarks by President Barack Obama, Hradcany Square, Prague, Czech Republic, April 5, 2009, www.whitehouse.gov/the_press_office/Remarks-By-President-Barack-Obama-In-Prague-As-Delivered.

46. Ibid.

47. For a similar assessment, see Terence Taylor, "Building on the Experience: Lessons from UNSCOM and UNMOVIC," *Disarmament Diplomacy*, No. 75 (January-February 2004), www.acronym.org.uk/dd/dd75/75tt.htm.

Chapter 1

1. David Albright and Kevin O'Neill, "The North Korean Nuclear Program: Unresolved Issues," ISIS Report, Institute for Science and International Security, June 6, 1994, http://isis-online.org/isis-reports/detail/the-north-korean-nuclear-program-unresolved-iussues/10.

2. This incident is related in Tim Trevan, *Saddam's Secrets: The Hunt for Iraq's Hidden Weapons* (London: HarperCollins Publishers, 1999), pp. 352–56.

3. Report by the Director General, "Implementation of the NPT Safeguards Agreement and Relevant Provisions of Security Council Resolutions in the Islamic Republic of Iran," GOV/2011/65, November 8, 2011, p. 7, www.iaea.org/sites/default/files/gov2011-65 .pdf.

4. Ibid., "Annex," p. 3.

5. Peter Crail, "IAEA Lays Out Iran Weapons Suspicions," *Arms Control Today*, Vol. 41, No. 10 (December 2011), pp. 21–31, http://armscontrol.org/act/2011_12/IAEA_Lays_ Out_Iran_Weapons_Suspicions.

6. The literature on monitoring and verification is extensive. See, for example, Allan S. Krass, *Verification: How Much Is Enough?* (London: Taylor and Francis, 1985); Kostas Tsipis, David W. Hafemeister, and Penny Janeway, eds., *Arms Control Verification: The Technologies That Make It Possible* (Washington, DC: Pergamon-Brassey's, 1986); Bhupendra Jasani and Toshibomi Sakata, eds., *Satellites for Arms Control and Crisis Monitoring* (Oxford: Oxford University Press for SIPRI, 1987); Jürgen Altman and Joseph Rotblat, eds., *Verification of Arms Reductions: Nuclear, Conventional and Chemical* (Berlin: Spriuger-Verlag, 1989); Frank Barnaby, *A Handbook of Verification Procedures* (London: Macmillan, 1990); United Nations, *Verification in All Its Aspects: Study on the Role of the United Nations in the Field of Verification* (A/45/372, August 28, 1990); Office of Technological Assessment, *Verification Technologies: Cooperative Aerial Surveillance in International Agreements* (Washington, DC: U.S. Government Printing Office, July 1991); United Nations, *Verification in All its Aspects, including the Role of the United Nations in the Field of Verification* (A/50/377, September 22, 1995); Joseph F. Pilat, "Arms Control, Verification, and Transparency," in Jeffrey A. Larsen and Gregory J. Rattray, eds., *Arms Control Toward the 21st Century* (Boulder, CO: Lynne Rienner Publishers, 1996), pp. 77–98; Nancy W. Gallagher, *The Politics of Verification* (Baltimore, MD: Johns Hopkins University Press Baltimore, 1999); Erwin Häckel and Gotthard Stein, eds., *Tightening the Reins: Towards a Strengthened International Nuclear Safeguards System*, German Society for Foreign Affairs (Berlin: Springer, 2000); Graham S. Pearson, *The UNSCOM Saga: Chemical and Biological Weapons Non-Proliferation* (Basingstoke: Palgrave, 2000); Michael May, ed., *Verifying the Agreed Framework*, A Joint Report by The Centre for International Security and Cooperation (CISAC), Stanford, CA, and The Center for Global Security Research (CGSR), Livermore, CA (April 2001); Joseph F. Pilat, "Verification and Transparency: Relics or Future Requirements?" in Jeffrey A. Larsen, ed., *Arms Control: Cooperative Security in a Changing Environment* (Boulder, CO: Lynne Rienner Publishers, 2002), pp. 79–96; and Jonathan B. Tucker, ed., *The Chemical Weapons Convention: Implementation Challenges and Solutions* (Monterey, CA: Centre for Non-Proliferation Studies, Monterey Institute of International Studies, April 2001).

7. The literature on compliance is also extensive. See, for example, Julie Dahlitz, *Avoidance and Settlement of Arms Control Disputes: Follow-up Studies Subsequent to the Symposium on the International Law of Arms Control and Disarmament* (New York: Unit-

ed Nations, 1994); Abram Chayes and Antonia Handler Chayes, *The New Sovereignty: Compliance with International Regulatory Agreements* (Cambridge, MA: Harvard University Press, 1998); Canadian Council on International Law and The Markland Group, *Treaty Compliance: Some Concerns and Remedies*, Nijhoff Law Specials, Vol. 32 (London: Kluwer Law International, 1998); Joseph Goldblat, *Ways to Improve the Implementation and Enforcement of Arms Control Agreements: Role of Verification*, Geneva Centre for Security Policy, Occasional Paper Series, No. 19, Geneva (August 2000); Harald Müller, "Compliance Politics: A Critical Analysis of Multilateral Arms Control Treaty Enforcement," *Nonproliferation Review*, Vol. 7, No. 2 (Summer 2000); and Michael Moodie and Amy Sands, "New Approaches to Compliance with Arms Control and Nonproliferation Agreements," *Nonproliferation Review*, Vol. 8, No. 1 (Spring 2001), pp. 1–9.

8. Verification, by providing information related to forces or activities, can provide political benefits to a state's intelligence apparatus, whether or not related to the verified accord. For this reason alone, states without strong intelligence capabilities might pursue more intrusive verification during treaty negotiations. On the other hand, states with intelligence assets may not have to rely on agreed verification provisions as much as others.

9. In addition to these international regimes, in some cases regional monitoring has been established via bilateral or by smaller multilateral agreements. The most important regional organizations include the European Atom Energy Community (EURATOM) and the Brazilian-Argentine Agency for Accounting and Control of Nuclear Materials (ABACC), though most of their activities are coordinated very closely with the IAEA. (See the "EURATOM" and "ABACC" entries in *Inventory of International Nonproliferation Organizations and Regimes*, Center for Nonproliferation Studies, May 10, 2013, http://cns.miis.edu/inventory/organizations.htm.)

10. David Fischer, *History of the International Atomic Energy Agency: The First Forty Years* (International Atomic Energy Agency, 1997), p. 246, www-pub.iaea.org/mtcd/pub lications/pdf/pub1032_web.pdf.

11. Quoted in ibid., p. 249.

12. Ibid.

13. Center for Nonproliferation Studies web database, Monterey Institute for International Studies, http://cns.miis.edu/db/china/iaeasg.htm. For the text of INFCIRC/66, see the IAEA web page: www.iaea.org/worldatom/Documents/Infcircs/Others/inf66r2 .shtml.

14. *Treaty on the Nonproliferation of Nuclear Weapons* (July 1, 1968), Article III, www .un.org/en/conf/npt/2005/npttreaty.html.

15. INFCIRC/153 places no specific requirements on the NWSs. This fact, however, was the cause of intense debate during the negotiations and for several years after the NPT was concluded and entered into force. Many of the nonnuclear-weapon states were concerned that the full scope safeguards would give the NWSs a competitive advantage

in their peaceful nuclear programs. In order to address these and other concerns, President Johnson offered in 1967 to apply safeguards to all nuclear activities in the United States other than those with direct national security significance. The U.S. offer entered into force in 1980. The United Kingdom, France, Russia, and China also subsequently made voluntary agreements, with varying degrees of coverage of civil facilities. None of these agreements involve safeguards on the nuclear-weapon programs in these states. For details on the U.S. agreement, see U.S. Department of State, *Agreement between the United States of America and the International Atomic Energy Agency for the Application of Safeguards in the United States (and Protocol Thereto)*, 1980, www.state.gov/t/isn/5209 .htm. For details on the commitment of the Soviet Union and China, see Fischer, *History of the International Atomic Energy Agency*, pp. 271–72.

16. International Atomic Energy Agency, "The Structure and Content of Agreements between the Agency and States Required in Connection with the Treaty on the Non-Proliferation of Nuclear Weapons," INFCIRC/153, June 1972, section I.7, www.iaea .org/Publications/Documents/Infcircs/Others/infcirc153.pdfINFCIRC/153.

17. Ibid., par. 72.

18. Ibid., par. 73.

19. Demetrius Perricos, interviewed in "Understanding the Lessons of Nuclear Inspections and Monitoring in Iraq: A Ten-Year Review: Perricos," conference hosted by the Institute for Science and International Security, June 14–15, 2001 (transcript date, August 28, 2001), http://isis-online.org/perricos.

20. Theodore Hirsch, "The IAEA Additional Protocol: What It Is and Why It Matters," *Nonproliferation Review*, Vol. 11, No. 13 (Fall–Winter, 2004), p. 142.

21. Ibid., pp. 142–43; Olli Heinonen, "The Case for an Immediate IAEA Special Inspection in Syria," *Policy Watch*, November 5, 2010, http://www.washingtoninstitute.org/ policy-analysis/view/the-case-for-an-immediate-iaea-special-inspection-in-syria.

22. Matthew Bunn, "International Safeguards: Summarizing 'Traditional' and 'New' Measures," MIT OpenCourseWare Web Site, Spring 2004, pp. 3–4, http://ocw.mit .edu/courses/nuclear-engineering/22-812j-managing-nuclear-technology-spring-2004/ lecture-notes/lec16notes.pdf.

23. "The 1997 IAEA Additional Protocol at a Glance," Arms Control Association, December 2012, www.armscontrol.org/factsheets/IAEAProtoco.

24. Ibid.

25. Ibid.

26. For a list of the countries that have signed and/or ratified the AP, see International Atomic Energy Agency, "Conclusion of Additional Protocols: Status as of 21 May 2014," May 21, 2014, www.iaea.org/safeguards/documents/AP_status_list.pdf.

27. As part of the terms outlined in the 2015 Joint Comprehensive Plan of Action, Iran will "provisionally apply the Additional Protocol to its Comprehensive Safeguards Agreement" and proceed with ratification of the AP on "Transition Day," which will occur eight

years after Adoption Day. (See Joint Comprehensive Plan of Action, July 14, 2015, paragraphs 13, 34.iv; Annex I, Section L; and Annex V, paragraph 15.10, www.eeas.europa.eu/statements-eeas/docs/iran_agreement/iran_joint-comprehensive-plan-of-action_en.pdf.)

28. Mark Hibbs, "The Unspectacular Future of the IAEA Additional Protocol," *Proliferation Analysis*, Carnegie Endowment for International Peace, April 26, 2012, p. 3, http://carnegieendowment.org/2012/04/26/unspectacular-future-of-iaea-additional -protocol/ahhz.

29. Herman Nackaerts, "Towards More Effective Safeguards: Learning Hard Lessons," Opening Plenary Address, INMM Annual Meeting, July 18, 2011, p. 3, www.inmm.org/AM/Template.cfm?Section=Evolving_the_IAEA_State_Level_Concept&Template=/CM/ContentDisplay.cfm&ContentID=2971.

30. Gene Aloise, "Nuclear Nonproliferation: IAEA Safeguards and Other Measures to Halt the Spread of Nuclear Weapons and Material," testimony before the Subcommittee on National Security, Emerging Threats, and International Relations, U.S. House of Representatives, September 26, 2006, www.gao.gov/new.items/d061128t.pdf.

31. Ibid.

32. Ibid.

33. See Jonathan B. Tucker, "Strengthening the Biological Weapons Convention," *Arms Control Today*, Vol. 25, No. 3 (April 1995), p. 9.

34. For a list of these countries, as well as a description of biological weapons proliferation, see Joseph Cirincione, Jon Wolfsthal, and Mirian Rajkumar, *Deadly Arsenals: Nuclear, Biological, and Chemical Threats* (Washington, DC: Carnegie Endowment for International Peace, 2005), ch. 4, pp. 57–82.

35. Laura H. Kahn, "The Biological Weapons Convention: Proceeding without a Verification Protocol," *Bulletin of the Atomic Scientists*, May 9, 2011, http://thebulletin .org/biological-weapons-convention-proceeding-without-verification-protocol. See also Filippa Lentzos, "Hard to Prove: The Verification Quandary of the Biological Weapons Convention," *Nonproliferation Review*, Vol. 18, No. 3 (November 2011), pp. 571–82.

36. John Hart and Vitaly Fedchenko, "Inspection and Verification Regimes," in Nathan E. Busch and Daniel H. Joyner, *Combating Weapons of Mass Destruction: The Future of International Nonproliferation Policy* (Athens: University of Georgia Press, 2009), p. 102.

37. For a comprehensive presentation of the Bush administration's position on the proposed BWC protocol, see Ambassador Donald Mahley, "Biological Weapons Convention," statement by the United States to the Ad Hoc Group of Biological Weapons Convention States Parties, Geneva, Switzerland, July 25, 2001, http://2001-2009.state .gov/t/ac/rls/rm/2001/5497.htm, accessed August 8, 2013.

38. Ibid.

39. Ibid., p. 2.

40. Ibid., p. 3.

41. Ibid., p. 6.

42. Ibid.

43. Ibid., p. 2.

44. See, for example, Jonathan B. Tucker, "Re-envisioning the Chemical Weapons Convention," *Bulletin of the Atomic Scientists*, May 2, 2011, http://thebulletin.org/re-en visioning-chemical-weapons-convention; Jonathan B. Tucker, "Growing Together: Biological and Chemical Threats," *Science Progress*, February 2, 2011, http://scienceprogress .org/2011/02/growing-together/.

45. Gregory D. Koblentz, "From Biodefense to Biosecurity: The Obama Administration's Strategy for Countering Biological Threats," *International Affairs*, Vol. 88, No. 1 (January 2012), p. 137.

46. Mark Lander, "Obama Administration Takes a New Approach to Biological Weapons," *New York Times*, December 8, 2009, www.nytimes.com/2009/12/09/world /09biowar.html, accessed August 8, 2013.

47. Ellen Tauscher, "Preventing Biological Weapons Proliferation and Bioterrorism," Address to the Annual Meeting of the States Parties to the Biological Weapons Convention, Geneva, Switzerland, December 9, 2009, www.state.gov/t/us/133335.htm, accessed August 8, 2013.

48. See Barack Obama, *National Strategy for Countering Biological Threats* (Washington, DC: National Security Council, November 2009), p. 1, www.whitehouse.gov/sites /default/files/National_Strategy_for_Countering_BioThreats.pdf.

49. Koblentz, "From Biodefense to Biosecurity," p. 132.

50. Bob Graham, Jim Talent, Graham Allison, Robin Cleveland, Steve Rademaker, Tim Roemer, Wendy Sherman, Henry Sokolski, and Rich Verma, *World at Risk: The Report of the Commission on the Prevention of WMD Proliferation and Terrorism* (New York: Vintage Books, 2008), p. 11.

51. Obama, *National Strategy for Countering Biological Threats*, pp. 8–9, 15–17.

52. Gregory Koblentz, "Pathogens as Weapons: The International Security Implications of Biological Warfare," *International Security*, Vol. 28, No. 3 (Winter 2003/4), pp. 98–99.

53. The Chemical Weapons Convention opened for signature in 1993 and entered into force on April 29, 1997. It prohibits the development, production, stockpiling, retention, transfer, and use of chemical weapons. It also bans engaging in any military preparation for use of CW and assisting any other states in developing them. At the time of this writing, the CWC had 192 states-parties. Israel has signed but not ratified the convention; North Korea has never signed the treaty. See Organization for the Prohibition of Chemical Weapons, "Non-Member States," n.d., www.opcw.org/about-opcw/ non-member-states.

54. Jonathan B. Tucker, "Verifying the Chemical Weapons Ban: Missing Elements," *Arms Control Today*, Vol. 37, No. 1 (January-February 2007), pp. 6–13, www.armscontrol .org/act/2007_01-02/Tucker.

55. "Guidelines for Schedules of Chemicals," OPCW website, www.opcw.org/?52,15,02,01,04,2007; Arms Control Association, "The Chemical Weapons Convention (CWC) at a Glance," September 2013, https://www.armscontrol.org/factsheets/cwcglance.

56. Tucker, "Verifying the Chemical Weapons Ban."

57. Organization for the Prohibition of Chemical Weapons, "Convention on the Prohibition of the Development, Production, Stockpiling and Use of Chemical Weapons and on Their Destruction (Chemical Weapons Convention)," OPCW website, www.opcw.org/chemical-weapons-convention.

58. Jonathan B. Tucker, "Introduction," in Jonathan B. Tucker, ed., *The Chemical Weapons Convention: Implementation Challenges and Solutions* (Monterey, CA: Monterey Institute for International Studies, April 2001), p. 4, http://cns.miis.edu/reports/pdfs/tuckcwc.pdf.

59. Tucker, "Verifying the Chemical Weapons Ban."

60. Ibid.

61. Ibid.

62. Ibid.

63. Ibid.

64. Ibid., p. 7.

65. Ibid., p. 8.

66. Kenneth E. Apt, "Verification of the Chemical Weapons Convention: Maximizing Technical Effectiveness," *Briefing*, Vol. 3, No. 3 (April 24, 1992), LA-UR-92-1187, Los Alamos National Laboratory, Center for National Security Studies, pp. 3–4.

67. Ibid.

68. Tucker, "Verifying the Chemical Weapons Ban."

69. Ibid.

70. Hart and Fedchenko, "Inspection and Verification Regimes," pp. 104–6.

71. Ibid., pp. 105–6.

72. UN Security Council Resolution 687, April 3, 1991. See also Ephraim Asculai, *Verification Revisited: The Nuclear Case* (Washington, DC: Institute for Science and International Security Press, 2002), p. 35; and "Iraq: The UNSCOM Experience," SIPRI Fact Sheet, Stockholm International Peace Research Institute, October 1998, p. 2, http://editors.sipri.se/pubs/Factsheet/UNSCOM.pdf. For the text of UNSCR 687, see www2.unog.ch/uncc/resolutio/res0687.pdf.

73. Graham S. Pearson, *The Search for Iraq's Weapons of Mass Destruction: Inspection, Verification, and Nonproliferation* (New York: Palgrave Macmillan, 2005), p. 28.

74. For detailed accounts of these events, see Pearson, *The Search for Iraq's Weapons of Mass Destruction*, pp. 26–95; Trevan, *Saddam's Secrets*, pp. 21–38; and Richard Butler, *The Greatest Threat: Iraq, Weapons of Mass Destruction, and the Growing Crisis of Global Security* (New York: PublicAffairs, 2000), pp. 200–222.

75. See *Letter Dated 15 December 1998 from the Secretary-General Addressed to the President of the Security Council*, S/1998/1172, December 15, 1998, www.un.org/Depts/uns com/s98-1172.htm. For a firsthand account of the events leading up to this report, see Butler, *The Greatest Threat*, pp. 200–222.

76. Hans Blix, "Oral Introduction of the 12th Quarterly Report of UNMOVIC," Report to the UN Security Council, March 7, 2003, www.un.org/Depts/unmovic/SC7asde livered.htm.

77. Jack Boureston and Yana Feldman, "Verifying Libya's Nuclear Dismantlement," *Verification Yearbook, 2004*, p. 87, www.vertic.org/media/Archived_Publications/Year books/2004/VY04_Boureston-Feldman.pdf.

78. Paula DeSutter, testimony, hearing before the Subcommittee on International Terrorism, Nonproliferation, and Human Rights, Subcommittee on International Relations, U.S. House of Representatives, September 22, 2004, http://www.state.gov/s/l/2004 /78305.htm.

79. Ibid.

80. For perhaps the best resource utilizing open-source satellite imagery to support monitoring and verification efforts, see the work of David Albright at the Institute for Science and International Security (ISIS), www.isis-online.org. See also Frank V. Pabian, "Evidence from Imagery: The Iran and Syrian Nuclear Programs—An Open and Shut Case?" Lecture given at the James Martin Center for Nonproliferation Studies, Monterey, CA, October 28, 2009, www.youtube.fcom/watch?v=JkXbbHMKpHk; Hui Zhang and Frank N. von Hippel, "Using Commercial Imaging Satellites to Detect the Operation of Plutonium-production Reactors and Gaseous-diffusion Plants?" *Science and Global Security*, Vol. 8, No. 3 (September 2000), pp. 219–71, http://belfercenter.ksg .harvard.edu/files/8_3newZhang.pdf; MITRE Corporation, "Open and Crowd-Sourced Data for Treaty Verification," JASON Program Office, JSR-14-TASK-015, October 2014, pp. 27–33, www.dtic.mil/dtic/tr/fulltext/u2/a614684.pdf.

81. MITRE, "Open and Crowd-Sourced Data," p. 35.

82. Olli Heinonen, "IAEA Safeguards—Evolving to Meet Today's Verification Undertakings," Conference Paper, Belfer Center for Science and International Affairs, July 12, 2013, http://belfercenter.ksg.harvard.edu/publication/23241/iaea_safeguards_evolving_to_meet_todays_verification_undertakings.html.

83. Ibid.

84. Apt, "Verification of the Chemical Weapons Convention," pp. 3–4.

85. Ibid., p. 6. See also Hans Blix, "The A-Bomb Squad," *World Monitor*, November 1991, pp. 18–21.

86. Apt, "Verification of the Chemical Weapons Convention," p. 6.

87. Ibid., p. 7.

88. Hart and Fedchenko, "Inspection and Verification Regimes," p. 102.

89. Gregory L. Schulte, "Strengthening the IAEA: How the Nuclear Watchdog Can

Regain Its Bark," *Strategic Forum*, No. 253 (March 2010), p. 3, www.ndu.edu/inss/docup-loaded/sf%20253_web.pdf, accessed August 8, 2013.

90. See Jack Shenker, "Cautious Reports on Tehran Nuclear Programme 'Were Framed to Avoid War,'" *Guardian*, March 31, 2010, www.guardian.co.uk/world/2010/mar/31/iran-nuclear-programme-cautious-language.

91. Tucker, "Introduction," p. 6.

92. Ibid.

Chapter 2

1. Mitchell Reiss, *Bridled Ambition: Why Countries Constrain Their Nuclear Capabilities* (Baltimore, MD: Johns Hopkins University Press, 1995), pp. 11–12.

2. Ibid., p. 7; Waldo Stumpf, "South Africa's Nuclear Weapons Program: From Deterrence to Dismantlement," *Arms Control Today*, Vol. 25, No. 10 (December 1995/January 1996), p. 3.

3. See, for example, U.S. Central Intelligence Agency, Directorate of Intelligence, "Prospects for Further Proliferation of Nuclear Weapons," October 2, 1974, classified interagency intelligence memorandum, partially declassified and released, Digital National Security Archive, http://nsarchive.chadwyk.com; U.S. Central Intelligence Agency, "South African Enrichment Program," August 1977, declassified document in the National Security Archive, www.gwu.edu/~nsarchiv/NSAEBB/NSAEBB181/sa16.pdf.

4. On South Africa's obligations to declare elements of past nuclear weapons, see Stumpf, "South Africa's Nuclear Weapons Program," p. 3. For discussions of South Africa's deception of the IAEA, including the camouflage and concealment of its nuclear weapons related facilities, see Frank V. Pabian, "The South African Denuclearization Exemplar: Insights for Nonproliferation," Los Alamos Unclassified Report, LA-UR # 12-25213, December 2012, pp. 20–23; Nuclear Proliferation International History Project, "NPIHP Releases 20 Documents on the South African Nuclear Program," Woodrow Wilson International Center for Scholars, February 1, 2012, www.wilsoncenter.org/article/npihp-releases-20-document-the-south-african-nuclear-program; David Albright, Paul Brannan, Zachary Laporte, Katherine Tajer, and Christina Walrond, "Rendering Useless South Africa's Nuclear Test Shafts in the Kalahari Desert," ISIS Report, Institute for Science and International Security, November 30, 2011, http://isis-online.org/uploads/isis-reports/documents/Vastrap_30November2011.pdf.

5. Reiss, *Bridled Ambition*, p. 7.

6. There have been instances of countries either giving up nuclear arsenals that they did not design or renouncing nuclear programs that had not yet developed an operational arsenal. For example, the former Soviet Bloc countries of Belarus, Kazakhstan, and Ukraine gave up the weapons they had inherited when the Soviet Union fragmented; Argentina and Brazil abandoned their nuclear programs by 1994; and Libya purportedly abandoned its WMD programs in 2003. However, South Africa is the only instance

of a country developing an operational nuclear arsenal and then later abandoning it. For analyses of these other cases, or of nuclear restraint generally, see Ariel E. Levite, "Never Say Never Again: Nuclear Reversal Revisited," *International Security*, Vol. 27, No. 3 (Winter 2002/3), pp. 59–88; Reiss, *Bridled Ambition*, pp. 45–182; Leonard S. Spector, "Repentant Nuclear Proliferants," *Foreign Policy*, No. 88 (Fall 1992), pp. 3–20; T. V. Paul, *Power vs. Prudence: Why States Forgo Nuclear Weapons* (Montreal: McGill-Queen's University Press, 2000); Etel Solingen, "The Political Economy of Nuclear Restraint," *International Security*, Vol. 19, No. 2 (Fall 1994), pp. 126–69; William C. Potter, *The Politics of Nuclear Renunciation: The Cases of Belarus, Kazakhstan, and Ukraine*, Occasional Paper No. 22 (Washington, DC: Henry L. Stimson Center, 1995); Nathan E. Busch and Joseph F. Pilat, "Disarming Libya? A Reassessment after the Arab Spring," *International Affairs*, Vol. 89, No. 2 (March 2013), pp. 451–75.

7. Adolf von Baeckmann, Gary Dillon, and Demetrius Perricos, "Nuclear Verification in South Africa," *IAEA Bulletin*, Vol. 37, No. 1 (January 1995), p. 42, www.iaea.org/Publications/Magazines/Bulletin/Bull371/37105394248.pdf.

8. Chandré Gould and Peter Folb, *Project Coast: Apartheid's Chemical and Biological Warfare Program* (Geneva: UN Institute for Disarmament Research and the Centre for Conflict Resolution, 2002), p. 1, www.unidir.org/files/publications/pdfs/project-coast -apartheid-s-chemical-and-biological-warfare-programme-296.pdf.

9. For numerous examples of the South African case being used as a "model" for these cases, see Hans Blix, interviewed in "Blix Speaks with Reporters," CNN, January 23, 2003, http://transcripts.cnn.com/TRANSCRIPTS/0301/23/se.05.html; Scott Firsing, "South Africa's Nuclear Dismantlement Continues to Astonish," *LSE Ideas*, London School of Economics and Political Science, December 2011, http: blogs.lse.ac.uk/2011/12; Amir Frayman, "Iran's Nuclear Program—Lessons from the South African Model," International Institute for Counter-Terrorism, September 15, 2005, www.ict.org.il; Sameh Aboul-Enein, "NPT 2010–2015: The Way Forward," *Proliferation Analysis*, Carnegie Endowment for International Peace, March 31, 2011, www.ceip.org; Sameh Aboul-Enein, "Middle East—Nuclear No-Go," *Diplomat*, May 2011, http://www.diplomatmagazine .com/issues/2011/may/452-middle-east-nuclear-no-go-v15-452.html; David Albright and Jacqueline Shire, with Paul Brannan and Andrea Scheel, "Nuclear Iran: Not Inevitable, Essential Background and Recommendations for the Obama Administration," Institute for Science and International Security, January 21, 2009, www.isisnucleariran.org/assets/pdf/Iran_paper_final_2.pdf; Joel Wit, "Dealing with North Korea's Nuclear Weapons Program," *Policy Forum* 98-13B, November 18, 1998, http://nautilus.org/napsnet/naps net-policy-forum/napsnet-forum-23-future-of-agreed-framework-2; Duk-ho Moon, "North Korea's Nuclear Weapons Program: Verification Priorities and New Challenges," Cooperative Monitoring Center Occasional Paper No. 32, December 2003, p. 21, www .cmc.sandia.gov/cmc-papers/sand2003-4558.pdf; Cheon Seongwhun and Tatsujiro Suzuki, "The Tripartite Nuclear-Weapon-Free Zone in Northeast Asia: A Long-Term Ob-

jective of the Six-Party Talks," *International Journal of Korean Unification Studies*, Vol. 12, No. 2 (December 2003), p. 56; Vilmos Cserveny, Josef Goldblat, Faawzy Hussein Hamad, Hannelore Hoppe, Jez Littlewood, Ibrahum Othman, Enrique Roman Morey, and Mohammed Kadry Said, "Building a Weapons of Mass Destruction Free Zone in the Middle East: Global Non-proliferation Regimes and Regional Experiences," UN Institute for Disarmament Research (UNIDIR), Geneva, UNIDIR/2004/24, 2004, p. 116, www.basel peaceoffice.org/sites/default/files/imce/menwfz/building_a_wmd_free_zone_in_the_ middle_east_unidir.pdf.

10. See, for example, Thomas Pickering, comments in panel session on "Preventing a Nuclear-Armed Iran," Arms Control Association Annual Meeting, Carnegie Endowment for International Peace, Washington, DC, June 4, 2012, www.armscontrol.org/events/Join-ACA-June-4-Our-Annual-Meeting%20#panel2.

11. For a similar assessment, see Jodi Lieberman, "Dismantling the South African Nuclear Weapons Program: Lessons Learned and Questions Unresolved," in Henry Sokolski, ed., *Nuclear Weapons Materials Gone Missing: What Does History Teach?* (Arlington, VA: Nonproliferation Policy Education Center, March 2014), p. 85, http://npolicy.org/books/2014muf/Nuclear%20Weapons%20Materials%20Gone%20Missing.pdf.

12. Reiss, *Bridled Ambition*, pp. 8–9; Stephen Burgess and Helen Purkitt, "The Secret Program: South Africa's Chemical and Biological Weapons," in Barry R. Schneider and Jim A. Davis, eds., *The War Next Time: Countering Rogue States and Terrorists Armed with Chemical and Biological Weapons* (Maxwell AFB, Alabama: USAF Counterproliferation Center, April 2004), p. 30.

13. F. W. de Klerk, quoted in J.W. de Villiers, Roger Jardine, and Mitchell Reiss, "Why South Africa Gave Up the Bomb," *Foreign Affairs*, Vol. 72, No. 5 (November–December 1993), p. 101.

14. For summaries of these events, see Reiss, *Bridled Ambition*, pp. 8–9; Burgess and Purkitt, "The Secret Program," pp. 28–30.

15. Burgess and Purkitt, "The Secret Program," p. 29.

16. de Klerk, quoted in de Villiers, Jardine, and Reiss, "Why South Africa Gave Up the Bomb," p. 101.

17. Burgess and Purkitt, "The Secret Program," p. 29.

18. For accounts of these measures and their effects on South Africa's pursuit of WMD, see de Villiers, Jardine, and Reiss, "Why South Africa Gave Up the Bomb," p. 101; Pabian, "The South African Denuclearization Exemplar," p. 7; Burgess and Purkitt, "The Secret Program," pp. 28–30.

19. Reiss, *Bridled Ambition*, pp. 15–16.

20. Chandré Gould and Peter I. Folb, "The South African Chemical and Biological Warfare Program: An Overview," *Nonproliferation Review* (Fall-Winter 2000), p. 11.

21. Burgess and Purkitt, "The Secret Program," p. 31.

22. P. Eric Louw, *The Rise, Fall, And Legacy of Apartheid* (Westport, CT: Praeger Publishers, 2004), p. 143.

23. Burgess and Purkitt, "The Secret Program," p. 30.

24. Reiss, *Bridled Ambition*, pp. 28–29.

25. Jeffrey M. Bale, "South Africa's Project Coast: 'Death Squads,' Covert State-Sponsored Poisonings, and the Dangers of CBW Proliferation," *Democracy and Security*, Vol. 2, No. 1 (January 2006), p. 34.

26. Ibid.

27. Burgess and Purkitt, "The Secret Program," p. 61, n. 13.

28. Bale, "South Africa's Project Coast," pp. 43–45.

29. See Thomas Cochran, "Highly Enriched Uranium Production for South African Nuclear Weapons," *Science and Global Security*, Vol. 4, No. 2 (Summer 1994), p. 34; Reiss, *Bridled Ambition*, p. 8.

30. Reiss, *Bridled Ambition*, pp. 11–12.

31. For details on South Africa's nuclear facilities, see "South Africa's Nuclear-Related Facilities," James Martin Center for Nonproliferation Studies, http://cns.miis.edu/safrica/facil.htm.

32. Reiss, *Bridled Ambition*, pp. 7, 11.

33. Ibid., p. 11.

34. World Nuclear Association, "Nuclear Power in South Africa," World Nuclear Association website, February 2013, www.world-nuclear.org/info/Country-Profiles/Countries-O-S-/South-Africa.

35. David Albright and Corey Hinderstein, "Pelindaba and Valindaba Facilities, South Africa," ISIS Report, Institute for Science and International Security, October 26, 2000, http://isis-online.org/isis-reports/detail/pelindaba-and-valindaba-facilities-south-africa/13.

36. Ibid.; see also David Albright, "South Africa's Secret Nuclear Weapons," ISIS Report, Institute for Science and International Security, May 1, 1994, p. 12, http://isis-online.org/isis-reports/detail/south-africas-secret-nuclear-weapons/13.

37. Albright, "South Africa's Secret Nuclear Weapons," p. 12.

38. Albright, "South Africa's Secret Nuclear Weapons," p. 9.

39. Reiss, *Bridled Ambition*, p. 10.

40. Ibid., p. 11.

41. Albright, "South Africa's Secret Nuclear Weapons," p. 12; David Albright and Corey Hinderstein, "South Africa's Weaponization Efforts: Success on a Small Scale," Institute for Science and International Security, September 13, 2001, http://isis-online.org/uploads/isis-reports/documents/safrica.pdf.

42. Reiss, *Bridled Ambition*, p. 12.

43. Peter Liberman, "Rise and Fall of the South African Bomb," *International Security*, Vol. 26. No. 2 (Fall 2001), p. 54; Verne Harris, Sello Hatang, and Peter Liberman,

"Unveiling South Africa's Nuclear Past," *Journal of Southern African Studies*, Vol. 30, No. 3 (September 2004), p. 459.

44. Albright, "South Africa's Secret Nuclear Weapons," p. 14.

45. Reiss, *Bridled Ambition*, p. 10.

46. Director of National Intelligence, Interagency Assessment, *South Africa: Policy Considerations Regarding a Nuclear Test*, August 18, 1977, declassified document, National Security Archive, www2.gwu.edu/~nsarchiv/NSAEBB/NSAEBB181/sa18.pdf.

47. For example, declassified files have revealed that William Bowdler, the U.S. ambassador to South Africa, sent a strongly worded memorandum on behalf of President Carter to Minister of Foreign Affairs Botha on August 18, 1977. The message warned that the detonation of a nuclear device "would have the most serious consequences for all aspects of our relations and would be considered by us as a serious threat to the peace." See "Message to Botha by Ambassador Bowlder," August 18, 1977, archived by the Cold War International History Project, Woodrow Wilson International Center for Scholars, www.wilsoncenter.org/program/cold-war-international-history-project.

48. Ibid.

49. Director of Central Intelligence, Interagency Intelligence Assessment, *The 22 September 1979 Event*, December 1979, declassified January 2003, posted in the National Security Archive, George Washington University, p. 5, www2.gwu.edu/~nsarchiv/NSAEBB/NSAEBB181/sa23.pdf.

50. Ibid., p. 11.

51. Ibid.

52. See Carey Sublette, "Report on the 1979 Vela Incident," Nuclear Weapons Archive, September 1, 2001, http://nuclearweaponarchive.org/Safrica/Vela.html.

53. Arms Control Association, "Biological Weapons Convention Signatories and States-Parties," April 2013, www.armscontrol.org/factsheets/bwcsig.

54. Gould and Folb, "The South African Chemical and Biological Warfare Program," p. 15; Stephen Burgess and Helen Purkitt, "The Rollback of South Africa's Chemical and Biological Warfare Program," USAF Counterproliferation Center, Air War College, Maxwell Air Force Base, Alabama, April 2001, www.au.af.mil/au/awc/awcgate/cpc-pubs/southafrica.pdf.

55. Gould and Folb, *Project Coast*, p. 1.

56. Burgess and Purkitt, "The Secret Program," p. 28.

57. Bale, "South Africa's Project Coast," p. 42; Gould and Folb, *Project Coast*, p. 8.

58. Bale, "South Africa's Project Coast," p. 42.

59. Gould and Folb, "The South African Chemical and Biological Warfare Program," p. 15.

60. Bale, "South Africa's Project Coast," p. 44; see also p. 45.

61. Burgess and Purkitt, "The Secret Program," p. 37; Gould and Folb, "The South African Chemical and Biological Warfare Program," p. 15.

62. Burgess and Purkitt, "The Secret Program," pp. 34–35.

63. Pabian, "The South African Denuclearization Exemplar," p. 23.

64. Reiss, *Bridled Ambition*, p. 20.

65. Ibid., pp. 20–21. See also Pabian, "South African Denuclearization Exemplar," pp. 23–25.

66. Reiss, *Bridled Ambition*, p. 17.

67. Ibid., pp. 17–19.

68. Burgess and Purkitt, "The Secret Program," p. 43.

69. Bale, "South Africa's Project Coast," p. 45.

70. Burgess and Purkitt, "The Secret Program," p. 43; Bale, "South Africa's Project Coast," p. 45.

71. Burgess and Purkitt, "The Secret Program," p. 43; Bale, "South Africa's Project Coast," p. 45.

72. Burgess and Purkitt, "The Secret Program," p. 47.

73. Ibid.

74. Zondi Masiza, "A Chronology of South Africa's Nuclear Program," *Nonproliferation Review*, Vol. 1, No. 1 (Fall 1993), p. 44.

75. David Albright, "South Africa and the Affordable Bomb," *Bulletin of the Atomic Scientists*, Vol. 50, No. 4 (July-August 1994), p. 46.

76. Waldo Stumpf, "Birth and Death of the South African Nuclear Weapons Programme," presentation at "50 Years after Hiroshima," conference hosted by the Union Scienziati per in disarm, Castiglioncello, Italy, September 28–October 2, 1995, www.fas.org/nuke/guide/rsa/stumpf.html.

77. Helen Purkitt and Stephan Burgess, *South Africa's Weapons of Mass Destruction* (Bloomington: Indiana University Press, 2005), p. 120.

78. Reiss, *Bridled Ambition*, pp. 18–19.

79. Ibid., p. 19. See also Purkitt and Burgess, *South Africa's Weapons of Mass Destruction*, p. 120.

80. Reiss, *Bridled Ambition*, p. 19.

81. Harris, Hatang, and Liberman, "Unveiling South Africa's Nuclear Past," p. 459.

82. Stumpf, "Birth and Death of the South African Nuclear Weapons Programme."

83. Villiers, Jardine, and Reiss, "Why South Africa Gave Up the Bomb," p. 104; Nuclear Threat Initiative, "South Africa Profile: Nuclear Overview," Nuclear Threat Initiative website, www.nti.org/e_research/profiles/SAfrica/Nuclear/index.html.

84. Bale, "South Africa's Project Coast," p. 46.

85. Burgess and Purkitt, "The Secret Program," p. 50.

86. Ibid., p. 48.

87. Ibid.

88. Gould and Folb, "The South African Chemical and Biological Warfare Program," p. 19.

89. Burgess and Purkitt, "The Secret Program," p. 50; Bale, "South Africa's Project Coast," p. 46.

90. Von Baeckmann, Dillon, and Perricos, "Nuclear Verification in South Africa," p. 42.

91. Stumpf, "South Africa's Nuclear Weapons Program," p. 3.

92. Von Baeckmann, Dillon, and Perricos, "Nuclear Verification in South Africa," p. 2.

93. International Atomic Energy Agency, "South Africa's Nuclear Capabilities," Report presented at the 36th General Conference, September 4, 1992, GC(XXXVI)/1015, www.iaea.org/About/Policy/GC/GC36/GC36Documents/English/gc-1015_en.pdf.

94. Ibid., p. 3.

95. Ibid.

96. Ibid., p. 5.

97. Von Baeckmann, Dillon, and Perricos, "Nuclear Verification in South Africa," p. 43.

98. International Atomic Energy Agency, "South Africa's Nuclear Capabilities," p. 5; von Baeckmann, Dillon, and Perricos, "Nuclear Verification in South Africa," 45.

99. International Atomic Energy Agency, "South Africa's Nuclear Capabilities," p. 7.

100. Ibid., p. 8.

101. Ibid., p. 5.

102. Ibid., p. 6; von Baeckmann, Dillon, and Perricos, "Nuclear Verification in South Africa," p. 42.

103. U.S. Department of State, "PAWG Draft Paper on South Africa's Nuclear Inventory," August 26, 1992, declassified document, National Security Archive, http://nsarchive.gwu.edu/NSAEBB/NSAEBB181/sa30a.pdf.

104. U.S. Department of State, "South Africa: Case Closed?" December 19, 1993, declassified document, National Security Archive, http://nsarchive.gwu.edu/NSAEBB/NSAEBB181/sa34.pdf.

105. Albright et al., "Rendering Useless South Africa's Nuclear Test Shafts in the Kalahari Desert," p. 1.

106. Ibid., p. 3.

107. International Atomic Energy Agency, "South Africa's Nuclear Capabilities," p. 8.

108. Pabian, "South African Denuclearization Exemplar," p. 22.

109. International Atomic Energy Agency, "South Africa's Nuclear Capabilities," pp. 8–9.

110. Pabian, "South African Denuclearization Exemplar," p. 23.

111. Albright, "South Africa's Secret Nuclear Weapons."

112. Ibid.

113. U.S. Department of State, "South Africa: Case Closed?" See also Pabian, "The South African Denuclearization Exemplar," p. 23.

114. International Atomic Energy Agency, "The Denuclearization of Africa," Report by the director at the 37th General Conference, GC(XXXVII)/1075, September 9, 1993, www.isea.org/About/Policy/GC/GC37/GC37Documents/English/gc37-1075.en.pdf, p. 2.

115. Ibid.

116. Ibid.; von Baeckmann, Dillon, and Perricos, "Nuclear Verification in South Africa," p. 48.

117. International Atomic Energy Agency, "The Denuclearization of Africa," pp. 2–3.

118. Ibid., p. 2.

119. Ibid., p. 3.

120. Ibid., p. 8.

121. Von Baeckmann, Dillon, and Perricos, "Nuclear Verification in South Africa," p. 45.

122. Ibid.

123. Ibid., p. 47. See also Albright et al., "Rendering Useless South Africa's Nuclear Test Shafts in the Kalahari Desert."

124. International Atomic Energy Agency, "Denuclearization of Africa," pp. 7, 11.

125. Ibid.

126. Bale, "South Africa's Project Coast," p. 46.

127. Burgess and Purkitt, "The Rollback of South Africa's Chemical and Biological Warfare Program," p. 57.

128. Gould and Folb, "The South African Chemical and Biological Warfare Program," p. 19.

129. Burgess and Purkitt indicate that he requested confirmation that South Africa had eliminated its CBW programs as a prerequisite for entering the nuclear nonproliferation treaty, but we are aware of no such requirements for NPT entry. More likely he was seeking confirmation prior to South Africa's entrance into the CWC.

130. Burgess and Purkitt, "The Rollback of South Africa's Chemical and Biological Warfare Program," 57.

131. Ibid., pp. 58–59.

132. Ibid., p. 64.

133. Gould and Folb, "The South African Chemical and Biological Warfare Program," p. 10.

134. Bale, "South Africa's Project Coast," p. 46.

135. Ibid., p. 48.

136. International Atomic Energy Agency, "The Denuclearization of Africa," p. 1.

137. Ibid., p. 11.

138. Von Baeckmann, Dillon, and Perricos, "Nuclear Verification in South Africa," p. 43.

139. International Atomic Energy Agency, "South Africa's Nuclear Capabilities," p. 5. This shut-down was reported to have been caused by "a catalytic reaction of the two gases used in the enrichment process-uranium hexafluoride (UF6) and hydrogen." See Cochran, "Highly Enriched Uranium Production," p. 36.

140. International Atomic Energy Agency, "The Denuclearization of Africa," pp. 10–11.

141. As a point of comparison, the IAEA considers one "significant quantity" of HEU (that is, enough HEU for a nuclear weapon) to be 25 kilograms. See International Atomic Energy Agency, "Limits to the Safeguards System," in *Against the Spread of Nuclear Weapons: IAEA Safeguards in the 1990s* (Vienna: International Atomic Energy Agency, December 1999, booklet 93-04459), www.iaea.org/Publications/Booklets/safe guards. However, other sources indicate that the IAEA found the reported Y-Plant HEU production was within 5–10 kilograms of the IAEA estimate. See David Albright, "South Africa's Nuclear Weapons Program," *Institute for Science and International Security*, March 2001.

142. Cochran, "Highly Enriched Uranium Production," p. 44.

143. Steve Fetter, "Verifying Nuclear Disarmament," Report prepared for the Henry L. Stimson Center's Project on Eliminating Weapons of Mass Destruction, March 12, 1998, p. 18, http://drum.lib.umd.edu/bitstream/1903/4023/1/1988-VerifyingNuclearDisarm ament.pdf.

144. Cochran, "Highly Enriched Uranium Production," p. 44.

145. International Atomic Energy Agency, "South Africa's Nuclear Capabilities," p. 6.

146. See, for example, the very large MUF in U.S. government estimates of domestic plutonium production in over the first fifty years of nuclear operations in U.S. Department of Energy, *Plutonium: The First Fifty Years: United States Plutonium Production, Acquisition and Utilization from 1944 to 1994* (Washington, DC: Department of Energy, February 1996), section 10.2, http://fissilematerials.org/library/doe96.pdf.

147. International Atomic Energy Agency, "South Africa's Nuclear Capabilities," p. 8.

148. This ties in with a broader issue relating to import and export of nuclear materials—and monitoring and verification generally. The Additional Protocol, which strengthens the authorities of the IAEA, requires both the supplier and the recipient of nuclear materials to provide information on the imports. But it does not require countries to provide information on import requests that have been denied. Although this information would be very helpful for international nonproliferation efforts—since it could help identify the nuclear intentions of a potential proliferator—the Nuclear Suppliers Group has not been prepared to take steps to address this issue.

149. International Atomic Energy Agency, "The Denuclearization of Africa," p. 8.

150. Ibid.

151. International Atomic Energy Agency, "South Africa's Nuclear Capabilities," pp. 8–9; Pabian, "South African Denuclearization Exemplar," pp. 22–23.

152. For these and other remaining questions about the South African nuclear program, see Reiss, *Bridled Ambition*, pp. 24–27.

153. Ibid., p. 25.

154. Olli Heinonen, "Verifying the Dismantlement of South Africa's Nuclear Weapons Program," in Henry Sokolski, ed., *Nuclear Weapons Materials Gone Missing: What Does History Teach?* (Arlington, VA: Nonproliferation Policy Education Center, March 2014), p. 95, http://npolicy.org/books/2014muf/Nuclear%20Weapons%20Materials%20Gone%20Missing.pdf.

155. Ibid.

156. International Atomic Energy Agency, "South Africa's Nuclear Capabilities," p. 7.

157. Recall, the declassified U.S. intelligence report stated that the declared HEU stockpile "corresponds to the mid-range of previous US estimates of actual plant production but is well below plant capacity." See U.S. Department of State, "South Africa: Case Closed?"

158. World Nuclear Association, "Nuclear Power in South Africa."

159. For a discussion of latency, see Scott D. Sagan, "Nuclear Latency and Nuclear Proliferation," in William Potter and Gaukhar Mukhatzhanova, eds., *Forecasting Nuclear Proliferation in the 21st Century* (Stanford: Stanford University Press, 2010), pp. 80–101.

160. Ibid., pp. 82–83.

161. International Panel on Fissile Materials, *Global Fissile Material Report 2009: A Path to Nuclear Disarmament*, October 2009, p. 14, http://fissilematerials.org/library/gfmr09.pdf.

162. Sverre Lodgaard, *Nuclear Disarmament and Non-Proliferation: Towards a Nuclear-Weapon-Free World?* (New York: Routledge, 2011), p. 120.

163. David Albright, "South Africa's Nuclear Weapons Program," Lecture given at the Massachusetts Institute of Technology, March 14, 2001, http://web.mit.edu/ssp/seminars/wed_archives01spring/albright.htm.

164. Committee on International Security and Arms Control, Monitoring Nuclear Weapons and Nuclear-Explosive Materials, National Academy of Sciences (Washington, DC: National Academies Press, 2005), p. 193, www.nap.edu/openbook.php?record_id=11265.

165. Ibid.

166. Heinonen, "Verifying the Dismantlement of South Africa's Nuclear Weapons Program," pp. 89–95.

167. For a similar assessment, see Lieberman, "Dismantling the South African Nuclear Weapons Program," p. 85.

168. One can see a similar approach to verification of U.S.-Russia strategic weapons reductions in the Moscow Treaty.

169. International Atomic Energy Agency, "South Africa's Nuclear Capabilities,"

pp. 1, 9; IAEA, "The Denuclearization of Africa," p. 2; von Baeckmann, Dillon, and Perricos, "Nuclear Verification in South Africa," pp. 42, 48.

170. As noted above, there are questions both about whether South Africa declared or dismantled everything, and whether the regime *voluntarily* admitted it had created a nuclear-weapon program or was compelled to do so by mounting domestic and international pressure.

171. Busch and Pilat, "Disarming Libya?" pp. 451–75.

172. Blix, "Blix Speaks with Reporters."

173. Pickering, comments in "Preventing a Nuclear-Armed Iran."

174. Seongwhun and Suzuki, "The Tripartite Nuclear-Weapon-Free Zone in Northeast Asia," p. 56.

175. Cserveny et al., "Building a Weapons of Mass Destruction Free Zone in the Middle East," p. 116.

176. Lieberman, "Dismantling the South African Nuclear Weapons Program," p. 85.

177. For a discussion of the deception and concealment activities of North Korea, Iran, and Syria, see Joseph F. Pilat and Nathan E. Busch, "WMD Monitoring and Verification Regimes: Lessons from Iraq," *Contemporary Security Policy*, Vol. 32, No. 2 (August 2011), pp. 404–6.

178. See, for example, Blix's own comments on Iraq in Hans Blix, "An Update on Inspection," Speech delivered to the UN Security Council, January 27, 2003, www.un.org/Depts/unmovic/Bx27.htm.

179. Christopher A. Ford, "Thinking about a Korean Denuclearization Treaty," Paper prepared for a "Track II" dialogue with North Korean officials, Aspen Institute Germany, Gut Klostermühle resort, Germany, March 31 and April 1, 2012, p. 6, reproduced by the Hudson Institute, www.hudson.org/files/publications/ChristopherFord—DPRKpaper042012.pdf.

180. Daryl G. Kimball, "Nuclear Disarmament: The South African Example," *Arms Control Now*, blog of the Arms Control Association, July 8, 2011, http://armscontrolnow.org/2011/07/08/nuclear-disarmament-the-south-african-example.

181. Committee on International Security and Arms Control, Monitoring Nuclear Weapons and Nuclear-Explosive Materials, National Academy of Sciences (Washington, DC: National Academies Press, 2005), p. 193.

182. Lieberman, "Dismantling the South African Nuclear Weapons Program," p. 85.

183. Indeed, as Sverre Lodgaard notes, the early 1990s, when South Africa renounced its nuclear arsenal, could be considered "the golden age of non-proliferation," when "non-proliferation seemed to be a winning proposition." Lodgaard, *Nuclear Disarmament and Non-proliferation*, p. 3.

Chapter 3

1. See, for example, Office of the Director of National Intelligence, "Background Briefing with Senior U.S. Officials on Syria's Covert Nuclear Reactor and North Korea's Involvement," April 24, 2008, www.cfr.org/syria/background-briefing-senior-us-offi cials-syrias-covert-nuclear-reactor-north-koreas-involvement/p16105; and The White House, "Statement by the Press Secretary," Office of the Press Secretary, April 24, 2008, http://georgewbush-whitehouse.archives.gov/news/releases/2008/04/20080424-14.html; David Albright and Paul Brannan, "The Al Kibar Reactor: Extraordinary Camouflage, Troubling Implications," Institute for Science and International Security, May 12, 2008, http://isis-online.org/uploads/isis-reports/documents/SyriaReactorReport_12May2008 .pdf; CBS News, "Smoking Gun Images of Syrian Nuke Reactor?" April 24, 2008, www .cbsnews.com/stories/2008/04/24/national/main4040170.shtml.

2. International Atomic Energy Agency, "Implementation of the NPT Safeguards Agreement in the Syrian Arab Republic," Report by the Director General, GOV/2008/60, November 19, 2008, www.globalsecurity.org/wmd/library/report/2008/syria_iaea_gov -2008-60_081119.htm.

3. "Diplomats Question Syrian Request for IAEA Aid," *Global Security Newswire*, November 17, 2008, http://gsn.nti.org/gsn/nw_20081117_8838.php.

4. Quoted in "ElBaradei Lashes Critics of Syrian Nuclear Aid Request," *Global Security Newswire*, Nuclear Threat Initiative, November 25, 2008, www.globalsecuritynews- wire.org/gsn/nw_20081125_8832.php.

5. Indeed, as James Acton of the Carnegie Endowment for International Peace pointed out at the time, ElBaradei was factually incorrect to say that the IAEA's stan- dards for nuclear noncompliance presume that a state is "innocent until proven guilty." The IAEA is obligated to find a state in noncompliance if "it is unable to verify the non-diversion of nuclear material. It does not have to prove there has been a diversion; it only needs to be unable to prove that there hasn't been one." See James Acton, "Can the IAEA Suspend Assistance to Syria?" comments posted on ArmsControlWonk.com, November 25, 2008, www.armscontrolwonk.com/2112/can-the-iaea-suspend-technical- cooperation-with-syria.

6. For just a few of these examples, see Charles Duelfer, "The Inevitable Failure of Inspections in Iraq," *Arms Control Today*, Vol. 32, No. 7 (September 2002), pp. 8–11; Daniel Byman, "A Farewell to Arms Inspections," *Foreign Affairs*, Vol. 79, No. 1 (January- February 2000), pp. 119–32; Gary Milhollin, "The Iraqi Bomb," *New Yorker*, February 1, 1993, pp. 47–56. For a summary of criticisms of monitoring and verification regimes given by Bush administration officials, see Joseph Cirincione, Jessica T. Mathews, and George Perkovich, "WMD in Iraq: Evidence and Implications," Carnegie Endowment for International Peace, January 2004, pp. 45–46, www.carnegieendowment.org/files/Iraq 3FullText.pdf.

7. See, for example, Hans Blix, *Disarming Iraq: The Search for Weapons of Mass Destruction* (London: Pantheon Books, 2004), p. 272. For similar assessments, see also George A. Lopez and David Cortright, "Containing Iraq: Sanctions Worked," *Foreign Affairs*, Vol. 83, No. 4 (July-August 2004), pp. 90–103; Frank Ronald Cleminson, "What Happened to Saddam's Weapons of Mass Destruction?" *Arms Control Today*, Vol. 33, No. 7 (September 2003), pp. 3–6; and Juan Cole, interviewed on MSNBC, September 28, 2009, www.msnbc.msn.com.

8. Blix, *Disarming Iraq*, p. 272. For similar assessments, see also Lopez and Cortright, "Containing Iraq," pp. 90–103; Cleminson, "What Happened to Saddam's Weapons of Mass Destruction?" pp. 3–6.

9. Jessica Tuchman Mathews, "We Can Stop Syria by Using Lessons from Iraq," op-ed, *Washington Post*, September 13, 2013, www.carnegie-mec.org/2013/09/13/we-can-stop-syria-by-using-lessons-from-iraq/gn63?reloadFlag=1. This reiterates what she had previously stated in 2004 and 2011. See Jessica Tuchman Mathews, "What Happened in Iraq?; The Success Story of United Nations Inspections," Keynote Speech to the International Peace Academy, March 5, 2004, www.carnegieendowment.org/publications/index.cfm?fa=view&id=1471; Jessica Tuchman Mathews, "The Lost Opportunity in Iraq," *Washington Post*, December 26, 2011, http://carnegieendowment.org/2011/12/26/lost-opportunity-in-iraq/8pik.

10. See Jack Shenker, "Cautious Reports on Tehran Nuclear Programme 'Were Framed to Avoid War,'" *Guardian*, March 31, 2010, www.guardian.co.uk/world/2010/mar/31/iran-nuclear-programme-cautious-language.

11. Dmitri Trenin, "Putin Takes Center Stage on Syria," *New York Times*, September 6, 2013, www.nytimes.com/2013/09/07/opinion/global/putin-takes-center-stage-on-syria.html.

12. C. J. Chivers, "The Secret Casualties of Iraq's Abandoned Chemical Weapons," *New York Times*, October 14, 2014, www.nytimes.com/interactive/2014/10/14/world/middleeast/us-casualties-of-iraq-chemical-weapons.html.

13. Ibid.

14. See John Hart and Vitaly Fedchenko, "Inspection and Verification Regimes," in Nathan E. Busch and Daniel H. Joyner, *Combating Weapons of Mass Destruction: The Future of International Nonproliferation Policy* (Athens: University of Georgia Press, 2009), pp. 95–117.

15. For detailed discussions of Iraq's lack of cooperation into the late 1990s, see Tim Trevan, *Saddam's Secrets: The Hunt for Iraq's Hidden Weapons* (London: HarperCollins Publishers, 1999); Richard Butler, *The Greatest Threat: Iraq, Weapons of Mass Destruction, and the Growing Crisis of Global Security* (New York: Public Affairs, 2000); and the December 15, 1998, UNSCOM Report, *Letter Dated 15 December 1998 from the Secretary-General Addressed to the President of the Security Council*, S/1998/1172, December 15, 1998, www.un.org/Depts/unscom/s98-1172.htm.

16. Iraq is believed to have begun its biological-weapon program as early as 1972 and production of chemical weapons in 1974. See Timothy V. McCarthy and Jonathan B. Tucker, "Saddam's Toxic Arsenal: Chemical and Biological Weapons in the Gulf Wars," in Peter R. Lavoy, Scott D. Sagan, and James J. Wirtz, eds., *Planning the Unthinkable: How New Powers Will Use Nuclear, Biological, and Chemical Weapons* (Ithaca, NY: Cornell University Press, 2000), p. 52; and Kenneth M. Pollack, *The Threatening Storm: The Case for Invading Iraq* (New York: Random House, 2002), p. 170.

17. On Iraqi use of WMD, see Thomas L. McNaugher, "Ballistic Missiles and Chemical Weapons: The Legacy of the Iran-Iraq War," *International Security*, Vol. 15, No. 2 (Autumn 1990), pp. 5–34; U.S. Department of State, "Saddam's Chemical Weapons Campaign: Halabja, March 16, 1988," Bureau of Public Affairs Washington, DC, March 14, 2003, www.state.gov/documents/organization/18817.pdf.

18. "Iraq: The UNSCOM Experience," SIPRI Fact Sheet, Stockholm International Peace Research Institute, October 1998, p. 2, http://editors.sipri.se/pubs/Factsheet/UNSCOM.pdf. For the text of UNSCR 687, see www2.unog.ch/uncc/resolutio/res0687.pdf.

19. Graham S. Pearson, *The Search for Iraq's Weapons of Mass Destruction: Inspection, Verification, and Nonproliferation* (New York: Palgrave Macmillan, 2005), p. 28.

20. Ibid., pp. 29–30.

21. For detailed accounts of these events, see Pearson, *The Search for Iraq's Weapons of Mass Destruction*, pp. 26–95; Trevan, *Saddam's Secrets*, pp. 21–38; and Butler, *The Greatest Threat*, pp. 200–222.

22. UN Security Council, *Letter Dated 17 December 1997 from the Executive Chairman of the Special Commission established by the Secretary-General pursuant to paragraph 9 (b) (i) of Security Council Resolution 687 (1991) addressed to the President of the Security Council, S/1997/987*, December 17, 1997.

23. Pearson, *The Search for Iraq's Weapons of Mass Destruction*, p. 57.

24. Mathews, "We Can Stop Syria by Using Lessons from Iraq."

25. Duelfer, "The Inevitable Failure of Inspections in Iraq," pp. 8–9.

26. Ibid., p. 9.

27. Ibid.

28. Ibid., p. 11.

29. Trevan, *Saddam's Secrets*, pp. 357–74; Butler, *The Greatest Threat*, pp. 104–10, 136–37, 221–28; Duelfer, "The Inevitable Failure of Inspections in Iraq," pp. 8–11. See also Pearson, *The Search for Iraq's Weapons of Mass Destruction*, pp. 94–95.

30. For an extended summary of these instances, see Anthony H. Cordesman, *Iraq and the War of Sanctions: Conventional Threats and Weapons of Mass Destruction* (Westport, CT: Praeger Publishers, 1999), pp. 181–210; and Jonathan B. Tucker, "Monitoring and Verification in a Noncooperative Environment: Lessons from the U.N. Experience in Iraq," *Nonproliferation Review*, Vol. 3, No. 3 (Spring–Summer 1996), pp. 6–7.

31. Cordesman, *Iraq and the War of Sanctions*, p. 212.

32. Tucker, "Monitoring and Verification in a Noncooperative Environment," p. 11; Rolf Ekeus, "Reassessment: The IISS Strategic Dossier on Iraq's Weapons of Mass Destruction," *Survival*, Vol. 46, No. 2 (Summer 2004), p. 74.

33. International Atomic Energy Agency, Board of Governors General Conference, GOV/2816/Add.1-GC(39)/10/Add.1, September 4, 1995, www.iaea.org/About/Policy/GC/GC39/GC39Documents/English/gc39-10-add1_en.pdf; Pollack, *The Threatening Storm*, p. 76; Asculai, *Verification Revisited*, p. 40. For the chronology of these events and the centrality of Kamel's defection to the Iraqi revelations, see United Nations, "UNSCOM: Chronology of Main Events," www.un.org/Depts/unscom/Chronology/resolution949.htm.

34. Asculai, *Verification Revisited*, p. 38.

35. For an extended discussion of the tensions between UNSCOM and the IAEA, see Trevan, *Saddam's Secrets*, pp. 96–102. See also Sharon A. Squassoni, "Iraq: U.N. Inspections for Weapons of Mass Destruction," CRS Report for Congress, Congressional Research Service, October 7, 2003; Tucker, "Monitoring and Verification in a Noncooperative Environment," p. 12; Paul Leventhal and Steven Dolley, "Iraq's Inspector Games," *Washington Post*, November 29, 1998, p. C01; Milhollin, "The Iraqi Bomb," pp. 47–56.

36. Trevan, *Saddam's Secrets*, p. 98.

37. International Atomic Energy Agency, Report by the Secretary-General, Board of Governors General Conference, August 2, 1995, GOV/2816-GC(39)/10, www.iaea.org/About/Policy/GC/GC39/GC39Documents/English/gc39-10_en.pdf.

38. International Atomic Energy Agency, Board of Governors General Conference, GOV/2816/Add.1-GC(39)/10/Add.1, September 4, 1995, www.iaea.org/About/Policy/GC/GC39/GC39Documents/English/gc39-10-add1_en.pdf; Cordesman, *Iraq and the War of Sanctions*, pp. 215–16; Pollack, *The Threatening Storm*, p. 76; Asculai, *Verification Revisited*, p. 40.

39. Squassoni, "Iraq," p. 4.

40. Ibid. For the official UNSCOM report outlining the unanswered questions about Iraq's proscribed programs (often called the Amorim Report), see *Final Report of the Panel of Disarmament and Current and Future Ongoing Monitoring and Verification Issues*, S/1999/356, March 30, 1999, www.un.org/Depts/unmovic/documents/Amorim%20Report.htm.

41. Cordesman, *Iraq and the War of Sanctions*, p. 628.

42. Mohamed ElBaradei, "Iraq's Nuclear File: Still Open," *Washington Post*, June 1, 1998, p. A17. For analysis of this letter, see Cordesman, *Iraq and the War of Sanctions*, p. 630.

43. See *Letter Dated 15 December 1998 from the Secretary-General Addressed to the President of the Security Council*, S/1998/1172, December 15, 1998, www.un.org/Depts/unscom/s98-1172.htm. For a firsthand account of the events leading up to this report, see Butler, *The Greatest Threat*, pp. 200–222.

44. Rolf Ekeus, "Shifting Priorities: UNMOVIC and the Future of Inspections in Iraq, An Interview with Ambassador Rolf Ekeus," *Arms Control Today*, Vol. 30, No. 2 (March 2000), pp. 3–6.

45. Pearson, *The Search for Iraq's Weapons of Mass Destruction*, p. 108.

46. Squassoni, "Iraq," p. 12. See also Gary Milhollin, "Hans the Timid," *Wall Street Journal*, November 26, 2002, p. A24; Asculai, *Verification Revisited*, pp. 38–41; Trevan, *Saddam's Secrets*, pp. 96–102.

47. For the text of UNSC Resolution 1441, see the UN website, www.un.org/Docs/ scres/2002/sc2002.htm.

48. Squassoni, "Iraq," p. 1; "Iraq Nuclear Chronology: 1990–2002," Nuclear Threat Initiative, www.nti.org/e_research/profiles/Iraq/Nuclear/2121_3293.html; "Attacking Iraq: Countdown Timeline," GlobalSecurity.org, www.globalsecurity.org/military/ops/iraq-time line.htm.

49. For similar arguments, see Squassoni, "Iraq," p. 10; Edward Ifft, "Iraq and the Value of On-Site Inspections," *Arms Control Today*, Vol. 34, No. 9 (November 2004), pp. 22–23.

50. See Duelfer, "The Inevitable Failure of Inspections in Iraq," p. 10. Trevor Findlay and Ben Mines, "UNMOVIC in Iraq: Opportunity Lost," in Trevor Findlay, ed., *Verification Yearbook 2003* (VERTIC, London, 2003), p. 55, www.vertic.org/media/Archived_ Publications/Yearbooks/2003/VY03_Findlay-Mines.pdf.

51. Richard Stone, "U.N. Inspectors Find Wisps of Smoke but No Smoking Guns," *Science*, Vol. 229 (March 28, 2003), p. 1968.

52. Squassoni, "Iraq," p. 9. See also Trevan, *Saddam's Secrets*, pp. 381–82.

53. Both UNMOVIC and the IAEA stated that this list was clearly incomplete, since it left off some scientists that UNSCOM had positively identified as part of Iraq's WMD programs. Iraq apparently did provide a more complete list, but, according to Blix, this was "at the end of February and early March 2003 and it was too late." See Hans Blix, "Inspecting Facts in Aftermath of War," op-ed, *Scotsman*, February 25, 2004, www.scotsman.com/news/inspecting-facts-in-aftermath-of-war-1-929453; and Hans Blix, Lecture given at the "Glocalisation, World Governance, and the Reform of the United Nations" workshop, Turin, Italy, March 13–14, 2004, p. 8, www.globusetlocus .org.

54. Hans Blix, "Oral Introduction of the 12th Quarterly Report of UNMOVIC," Report to the UN Security Council, March 7, 2003, www.un.org/Depts/unmovic/SC7as delivered.htm. For analysis of this issue, see Squassoni, "Iraq," p. 11.

55. Stone, "U.N. Inspectors Find Wisps of Smoke but No Smoking Guns," p. 1968.

56. Squassoni, "Iraq," Summary, p. I; Findlay and Mines, "UNMOVIC in Iraq," pp. 54–55.

57. See Hans Blix, "An Update on Inspection," Report to the Security Council, January 27, 2003, www.un.org/Depts/unmovic/Bx27.htm.

58. Hans Blix, Briefing of the Security Council, February 14, 2003, www.un.org/
Depts/unmovic/blix14Febasdel.htm.

59. Ibid.

60. Ibid.

61. Blix, "Oral Introduction of the 12th Quarterly Report of UNMOVIC."

62. Ibid.

63. Ibid.

64. UNMOVIC, "Unresolved Disarmament Issues: Iraq's Proscribed Weapons Programs," UNMOVIC Working Document, March 6, 2003, www.un.org/Depts/unmovic/
documents/UNMOVIC%20UDI%20Working%20Document%206%20March%2003
.pdf. See also Findlay and Mines, "UNMOVIC in Iraq," p. 55.

65. Mohamed ElBaradei, "The Status of Nuclear Inspections in Iraq," Report to the
UN Security Council, January 27, 2003, www.un.org/News/dh/iraq/elbaradei27jan03
.htm.

66. Ibid.

67. See, for example, ElBaradei's statement in "Press Encounter with Hans Blix and
Mohamed ElBaradei." UN News Centre, January 9, 2003, http://www.iraqwatch.org/un/
unmovic/unmovic-blixelbaradei-010903.htm.

68. Mohamed ElBaradei, "Transcript of ElBaradei's U.N. Presentation," CNN.com,
March 7, 2003, www.cnn.com/2003/US/03/07/sprj.irq.un.transcript.elbaradei/.

69. Mohamed ElBaradei, interviewed on *HardTalk*, British Broadcasting Corporation (BBC) News, August 29, 2003, http://news.bbc.co.uk/1/hi/programmes/hardtalk/319
0731.stm.

70. Ibid.

71. Ibid., emphasis added.

72. Quoted in Online News Hour, PBS, October 7, 2005, www.pbs.org/newshour/
updates/nobel_10-07-05.html.

73. Hans Blix, interviewed in "Verifying Arms Control Agreements: An Interview
with Hans Blix," *Arms Control Today*, Vol. 33, No. 6 (July-August. 2003), p. 12.

74. Hans Blix, in "Transcript of the Interview with IAEA Director General Mohamed ElBaradei and Dr. Hans Blix, former head of UNMOVIC," CNN Late Edi-
tion with Wolf Blitzer, March 21, 2004, www.iaea.org/NewsCenter/Transcripts/2004/
cnn21032004.html. See also a similar formulation in "Getting It Right the Next Time: An
Interview with Hans Blix," Arms Control Association, June 19, 2004, www.armscontrol
.org/interviews/20040619_Blix.asp.

75. Blix, *Disarming Iraq*, p. 215.

76. Demetrius Perricos, "Acting Executive Chairman's Speaking Notes—Security
Council, 29 June 2007," Briefing given to the UN Security Council, June 29, 2007, www
.un.org/Depts/unmovic/new/pages/security_council_briefings.asp#11.

77. Ibid.

78. For a good discussion of the ISG, see Pearson, *The Search for Iraq's Weapons of Mass Destruction*, pp. 176–86.

79. Kenneth Katzman, "Iraq: U.S. Regime Change Efforts and Post-Saddam Governance," CRS Report to Congress, Congressional Research Service, April 26, 2005, p. 14, http://digital.library.unt.edu/govdocs/crs//data/2005/upl-meta-crs-6454/RL31339_2005 Apr26.pdf.

80. David A. Kay, *Statement on the Interim Progress Report on the Activities of the Iraq Survey Group (ISG)*, Speech before the House Permanent Select Committee on Intelligence, the House Committee on Appropriations, Subcommittee on Defense, and the Senate Select Committee on Intelligence, October 2, 2003, https://www.cia.gov/news -information/speeches-testimony/2003/david_kay_10022003.html.

81. Charles Duelfer, *Testimony of Charles Duelfer, Special Advisor to the DCI for Iraqi Weapons of Mass Destruction*, Report to the U.S. Congress, March 30, 2004, https://www .cia.gov/news-information/speeches-testimony/2004/tenet_testimony_03302004.html; Charles Duelfer, *Hide and Seek: The Search for Truth in Iraq* (New York: Public Affairs, 2009), pp. 441–60, 469–71.

82. For a small list of such headlines, see "Report Concludes No WMD in Iraq," BBC News, October 7, 2004, http://news.bbc.co.uk/2/hi/middle_east/3718150.stm; Julian Borger, "Iraq Had No WMD: The Final Verdict," *Guardian*, September 18, 2004, http:// politics.guardian.co.uk/iraq/story/0,12956,1307530,00.html; John W. Dean, "Is Lying about the Reason for a War an Impeachable Offense?" CNN.com, June 6, 2003; James Risen and Judith Miller, "No Illicit Arms Found in Iraq, U.S. Inspector Tells Congress," *New York Times*, October 3, 2003, p. A1; Bryan Bender, "Probe Finds No Illicit Iraq Arms; Program Halted after Gulf War, Inspector Says," *Boston Globe*, October 7, 2004.

83. Kay, *Interim Progress Report.*

84. Duelfer, *Testimony of Charles Duelfer.*

85. Ibid.

86. *The Comprehensive Report of the Special Advisor to the DCI on Iraq's WMD* (aka. the Duelfer Report), Vol. 2, September 30, 2004, p. 7, www.foia.cia.gov/sites/default/files/ document_conversions/89801/DOC_0001156442.pdf.

87. Kay, *Interim Progress Report.*

88. Ibid.

89. Duelfer, *Testimony of Charles Duelfer.*

90. Ibid.

91. Kay, Interim Progress Report.

92. Pearson, *The Search for Iraq's Weapons of Mass Destruction*, pp. 229–30.

93. Rolf Ekeus, "Iraq's Real Weapons Threat," *Washington Post*, June 29, 2003, p. B7. Ekeus adds that "[m]any hundreds of chemical engineers and production and process engineers worked to develop nerve agents, especially VX, with the primary task being to stabilize the warfare agents in order to optimize a lasting lethal property." Given the

regime's emphasis on stabilizing VX, it may not be surprising, then, that the ISG found plans for a large-scale program to produce a chemical that Iraq had previously used as a stabilizing agent for VX.

94. Duelfer Report, Vol. 1, "Scope Note," pp. 1–5, www.foia.cia.gov/duelfer/Iraqs_WMD_Vol1.pdf.

95. Kay, *Interim Progress Report*. He further noted that "Iraqi practice was not to mark much of their chemical ordinance and to store it at the same ASPs that held conventional rounds," so much of the ordinance could have been stored at these sites (Ibid.)

96. Duelfer Report, Vol. 1, "Scope Note," pp. 2–3.

97. Ibid.

98. Ibid. Rolf Ekeus similarly argued in June 2003 that "[i]t is understandable that the U.N. inspectors and even more, the military search teams, have had difficulty penetrating the sophisticated, well-rehearsed and protected WMD program in Iraq. The task was made infinitely more challenging by the fact that Iraq was, and indeed still is, a 'republic of fear.' Through my indirect contact with some senior Iraqi weapons scientists, I have been given to understand that the reign of terror is still in place." Ekeus, "Iraq's Real Weapons Threat," p. B7.

99. See, for example, Cameron Hunter and Sammy Salama, "Iraq's WMD Scientists in the Crossfire," Nuclear Threat Initiative, May 2006, www.nti.org/analysis/articles/iraqs-wmd-scientists-crossfire.

100. Kay, Interim Progress Report.

101. George J. Tenet, "Remarks as Prepared for Delivery at Georgetown University," February 5, 2004, https://www.cia.gov/news-information/speeches-testimony/2004/tenet_georgetownspeech_02052004.html.

102. Duelfer Report, Vol. 1, "Scope Note," pp. 1–2.

103. Charles Duelfer, interview, on *NewsHour with Jim Lehrer*, April 27, 2005, www.pbs.org/newshour/bb/middle_east/jan-june05/duelfer_4-27.html.

104. Ibid.

105. *Addendums to the Comprehensive Report of the Special Advisor to the DCI on Iraq's WMD*, March 2005, p. 1, https://www.cia.gov/library/reports/general-reports-1/iraq_wmd_2004/addenda.pdf.

106. Some former Iraqi military leaders later stated that Iraqi weapons and equipment had been transferred to Syria, though it is unclear how reliable these statements are. See, for example, Georges Sada, *Saddam's Secrets: How an Iraqi General Defied and Survived Saddam Hussein* (Brentwood, TN: Integrity Publishers, 2006), pp. 250–64. The former head Israeli general during Operation Iraqi Freedom made similar claims at about the same time. See Ira Stoll, "Saddam's WMD Moved to Syria, an Israeli Says," *New York Sun*, December 15, 2005, www.nysun.com/article/24480.

107. See, for example, Melanie Phillips, "I Found Saddam's WMD Bunkers," *Spectator*, April 20, 2007, www.spectator.co.uk; Douglas Hanson, "Case Not Closed: Iraq's

WMD Stockpiles," *American Thinker*, March 2, 2004, www.americanthinker.com/2004 /03/case_not_closed_iraqs_wmd_stoc.html.

108. See Duelfer Report, Vol. 1, "Regime Strategic Intent," pp. 3, 24–35.

109. UN Monitoring Verification and Inspection Commission, "Initial Comments on the Report of the US-Led Iraq Survey Group (ISG) Searching for WMD in Iraq," Document S/2004/924, November 2004, p. 12, www.un.org/Depts/unmovic/new/docu ments/technical_documents/s-2004-924-comments_on_ISG.pdf.

110. Julian E. Barnes, "Sunni Extremists in Iraq Occupy Hussein's Chemical Weapons Facility," *Wall Street Journal*, June 19, 2014, http://online.wsj.com/articles/sunni-extremists -in-iraq-occupy-saddams-chemical-weapons-facility-1403190600; Damien McElroy, "ISIS Storms Saddam-Era Chemical Weapons Complex in Iraq," *Telegraph*, June 19, 2014, www .telegraph.co.uk/news/worldnews/middleeast/iraq/10913275/Isis-storms-Saddam-era -chemical-weapons-complex-in-Iraq.html; Nick O'Malley, "US Concern as ISIL Militants Seize Former Chemical Weapons Plant," *Sydney Morning Herald*, June 20, 2014, http://m .smh.com.au/world/us-concern-as-isil-militants-seize-former-chemical-weapons-plant -20140620-zsfmr.html; Liz Sly, "Embattled Iraqi Prime Minister Nouri al-Maliki 'Will Not Go Quietly,' Foes and Friends Say," *Washington Post*, June 21, 2014, www.washingtonpost .com/world/islamic-militants-bear-down-on-iraqi-forces-seize-chemical-weapons-facili ty/2014/06/20/b69df9c2-8301-461a-9258-bb1fa1c470eb_story.html.

111. McElroy, "ISIS Storms Saddam-Era Chemical Weapons Complex in Iraq."

112. Duelfer Report, "Al Muthanna Chemical Weapons Complex: Iraq's Chemical Warfare Program—Annex B," https://www.cia.gov/library/reports/general-reports-1/iraq _wmd_2004.

113. Ibid.

114. Ibid. See also a 2004 report on the bunkers by the Associated Press, "Chemi-cal Weapons Bunker Was Looted," October 31, 2004, http://cjonline.com/stories/103104/ pag_bunker.shtml.

115. Quoted in Barnes, "Sunni Extremists in Iraq Occupy Hussein's Chemical Weapons Facility."

116. Charles Duelfer, "Extremists at Former Saddam CW Facility," Duelfer Blog, June 19, 2014, www.charlesduelfer.com/blog/.

117. Chivers, "Secret Casualties."

118. Ibid.

119. Ibid.

120. Ted Thornhill, "Has ISIS Looted Chemical Weapons from Former Iraqi Nerve Agent Factory That US Failed to Destroy?" *Daily Mail*, October 15, 2014, www.dailymail .co.uk/news/article-2793731/will-rusting-chemical-weapons-cache-ignored-americans -fall-isis-hands-iraq-claims-2-500-rockets-containing-deadly-sarin-hands-terrorists .html.

121. Michelle Nichols, "Exclusive—Iraq Tells U.N. That 'Terrorist Groups' Seized Nuclear Materials," *Reuters*, July 10, 2014, http://in.reuters.com/article/2014/07/09/us-iraq -security-nuclear-idINKBN0FE2L620140709.

122. Matthew Bunn, "ISIS Seizes Nuclear Material—But That's Not the Reason to Worry," op-ed, *National Interest*, July 11, 2014, http://nationalinterest.org/feature/isis-seizes -nuclear-material—that's-not-the-reason-worry-10849.

123. Ibid. See also "UPDATE 4—Seized Nuclear Material in Iraq 'Low Grade'"—UN Agency," *Reuters*, July 10, 2014, http://uk.reuters.com/article/2014/07/10/iraq-security-iaea -idUKL6N0PL1RM20140710.

124. That perspective remains to this day. See, for example, Mathews, "We Can Stop Syria by Using Lessons from Iraq."

125. See, for example, Mohamed ElBaradei, interview by the Academy of Achievement, Washington, DC, June 3, 2006, p. 6, www.achievement.org/autodoc/page/elboint-1; "Interview with Hans Blix," *El Pais*, April 9, 2003, www.globalpolicy.org/security/issues/ iraq/unmovic/2003/0409lostpatience.htm.

126. The authors thank William Perry for this important insight. See also Michael O'Hanlon, "Blix Blames Politicians, Not Intelligence, for Iraq," *New York Times*, March 20, 2004, p. B11.

127. Perricos, "Acting Executive Chairman's Speaking Notes."

128. For example, despite reporting that Iran's provision of "changing or contradictory information" left major issues unresolved and clear evidence that Iran was not fully cooperating with the IAEA, ElBaradei reported after its visit to Natanz in 2003 that there was "no evidence" that Iran was pursuing nuclear weapons. ElBaradei and the IAEA also repeatedly stated that the IAEA had found "no credible evidence" of Iranian weaponization activities. These claims effectively set a new threshold for proof of noncompliance by raising the bar by demanding proof of weaponization or other evidence beyond the concealment of facilities, covert activities, or inconsistent and contradictory reporting. Moreover, the IAEA itself reported that it has limited legal authority to search for weaponization indicators, unless the diversion of nuclear material is also a possibility. One might wonder how could such claims about weaponization be made with only a limited mandate and capability to look for such weaponization activities. See International Atomic Energy Agency, "Implementation of the NPT Safeguards Agreement in the Islamic Republic of Iran," Report by the Director, November 10, 2003, GOV/2003/75, par. 52, www.iaea.org/Publications/Documents/Board/2003/gov2003-75.pdf; International Atomic Energy Agency, "Implementation of the NPT Safeguards Agreement in the Islamic Republic of Iran," Report by the Director, June 1, 2004, GOV/2004/34, par. 47, www.fas.org/nuke/guide/iran/iaea0604.pdf; International Atomic Energy Agency, "Implementation of the NPT Safeguards Agreement in the Islamic Republic of Iran," Report by the Director, September 2, 2005, GOV/2005/67, p. 11, par. 49, www.iaea.org/Publications/Documents/Board/2005/gov2005-67.pdf.

129. UN Monitoring Verification and Inspection Commission, *Compendium of Iraq's Proscribed Weapons Programmes in the Chemical, Biological and Missile Areas*. June 2007, http://www.un.org/depts/unmovic/new/pages/compendium.asp, pp. 1100–1102.

130. "CWC: Key Challenges and the Road Ahead," WMD411, Nuclear Threat Initiative, July 2010, www.nti.org/f_wmd411/f203.html. For an excellent discussion of the verification challenges of the BWC, see Jonathan B. Tucker, "Seeking Biosecurity Without Verification: The New U.S. Strategy on Biothreats," *Arms Control Today*, Vol. 41, No. 1 (January-February 2010), pp. 8–14.

131. Duelfer Report, Vol. 1, "Scope Note," pp. 1–5.

132. Blix, "Oral Introduction of the 12th Quarterly Report of UNMOVIC."

133. Bruce W. Jentleson and Christopher A. Whytock, "Who 'Won' Libya?: The Force-diplomacy Debate and Its Implications for Theory and Policy," *International Security*, Vol. 30, No. 3 (Winter 2005/6), pp. 47–86.

134. Trevor Findlay, "LOOKING BACK: The UN Monitoring, Verification, and Inspection Commission," *Arms Control Today*, Vol. 35, No. 7 (September 2005), pp. 45–48; Ron Cleminson, "International Verification of WMD Proliferation: Applying UNMOVIC's Legacy," *Journal of Military and Strategic Studies*, Vol. 9, No. 3 (Spring 2006/7), www.jmss.org/jmss/index.php/jmss/article/view/104; Richard Butler, "Don't Kick the Inspectors Out of the U.N.," *New York Times*, June 29, 2007, p. A27.

135. Mathews, "We Can Stop Syria by Using Lessons from Iraq."

Chapter 4

1. "Libya: Stockpiles of Chemical Weapons Found," *Telegraph*, October 27, 2011, www.telegraph.co.uk/news/worldnews/africaandindianocean/libya/8851973/Libya-stockpiles-of-chemical-weapons-found.html.

2. Chris Schneidmiller, "OPCW Verifies Secret Libyan Chemical Arms," *Global Security Newswire*, January 20, 2012, www.nti.org/gsn/article/opcw-verifies-secret-libyan-chemical-arms.

3. Mark Oliver, "Blair Meets Gadafy," *Guardian*, March 25, 2004, www.guardian.co.uk/world/2004/mar/25/libya.politics.

4. Commission on Presidential Debates, "Transcript of the First Bush-Kerry Presidential Debate," University of Miami, September 30, 2004, www.debates.org/index.php?page=september-30-2004-debate-transcript.

5. Gawdat Bahgat, "Nonproliferation Success: The Libyan Model," *World Affairs*, Vol. 168, No. 1 (Summer 2005), pp. 3–12; "U.S. Points to Libya as Disarmament Model," *Arms Control Today*, Vol. 34, No. 3 (April 2004), p. 29; Paul Kerr, "Libya's Disarmament: A Model for U.S. Policy?" *Arms Control Today*, Vol. 34, No. 5 (June 2004), pp. 34–38.

6. David Cameron, quoted in Patrick Wintour, "UK to Investigate Libya's Chemical Weapons," *Guardian*, November 14, 2011, p. 2.

7. Commission on the Intelligence Capabilities of the United States Regarding Weapons of Mass Destruction, Report to the President of the United States (also known as the Robb-Silberman Report), Government Printing Office, March 31, 2005, p. 263, www.gpo.gov/fdsys/pkg/GPO-WMD/pdf/GPO-WMD.pdf.

8. Ibid.

9. Sharon Squassoni, "Disarming Libya: Weapons of Mass Destruction," CRS Report to Congress, Congressional Research Service, September 22, 2006, http://fpc.state .gov/documents/organization/78338.pdf; Michael Evans, "Libya Knew Game Was Up before Iraq War," *Times*, March 13, 2004, p. 8.

10. Robert G. Joseph, *Countering WMD: The Libyan Experience* (National Institute Press, 2009), p. 55.

11. Jack Boureston and Yana Feldman, "Verifying Libya's Nuclear Dismantlement," in Trevor Findlay, *Verification Yearbook, 2004* (London: Verification Research, Training, Information Centre, 2005), p. 87, www.vertic.org/media/Archived_Publications/Year books/2004/VY04_Boureston-Feldman.pdf, accessed February 4, 2013. See also Joseph, *Countering WMD*, pp. 55–56.

12. Joseph, *Countering WMD*, p. 56.

13. Ibid. According to one account, the United States provided Libyan officials with a compact disc "containing intercepts of a conversation about Libya's nuclear weapons program between Libya's nuclear chief and A. Q. Khan—that reinforced Col. Gadhafi's decision to reverse course on WMD." See Judith Miller, "How Gadhafi Lost His Groove: The Complex Surrender of Libya's WMD," *Wall Street Journal*, May 16, 2006.

14. For an insider's account of the negotiations during this period, see Joseph, *Countering WMD*, pp. 59–69.

15. Boureston and Feldman, "Verifying Libya's Nuclear Dismantlement," p. 87.

16. Paula DeSutter, testimony, Hearing before the Subcommittee on International Terrorism, Nonproliferation, and Human Rights, Subcommittee on International Relations, U.S. House of Representatives, September 22, 2004, www.state.gov/s/l/2004/78305 .htm, accessed February 7, 2013.

17. Bahgat, "Nonproliferation Success," pp. 3–12; "U.S. Points to Libya as Disarmament Model," p. 29; Kerr, "Libya's Disarmament" pp. 34–38.

18. Robert Litwak, *Regime Change: U.S. Strategy through the Prism of 9/11* (Washington, DC: Woodrow Wilson Center Press, 2007).

19. For a discussion of the so-called force-diplomacy debate, see Bruce W. Jentleson and Christopher A. Whytock, "Who 'Won' Libya?: The Force-Diplomacy Debate and Its Implications for Theory and Policy," *International Security*, Vol. 30, No. 3 (Winter 2005/6), pp. 47–86; Malfrid Braut-Hegghammer, "Libya's Nuclear Turnaround: Perspectives from Tripoli," *Middle East Journal*, Vol. 20, No. 1 (Winter 2008); Dafna Hochman, "Rehabilitating a Rogue: Libya's WMD Reversal and Lessons for U.S. Policy," *Parameters*, Vol. 36, No. 1 (Spring 2006), pp. 63–77; Malfrid Braut-Hegghammer, "Libya's

Nuclear Intentions: Ambition and Ambivalence," *Strategic Insights*, Vol. 8, No. 2 (April 2009), http://mercury.ethz.ch/serviceengine/Files/ISN/99275/ichaptersection_singledoc ument/f8d73531-da35-4f61-b3ed-61e0f4f0a713/en/12_braut-hegghammerApr09.pdf; Martin S. Indyk, "Was Kadafi Scared Straight? The Record Says No," *Los Angeles Times*, March 28, 2004.

20. Joseph Cirincione, "How We Dodged Libya's Nuclear Bullet," Huffington Post, March 11, 2011.

21. Herman Nackaerts, "Towards More Effective Safeguards: Learning Hard Lessons," Opening Plenary Address, Institute of Nuclear Materials Management (INMM) Annual Meeting, July 18, 2011, p. 1, www.inmm.org/AM/Template.cfm?Section=Evolving_the_ IAEA_State_Level_Concept&Template=/CM/ContentDisplay.cfm&ContentID=2971.

22. Cirincione, "How We Dodged Libya's Nuclear Bullet."

23. Bruce W. Jentleson, quoted in Miller, "How Gadhafi Lost His Groove." For a more extensive discussion of this argument, see Jentleson and Whytock, "Who 'Won' Libya?" pp. 47–86.

24. Ibid.

25. For discussions of Libya's renunciation of its WMD programs, see Wyn Q. Bowen, "Libya and Nuclear Proliferation," *Adelphi Paper*, No. 380 (May 2006); Joseph, *Countering WMD*; Jentleson and Whytock, "Who 'Won' Libya?" pp. 47–86. For a discussion of "cooperative" vs. "coercive" verification regimes, see Joseph F. Pilat and Nathan E. Busch, "WMD Monitoring and Verification Regimes: Lessons from Iraq," *Contemporary Security Policy*, Vol. 32, No. 2 (August 2011), pp. 401–31.

26. See John Hart and Vitaly Fedchenko, "Inspection and Verification Regimes," in Nathan E. Busch and Daniel H. Joyner, *Combating Weapons of Mass Destruction: The Future of International Nonproliferation Policy* (Athens: University of Georgia Press, 2009), pp. 95–117.

27. For detailed discussions of Iraq's lack of cooperation into the late 1990s, see Tim Trevan, *Saddam's Secrets: The Hunt for Iraq's Hidden Weapons* (London: HarperCollins Publishers, 1999); Richard Butler, *The Greatest Threat: Iraq, Weapons of Mass Destruction, and the Growing Crisis of Global Security* (New York: Public Affairs, 2001); Pilat and Busch, "WMD Monitoring and Verification Regimes," pp. 401–31.

28. Paula DeSutter, testimony before the Committee on Foreign Relations, U.S. Senate, February 26, 2004, www.access.gpo.gov/congress/senate.

29. Joseph, *Countering WMD*, pp. 93–94.

30. Ibid., p. 57.

31. DeSutter, September 2004 testimony.

32. Ibid.

33. Bowen, "Libya and Nuclear Proliferation," p. 72.

34. Patrick E. Tyler, "Libya's Atom Bid in Early Phases," *New York Times*, December 30, 2003, p. A9.

35. Joseph, *Countering WMD*, p. 51. See also, Tyler, "Libya's Atom Bid in Early Phases," p. A9.

36. Squassoni, "Disarming Libya," p. 3.

37. David Albright, "Libya: A Major Sale at Last," ISIS Special Report, Institute for Science and International Security, December 1, 2010, p. 41, http://isis-online.org/up loads/isis-reports/documents/Libya_and_the_Khan_Network_1Dec2010.pdf. See also Joseph, *Countering WMD*, p. 51.

38. Joby Warrick and Peter Slevin, "Libyan Arms Designs Traced Back to China," *Washington Post*, February 15, 2004, p. A1; "Warhead Blueprints Link Libya Project to Pakistan Figure," *New York Times*, February 4, 2004, p. A1, www.nytimes.com/2004/02/04/ world/warhead-blueprints-link-libya-project-to-pakistan-figure.html; Bates Gill, "China's Role in Nonproliferation," in Nathan E. Busch and Daniel H. Joyner, *Combating Weapons of Mass Destruction: The Future of International Nonproliferation Policy* (Athens: University of Georgia Press, 2009), p. 247.

39. Joseph, *Countering WMD*, p. 76; DeSutter, September 2004 testimony.

40. Joseph, *Countering WMD*, p. 76.

41. Albright, "Libya," p. 10.

42. Ibid., p. 7.

43. Sammy Salama, "Was Libyan WMD Disarmament a Significant Success for Nonproliferation?" Center for Nonproliferation Studies (CNS) Monterey Institute of International Studies, September 2004, www.nti.org/analysis/articles/was-libyan-wmd -disarmament-success/.

44. The uranium enrichment throughput of a P-2 centrifuge is reportedly estimated to be about 2.5 times greater than that of the P-1 centrifuge. See David Albright and Jacqueline Shire, "Iran Installing More Advanced Centrifuges at Natanz Pilot Enrichment Plant: Factsheet on the P-2/IR-2 Centrifuge," Institute for Science and International Security (ISIS), February 7, 2008, www.isis-online.org/publications/iran/ISIS_Iran_ P2_7Feb2008.pdf, accessed February 7, 2013.

45. Joseph, *Countering WMD*, p. 51.

46. Albright, "Libya," p. 10.

47. Ibid., pp. 13, 41.

48. John Deutch, "Worldwide Threat Assessment," brief to the Senate Select Committee in Intelligence, February 22, 1996, www.dtic.mil/cgi-bin/GetTRDoc?Location=U 2&doc=GetTRDoc.pdf&AD=ADA312173, accessed February 7, 2013; George Tenet, testimony before the Senate Select Committee on Intelligence, February 5, 1997, https:// www.cia.gov/news-information/speeches-testimony/1997/dci_testimony_020597.html, accessed February 7, 2013; George Tenet, "The Worldwide Threat in 2000: Global Realities to Our National Security," testimony before the Senate Foreign Relations Committee, March 21, 2000, https://www.cia.gov/news-information/speeches-testimony/2000/ dci_speech_032100.html, accessed February 7, 2013.

49. Joshua Sinai, "Libya's Pursuit of Weapons of Mass Destruction," *Nonproliferation Review*, Vol. 4, No. 3 (Spring–Summer 1997), p. 95, http://cns.miis.edu/npr/pdfs/sinai 43.pdf.

50. Salama, "Was Libyan WMD Disarmament a Significant Success for Nonproliferation?"; Jonathan B. Tucker, "The Rollback of Libya's Chemical Weapons Program," *Nonproliferation Review*, Vol. 16, No. 3 (November 2009), p. 366, www.tandfonline.com/doi/pdf/10.1080/10736700903255060.

51. Tucker, "The Rollback of Libya's Chemical Weapons Program," p. 375.

52. Joseph, *Countering WMD*, p. 57; Tucker, "The Rollback of Libya's Chemical Weapons Program," p. 366.

53. Joseph, *Countering WMD*, p. 52.

54. Tucker, "The Rollback of Libya's Chemical Weapons Program," p. 376.

55. Ibid., pp. 376–79; DeSutter, September 2004 testimony.

56. U.S. Department of State, "Adherence to and Compliance with Arms Control and Nonproliferation Agreements and Commitments," Washington, DC, 2001, p. 11, www.state.gov/documents/organization/22466.pdf.

57. Office of the Secretary of Defense, "Proliferation: Threat and Response," U.S. Department of State, April 1996, www.dod.mil/pubs/prolif.

58. Office of the Director of Central Intelligence, "Unclassified Report to Congress on the Acquisition of Technology Relating to Weapons of Mass Destruction and Advanced Conventional Munitions, 1 January Through 30 June 2003," November 2004, https://www.cia.gov/library/reports/archived-reports-1/jan_jun2003.pdf.

59. Paula DeSutter, "Libya, WMDs, and Musa Kusa," *National Review*, April 4, 2011, www.nationalreview.com/blogs/print/263744; Robb-Silberman Report, p. 256.

60. Robb-Silberman Report, p. 256.

61. Paul Kerr, "Commission Slams WMD Intelligence," *Arms Control Today*, Vol. 35, No. 4 (May 2005), p. 29.

62. Judith Miller, "U.S. Says Libya Will Convert Missiles to Defensive Weapons," *New York Times*, April 11, 2004, p. N6; Paul Kerr, "Libya to Keep Limited Missile Force," *Arms Control Today*, Vol. 34, No. 4 (May 2004), p. 28.

63. For an excellent summary of the events involving Libya's SCUD-B missiles, see Jeffrey Lewis, "Libya's Scud-B Force," *Arms Control Wonk*, August 22, 2011, http://lewis.armscontrolwonk.com/archive/4383/libyas-scud-b-force. See also DeSutter, September 2004 testimony; U.S. Department of State, "Libya: Securing Stockpiles Promotes Security," Office of the Spokesperson, Washington, DC, August 26, 2011, www.state.gov/r/pa/prs/ps/2011/08/171101.htm.

64. Oliver, "Blair Meets Gadafy."

65. DeSutter, September 2004 testimony. For more information on the missile classifications of the Missile Technology Control Regime (MTCR), see "MTCR Guidelines

and the Equipment, Software and Technology Annex," Missile Technology Control Regime website, www.mtcr.info/english/guidelines.html, accessed February 7, 2013.

66. Mohamed ElBaradei, Report of the Director General, "Implementation of the NPT Safeguards Agreement in the Socialist People's Libyan Arab Jamahiriya," IAEA, GOV/2008/39, p. 7, www.iaea.org/Publications/Documents/Board/2008/gov2008-39 .pdf, accessed February 7, 2013.

67. Ibid.

68. Alex Bollfrass, "Libya Backs Out of CW Destruction Agreement," *Arms Control Today*, Vol. 37, No. 6 (July-August 2007), p. 29; Alex Bollfrass, "Details Bedevil Libyan Grand Bargain," *Arms Control Today*, Vol. 37, No. 8 (October 2007), pp. 33–34; Max Fisher, "A Nuclear Standoff with Libya," *Atlantic*, November 2010, www.theatlantic.com/ international/archive/2012/11/a-nuclear-standoff-with-libya/67076; and Lewis, "Libya's Scud-B Force."

69. Bollfrass, "Libya Backs Out of CW Destruction Agreement," p. 29; Bollfrass, "Details Bedevil Libyan Grand Bargain," pp. 33–34.

70. Jean Pascal Zanders, "Destroying Libya's Chemical Weapons: Deadlines and Delays," WMD Junction, James Martin Center for Nonproliferation Studies, May 19, 2011, http://cns.miis.edu/wmdjunction/110519_destroying_libya_cw.htm.

71. Ibid.

72. See Bollfrass, "Details Bedevil Libyan Grand Bargain"; and U.S. Department of State, "Libya."

73. Fisher, "A Nuclear Standoff with Libya."

74. U.S. Department of State, "Libya"; Lewis, "Libya's Scud-B Force."

75. U.S. Department of State, "Securing Stockpiles." See also Nuclear Threat Initiative, "Weapons Stocks Still a Worry in Post-Qadhafi Libya," *Global Security Newswire*, October 21, 2011, www.nti.org/gsn/article/weapons-stocks-still-a-worry-in-post-qadhafi -libya/.

76. Organization for the Prohibition of Chemical Weapons, "OPCW Inspectors Verify Newly Declared Chemical Weapons Materials in Libya," OPCW website, January 20, 2012, www.opcw.org/news/article/opcw-inspectors-verify-newly-declared-chemical -weapons-materials-in-libya.

77. See, for example, Bilal Y. Saab, "Can Libya Be Locked Down?: In a Post-Qaddafi Era, Who Will Secure Libya's Chemical and Biological Weapons Materials?" WMD Junction, James Martin Center for Nonproliferation Studies, September 22, 2011, http://cns .miis.edu/wmdjunction/110922_libya_lockdown.htm; Fredrik Dahl, "Nuclear Experts Warn of Libya 'Dirty Bomb' Material," Reuters, August 24, 2011.

78. Carlo Munoz, "US Should Help Secure Libyan WMD, House Intel Chief Says," AolDefense.com, September 16, 2011, http://defense.aol.com/2011/09/16/u-s-should-help -secure-libyan-wmd-house-intel-chief-says/, accessed February 7, 2013; Mike Rogers,

interviewed in "Libyan Weapons Stockpiles Remain a Concern," National Public Radio, August 24, 2011, www.npr.org/2011/08/24/139923591/libyan-weapons-stockpiles-remain -a-concern, accessed February 26, 2013.

79. Carter Ham, "TRANSCRIPT: AFRICOM Commander Ham Discusses African Security with Defense Writers," U.S. AFRICOM Public Affairs, September 15, 2011, www .africom.mil/Newsroom/Article/8587/transcript-africom-commander-ham-discusses -african, accessed February 7, 2013.

80. R. Jeffery Smith, Joby Warrick, and Colum Lynch, "Iran May Have Sent Libya Shells for Chemical Weapons," *Washington Post*, November 20, 2011.

81. Ibid.

82. Organization for the Prohibition of Chemical Weapons, "OPCW Inspectors Verify Newly Declared Chemical Weapons Materials in Libya."

83. Schneidmiller, "OPCW Verifies Secret Libyan Chemical Arms."

84. Organization for the Prohibition of Chemical Weapons, "OPCW Inspectors Verify Newly Declared Chemical Weapons Materials in Libya."

85. Jill Reilly, "Revealed: International Inspectors Discover Gaddafi's Secret Stock-pile of Chemical Weapons," *Daily Mail*, January 21, 2012.

86. Eric Schmitt, "Libya's Cache of Toxic Arms All Destroyed," *New York Times*, Feb-ruary 2, 2014, www.nytimes.com/2014/02/03/world/africa/libyas-cache-of-toxic-arms-all -destroyed.html; Jomana Karadsheh, "Libya Destroys Chemical Weapons," *CNN*, Febru-ary 4, 2014, www.cnn.com/2014/02/04/world/africa/libya-chemical-weapons.

87. Karadsheh, "Libya Destroys Chemical Weapons."

88. Schmitt, "Libya's Cache of Toxic Arms All Destroyed"; Karadsheh, "Libya De-stroys Chemical Weapons."

89. Karadsheh, "Libya Destroys Chemical Weapons."

90. Smith, Warrick, and Lynch, "Iran May Have Sent Libya Shells for Chemical Weapons."

91. Robb-Silberman Report, pp. 263–65.

92. Nackaerts, "Towards More Effective Safeguards," p. 1.

93. Pilat and Busch, "WMD Monitoring and Verification Regimes," pp. 419–20.

94. Bowen, "Libya and Nuclear Proliferation," p. 73.

95. Joseph, *Countering WMD*, p. 91.

96. As noted in Chapter 1 of this book, there have been some efforts to strengthen the BWC over the years, most notably in the lead-up to the fifth review conference, held in December 2001, in which a number of countries attempted to model a strengthened BWC on the significantly expanded authorities granted to the IAEA by the AP. However, the United States (among other countries) rejected the draft protocol, arguing that such steps would be prohibitively costly, unacceptably intrusive—and probably ineffective. More recently, the Obama administration has promoted a somewhat new approach that emphasizes the importance of getting the life sciences community (including doctors, bi-

ologists, and the pharmaceutical industry) involved in preventing BW development and use. See Donald A. Mahley, "Statement of the United States to the Ad Hoc Group of Biological Weapons Convention States Parties," Geneva, July 25, 2001, http://2001-2009.state .gov/t/ac/rls/rm/2001/5497.htm, accessed February 7, 2013; Jonathan B. Tucker, "Seeking Biosecurity without Verification: The New U.S. Strategy on Biothreats," *Arms Control Today*, Vol. 41, No. 1 (January-February 2010), pp. 8–14; Gregory D. Koblentz, "From Biodefense to Biosecurity: The Obama Administration's Strategy for Countering Biological Threats," *International Affairs*, Vol. 88, No. 1 (January 2012), pp. 131–48.

97. Bowen, "Libya and Nuclear Proliferation," p. 83.

98. Herman Nackaerts, "A Changing Nuclear Landscape: Preparing for Future Verification Challenges," International Forum on Peaceful Use of Nuclear Energy and Nuclear Non-Proliferation, Vienna, Austria, February 2, 2011, www.iaea.org/newscenter/ statements/ddgs/2011/nackaerts020211.html.

99. Special inspections have been invoked only twice. In the first instance, Romania requested that the IAEA verify unreported plutonium experiments conducted by the Ceausescu regime. In the second instance, the IAEA requested a special inspection in North Korea in 1993 but was denied access. See Heinonen, "Special Inspection in Syria"; Jack Boureston and Charles D. Ferguson, "Strengthening Nuclear Safeguards: Special Committee to the Rescue?" *Arms Control Today*, Vol. 35, No. 10 (December 2005), p. 20.

100. Organization for the Prohibition of Chemical Weapons, "The Chemical Weapons Convention," OPCW website, www.opcw.org/chemical-weapons-convention.

101. Ambassador Ahmet Üzümcü, OPCW Director General, "Organisation for the Prohibition of Chemical Weapons," John Gee Memorial Lecture, Australian National University, Canberra, Australia, July 26, 2012, p. 12, www.opcw.org/index.php?eID=dam_ frontend_push&docID=15594, accessed February 7, 2013.

102. For some of these concerns, see Jonathan B. Tucker, "Verifying the Chemical Weapons Ban: Missing Elements," *Arms Control Today*, Vol. 37, No. 1 (January-February 2007), pp. 6–13, www.armscontrol.org/act/2007_01-02/Tucker, pp. 11–12.

103. Nackaerts, "Towards More Effective Safeguards," p. 3.

104. Commission on the Intelligence Capabilities of the United States Regarding Weapons of Mass Destruction, Report to the President of the United States, March 31, 2005, p. 263.

105. Joseph, *Countering WMD*, pp. 93–94.

106. Bowen, "Libya and Nuclear Proliferation," p. 74.

107. Joseph, *Countering WMD*, pp. 93–94.

108. One can see a similar approach to verification of U.S.-Russia strategic weapons reductions in the Moscow Treaty.

109. ElBaradei, Report of the Director General, "Implementation of the NPT Safeguards Agreement in the Socialist People's Libyan Arab Jamahiriya," p. 7.

110. International Atomic Energy Agency, "Status List: Conclusion of Safeguards

Agreements, Additional Protocols and Small Quantities Protocols," IAEA website, February 20, 2012, www.iaea.org/OurWork/SV/Safeguards/documents/sir_table.pdf. As part of the requirements established by the 2015 Joint Comprehensive Plan of Action, Iran has committed to apply the AP "provisionally" until 2023, and to "seek" the ratification of the AP after that date.

111.   Aloise, Government Accountability Office, "Nuclear Nonproliferation."

112.   As we have seen in Chapter 2, similar questions could be raised about South Africa's renunciation and dismantlement of its nuclear-weapon program in the early 1990s. Because South Africa unilaterally dismantled its program and brought in the International Atomic Energy Agency only after the dismantlement was complete, information vital to the verification process was lost. As Mitchell Reiss later wrote: "[A] complete accounting of South Africa's enriched uranium inventory may never be known." See Mitchell Reiss, *Bridled Ambition: Why Countries Constrain Their Nuclear Capabilities* (Baltimore, MD: Johns Hopkins University Press, 1995), p. 25.

113.   Robb-Silberman Report, p. 256.

114.   Smith, Warrick, and Lynch, "Iran May Have Sent Libya Shells for Chemical Weapons."

115.   Author's interviews with technical monitoring and verification experts, including safeguards professionals, Washington, DC, and Los Alamos, NM, March–June 2012.

116.   Chris Schneidmiller, "No Sign of Changes to Libyan Chemical Arms Security after Benghazi Attack," *Global Security Newswire*, September 14, 2012, www.nti.org/gsn/article/no-sign-changes-libya.

117.   Schmitt, "Libya's Cache of Toxic Arms All Destroyed"; Karadsheh, "Libya Destroys Chemical Weapons."

118.   See Jeffrey White, "The Assad Regime Winning by Inches?" *PolicyWatch* 2221, Washington Institute, March 11, 2014, www.washingtoninstitute.org/policy-analysis/view/the-assad-regime-winning-by-inches; Leonard Spector, "Assad's Chemical Romance," *Foreign Policy*, August 23, 2011, www.foreignpolicy.com/articles/2011/08/23/assads_chemical_romance.

119.   See, for example, Barack Obama, "Press Conference by the President," Office of the Press Secretary, The White House, March 6, 2012, http:www.whitehouse.gov/the-press-office/2012/03/06/press-conference-president; and Barack Obama, "State of the Union Address, 2011," U.S. Capitol, Washington, DC, January 25, 2011, www.thewhitehouse.gov/the-press-office/2011/01/25/remarks-president-state-union-address.

120.   "Syria May Still Have Hidden Chemical Weapons, OPCW Admits," Channel 4 News, June 25, 2014, www.channel4.com/news/syria-chemical-weapons-may-still-have-assets-opcw-assad.

121.   Joseph, *Countering WMD*, pp. 55–56.

Chapter 5

1.   George P. Shultz, William J. Perry, Henry A. Kissinger and Sam Nunn, "A World Free of Nuclear Weapons," *Wall Street Journal*, January 4, 2007, www.nuclearsecurity project.org/publications/a-world-free-of-nuclear-weapons; George P. Shultz, William J. Perry, Henry A. Kissinger and Sam Nunn, "Toward a Nuclear-Free World," *Wall Street Journal*, January 15, 2008, www.nuclearsecurityproject.org/publications/toward-a-nuclear-free-world; George P. Shultz, William J. Perry, Henry Kissinger, and Sam Nunn, "Deterrence in the Age of Proliferation," *Wall Street Journal*, March 7, 2011, http://online .wsj.com/article/SB10001424052748703300904576178760530169414.html.

2.   Remarks by President Barack Obama, Hradcany Square, Prague, Czech Republic, April 5, 2009, www.whitehouse.gov/the_press_office/Remarks-By-President-Barack -Obama-In-Prague-As-Delivered.

3.   Ibid.

4.   U.S. Department of Defense, *Nuclear Posture Review Report*, April 2010, www .defense.gov/npr/docs/2010%20nuclear%20posture%20review%20report.pdf.

5.   Ibid.

6.   Tanya Ogilvie-White and David Santoro, "Disarmament and Non-Proliferation: Towards More Realistic Bargains," *Survival*, Vol. 53, No. 3 (June 2011), p. 101. The Non-Aligned Movement consists of 115 countries and aims to represent the interests of developing countries. For more on the NAM's growing disappointment with Obama's Prague agenda, see Harald Müller, "The NPT Review Process and Strengthening the Treaty: Disarmament," EU Non-Proliferation Consortium, Non-Proliferation Papers, No. 10 (February 2012), www.nonproliferation.eu/documents/nonproliferationpapers/harald muller4f797b677acbf.pdf. For the text of the NPT, see "Treaty on the Non-Proliferation of Nuclear Weapons (NPT)," UN Office for Disarmament Affairs, www.un.org/disarma ment/WMD/Nuclear/NPTtext.shtml.

7.   In its press release, the Nobel Committee stated that "the Committee has attached special importance to Obama's vision of and work for a world without nuclear weapons," and that "Obama has as President created a new climate in international politics." See "The Nobel Peace Prize for 2009," Nobelprize.org, www.nobelprize.org/ nobel_prizes/peace/laureates/2009/press.html, accessed June 15, 2003.

8.   See Barack Obama, "Remarks by President Obama at the Brandenburg Gate—Berlin, Germany," Office of the Press Secretary, The White House, June 19, 2013, www .whitehouse.gov/the-press-office/2013/06/19/remarks-president-obama-brandenburg -gate-berlin-germany.

9.   As Sverre Lodgaard notes, there is considerable ambiguity in what "disarmament" (or even terms such as "zero," "abolition," or "elimination") actually means in this context. Is it referring to steep reductions? No deployed nuclear weapons? No assembled warheads? No latent capabilities? Each of these possibilities would bring its own veri-

fication challenges, increasing in scope and difficulty as one proceeded along the possibilities. See Sverre Lodgaard, *Nuclear Disarmament and Non-Proliferation: Towards a Nuclear-Weapon-Free World?* (New York: Routledge, 2011), pp. 200–202.

10. For a summary of the "series of disappointments" that have undermined the momentum of President Obama's vision of a nuclear-free world, see Michael Nacht, "The Global Nuclear Environment: President Obama's Vision amid Emerging Nuclear Threats," in Joseph F. Pilat and Nathan E. Busch, eds., *The Routledge Handbook of Nuclear Proliferation and Policy* (New York: Routledge, 2015). See also Ogilvie-White and Santoro, "Disarmament and Non-Proliferation," p. 101.

11. George Perkovich and James M. Acton, "Verifying the Transition to Zero," in George Perkovich and James M. Acton, eds., *Abolishing Nuclear Weapons: A Debate* (Washington, DC: Carnegie Endowment for International Peace, 2009), p. 55, http://carnegieendowment.org/files/abolishing_nuclear_weapons_debate.pdf, accessed June 15, 2013. See also Steve Fetter, "Stockpile Declarations," in Nicholas Zarimpas, ed., *Transparency in Nuclear Warheads and Materials: The Political and Technical Dimensions* (Oxford: Oxford University Press, 2003), pp. 129–50, http://editors.sipri.se/pubs/zarimpas.html, accessed June 11, 2013.

12. Jay Solomon, "U.S. Declares Size of Nuclear Arsenal," *Wall Street Journal*, May 4, 2010, http://online.wsj.com/article/SB10001424052748704342604575222121497753864.html, accessed June 11, 2013.

13. Alexander Glaser, "Facilitating Nuclear Disarmament: Verified Declarations of Fissile Material Stocks and Production," *Nonproliferation Review*, Vol. 19, No. 1 (June 2012), p. 126.

14. Fetter, "Stockpile Declarations," p. 130.

15. China's arsenal had long been estimated to consist of about 400 weapons, but some more recent estimates have placed the arsenal size at around 1,300, or even as large as 3,000. See Bret Stephens, "How Many Nukes Does China Have? Plumbing the Secret Underground Great Wall," *Wall Street Journal*, October 24, 2011, http://online.wsj.com/article/SB10001424052970204346104576639502894496030.html, accessed June 6, 2013.

16. See, for example, David Albright, "India's Military Plutonium Inventory, End 2004," Institute for Science and International Security, May 7, 2005, http://isis-online.org/uploads/isis-reports/documents/india_military_plutonium.pdf.

17. Perkovich and Acton, "Verifying the Transition to Zero," p. 60.

18. Ibid., p. 55.

19. For details on the PNIs, see Arms Control Association, "The Presidential Nuclear Initiatives (PNIs) on Tactical Nuclear Weapons at a Glance," August 2012, https://www.armscontrol.org/factsheets/pniglance.

20. Ibid.

21. Christopher A. Ford, "Deterrence to—and through—'Zero': Challenges of Disarmament and Proliferation," presented to the Nonproliferation Forum, sponsored by

the Woodrow Wilson Center and the Los Alamos National Laboratory, Ronald Reagan International Building, Washington, DC, November 14, 2008, p. 11. For a similar assessment, see Jay Davis, "Technical and Policy Issues for Nuclear Weapons Reductions," *Physics and Society*, January 2012, www.aps.org/units/fps/newsletters/201201/davis.cfm, accessed June 8, 2013.

22. Patricia Lewis, "Verification, Compliance, and Enforcement," in George Perkovich and James M. Acton, eds., *Abolishing Nuclear Weapons: A Debate* (Washington, DC: Carnegie Endowment for International Peace, 2009), p. 236.

23. Theodore B. Taylor, "Verified Elimination of Nuclear Warheads," *Science and Global Security*, Vol. 1, No. 1–2 (1989), p. 11, http://scienceandglobalsecurity.org/archive/sgs01taylor.pdf; Christopher A. Ford, "Why Not Nuclear Disarmament?" *New Atlantis*, No. 27 (Spring 2010), pp. 7–8, www.thenewatlantis.com/publications/why-not-nuclear-disarmament, accessed August 6, 2014.

24. Emily C. Saunders, Ariana N. Rowley, and Bryan L. Fearey, "Towards a Tactical Nuclear Weapons Treaty," Paper presented at the Midwest Political Science Association Annual Conference, April 13, 2013, p. 8.

25. Lewis, "Verification, Compliance, and Enforcement," p. 234.

26. For a discussion of this method, see James Fuller, "Verification on the Road to Zero: Issues for Nuclear Warhead Dismantlement," *Arms Control Today*, Vol. 40, No. 10 (December 2010), pp. 19–27, www.armscontrol.org/act/2010_12/%20Fuller.

27. See, for example, David Cliff, Hassan Elbahtimy, and Andreas Persbo, "Verifying Warhead Dismantlement: Past, Present, Future," *VerificationMatters*, VERTIC Research Reports, No. 9 (September 2010), p. 55, www.vertic.org/media/assets/Publications/VM9.pdf.

28. Saunders, Rowley, and Fearey, "Towards a Tactical Nuclear Weapons Treaty," p. 8.

29. Perkovich and Acton, "Verifying the Transition to Zero," p. 58.

30. Eric R. Gerdes, Roger G. Johnston, and James E. Doyle, "A Proposed Approach for Monitoring Nuclear Warhead Dismantlement," *Science & Global Security*, Vol. 9 (2001), p. 115.

31. Ibid., p. 128.

32. Thomas E. Shea, "The Trilateral Initiative: A Model for the Future?" *Arms Control Today*, Vol. 38, No. 4 (May 2008), pp. 17–18, www.armscontrol.org/act/2008_05/Persbo Shea.

33. James Martin Center for Nonproliferation Studies, "The Moscow Summit: Mayak Fissile Material Storage Facility," n.d., http://cns.miis.edu/archive/summit/mayak.htm.

34. Ibid.

35. Government Accounting Office, "Weapons of Mass Destruction: Effort to Reduce Russian Arsenals May Cost More, Achieve Less than Planned," Report to the Chair-

man and Ranking Minority Member, Committee on Armed Services, House of Representatives, April 1999, www.gao.gov/assets/230/227235.pdf.

36.   For similar concerns, see Ford, "Deterrence to—and through—'Zero,'" p. 11; and Saunders, Rowley, and Fearey, "Towards a Tactical Nuclear Weapons Treaty," p. 8.

37.   Ford, "Deterrence to—and through—'Zero,'" p. 11.

38.   Pavel Podvig, "Disposition of Excess Military Nuclear Material," UN Institute for Disarmament Research (UNIDIR), February 2012, www.unidir.org/files/publications /pdfs/disposition-of-excess-military-nuclear-material-388.pdf.

39.   Ibid. See also Elena Sokova, "Plutonium Disposition," Nuclear Threat Initiative, September 16, 2010, www.nti.org/analysis/articles/plutonium-disposition-14.

40.   Daniel Horner, "U.S. Revisits Plutonium Disposition Plan," *Arms Control Today*, Vol. 43, No. 4 (May 2013), pp. 29–30, www.armscontrol.org/print/5770; Rob Pavey, "Layoff Notices Coming for MOX Workers," *Augusta Chronicle*, June 3, 2013, http://chronicle.au gusta.com/news/metro/2013-06-03/layoff-notices-coming-mox-workers?v=1370305450; Roland Oliphant, "'Cancel Sanctions and Scale Back Nato' Russia Tells US as Vladimir Putin Scraps Nuclear Control Deal," Daily Telegraph, October 3, 2016, http://www.tele graph.co.uk/news/2016/10/03/putin-scraps-deal-to-dispose-of-bomb-grade-plutonium -in-swipe-at.

41.   "The United-Kingdom—Norway Initiative: Further Research into Managed Access of Inspectors during Warhead Dismantlement Verification," Ministry of Defense, United Kingdom, March 31, 2010, p. 11, https://www.gov.uk/government/uploads/system /uploads/attachment_data/file/28424/20120426_2010_ukni_man_access_exercise.pdf, accessed June 11, 2013.

42.   David Cliff, "Multilateral Approaches to Future Dismantlement Verification," Paper presented at the UK PONI Annual Conference, *Nuclear Stability: From the Cuban Crisis to the Energy Crisis*, Royal United Services Institute, Great Britain, May 10, 2012, www.rusi.org/downloads/assets/UK_PONI_2012_-_Cliff_-_Multilateral_Disarmament _Verification.pdf, accessed June 11, 2013.

43.   "The United-Kingdom—Norway Initiative," p. 3.

44.   Ibid., p. 4.

45.   Ford, "Why Not Nuclear Disarmament?" pp. 6–7.

46.   "The United-Kingdom—Norway Initiative," p. 11.

47.   See, for example, Shea, "The Trilateral Initiative"; Cliff, Elbahtimy, and Persbo, "Verifying Warhead Dismantlement," pp. 49–54, 64–84.

48.   Brian Anderson, Hugh Beach, John Finney, Nick Ritchie, Ruben Saakyan, and Christopher Watson, "Verification of Nuclear Weapon Dismantlement: Peer Review of the UK MoD Programme," British Pugwash, p. 4, www.britishpugwash.org/documents/ BPG%20Verification%20Report.pdf, accessed June 14, 2013.

49.   Treaty on the Nonproliferation of Nuclear Weapons, July 1, 1968, Articles I–II, www.un.org/en/conf/npt/2005/npttreaty.html.

50. Anderson et al., "Verification of Nuclear Weapon Dismantlement," p. 4.

51. For details on the Conference on Disarmament, see Nuclear Threat Initiative, "Conference on Disarmament (CD)," updated June 2014, www.nti.org/treaties-and -regimes/conference-on-disarmament. For a discussion of both the role that an FMCT could play in laying the basis for nuclear disarmament and the challenges of negotiating an FMCT, see Zia Mian and Frank N. von Hippel, "Policy and Technical Issues Facing a Fissile Material (Cutoff) Treaty," in Joseph F. Pilat and Nathan E. Busch, eds., *The Routledge Handbook of Nuclear Proliferation and Policy* (New York: Routledge, 2015).

52. Glaser, "Facilitating Nuclear Disarmament," p. 126.

53. Ibid., p. 127.

54. Ibid., p. 130. See also Ford, "Deterrence to—and through—'Zero,'" p. 11.

55. For detailed examinations of the vulnerabilities in Russia's nuclear security system in the 1990s and early 2000s, see Nathan E. Busch, *No End in Sight: The Continuing Menace of Nuclear Proliferation* (Lexington: University Press of Kentucky, 2004), pp. 117–30; Nathan Busch, "Russian Roulette: The Continuing Relevance of Russia to the Nuclear Proliferation Debate," *Security Studies*, Vol. 11, No. 3 (Spring 2002), pp. 44–90.

56. Matthew Bunn, Eben Harrell, and Martin B. Malin, "Progress on Securing Nuclear Weapons and Materials: The Four-Year Effort and Beyond," Project on Managing the Atom, Belfer Center for Science and International Affairs, Harvard Kennedy School, March 2012, p. 10, http://nrs.harvard.edu/urn-3:HUL.InstRepos:10592471, accessed June 10, 2013.

57. For more detailed discussions of the accounting and control systems for China, India, and Pakistan, see Busch, *No End in Sight*, pp. 153–71, 211–23.

58. Glaser, "Facilitating Nuclear Disarmament," p. 129.

59. This possibility was raised in the case of South Africa in Chapter 2 of this book.

60. Perkovich and Acton, "Verifying the Transition to Zero," p. 62.

61. For one of the first systematic discussions of "nuclear archeology," see Steve Fetter, "Nuclear Archaeology: Verifying Declarations of Fissile Material Production," *Science & Global Security*, Vol. 3, Nos. 3–4 (1993), pp. 237–59.

62. For the authorities outlined in INFCIRC/153 and INFCIRC/540, see International Atomic Energy Agency, "The Structure and Content of Agreements between the Agency and States Required in Connection with the Treaty on the Non-Proliferation of Nuclear Weapons," INFCIRC/153 (Corrected), June 1972, www.iaea.org/Publications/ Documents/Infcircs/Others/infcirc153.pdf; International Atomic Energy Agency, "Model Protocol Additional to the Agreement(s) between State(s) and the International Atomic Energy Agency for the Application of Safeguards," INFCIRC/540 (Corrected), September 1997, www.iaea.org/Publications/Documents/Infcircs/1997/infcirc540c.pdf.

63. Perkovich and Acton, "Verifying the Transition to Zero," p. 62.

64. Glaser, "Facilitating Nuclear Disarmament," p. 131.

65. Perkovich and Acton, "Verifying the Transition to Zero," p. 62.

66. Glaser, "Facilitating Nuclear Disarmament," p. 131.

67. Ibid.

68. Steve Fetter, "Verifying Nuclear Disarmament," Report prepared for the Henry L. Stimson Center's Project on Eliminating Weapons of Mass Destruction, March 12, 1998, p. 18, accessed April 4, 2013, http://drum.lib.umd.edu/bitstream/1903/4023/1/1998 -VerifyingNuclearDisarmament.pdf.

69. Perkovich and Acton, "Verifying the Transition to Zero," p. 59.

70. Ibid.

71. For a detailed discussion of the various methods of fissile material disposition, see Matthew Bunn and John P. Holdren, "Managing Military Uranium and Plutonium in the United States and the Former Soviet Union," *Annual Review of Energy and the Environment*, Vol. 22 (1997), pp. 443–63, http://belfercenter.ksg.harvard.edu/files/mmup .pdf. See also Perkovich and Acton, "Verifying the Transition to Zero," p. 59.

72. Glaser, "Facilitating Nuclear Disarmament," p. 132.

73. Ford, "Why Not Nuclear Disarmament?" p. 8.

74. For a discussion of standard MPC&A systems, standards established by IAEA agreements, and the U.S.-Russia MPC&A program, see Busch, *No End in Sight*, pp. 19–24, 65–76, 315–30.

75. Joseph F. Pilat, "Report of a Workshop on IAEA Safeguards, Arms Control and Disarmament," Woodrow Wilson International Center for Scholars, Washington, DC, October 3, 2011, pp. 8–9.

76. Ibid., p. 9.

77. Ford, "Why Not Nuclear Disarmament?" p. 9.

78. Herman Nackaerts, "Towards More Effective Safeguards: Learning Hard Lessons," Opening Plenary Address, Institute of Nuclear Materials Management (INMM) Annual Meeting, July 18, 2011, p. 1, www.inmm.org/AM/Template.cfm?Section=Evolving_the_ IAEA_State_Level_Concept&Template=/CM/ContentDisplay.cfm&ContentID=2971.

79. For a detailed study of the A. Q. Khan smuggling network, see David Albright, "Libya: A Major Sale at Last," ISIS Special Report, Institute for Science and International Security, http://isis-online.org/uploads/isis-reports/documents/Libya_and_the_Khan_ Network_1Dec2010.pdf.

80. Kelley Sayler, "Malaysia, Export Controls, and the Nuclear Black Market," Center for Strategic and International Studies, March 24, 2011, http://csis.org/blog/malaysia -export-controls-and-nuclear-black-market.

81. David Albright and Andrea Stricker, "Major U.S. Sting Operation Arrests Iranian in Nuclear Smuggling Network," ISIS Report, Institute for Science and International Security, August 12, 2012, http://isis-online.org/uploads/isis-reports/documents/ US_case_gas_centrifuge_equipment.pdf.

82. Andrea Stricker, "United States Prosecutes U.S.-Based Smuggler Working for Iran," ISIS Report, Institute for Science and International Security, October 26, 2012, p. 1, http:// isis-online.org/uploads/isis-reports/documents/Yip_smuggling_case_26Oct2012.pdf.

83. Andrea Stricker, "Case Study: United States Busts Likely North Korean Transshipment Scheme," ISIS Report, Institute for Science and International Security, May 24, 2013, p. 1, http://isis-online.org/uploads/isis-reports/documents/Tsai_casestudy_24May2013.pdf.

84. David Albright, Andrea Stricker, Daniel Schnur, and Sarah Burkhard, "Additional Taiwan-Based Element of Iranian Military Goods Procurement Network Exposed," ISIS Report, Institute for Science and International Security, September 16, 2015, http://isis-online.org/uploads/isis-reports/documents/Hsieh_case_study_16Sept2015 -final.pdf.

85. See, for example, David Albright and Paul Brannan, "If Not Now, When? Time for an IAEA Special Inspection in Syria," ISIS Report, Institute for Science and Global Security, September 6, 2010, http://isis-online.org/isis-reports/detail/if-not-now-when -time-for-an-iaea-special-inspection-in-syria/; David Albright and Robert Avagyan, "Taking Stock and Moving Forward on the Issue of the Parchin High Explosives Test Site," ISIS Report, Institute for Science and Global Security, January 25, 2013, http://isis -online.org/uploads/isis-reports/documents/Parchin_site_brief_25Jan2013-final.pdf.

86. See John Carlson, "IAEA Safeguards Additional Protocol," Department of Foreign Affairs and Trade, Australian Government, January 20, 2009, https://www.dfat.gov .au/asno/publications/iaea-safeguards-additional-protocol.html.

87. For details on this initiative, see National Nuclear Security Administration, "NNSA Next Generation Safeguards Initiative: Fact Sheet," U.S. Department of Energy, January 2, 2009, http://nnsa.energy.gov/mediaroom/factsheets/nextgenerationsafeguards.

88. Perkovich and Acton, "Verifying the Transition to Zero," p. 66.

89. As noted elsewhere in this book (especially Chapters 1 and 5), national technical means and other third-party information has been essential for the IAEA's activities, especially in such cases as Iraq, North Korea, Iran, and Syria, where the states are not co-operating. See also Report by the Director General, "Implementation of the NPT Safeguards Agreement and Relevant Provisions of Security Council Resolutions in the Islamic Republic of Iran," International Atomic Energy Agency, GOV/2011/65, November 8, 2011, Annex, paragraphs 6, 9, and 12, www.iaea.org/sites/default/files/gov2011-65.pdf; Director General, "NPT Safeguards Agreement in Syria," GOV/2008/60, p. 4; David Albright and Paul Brannan, "Satellite Image Shows Suspected Uranium Conversion Plant in Syria," ISIS Report, Institute for Science and International Security, February 2011, http://isis-online.org/isis-reports/detail/satellite-image-shows-suspected-uranium-conversion-plant-in-syria1/; Daniel H. Joyner, "More Gold from Blix on the IAEA's Use of Information from National Intelligence Agencies," Arms Control Law blog, March 8, 2013, http://armscontrollaw.com/2013/03/08/more-gold-from-blix-on-the-iaeas-use-of -information-from-national-intelligence-agencies/.

90. See, for example, Michael J. Mazarr, ed., *Nuclear Weapons in a Transformed World: The Challenge of Virtual Nuclear Arsenals* (New York: St. Martin's Press, 1997).

91. Josef Joffe and James W. Davis, "Less than Zero: Bursting the New Disarmament

Bubble," *Foreign Affairs*, January-February, 2011, www.foreignaffairs.com/articles/67034/josef-joffe-and-james-w-davis/less-than-zero.

92. For a discussion of the challenges of a CTBT, including the difficulties of detecting low-yield tests, see Paul Robinson, "A New Path Forward for the CTBT," in Joseph F. Pilat and Nathan E. Busch, eds., *The Routledge Handbook of Nuclear Proliferation and Policy* (New York: Routledge, 2015).

93. Perkovich and Acton, "Verifying the Transition to Zero," p. 52.

94. Lewis, "Verification, Compliance, and Enforcement," p. 234.

95. Ibid., p. 235.

96. Perkovich and Acton, "Verifying the Transition to Zero," p. 55.

Chapter 6

1. Herman Nackaerts, Keynote Address, "IAEA Safeguards: Cooperation as the Key to Change," Institute for Nuclear Materials Management 52nd Annual Meeting, July 18, 2011, www.iaea.org/safeguards/statements-repository/Key_to_Change.pdf.

2. Barack Obama, "Statement by the President on the Completion by the M/V Cape Ray of the Destruction of Syria's Chemical Weapons," Office of the Press Secretary, The White House, August 18, 2014, www.whitehouse.gov/the-press-office/2014/08/18/statement-president-completion-mv-cape-ray-destruction-syria-s-declared-; Rick Gladstone, "Syria May Have Hidden Chemical Arms, U.S. Says," *New York Times*, September 4, 2014, www.nytimes.com/2014/09/05/world/middleeast/syria-may-have-hidden-chemical-arms-us-says.html.

3. Joseph Cirincione, Jon Wolfsthal, and Mirian Rajkumar, *Deadly Arsenals: Nuclear, Biological, and Chemical Threats* (Washington, DC: Carnegie Endowment for International Peace, 2005), p. 244.

4. International Atomic Energy Agency, "IAEA and DPRK: Fact Sheet on DPRK Nuclear Safeguards," May 2003, www.iaea.org/newscenter/focus/iaeadprk/fact_sheet_may2003.shtml.

5. Cirincione et al., *Deadly Arsenals*, p. 245.

6. Ibid., p. 246.

7. Ibid.

8. Larry A. Niksch, "North Korea's Nuclear Weapons Program," Congressional Research Service Brief for Congress, December 6, 2001, p. 6, http://www.fas.org/nuke/guide/dprk/nuke/nk1.pdf.

9. Paul Kerr, "North Korea Admits Secret Nuclear Weapons Program," *Arms Control Today*, Vol. 32, No. 9 (November 2002), pp. 19, 24, www.armscontrol.org/act/2002_11/nkoreanov02; see also "North Korea's Secret Nuclear Weapons Program: A Serious Violation of North Korea's International Commitments?" *Proliferation Analysis*, Carnegie Endowment for International Peace, October 25, 2002, http://carnegieendowment

.org/2002/10/25/north-korea-s-secret-nuclear-weapons-program-serious-violation-of
-north-korea-s-international-commitments/25fg.

10. Niksch, "North Korea's Nuclear Weapons Program," p. 8. For a more detailed discussion of the Agreed Framework, see Cirincione et al., *Deadly Arsenals*, pp. 246–49; and David Albright and Kevin O'Neill, *Solving the North Korean Nuclear Puzzle* (Washington, DC: Institute for Science and International Security, 2000), pp. 31–55.

11. Office of the Spokesman, "North Korea—Denuclearization Action Plan," U.S. Department of State, Washington, DC, February 13, 2007, www.state.gov/r/pa/prs/ps /2007/february/80479.htm.

12. See "North Korea Digs In," *Strategic Comments*, Vol. 14, No. 10 (November 2008), p. 2; Choe Sang-Hun, "North Korea Limits Tests of Nuclear Site," *New York Times*, November 13, 2008, p. A8; Helene Cooper, "Nuclear Inspectors Barred from North Korean Site," *New York Times*, October 10, 2008, p. A16; Bruce Klinginger and Walter Lohman, "Securing U.S. Objectives in North Korea: A Memo to President-Elect Obama," Heritage Foundation, January 6, 2009, http: heritage.org/Research/AsiaandthePacific/sr0037.cfm.

13. For a list of these events, see "Chronology of North Korea's Missile Program," Associated Press, July 6, 2009, www.ledger-enquirer.com/252/story/769237.html.

14. Blaine Harden, "North Korea Says It Will Start Enriching Uranium: Weapons Move Is 'Retaliation' for Sanctions," *Washington Post*, June 14, 2009; Blaine Harden, "North Korea: Uranium Program Near Completion," *Washington Post*, September 4, 2009.

15. Siegfried S. Hecker, "What I Found in North Korea," *Foreign Affairs*, December 9, 2010, www.foreignaffairs.com/articles/67023/siegfried-s-hecker/what-i-found-in -north-korea.

16. Ibid.

17. For summaries of these activities, see "Timeline of North Korea's Nuclear Program," *New York Times*, April 4, 2013, http://nytimes.com/interactive/2013/02/05/world/ asia/northkorea-timeline.html; Steven Lee Myers, "North Koreans Agree to Freeze Nuclear Work; U.S. to Give Aid," *New York Times*, February 29, 2012, www.nytimes.com/2012 /03/01/world/asia/us-says-north-korea-agrees-to-curb-nuclear-work.html.

18. "Timeline: North Korea Nuclear Stand-Off," BBC News, April 2013, www.bbc .co.uk/news/world-asia-pacific-11811861.

19. Elisa D. Harris, "Threat Reduction and North Korea's CBW Programs," *Nonproliferation Review*, Vol. 11, No. 3 (February 2008), pp. 86–87.

20. Ibid., p. 87.

21. General Thomas A. Schwartz, testimony before the Committee on Armed Services, U.S. Senate, 107th Congress, March 5, 2002, http://wfile.ait.org.tw/wf-archive /2002/020306/epf310.htm.

22. Director of National Intelligence, *Unclassified Report to Congress on the Acquisi-*

tion of Technology Relating to Weapons of Mass Destruction and Advanced Conventional Munitions, Covering 1 January to 31 December 2011, p. 5, http: www.fas.org/irp/threat/ wmd-acq2011.pdf.

23. Schwartz, 2002 Senate testimony.

24. Director of National Intelligence, *Unclassified Report to Congress on the Acquisition of Technology Relating to Weapons of Mass Destruction and Advanced Conventional Munitions, Covering 1 January to 31 December 2011*, p. 6.

25. See Marcus Noland, "Why North Korea Will Muddle Through," *Foreign Affairs*, Vol. 76, No. 4 (July-August 1997), pp. 105–18. For more recent assessments of North Korea's instability and potential collapse, see Kent Harrington and Bennett Ramberg, "Managing North Korea's Collapse," *Japan Times*, January 23, 2015, www.japantimes .co.jp/opinion/2015/01/23/commentary/world-commentary/managing-north-koreas -collapse; Guy Taylor, "U.S., China, South Korea Should Prepare for North Korea's Collapse, Ex-Envoy Says," *Washington Times*, March 4, 2015, www.washingtontimes.com/ news/2015/mar/4/us-china-south-korea-should-prepare-north-koreas-c; Paula Hancocks, "North Korean Defector: Kim Will Lose Power within Three Years," *CNN*, May 12, 2015, www.cnn.com/2015/05/12/asia/north-korea-defector-kim-power.

26. For detailed discussions of the inherent instability of the North Korean regime, see Nathan E. Busch, *No End in Sight: The Continuing Menace of Nuclear Proliferation* (Lexington: University Press of Kentucky, 2004), pp. 258–64; Scott Snyder, "North Korea's Challenge of Regime Survival: Internal Problems and the Implications for the Future," *Pacific Affairs*, Vol. 73, No. 4 (Winter 2000/1), pp. 517–33; Jei Guk Jeon, "North Korean Leadership: Kim Jong Il's Balancing Act in the Ruling Circle," *Third World Quarterly*, Vol. 21, No. 5 (October 2000), pp. 761–79; Rupert Wingfield-Hayes, "The Plight of North Korea's Refugees," BBC News, September 5, 2002; George Wehrfritz and Hideko Takayama, "Riding the Seoul Train: An Underground Railroad Leads North Korean Refugees to the South," *Newsweek International*, March 5, 2001, p. 26, www.newsweek.com/ riding-seoul-train-148821.

27. For some of these lessons, see Mitchell Reiss, *Bridled Ambition: Why Countries Constrain Their Nuclear Capabilities* (Baltimore, MD: Johns Hopkins University Press, 1995); William C. Potter, *The Politics of Nuclear Renunciation: The Cases of Belarus, Kazakhstan, and Ukraine*, Occasional Paper No. 22 (Washington, DC: Henry L. Stimson Center, 1995); Leonard S. Spector, "Repentant Nuclear Proliferants," *Foreign Policy*, No. 88 (Fall 1992), pp. 3–20.

28. In November 2003, the IAEA stated that Iran had been concealing parts of its nuclear program for nearly two decades. See Paul Kerr, "The IAEA's Report on Iran: An Analysis," *Arms Control Today*, Vol. 33, No. 10 (December 2003), www.armscontrol.org /act/2003_12/IAEAreport; Paul K. Kerr, "Iran's Nuclear Program: Status," CRS Report to Congress, Congressional Research Service, November 20, 2008, www.fas.org/sgp/crs/ nuke/RL34544.pdf.

29. International Atomic Energy Agency, "Implementation of the NPT Safeguards Agreement in the Islamic Republic of Iran," Report by the Director, June 1, 2004, GOV/2004/34, par. 47, www.fas.org/nuke/guide/iran/iaea0604.pdf; David Albright, Christina Walrond, and Andrea Stricker, "ISIS Analysis of IAEA Safeguards Report of May 22, 2013," ISIS Report, Institute for Science and International Security, May 22, 2013, http://isis-online.org/uploads/isis-reports/documents/ISIS_Analysis_IAEA_Safe guards_Report_22May2013.pdf.

30. Report by the Director General, "Implementation of the NPT Safeguards Agreement and Relevant Provisions of Security Council Resolutions in the Islamic Republic of Iran," International Atomic Energy Agency, GOV/2011/65, November 8, 2011, p. 7, www.iaea.org/sites/default/files/gov2011-65.pdf.

31. Report by the Director General, "Implementation of the NPT Safeguards Agreement and Relevant Provisions of Security Council Resolutions in the Islamic Republic of Iran," International Atomic Energy Agency, GOV/2013/3, May 22, 2013, p. 8, www.iaea .org/Publications/Documents/Board/2013/gov2013-6.pdf.

32. The Bushehr reactor became operational in September 2011. There is a widespread belief that because Bushehr is a light-water reactor and produces "reactor-grade" plutonium, it is less of a proliferation risk than heavy-water reactors such as Iran's Arak reactor which, once completed, could be used to produce "weapon-grade" plutonium. However, not only does the plutonium production depend on the reactor's operation, which determines whether the consequent product is reactor- or weapon-grade, but there is reason to believe that reactor-grade plutonium can be used in nuclear weapons. As indicated in an unclassified report by the Department of Energy, while the technical hurdles for producing a nuclear weapon are higher with reactor-grade (as opposed to weapon-grade) plutonium, they are not insurmountable and, "in short, reactor-grade plutonium is weapons-usable, whether by unsophisticated proliferators or by advanced nuclear weapon states" (see U.S. Department of Energy, "Nonproliferation and Arms Control Assessment of Weapons-Usable Fissile Material Storage and Excess Plutonium Disposition Alternatives," DOE/NN-0007, January 1, 1997, p. 39, www.osti.gov/scitech/ servlets/purl/425259). Furthermore, because Bushehr uses low-enriched uranium as its fuel, it has also been used to justify Iran's enrichment program.

33. David Albright and Corey Hinderstein, "The Iranian Gas Centrifuge Uranium Enrichment Plant at Natanz: Drawing from Commercial Satellite Images," Institute for Science and International Security (ISIS), March 14, 2003, www.isis-online.org/publica tions/iran/natanz03_02.html.

34. Joby Warrick and Glenn Kessler, "Iran's Nuclear Program Speeds Ahead," *Washington Post*, March 10, 2003, p. A01.

35. Iran Watch, "Natanz," Wisconsin Project on Nuclear Arms Control, July 14, 2014, www.iranwatch.org/iranian-entities/natanz; David Albright, Paulina Izewicz, Andrea Stricker, and Serena Kelleher-Vergantini, "ISIS Analysis of IAEA Iran Safeguards Re-

port," ISIS Report, Institute for Science and International Security, May 23, 2014, p. 2, http://isis-online.org/uploads/isis-reports/documents/ISIS_Analysis_IAEA_Safeguards _Report_23May2014-finaldoc.pdf.

36. Albright et al., "ISIS Analysis of IAEA Iran Safeguards Report," p. 3.

37. Ibid., p. 2. See also David Albright and Christina Walrond, "Iran's Critical Capability in 2014: Verifiably Stopping Iran from Increasing the Number and Quality of Its Centrifuges," ISIS Report, July 17, 2013, pp. 2–3, http://isis-online.org/uploads/isis-reports /documents/Iran_critical_capability_17July2013.pdf.

38. Heavy water, which is ordinary water enriched in the hydrogen isotope deuterium, is used as a moderator in one type of nuclear reactor. David Albright and Corey Hinderstein, "Iran Building Nuclear Fuel Cycle Facilities: International Transparency Needed," *ISIS Issue Brief*, Institute for Science and International Security, December 12, 2002, www.isis-online.org/publications/iran/iranimages.html.

39. Albright et al., "ISIS Analysis of IAEA Iran Safeguards Report," p. 1; Report by the Director General, "Implementation of the NPT Safeguards Agreement and Relevant Provisions of Security Council Resolutions in the Islamic Republic of Iran," International Atomic Energy Agency, GOV/2013/3, May 22, 2013, p. 7, http://www.iaea.org/Pub lications/Documents/Board/2013/gov2013-6.pdf.

40. David Albright and Christina Walrond, "Update on the Arak Reactor," ISIS Report, Institute for Science and International Security, July 15, 2013, p. 8, www.isis-online .org/uploads/isis-reports/documents/Iran_critical_capability_17July2013.pdf.

41. In its initial configuration, once completed the reactor was estimated to be capable of producing about 9 kilograms of weapon-grade plutonium annually, reportedly enough for about two nuclear weapons per year. See Institute for Science and International Security, "Compendium of ISIS's Reports and Recommendations on the P5+1/ Iran Long-Term Deal Negotiations," September 22, 2014, p. 5, www.isis-online.org/ uploads/isis-reports/documents/Compendium_of_ISISs_Reports_and_Recommenda tions_on_the_P51-Iran_Long-Term_Deal_Negotiations.pdf.

42. Barack Obama, official statement at the G-20 Summit, Pittsburgh, PA, September 25, 2009, transcript posted at www.nytimes.com/2009/09/26/world/middleeast/26nuke .text.html; Official U.S. Government Statement, "Public Points for Qom Disclosure," posted at the "Nuclear Iran" site of the Institute for Science and International Security, September 25, 2009, www.isisnucleariran.org/assets/pdf/Official_Comments_Qom_ Disclosure.pdf; Office of the Press Secretary, "Background Briefing by Senior Administration Officials on Iranian Nuclear Facility," September 25, 2009, www.whitehouse .gov/the_press_office/Background-Briefing-By-Senior-Administration-Officials-On -Iranian-Nuclear-Facility.

43. Iranian officials did indicate the existence of an additional facility in a letter to the IAEA a few days before the September 2009 announcement. Iranian officials therefore claimed that that Iran had not violated its safeguards agreement because they had

declared the facility prior to introducing nuclear material into the site. This claim is unconvincing, however, because Iran was bound by a 1992 agreement with the IAEA to declare any site upon the *decision to build* that site. Although Iran unilaterally withdrew from the 1992 agreement in 2007 (a step that was never recognized by the IAEA), the construction of the site nevertheless began well before 2007 and thus would still constitute a violation of the agreement. See David E. Sanger and William J. Broad, "U.S. and Allies Warn Iran over Nuclear 'Deception,'" *New York Times*, September 25, 2009; Office of the Press Secretary, "Background Briefing by Senior Administration Officials on Iranian Nuclear Facility."

44. Albright et al., "ISIS Analysis of IAEA Iran Safeguards Report," pp. 4–5.

45. David Albright, Christina Walrond, and Andrea Stricker, "ISIS Analysis of IAEA Safeguards Report of May 22, 2013," ISIS Report, Institute for Science and International Security, May 22, 2013, http://isis-online.org/uploads/isis-reports/documents/ISIS_Analysis_IAEA_Safeguards_Report_22May2013.pdf.

46. Report by the Director General, "Implementation of the NPT Safeguards Agreement and Relevant Provisions of Security Council Resolutions in the Islamic Republic of Iran," International Atomic Energy Agency, GOV/2013/27, May 22, 2013, pp. 10–11, http://www.iaea.org/Publications/Documents/Board/2013/gov2013-27.pdf.

47. Report by the Director General, "Implementation of the NPT Safeguards Agreement and Relevant Provisions of Security Council Resolutions in the Islamic Republic of Iran," International Atomic Energy Agency, GOV/2013/3, May 22, 2013, p. 10, www.iaea.org/Publications/Documents/Board/2013/gov2013-6.pdf.

48. Director General, "Implementation of the NPT Safeguards Agreement," GOV/2013/27, May 22, 2013, p. 11, http://www.iaea.org/Publications/Documents/Board/2013/gov2013-27.pdf.

49. Albright et al., "ISIS Analysis of IAEA Safeguards Report of May 22, 2013," p. 6.

50. George Jahn, "U.N. Nuclear Group Clears Iran," Associated Press, September 21, 2015, http://bigstory.ap.org/article/72239ef269414e33a4983e6d91fbf43f/iran-gives-samples-military-site-nuclear-inspectors.

51. Jay Solomon, "Uranium Provides New Clue on Iran's Past Nuclear Arms Work," *Wall Street Journal*, June 19, 2016, http://www.wsj.com/articles/uranium-provides-new-clue-on-irans-past-nuclear-arms-work-1466380760.

52. Olli Heinonen, "Uranium Particles at Parchin Indicate Possible Undeclared Iranian Nuclear Activities," Foundation for Defense of Democracies, July 1, 2016, http://www.defenddemocracy.org/media-hit/olli-heinonen1-uranium-particles-at-parchin-indicate-possible-undeclared-iranian-nuclear-a.

53. William H. Tobey, "Testing a Nuclear Deal with Tehran," op-ed, *Foreign Policy*, November 13, 2013, http://belfercenter.ksg.harvard.edu/publication/23616/testing_a_nuclear_deal_with_tehran.html.

54. Ibid. For the text of the 2011 IAEA report on Iran, see Report by the Director

General, "Implementation of the NPT Safeguards Agreement and Relevant Provisions of Security Council Resolutions in the Islamic Republic of Iran," International Atomic Energy Agency, GOV/2011/65, November 8, 2011, p. 7, www.iaea.org/sites/default/files/gov 2011-65.pdf.

55. Julian Borger, "Iran Nuclear Report: IAEA Claims Tehran Working on Advanced Warhead," *Guardian*, November 7, 2011, www.theguardian.com/world/2011/nov/07/iran -working-on-advanced-nuclear-warhead.

56. Report by the Director General, "Implementation of the NPT Safeguards Agreement and Relevant Provisions of Security Council Resolutions in the Islamic Republic of Iran," International Atomic Energy Agency, GOV/2013/56, November 14, 2013, p. 11, www.iaea.org/Publications/Documents/Board/2013/gov2013-56.pdf.

57. David E. Sanger, "Long Absent, Nuclear Expert Still Has Hold on Iran Talks," *New York Times*, June 24, 2014, www.nytimes.com/2014/06/25/world/middleeast/top -scientist-from-iran-hinders-talks-with-absence.html.

58. JPCOA, par. 14. See Yukiya Amano, "IAEA Director General's Statement and Road-map for the Clarification of Past & Present Outstanding Issues regarding Iran's Nuclear Program," International Atomic Energy Agency, July 14, 2015, https://www.iaea .org/newscenter/statements/iaea-director-generals-statement-and-road-map-clarifica tion-past-present-outstanding-issues-regarding-irans-nuclear-program.

59. International Atomic Energy Agency, "Final Assessment on Past and Present Outstanding Issues regarding Iran's Nuclear Programme," Report by the Director General, GOV/2015/68, December 2, 2015, https://www.iaea.org/sites/default/files/gov-2015 -68.pdf.

60. International Atomic Energy Agency, "Implementation of the NPT Safeguards Agreement in the Islamic Republic of Iran," Report by the Director General, GOV/2003/40, June 6, 2003, p. 6, https://www.iaea.org/sites/default/files/gov2003-40 .pdf.

61. For an excellent discussion of the history of the negotiations with Iran, see Gregory F. Giles, "Iran," in Joseph F. Pilat and Nathan E. Busch, eds., *The Routledge Handbook of Nuclear Proliferation & Policy* (New York: Routledge, 2015), pp. 43–45.

62. Ibid., p. 43.

63. Ibid.

64. Institute for Science and International Security, "ISIS Imagery Brief: Destruction at Iranian Site Raises New Questions about Iran's Nuclear Activities," ISIS Report, June 17, 2004, http://isis-online.org/isis-reports/detail/isis-imagery-brief-destruction -at-iranian-site-raises-new-questions-about-i/8.

65. Giles, "Iran," p. 44. See also International Atomic Energy Agency, "Implementation of the NPT Safeguards Agreement in the Islamic Republic of Iran," GOV/2004/60, September 1, 2004, p. 8, www.iaea.org/Publications/Documents/Board/2004/gov2004 -60.pdf; International Atomic Energy Agency, "Implementation of the NPT Safeguards

Agreement in the Islamic Republic of Iran," GOV/2004/83, November 15, 2004, pp. 21–22, http://iaea.org/Publications/Documents/Board/2004/gov2004-83.pdf.

66. Paul Kerr, "IAEA Cites Iran on Safeguards Failures," *Arms Control Today*, October 2005, www.armscontrol.org/print/1900.

67. Zachary Laub, "International Sanctions on Iran," CFR Backgrounder, Council on Foreign Relations, July 8, 2015, www.cfr.org/iran/international-sanctions-iran/p20258.

68. Ibid.

69. Kenneth Katzman, "Iran Sanctions," Congressional Research Service Report, RS20871, April 21, 2015, Summary, https://fas.org/sgp/crs/mideast/RS20871.pdf.

70. Anne Penketh, "Iran Nuclear Deal: Historic Agreement Reached with US and Other World Powers," *Telegraph*, November 25, 2013, www.independent.co.uk/news/world/middle-east/iran-nuclear-deal-historic-agreement-reached-with-us-and-other-world-powers-in-geneva-8960434.html; PBS *NewsHour*, "U.S. and Iran Reach Historic Agreement over Nuclear Program," November 25, 2013, www.pbs.org/newshour/extra/daily_videos/u-s-and-iran-reach-historic-agreement-over-nuclear-program/; ABC News, "New Details on Historic Agreement to Freeze Iran's Nuclear Program," ABCnews.com, http://abcnews.go.com/GMA/video/details-historic-agreement-freeze-irans-nuclear-program-21003905; Anne Gearan and Joby Warrick, "Iran, World Powers Reach Historic Nuclear Deal," *Washington Post*, November 23, 2013, www.washingtonpost.com/world/national-security/kerry-in-geneva-raising-hopes-for-historic-nuclear-deal-with-iran/2013/11/23/53e7bfe6-5430-11e3-9fe0-fd2ca728e67c_story.html.

71. Shortly after this agreement was announced, the White House published a fact sheet purporting to outline the agreement (see White House, "Fact Sheet"). This fact sheet was disputed by Iran as "mis-leading," however, and the Iranian regime published what it claimed were the actual terms of agreement (see "Full Text of Nuclear Deal between Iran, Six World Powers," *Alalam*, November 24, 2013, http://en.alalam.ir/news/1537590). Two important areas of disagreement appear to involve whether Iran has the right to enrich uranium and whether the Interim Agreement stipulates any requirements relating to enrichment of 3.5 percent U-235.

72. Kenneth Katzman and Paul K. Kerr, "Interim Agreement on Iran's Nuclear Program," Congressional Research Service, December 11, 2013, p. 7, www.fas.org/sgp/crs/nuke/R43333.pdf. Until the facility was completed, Iran's stockpile of 5 percent enriched uranium temporarily increased. See "Iran's Uranium Stocks Could Grow under Nuclear Accord," *Global Security Newswire*, January 22, 2014, www.nti.org/gsn/article/iran-uranium-stocks-could-grow-under-interim-accord.

73. CNN Staff, "The Iran Nuclear Deal: Full Text," CNN.com, November 24, 2013, www.cnn.com/2013/11/24/world/meast/iran-deal-text/; Katzman and Kerr, "Interim Agreement on Iran's Nuclear Program," p. 8.

74. Olli Heinonen, "The Verification Devil in the Details," Belfer Center for Science

and International Affairs, November 26, 2013, http://iranmatters.belfercenter.org/blog/verification-devil-details.

75. Frederick Dahl and Justyna Pawlak, "West, Iran Activate Landmark Nuclear Deal," *Reuters*, January 20, 2014, www.reuters.com/article/2014/01/20/us-iran-nuclear-id USBREA0J00420140120.

76. "Iran Reduces Sensitive Uranium Stocks by Half, Envoys Say," *Global Security Newswire*, April 16, 2014, http://nti.org/gsn/article/iran-slashes-sensitive-uranium-half.

77. "Iran Nuclear Talks Deadline Extended until November," BBC News, July 19, 2014, www.bbc.com/news/world-middle-east-28381608; Gary Samore, "Will Iran Strike a Nuclear Deal by July?" *Politico Magazine*, June 2, 2014, www.politico.com/magazine/story/2014/06/will-iran-strike-a-nuclear-deal-by-july-107250.html; Jofi Joseph, "Challenges in Extending the Joint Plan of Action," Iran Matters, Belfer Center for Science and International Affairs, June 25, 2014, http://iranmatters.belfercenter.org/blog/challenges-extending-joint-plan-action; "Key Envoy: Iran Talks May Drag into 2015," *Global Security Newswire*, June 10, 2014, www.nti.org/gsn/article/iran-talks-may-drag-2015-key-envoy-says/?mgs1=d8c9gbrDRS.

78. On the technical steps for converting UO2 back to UF6, which are described as not time consuming, not necessarily detectable, and not particularly technically demanding, see Olli Heinonen and Simon Henderson, "On Iran," op-ed, *Economist*, July 6, 2013, http://belfercenter.ksg.harvard.edu/publication/23213/on_iran.html.

79. David Albright, "The Rocky Path to a Long-Term Settlement with Iran," op-ed, *Washington Post*, November 25, 2013, www.washingtonpost.com/opinions/reaching-a-final-iran-deal-will-be-a-tough-road/2013/11/25/dcc2f752-55ef-11e3-ba82-16ed0368 1809_story .html.

80. See Barack Obama, Presidential Debate with Mitt Romney, Commission on Presidential Debates, October 22, 2012, http://debates.org/index.php?page=october-22-2012-the-third-obama-romney-presidential-debate; John Kerry, "The P5+1's First Step Agreement with Iran on its Nuclear Program," Opening Remarks before the House Foreign Affairs Committee, Washington, DC, December 10, 2013, www.state.gov/secretary/remarks/2013/12/218578.htm; Wendy Sherman, quoted in "Lead Negotiator: U.S. Would Consider Limited Enrichment by Iran with Conditions," *Public Broadcasting Service*, December 4, 2013, www.pbs.org/newshour/bb/world-july-dec13-sherman_12-04; Editorial Board, "Obama's Iran Deal Falls Far Short of His Own Goals," op-ed, *Washington Post*, April 2, 2015, https://www.washingtonpost.com/opinions/obamas-iran-deal-falls-well-short-of-his-own-goals/2015/04/02/7974413c-d95c-11e4-b3f2-607bd612aeac_story.html.

81. Joint Comprehensive Plan of Action, Annex 1, par. 37–38.

82. International Atomic Energy Agency, "Final Assessment," pp. 10, 12, 14.

83. Joint Comprehensive Plan of Action, Annex I, paragraphs 75–78.

84. Gary Samore et al., *The Iran Nuclear Deal: A Definitive Guide*, Belfer Center for

Science and International Affairs, August 2015, p. 58, http://belfercenter.ksg.harvard.edu/files/IranDealDefinitiveGuide.pdf.

85. Ambassador Christopher Ford, interview with authors, Los Alamos, New Mexico, October 14, 2015.

86. Samore et al., *The Iran Nuclear Deal*, p. 60.

87. Ibid.

88. Alissa J. Rubin, "After Deal, Europeans Are Eager to Do Business in Iran," *New York Times*, August 1, 2015, www.nytimes.com/2015/08/02/world/europe/after-deal-europeans-are-eager-to-do-business-in-iran.html.

89. Joint Comprehensive Plan of Action, par. 36–37.

90. Ibid., par. 37.

91. Rubin, "After Deal"; Hillel Fradkin and Lewis Libby, "Enforcing the Iran Deal: Another Gaping Hole," Hudson Institute, August 25th, 2015, www.hudson.org/research/11556-enforcing-the-iran-deal-another-gaping-hole.

92. Jack Shenker, "Cautious Reports on Tehran Nuclear Programme 'Were Framed to Avoid War,'" *Guardian*, March 31, 2010, www.guardian.co.uk/world/2010/mar/31/iran-nuclear-programme-cautious-language; Julian Borger and Katy Roberts, "Nuclear Watchdog Chief Accused of Pro-Western Bias over Iran," *Guardian*, March 22, 2012, www.theguardian.com/world/2012/mar/22/nuclear-watchdog-iran-iaea.

93. Joint Comprehensive Plan of Action, paragraphs 13, 34.iv; Annex I, Section L; and Annex V, paragraph 15.10.

94. Barack Obama, "Statement by the President on Iran," The White House, Office of the Press Secretary, July 14, 2015, https://www.whitehouse.gov/the-press-office/2015/07/14/statement-president-iran.

95. For this reason, Security Council resolutions have called for additional verification measures beyond the Additional Protocol. See, for example, UN Security Council Resolution 1696, which calls upon Iran to "act in accordance with the provisions of the Additional Protocol *and* to implement without delay all transparency measures as the IAEA may request in support of its ongoing investigations" (emphasis added). See UN Security Council, *Resolution 1696 (2006)*, July 31, 2006, pp. 2–3, www.iaea.org/newscenter/focus/iaeairan/unsc_res1696-2006.pdf.

96. The White House, "The Historic Deal That Will Prevent Iran from Acquiring a Nuclear Weapon," Fact Sheet, n.d., https://www.whitehouse.gov/issues/foreign-policy/iran-deal.

97. Upon such a request, Iran (in consultation with the Joint Commission) has fourteen days to resolve those concerns. In the absence of an agreement, the members of the Joint Commission would have seven days to advise on the necessary means to resolve the IAEA's concerns by consensus or by a vote of five or more of its eight members, and Iran would be required to implement the necessary means within three additional days.

98. Institute for Science and International Security, "Verification of the Joint Com-

prehensive Plan of Action," ISIS Report, July 28, 2015, p. 5, http://isis-online.org/uploads/isis-reports/documents/Verification_of_Iran_JCPOA_Final.pdf.

99. Mike Pompeo and Tom Cotton, "Pompeo, Cotton Urge Disclosure of Complete Iran Nuclear Deal," Press Release, July 21, 2015, http://pompeo.house.gov/news/documentsingle.aspx?DocumentID=398509.

100. U.S. Congress, "H.R.1191—Iran Nuclear Agreement Review Act of 2015," Public Law No. 114-17, 114th Congress, May 22, 2015, Sec. 2(a)(1), https://www.congress.gov/bill/114th-congress/house-bill/1191/text/pl. See also Marc A. Thiessen, "Obama's Secret Iran Deals Exposed," *Washington Post*, July 27, 2015, https://www.washingtonpost.com/opinions/obamas-secret-iran-deals-exposed/2015/07/27/26d14dbc-3460-11e5-8e66-07b4603ec92a_story.html.

101. Associated Press, "Text of Draft Agreement between IAEA, Iran," August 20, 2015, http://bigstory.ap.org/article/bedd428e26924eed95c5ceaeec72d3a4/text-draft-agreement-between-iaea-iran; George Jahn, "Officials: Iran May Take Own Samples at Alleged Nuclear Site," Associated Press, July 28, 2015, http://bigstory.ap.org/article/e1ccf648e18a4788ac94861a3bc1b966/officials-iran-may-take-own-samples-alleged-nuclear-site.

102. A former IAEA inspector called into question the authenticity of the Associated Press story when he published an annotated version of the document. (See "Not Authentic," *Atomic Reporters*, August 21, 2015, http://atomicreporters.com/2015/08/21/aps-supposed-iran-deal-leak-full-of-holes.) The Associated Press did publish a correction to its story, but the correction read: "The Associated Press erroneously referred to Parchin as a 'nuclear site.' In fact, it's a military site where some believe nuclear work occurred." The Associated Press did not retract any of its report on the draft agreement, but instead stated that AP reporters had received confirmation that the reported agreement was accurate. See George Jahn, "Correction: Iran-Nuclear story," Associated Press, August 28, 2015, www.startribune.com/ap-exclusive-un-to-let-iran-inspect-alleged-nuke-work-site/322301801.

103. Yukiya Amano, "IAEA Director General's Remarks to the Press on Visit to Iran," International Atomic Energy Agency, September 21, 2015, https://www.iaea.org/newscenter/statements/iaea-director-generals-remarks-press-visit-iran. For an analysis of Amano's speech and the IAEA's visit to Parchin, see David Albright, Olli Heinonen, and Serena Kelleher-Vergantini, "IAEA Visit to the Parchin Site," ISIS Report, Institute for Science and International Security, September 22, 2015, http://isis-online.org/uploads/isis-reports/documents/IAEA_Visit_to_the_Parchin_Site_September_22_2015_Final_1.pdf.

104. Jahn, "U.N. Nuclear Group Clears Iran."

105. Ibid.

106. Albright, Heinonen, and Kelleher-Vergantini, "IAEA Visit to the Parchin Site," p. 3.

107. Jahn, "U.N. Nuclear Group Clears Iran."

108. International Atomic Energy Agency, "Final Assessment on Past and Present Outstanding Issues regarding Iran's Nuclear Programme."

109. John Kerry, "Secretary Kerry's Press Availability," Press Briefing, U.S. Department of State, June 16, 2015, www.state.gov/secretary/remarks/2015/06/243892.htm.

110. Michael Hayden, "John Kerry's Unreliable Words Undermine Iran Talks," op-ed, *Washington Times*, June 17, 2015, www.washingtontimes.com/news/2015/jun/17/michael-hayden-john-kerrys-unreliable-words-underm.

111. Albright, Heinonen, and Kelleher-Vergantini, "IAEA Visit to the Parchin Site," p. 3.

112. Obama, "Statement by the President on Iran."

113. Joint Comprehensive Plan of Action, Annex V, 15.1.

114. Eric Lorber and Peter Feaver, "Do the Iran Deal's 'Snapback' Sanctions Have Teeth?" *Foreign Policy*, July 21, 2015, http://foreignpolicy.com/2015/07/21/do-the-iran-deals-snapback-sanctions-have-teeth.

115. Matthew Levitt, "The Implications of Sanctions Relief under the Iran Agreement," testimony submitted to the Senate Committee on Banking, Housing, and Urban Affairs, August 5, 2015, https://www.washingtoninstitute.org/uploads/Documents/testimony/LevittTestimony20150805.pdf.

116. Ibid., par. 37.

117. Rubin, "After Deal"; Fradkin and Libby, "Enforcing the Iran Deal: Another Gaping Hole."

118. Colum Lynch, "Shutting Down Iran's Nuclear Smugglers," *Foreign Policy*, July 1, 2015, http://foreignpolicy.com/2015/07/01/shutting-down-irans-tehran-nuclear-smugglers-security-council-united-nations.

119. Chaim Braun and Christopher F. Chyba, "Proliferation Rings: New Challenges to the Nuclear Nonproliferation Regime," *International Security*, Vol. 29, No. 2 (Fall 2004), pp. 5–49; Lynch, "Shutting Down Iran's Nuclear Smugglers"; David Albright, Andrea Stricker, Daniel Schnur, and Sarah Burkhard, "Additional Taiwan-Based Element of Iranian Military Goods Procurement Network Exposed," ISIS Report, Institute for Science and International Security, September 16, 2015, http://isis-online.org/uploads/isis-reports/documents/Hsieh_case_study_16Sept2015-final.pdf. For a brief list of some arrests related to nuclear smuggling, see Chapter 5 of this book.

120. Joint Comprehensive Plan of Action, Annex IV, par. 6.1–6.1.1.

121. Samore et al., *The Iran Nuclear Deal*, p. 48.

122. Ibid., p. 49.

123. David Albright and Andrea Stricker, "Preliminary Assessment of the JCPOA Procurement Channel: Regulation of Iran's Future Nuclear and Civil Imports and Considerations for the Future," ISIS Report, Institute for Science and International Security, August 31, 2015, p. 2, http://isis-online.org/uploads/isis-reports/documents/Procurement_Channel_JCPOA_analysis_31Aug2015_final_1.pdf.

124. Ibid., pp. 50–51.

125. Ibid., p. 2.

126. David Albright, "Technical Note: Making Sense out of the IR-8 Centrifuge," ISIS Report, Institute for Science and International Security, September 23, 2014, http://isis-online.org/isis-reports/detail/technical-note-making-sense-out-of-the-ir-8-centrifuge/8.

127. Ibid.

128. Samore et al., *The Iran Nuclear Deal*, p. 20.

129. Ibid., p. 22.

130. A proposal to reduce the risks at Bushehr is presented in Henry Sokolski, "The Iran Deal: An Omission We Still Can Fix," Nonproliferation Policy Education Center, October 15, 2015, www.npolicy.org/article.php?aid=1295&tid=4.

131. Bob Menendez, "Menendez Delivers Remarks on Iran Nuclear Deal at Seton Hall University's School of Diplomacy and International Relations," Press Release, August 18, 2015, www.menendez.senate.gov/news-and-events/press/menendez-delivers-remarks-on-iran-nuclear-deal-at-seton-hall-universitys-school-of-diplomacy-and-international-relations.

132. John Kerry, "Iran Nuclear Agreement Review," testimony before the Senate Foreign Relations Committee, Washington, DC, July 23, 2015, www.state.gov/secretary/remarks/2015/07/245221.htm.

133. Anthony H. Cordesman and Adam C. Seitz, "Iranian Weapons of Mass Destruction: Biological Weapons Programs," Center for Strategic and International Studies, October 28, 2008, p. pp. 3–4, http://csis.org/files/media/csis/pubs/081028_iranbw_chapterrev.pdf; "Iran: Chemical," Country Profiles, Nuclear Threat Initiative, February 2013, www.nti.org/country-profiles/iran/chemical/.

134. Director of Central Intelligence, *Unclassified Report to Congress on the Acquisition of Technology Relating to Weapons of Mass Destruction and Advanced Conventional Munitions, 1 July through 31 December 2003*, p. 3, https://www.cia.gov/library/reports/archived-reports-1/721report_july_dec2003.pdf.

135. Director of National Intelligence, *Unclassified Report to Congress on the Acquisition of Technology Relating to Weapons of Mass Destruction and Advanced Conventional Munitions, Covering 1 January to 31 December 2011*, http: www.fas.org/irp/threat/wmd-acq2011.pdf.

136. James Ball, "Syria Has Expanded Chemical Weapons Supply with Iran's Help, Documents Show," *Washington Post*, July 27, 2012, www.washingtonpost.com/world/national-security/syria-has-expanded-chemical-weapons-supply-with-irans-help-documents-show/2012/07/27/gJQAjJ3EEX_story.html.

137. Ibid.

138. International Institute for Strategic Studies, *Iran's Nuclear, Chemical and Biological Capabilities: A Net Assessment*, ch. 3 summary, www.iiss.org/en/publications/stra

tegic%20dossiers/issues/iran—39-s-nuclear—chemical-and-biological-capabilities—a-net-assessment-44f8/incbc-05-chapter-3-dc5a.

139. Ibid.

140. Cordesman and Seitz, "Iranian Weapons of Mass Destruction," pp. 3–4.

141. Central Intelligence Agency, "Current and Projected National Security Threats to the United States and Its Interests Abroad," written responses to questions before the Select Committee on Intelligence of the United States Senate, Hearing 104-510, www.fas.org. For a summary of evolving (unclassified) intelligence briefings on Iran's BW program, see Cordesman and Seitz, "Iranian Weapons of Mass Destruction," pp. 5–8; and Nuclear Threat Initiative, Iran: Biological," Country Profiles, February 2013, www.nti.org/country-profiles/iran/biological/.

142. Director of National Intelligence, *Unclassified Report to Congress on the Acquisition of Technology Relating to Weapons of Mass Destruction and Advanced Conventional Munitions, Covering January 1 to December 31, 2011*, p. 4, http: www.fas.org/irp/threat/wmd-acq2011.pdf.

143. For a lengthier discussion of the shortcomings of the AP, see Chapter 1 of this book.

144. Patrick Migliorini, David Albright, Houston Wood, and Christina Walrond, "Iranian Breakout Estimates, Updated September 2013," ISIS Report, Institute for Science and International Security, October 24, 2013, http://isis-online.org/uploads/isis-reports/documents/Breakout_Study_Summary_24October2013.pdf.

145. Albright et al., "ISIS Analysis of IAEA Iran Safeguards Report," p. 6.

146. David Albright, "The Rocky Path to a Long-Term Settlement with Iran."

147. Heinonen, "The Verification Devil in the Details."

148. Alan J. Kuperman, "The Iran Deal's Fatal Flaw," *New York Times*, June 23, 2015, www.nytimes.com/2015/06/23/opinion/the-iran-deals-fatal-flaw.html.

149. David Albright, Houston Wood, and Andrea Stricker, "Breakout Timelines under the Joint Comprehensive Plan of Action," ISIS Report, Institute for Science and International Security, August 18, 2015, p. 1, www.isis-online.org/uploads/isis-reports/documents/Iranian_Breakout_Timelines_and_Issues_18Aug2015_final.pdf.

150. Barack Obama, cited in "Transcript: President Obama's Full NPR Interview on Iran Nuclear Deal," National Public Radio, April 7, 2015, www.npr.org/2015/04/07/397933577/transcript-president-obamas-full-npr-interview-on-iran-nuclear-deal.

151. See his 2010 interview with Jack Shenker of the *Guardian*. See Shenker, "Cautious Reports on Tehran Nuclear Programme 'Were Framed to Avoid War.'"

152. John L. Esposito, "Introduction: From Khomeini to Khatami," in John L. Esposito and R. K. Ramazani, eds., *Iran at the Crossroads* (New York: Palgrave, 2001), p. 2.

153. Mohsen Milani, "Reform and Resistance in the Islamic Republic of Iran," in John L. Esposito and R. K. Ramazani, eds., *Iran at the Crossroads* (New York: Palgrave, 2001), p. 30; Shahram Chubin, *Whither Iran? Reform, Domestic Politics and National*

Security, Adelphi Paper, No. 342 (New York: Oxford University Press, 2002); Bijan Khajehpour, "Iran's Economy: Twenty Years after the Islamic Revolution," in John L. Esposito and R. K. Ramazani, eds., *Iran at the Crossroads* (New York: Palgrave, 2001), p. 111; Mark Downes, *Iran's Unresolved Revolution* (Aldershot: Ashgate Publishing Company, 2002).

154. George Tenet, Director of U.S. Central Intelligence, "The Worldwide Threat in 2003: Evolving Dangers in a Complex World," Speech delivered before the Senate Select Committee on Intelligence, February 11, 2003, http://fas.org/irp/congress/2003_hr /021103tenet.html.

155. Jonathan Manthorpe, "Anger at Clerics Threatens to Bring Iran to the Boil," *Vancouver Sun,* November 23, 2002, p. A27;; Wendell Steavenson, "Iranian Protest Widens: 10,000 at Demo.," *Gazette* (Montreal, Quebec), December 9, 2002, p. A13; Karl Vick, "Iranian Apathy May Hinder U.S. Bid to Foment Unrest," *Washington Post,* May 29, 2003, p. A14; Neil MacFarquhar, "Student Protests in Tehran Become Nightly Fights for Freedom," *New York Times,* June 14, 2003, p. A3; Adam Daifallah, "General Strike Set in Iran in Bid to Topple Mullahs," *New York Sun,* April 24, 2003, p. A1.

156. Holly Dagres, "Viewpoint: Three Years In, Is Iran's Green Revolution Still Going?" *Middle East Voices,* June 13, 2009, http://middleeastvoices.com/2012/06/viewpoint -three-years-in-is-irans-green-revolution-still-going.

157. Michael Elleman, Dina Esfandiary, and Emile Hokayem, "Syria's Proliferation Challenge and the European Union's Response," EU Non-Proliferation Consortium, *Nonproliferation Papers,* No. 20 (July 2012), p. 1, www.sipri.org/research/disarmament/ eu-consortium/publications/Nonproliferation-paper-20.

158. Ibid.

159. See, for example, Graham Allison and Olli Heinonen, "Break the Silence on Syria's Nuclear Program," op-ed, *Wall Street Journal,* December 4, 2010, http://online.wsj .com/news/articles/SB10001424052748703377504575651130446186898.

160. See Report by the Director General, "Implementation of the NPT Safeguards Agreement in the Syrian Arab Republic," International Atomic Energy Agency, GOV/2009/36, June 5, 2009, www.iaea.org/Publications/Documents/Board/2009/ gov2009-36.pdf. See also David Albright and Paul Brannan, "IAEA Report on Syria: Undeclared Uranium Particles Found in Hot Cell Facility in Damascus; Syria Not Answering IAEA's Questions," ISIS Report, June 5, 2009, http://isis-online.org/publications/ syria/Syria_IAEA_Report_Analysis_5June2009.pdf.

161. Frank V. Pabian, "Evidence from Imagery: The Iran and Syrian Nuclear Programs—An Open and Shut Case?" Lecture given at the James Martin Center for Nonproliferation Studies, Monterey, CA, October 28, 2009, www.youtube.fcom/watch ?v=JkXbbHMKpHk.

162. Ibid.

163. Report by the Director General, "Implementation of the NPT Safeguards Agree-

ment in the Syrian Arab Republic," International Atomic Energy Agency, GOV/2011/30, May 24, 2011, p. 8, www.iaea.org/Publications/Documents/Board/2011/gov2011-30.pdf.

164. Report by the Director General, "Implementation of the NPT Safeguards Agreement in the Syrian Arab Republic," GOV/2008/60, November 19, 2008, www.iaea.org/Publications/Documents/Board/2008/gov2008-60.pdf.

165. David Albright and Paul Brannan, "Satellite Image Shows Suspected Uranium Conversion Plant in Syria," ISIS Report, Institute for Science and International Security, February 23, 2011, http://isis-online.org/isis-reports/detail/satellite-image-shows-suspected-uranium-conversion-plant-in-syria1/.

166. Director General, "NPT Safeguards Agreement in Syria," GOV/2008/60, p. 3.

167. Albright and Brannan, "Satellite Image Shows Suspected Uranium Conversion Plant in Syria."

168. Report by the Director General, "Implementation of the NPT Safeguards Agreement in the Syrian Arab Republic," International Atomic Energy Agency, GOV/2009/36, June 5, 2009, p. 3, www.iaea.org/Publications/Documents/Board/2011/gov2011-30.pdf.

169. Albright and Brannan, "IAEA Report on Syria."

170. Report by the Director General, "Implementation of the NPT Safeguards Agreement in the Syrian Arab Republic," International Atomic Energy Agency, GOV/2011/30, May 24, 2011, p. 8, www.iaea.org/Publications/Documents/Board/2011/gov2011-30.pdf.

171. David Albright and Paul Brannan, "If Not Now, When? Time for an IAEA Special Inspection in Syria," ISIS Report, Institute for Science and International Security, September 6, 2010, http://isis-online.org/isis-reports/detail/if-not-now-when-time-for-an-iaea-special-inspection-in-syria/; Olli Heinonen, "The Case for an Immediate IAEA Special Inspection in Syria," *Policy Watch*, November 5, 2010, www.washingtoninstitute.org/policy-analysis/view/the-case-for-an-immediate-iaea-special-inspection-in-syria; James M. Acton, Mark Fitzpatrick, and Pierre Goldschmidt, "The IAEA Should Call for a Special Inspection in Syria," *Proliferation Analysis*, Carnegie Endowment for International Peace, February 26, 2009, www.carnegieendowment.org/publications/index.cfm?fa=view&id=22791; Jay Solomon, "U.S. Considers Push for U.N. Action in Syria," *Wall Street Journal*, August 6, 2010, http://online.wsj.com/article/SB100014240527487046 57504575411762167580080.html.

172. Report by the Director General, "Implementation of the NPT Safeguards Agreement in the Syrian Arab Republic," International Atomic Energy Agency, GOV/2012/42, August 30, 2012, p. 2, www.iaea.org/Publications/Documents/Board/2012/gov2012-42.pdf.

173. Mary Beth Nikitin, Andrew Feickert, and Paul K. Kerr, "Syria's Chemical Weapons: Issues for Congress," Congressional Research Service, May 31, 2013, pp. 4–5, www.fas.org/sgp/crs/nuke/R42848.pdf.

174. See, for example, Dennis C. Blair, "Annual Threat Assessment of the US Intelligence Community for the Senate Select Committee on Intelligence," Report by

the Director of National Intelligence, February 2, 2010, p. 26, www.intelligence.senate
.gov/100202/blair.pdf; U.S. Director of National Intelligence, "Unclassified Report to
Congress on the Acquisition of Technology Relating to Weapons of Mass Destruction and Advanced Conventional Munitions, Covering 1 January to 31 December 2010,"
pp. 5–6, https://www.fas.org/irp/threat/wmd-acq2010.pdf.; U.S. Director of National
Intelligence, "Unclassified Report to Congress on the Acquisition of Technology Relating to Weapons of Mass Destruction and Advanced Conventional Munitions, Covering
1 January to 31 December 2009," pp. 6–7, https://www.fas.org/irp/threat/wmd-acq2009
.pdf.

175. Daryl Kimball and Kelsey Davenport, "Chemical Weapons: Frequently Asked
Questions," Arms Control Association, October 2013, www.armscontrol.org/factsheets/
Chemical-Weapons-Frequently-Asked-Questions. There have been instances of nonstate
actors using chemical weapons, most notably Aum Shinrikyo's use of sarin in a Tokyo
subway in 1995, and there have been more reports of chemical weapons used by Turk-
ish troops against Kurdish separatists in 2009, but these remain unproven. See Daniel
Steinvorth and Yassin Musharbash, "Shocking Images of Dead Kurdish Fighters: Turkey
Accused of Using Chemical Weapons against PKK," *Der Spiegel*, August 12, 2010, www
.spiegel.de/international/world/shocking-images-of-dead-kurdish-fighters-turkey
-accused-of-using-chemical-weapons-against-pkk-a-711536.html.

176. CBS News, "Sec. of State John Kerry Voices Concern over Syria Chemical
Weapons," September 21, 2014, www.cbsnews.com/news/sec-of-state-john-kerry-voices
-concern-over-syria-chemical-weapons; Organization for the Prohibition of Chemical Weapons, "OPCW Fact Finding Mission: 'Compelling Confirmation' That Chlorine Gas Used as Weapon in Syria," Press Release, September 10, 2014, www.opcw
.org/news/article/opcw-fact-finding-mission-compelling-confirmation-that-chlorine
-gas-used-as-weapon-in-syria; William Branigin and Anne Gearan, "Last of Syria's
Chemical Weapons Handed Over for Destruction, International Body Says," *Washington Post*, June 23, 2014, www.washingtonpost.com/world/middle_east/agency-last
-of-syrias-chemical-weapons-handed-over-for-destruction/2014/06/23/4eb9a138
-fad9-11e3-8176-f2c941cf35f1_story.html; Adam Entous, "Assad Chemical Threat Mounts,"
Wall Street Journal, June 28, 2015, www.wsj.com/articles/assad-chemical-threat-mounts
-1435535977.

177. "Obama Warns Syria Not to Cross 'Red Line,'" *CNN*, August 21, 2013, www.cnn
.com/2012/08/20/world/meast/syria-unrest.

178. "France: Assad Launched 14 Chemical Strikes since October," *Global Security
Newswire*, May 14, 2014, www.nti.org/gsn/article/france-assad-launched-14-chemical
-strikes-after-september; Diane Barnes, "Kerry Says 'Raw Data' Points to New Syria
Chemical Strikes," *Global Security Newswire*, May 15, 2014, www.nti.org/gsn/article/hagel
-holds-off-endorsing-claims-new-syria-chemical-strikes.

179. Colum Lynch and Joby Warrick, "In Syrian Chemical Weapons Claim, Criticism

about Lack of Transparency," June 20, 2013, http://articles.washingtonpost.com/2013-06 -20/world/40091001_1_chemical-weapons-obama-administration-rebel-claims.

180. Ibid.

181. Colum Lynch, "U.S. Claims of Chemical Weapons against Syrian Rebels Meet Caution at U.N.," *Washington Post*, June 14, 2013, http://articles.washingtonpost.com /2013-06-14/world/39976895_1_chemical-weapons-syrian-government-government -forces.

182. Ibid.

183. Secretary-General Ban Ki-moon, "Off-the-Cuff: Secretary-General's press encounter on the Report of the Mission to Investigate Allegations of the Use of Chemical Weapons in the Syrian Arab Republic: Report on the incident of 21 August 2013 in the Ghouta area of Damascus," United Nations, September 16, 2013, www.un.org/sg/offthe cuff/index.asp?nid=2985.

184. The White House, "Government Assessment of the Syrian Government's Use of Chemical Weapons on August 21, 2013," Office of the Press Secretary, August 30, 2013, www.whitehouse.gov/the-press-office/2013/08/30/government-assessment-syrian-gov ernment-s-use-chemical-weapons-august-21; "French Report Concludes Syria Regime Used Chemical Weapons," Associated Press, September 2, 2013, www.cbsnews.com /news/ french-report-concludes-syria-regime-used-chemical-weapons/; Erin Pelton, "United Nations Releases Report on the Use of Chemical Weapons in Syria," White House Blog, September 18, 2013, www.whitehouse.gov/blog/2013/09/18/united-nations-releases-report -use-chemical-weapons-syria.

185. Vladimir Putin, "A Plea for Caution from Russia," op-ed, *New York Times*, September 11, 2013, www.nytimes.com/2013/09/12/opinion/putin-plea-for-caution-from -russia-on-syria.html.

186. Charles Crawford, "Syria, Chemical Weapons, and the Worst Day in Western Diplomatic History," *Telegraph*, September 10, 2013, http://blogs.telegraph.co.uk/news/ charlescrawford/100235250/syria-chemical-weapons-and-the-worst-day-in-western -diplomatic-history/.

187. "Secretary-General Receives Syria's Formal Accession to Treaty Banning Chemical Weapons," UN News Centre, September 14, 2014, www.un.org/apps/news/story .asp?NewsID=45852#.U72RdPldXhE.

188. UN Security Council, Resolution 2118 (2013), S/RES/2118 (2013), September 27, 2013, www.securitycouncilreport.org/atf/cf/%7B65BFCF9B-6D27-4E9C-8CD3-CF6E4FF 96FF9%7D/s_res_2118.pdf.

189. Organization for the Prohibition of Chemical Weapons, "Syria Submits Its Initial Declaration and a General Plan of Destruction of Its Chemical Weapons Programme," OPCW website, October 27, 2013, www.opcw.org/index.php?id=242&tx_tt news%5Btt_news%5D=1776&cHash=02addbd970a75957d30033ec257b66c6.

190. C. Todd Lopez, "Army to Destroy Syrian Chemical Weapons Aboard Ship,"

Army News Service, Department of Defense, January 3, 2014, www.defense.gov/news/newsarticle.aspx?id=121428.

191. Organization for the Prohibition of Chemical Weapons, "Syria Completes Destruction Activities to Render Inoperable Chemical Weapons Production Facilities and Mixing/Filling Plants," Press Release, OPCW website, October 31, 2013, www.opcw.org/news/article/syria-completes-destruction-activities-to-render-inoperable-chemical-weapons-production-facilities-a/.

192. Mike Corder, "All Syrian Chemical Weapons Munitions Destroyed," *USA Today*, December 6, 2013, www.usatoday.com/story/news/world/2013/12/06/all-syrian-chemical-weapons-munitions-destroyed/3892017/.

193. Ahmet Üzümcü, "Announcement to Media on Last Consignment of Chemicals Leaving Syria," Organization for the Prohibition of Chemical Weapons, June 23, 2014, http://www.opcw.org/news/article/announcement-to-media-on-last-consignment-of-chemicals-leaving-syria/; Organization for the Prohibition of Chemical Weapons, "OPCW: All Category 1 Chemicals Declared by Syria Now Destroyed," Press Release, August 28, 2014, https://www.opcw.org/news/article/opcw-all-category-1-chemicals-declared-by-syria-now-destroyed.

194. Robert P. Mikulak, "Statement to the Fortieth Meeting of the Executive Council," U.S. Delegation to the Executive Council, The Hague, Netherlands, April 29, 2014, http:www.state.gov/t/avc/rls/2014/225340.htm.

195. Ahmet Üzümcü, quoted in Ashley Fantz and Diana Magnay, "Global Watchdog: Syria Has Shipped Out Its Last 'Declared' Chemical Weapons," CNN.com, www.cnn.com/2014/06/23/world/meast/syria-chemical-weapons.

196. See, for example, Ashley Fantz and Diana Magnay, "Global Watchdog: Syria Has Shipped Out Its Last 'Declared' Chemical Weapons," CNN.com, www.cnn.com/2014/06/23/world/meast/syria-chemical-weapons; "Syria May Still Have Hidden Chemical Weapons, OPCW Admits," Channel 4 News, June 25, 2014, www.channel4.com/news/syria-chemical-weapons-may-still-haveassets-opcw-assad.

197. Organization for the Prohibition of Chemical Weapons, "Letter dated 28 March 2016 from the Secretary-General addressed to the President of the Security Council," United Nations Security Council, S/2016/285, March 29, 2016, p. 4, http://reliefweb.int/sites/reliefweb.int/files/resources/N1608678.pdf.

198. Robert Mikulak, "Statement to the Fortieth Meeting of the Executive Council."

199. Alex Spillius, "Syria: Bashar al-Assad Has 'Spread Chemical Weapons around 50 Sites,'" *Telegraph*, September 13, 2013, www.telegraph.co.uk/news/worldnews/middleeast/syria/10306852/Syria-Bashar-al-Assad-has-spread-chemical-weapons-around-50-sites.html. It is possible that the apparent discrepancies between the reported U.S. estimates and Syria's CW declaration could be partially explained if the United States is counting individual buildings at chemical weapons sites and the Syrian government declared CW sites that can contain more than one building.

200. Inna Lazareva, "Israelis Keep Gas Masks against Syrian Threat," *Sunday Times*, December 15, 2013, p. 36, www.thesundaytimes.co.uk/sto/news/world_news/Middle_East/article1352661.ece.

201. Colum Lynch, John Hudson, and Yochi Dreazen, "Exclusive: Syria Pushes to Keep Its Chemical Weapons Factories," *Foreign Policy*, October 31, 2013, http://thecable .foreignpolicy.com/posts/2013/10/31/exclusive_syria_tries_to_hold_on_to_its_chemi cal_weapons_factories#sthash.74Fx6MXX.dpbs.

202. Ernesto Londoño and Greg Miller, "U.S. officials say Syria is using remaining chemical weapons stockpile as leverage," *Washington Post*, April 30, 2014, www.washing tonpost.com/world/national-security/us-officials-say-syria-is-using-remaining-chem ical-weapons-stockpile-as-leverage/2014/04/30/1dd68c8a-d0a8-11e3-9e25-188ebe1fa93b_ story.html; "U.S. Insiders: Assad Turns Last Chemical Arms Into Bargaining Chip," May 1, 2014, www.nti.org/gsn/article/us-insiders-assad-turns-last-chemical-arms-bargaining-chip; Bendavid and Abi-Habib, "Syria Pact in Peril," p. A1.

203. Lynch, Hudson, and Dreazen, "Exclusive: Syria Pushes to Keep Its Chemical Weapons Factories."

204. Associated Press, "Global Watchdog: 2 Syrian Chemical Weapons Facilities Destroyed, All 12 Destroyed This Summer," March 2, 2015, www.foxnews.com/world /2015/03/02/global-watchdog-2-syrian-chemical-weapons-facilities-destroyed-all -12-destroyed.

205. Organization for the Prohibition of Chemical Weapons, "Letter dated 28 March 2016," p. 2.

206. Anthony Deutsch, "Exclusive: Syria Has Shipped out Less than 5 Percent of Chemical Weapons," *Reuters*, January 29, 2014, www.reuters.com/article/2014/01/29/ us-syria-crisis-chemical-idUSBREA0S19720140129; Julian Borger, "Syria to Hand Over Chemical Weapons but Doubts Linger over Full Arsenal," *Guardian*, April 24, 2014, www .theguardian.com/world/2014/apr/24/syria-chemical-weapons-doubts-chlorine. See also Naftali Bendavid and Maria Abi-Habib, "Syria Pact in Peril—Regime Faces Allegations It Violated Agreement with Chlorine Gas Attacks," *Wall Street Journal*, May 15, 2014, p. A1; and "British Insiders Accuse Assad of Withholding Chemical-Arms Materials," *Global Security Newswire*, April 25, 2014, www.nti.org/gsn/article/british-insiders-accuse-assad -withholding-chemical-arms-materials.

207. Naftali Bendavid, "Syria Chemical Weapons Inspections Hit Snag," *Wall Street Journal*, October 28, 2013, http://online.wsj.com/news/articles/SB1000142405270230447 0504579163730984986434; "Fidelity of Syrian Chemical Disclosure Questioned," *Global Security Newswire*, November 1, 2013, www.nti.org/gsn/article/questions-remain-about -fidelity-syrian-chemical-disclosure/.

208. *The Comprehensive Report of the Special Advisor to the DCI on Iraq's WMD* (aka. the Duelfer Report), Vol. 1, "Scope Note," pp. 2–3, www.foia.cia.gov/sites/default/files/ document_conversions/89801/DOC_0001156395.pdf.

209. Also, the security situation will potentially make it more difficult to acquire information (including from third parties) that would be required to initiate a challenge inspection.

210. Corder, "All Syrian Chemical Weapons Munitions Destroyed."

211. Organization for the Prohibition of Chemical Weapons, "Syria Completes Destruction Activities to Render Inoperable Chemical Weapons Production Facilities and Mixing/Filling Plants"; Bendavid, "Syria Chemical Weapons Inspections Hit Snag"; Global Security Newswire, "Fidelity of Syrian Chemical Disclosure Questioned."

212. Bendavid, "Syria Chemical Weapons Inspections Hit Snag"; Global Security Newswire, "Fidelity of Syrian Chemical Disclosure Questioned."

213. The experience in Libya, for example, illustrates this problem.

214. For example, this difficulty can be seen in the steps taken by France, China, and Russia to prevent Security Council action in Iraq, despite significant evidence of obstructionism documented by UNSCOM—or, for that matter, Russia's denial of chemical weapon use by Syria in 2013.

215. Mike Hoffman, "Syria Airstrike in Iraq Complicates ISIL Equation," DefenseTech, June 25, 2014, http://defensetech.org/2014/06/25/syria-airstrike-in-iraq-complicates-isil -equation; Luke Harding, "Syria Misses Chemical Weapons Deadline," *Guardian*, December 31, 2013, www.theguardian.com/world/2013/dec/31/syria-misses-chemical-weapons -deadline. Of course, ISIL's gains may produce the opposite effect, spurring U.S. support of moderate rebel groups to a degree not yet seen. See Lesley Wroughton, "Kerry in Saudi, Says Syrian Opposition Has Key Role against ISIL," *Reuters*, June 27, 2014, http:// in.reuters.com/article/2014/06/27/uk-iraq-crisis-kerry-saudi-idINKBN0F218Q20140627.

216. "France: Assad Launched 14 Chemical Strikes since October," *Global Security Newswire*, May 14, 2014, www.nti.org/gsn/article/france-assad-launched-14-chemical- strikes-after-september.

217. Barnes, "Kerry Says 'Raw Data' Points to New Syria Chemical Strikes."

218. Organization for the Prohibition of Chemical Weapons, "OPCW Fact Finding Mission."

219. CBS News, "Sec. of State John Kerry Voices Concern over Syria Chemical Weapons."

220. UN Security Council, "Security Council Condemns Use of Chlorine Gas as Weapon in Syria," Resolution 2209 (2015), 7401st Meeting, March 5, 2015, www.un.org/ press/en/2015/sc11810.doc.htm.

221. Anne Barnard and Somini Senguptamay, "Syria Is Using Chemical Weapons Again, Rescue Workers Say," *New York Times*, May 6, 2015, www.nytimes.com/2015/05/07/ world/middleeast/syria-chemical-weapons.html.

222. Associated Press, "US Seeks Security Council Action to Identify Perpetrators of Chemical Weapons Attacks in Syria," July 9, 2015, www.usnews.com/news/world/articles /2015/07/09/us-seeks-un-action-on-chemical-weapon-attacks-in-syria.

223. Nikitin and Kerr, "Syria's Chemical Weapons," pp. 7–8; Jeremy M. Sharp and Christopher M. Blanchard, "Armed Conflict in Syria: U.S. and International Response," Congressional Research Service, June 14, 2013, www.fas.org/sgp/crs/mideast/RL33487 .pdf, p. 16.

224. Nikitin, Feickert, and Kerr, "Syria's Chemical Weapons," pp. 4–8; Sharp and Blanchard, "Armed Conflict in Syria," p. 16; Ben Rhodes, "Statement by Deputy National Security Advisor for Strategic Communications on Syrian Chemical Weapons Use," The White House, Office of the Press Secretary, June 13, 2013, www.whitehouse .gov/the-press-office/2013/06/13/statement-deputy-national-security-advisor-strategic -communications-ben-; Ruth Maclean, "Syrian Regime Moves to Secure Its Chemical Weapons," *Times* (London), September 29, 2012, www.thetimes.co.uk/tto/news/world/ middleeast/article3553190.ece; Sharp and Blanchard, "Armed Conflict in Syria," p. 17.

225. Busch, *No End in Sight*, pp. 282–83; Peter Stein and Peter D. Feaver, *Assuring Control of Nuclear Weapons: The Evolution of Permissive Action Links* (Lanham, MD: University Press of America, 1987), pp. 7–8; Peter Feaver, "Command and Control in Emerging Nuclear Nations," *International Security*, Vol. 17, No. 3 (Winter 1992/93), pp. 164–66.

226. International Atomic Energy Agency, "Conclusion of Additional Protocols: Status as of 21 May 2014," IAEA website, accessed July 15, 2014, www.iaea.org/safeguards/ documents/sir_table.pdf.

227. For a fascinating discussion on the origins of and negotiations over the information on al-Kibar, see Elliott Abrams, "Bombing the Syrian Reactor: The Untold Story," *Commentary*, Vol. 135, No. 2 (February 2013), pp. 18–24, http://commentarymaga zine.com/article/bombing-the-syrian-reactror-the-untold-story.

228. Peter Crail, "IAEA Sends Syria Nuclear Case to the UN," *Arms Control Today*, Vol. 41, No. 6 (July-August 2011), pp. 22–24, www.armscontrol.org/print/4948.

229. Abrams, "Bombing the Syrian Reactor."

230. Michael Singh, "Syria's Lessons for the Iran Nuclear Talks," Policy Analysis, Washington Institute for Near East Policy, September 20, 2013, https://www.washington institute.org/policy-analysis/view/syrias-lessons-for-the-iran-nuclear-talks.

231. Paul F. Walker, "Myanmar Ratifies Chemical Weapons Convention," *Arms Control Now*, blog of the Arms Control Association, January 28, 2015, https://www.armscon trol.org/blog/ArmsControlNow/2015-01-28/Myanmar-Ratifies-Chemical-Weapons -Convention.

232. "Myanmar Overview," Nuclear Threat Initiative, July 2013, www.nti.org/ country-profiles/myanmar/. For a report on accusations of CW use, see "Burma Used Chemicals on Rebels," BBC News, April 25, 2005, http://news.bbc.co.uk/2/hi/asia-pacific /4467471.stm.

233. Peter Crail, "Report Alleges Secret Myanmar Nuclear Work," *Arms Control Today*, Vol. 40, No. 6 (July-August, 2010), p. 44.

234. David Albright and Christina Walrond, "Technical Note: Revisiting Bomb Reactors in Burma and an Alleged Burmese Nuclear Weapons Program," ISIS Report, Institute for Science and International Security, April 11, 2011, http://isis-online.org/uploads/isis-reports/documents/Burma_Analysis_Bomb_Reactors_11April2011.pdf.

235. British Broadcasting Corporation, "Myanmar's 2015 Landmark Elections Explained," December 3, 2015, http://www.bbc.com/news/world-asia-33547036.

236. See, for example, David Albright and Andrea Stricker, "Burma's Nuclear Aspirations: Less Reason Now for Concern," ISIS Report, Institute for Science and International Security, December 12, 2011, http://isis-online.org/isis-reports/detail/burmas-nuclear-aspirations-less-reason-now-for-concern/; David Albright and Andrea Stricker, "Myanmar Says Halted Nuclear Research Program: Verification Critical," ISIS Report, Institute for Science and International Security, June 3, 2011, http://isis-online.org/isis-reports/detail/myanmar-says-halted-nuclear-research-program-verification-critical/; David Albright and Andrea Stricker, "In Positive Move, Burma to Sign Additional Protocol," ISIS Report, Institute for Science and International Security, November 19, 2012, http://isis-online.org/isis-reports/detail/in-positive-move-burma-to-sign-additional-protocol/.

237. Andrea Stricker and Serena Kelleher-Vergantini, "Myanmar Government Must Close Down Military Ties with North Korea," ISIS Report, Institute for Science and International Security, July 5, 2013, http://isis-online.org/isis-reports/detail/myanmar-government-must-close-down-military-ties-with-north-korea/.

238. For Myanmar's alleged preparations to ratify the CWC, see Khin Maung Soe, "Myanmar Prepares to Ratify Chemical and Biological Weapons Treaties," December 11, 2013, www.rfa.org/english/news/myanmar/weapons-12112013192030.html; Shwe Aung, "Burma Preparing to Ratify Chemical Weapons Ban: Ye Htut," DVB, February 14, 2014, https://www.dvb.no/news/Burma-preparing-to-ratify-chemical-weapons-ban-ye-htut-burma-myanmar/37250.

239. Jeffrey Lewis and Catherine Dill, "Myanmar's Unrepentant Arms Czar," *Foreign Policy*, May 9, 2014, www.foreignpolicy.com/articles/2014/05/09/myanmar_north_korea_thein_htay_chemical_weapons; Catherine Dill and Jeffrey Lewis, "Suspect Defense Facility in Myanmar," James Martin Center for Nonproliferation Studies, May 9, 2014, www.nonproliferation.org/suspect-defense-facility-in-myanmar; "Myanmar Brushes Off Analysis of Alleged Chemical-Arms Site," *Global Security Newswire*, May 19, 2014, www .nti.org/gsn/article/myanmar-expert-concerns-alleged-chemical-arms-site.

240. Dill and Lewis, "Suspect Defense Facility in Myanmar."

241. Jeffrey Lewis, "Note from a Small Organization," Arms Control Wonk, May 16, 2014, http://lewis.armscontrolwonk.com/archive/7328/note-from-a-small-organization.

242. Nicholas Blanford, "Why President Bashar al-Assad's Rule May Endure," *Christian Science Monitor*, January 5, 2014, www.csmonitor.com/World/Middle-East/2014/0105/Why-President-Bashar-al-Assad-s-rule-may-endure.

243. Busch, *No End in Sight*, p. 227; Joseph Bermudez, Jr., "The Democratic People's

Republic of Korea and Unconventional Weapons," in *Planning the Unthinkable: How New Powers Will Use Nuclear, Biological, and Chemical Weapons* (Ithaca, NY: Cornell University Press, 2000), p. 199.

244. See Busch, *No End in Sight*, pp. 84–131; Bermudez, "The Democratic People's Republic of Korea and Unconventional Weapons," p. 200.

245. For more extensive discussions of "denial and deception," see Busch, *No End in Sight*, pp. 30–31, 256; Roy Godson and James J. Wirtz, "Strategic Denial and Deception," in Roy Godson and James J. Wirtz, eds., *Strategic Denial and Deception: The Twenty-First Century Challenge* (New Brunswick, NJ: Transaction Publishers, 2002); Jonathan B. Tucker, "Monitoring and Verification in a Noncooperative Environment: Lessons from the U.N. Experience in Iraq," *Nonproliferation Review*, Vol. 3, No. 3 (Spring-Summer 1996), pp. 1–14; David A. Kay, "Denial and Deception Practices of WMD Proliferators: Iraq and Beyond," *Washington Quarterly*, Vol. 18, No. 1 (Winter 1995), pp. 85–105.

246. Colleen Curry, "U.S. Wargames North Korean Regime Collapse, Invasion to Secure Nukes," ABC News, March 29, 2013, http://abcnews.go.com/International/us-war games-north-korean-regime-collapse-invasion-secure/storynew?id=18822930.

247. See, for example, Jon Lee Anderson, "Obama's Syria Problem," *New Yorker*, December 14, 2012, www.newyorker.com/online/blogs/comment/2012/12/obamas-syria -problem.html; "Securing Syrian Chemical Sites May Require 75,000 Troops: U.S. Military," *Global Security Newswire*," November 16, 2012, www.nti.org/gsn/article/securing -syrian-chemical-sites-may-require-75000-troops-us-military/.

248. Andrew C. Weber and Anya Erokhina, "Cooperative Threat Reduction and Its Lessons," in Joseph F. Pilat and Nathan E. Busch, eds., *The Routledge Handbook of Nuclear Proliferation and Policy* (New York: Routledge, 2015), p. 463.

249. Nackaerts, "IAEA Safeguards: Cooperation as the Key to Change."

250. Scott D. Sagan, "Nuclear Latency and Nuclear Proliferation," in William Potter and Gaukhar Mukhatzhanova, eds., *Forecasting Nuclear Proliferation in the 21st Century* (Stanford: Stanford University Press, 2010), pp. 82–83.

251. International Atomic Energy Agency, "Conclusion of Additional Protocols: Status as of 31 December 2013," December 31, 2013, www.iaea.org/safeguards/documents/ AP_status_list.pdf. According to some reports, Myanmar may soon ratify the CWC, but it has yet to do so at the time of this writing. See Soe, "Myanmar Prepares to Ratify Chemical, Biological Weapons Treaties."

252. For the role of third-party information in identifying clandestine activities and facilities, see, for example, Report by the Director General, "Implementation of the NPT Safeguards Agreement and Relevant Provisions of Security Council Resolutions in the Islamic Republic of Iran," International Atomic Energy Agency, GOV/2011/65, November 8, 2011, Annex, paragraphs 6, 9, and 12, www.iaea.org/sites/default/files/gov2011-65 .pdf; Director General, "NPT Safeguards Agreement in Syria," p. 4; Albright and Brannan, "Satellite Image Shows Suspected Uranium Conversion Plant in Syria."

Conclusion

1. For a detailed discussion of the Soviet Union's covert BW program, written by the former director of the program, see Kenneth Alibek, *Biohazard* (New York: Random House, 1999).

2. Arms Control Association, "The Chemical Weapons Convention (CWC) at a Glance," September 2013, https://www.armscontrol.org/factsheets/cwcglance.

3. Jonathan B. Tucker, "Putting Teeth in the Biological Weapons Convention," *Issues in Science and Technology*, Vol. 18, No. 3 (Spring 2002), http://issues.org/18-3/tucker.

4. See, for example, Laura Rockwood, "The IAEA and International Safeguards," in Joseph F. Pilat and Nathan E. Busch, eds., *The Routledge Handbook of Nuclear Proliferation and Policy* (New York: Routledge, 2015); Theodore Hirsch, "The IAEA Additional Protocol: What It Is and Why It Matters," *Nonproliferation Review*, Vol. 11, No. 13 (Fall–Winter 2004), p. 142; Matthew Bunn, "International Safeguards: Summarizing 'Traditional' and 'New' Measures," MIT OpenCourseWare Web Site, Spring 2004, pp. 3–4, http://ocw.mit.edu/courses/nuclear-engineering/22-812j-managing-nuclear-technology-spring-2004/lecture-notes/lec16notes.pdf.

5. Arms Control Association, "The Chemical Weapons Convention (CWC) at a Glance"; Tucker, "Putting Teeth in the Biological Weapons Convention."

6. Report by the Director General, "Implementation of the NPT Safeguards Agreement in the Syrian Arab Republic," International Atomic Energy Agency, GOV/2011/30, May 24, 2011, p. 8, www.iaea.org/Publications/Documents/Board/2011/gov2011-30.pdf; Herman Nackaerts, "Towards More Effective Safeguards: Learning Hard Lessons," Opening Plenary Address, Institute of Nuclear Materials Management (INMM) Annual Meeting, July 18, 2011, pp. 1–2, www.inmm.org/AM/Template.cfm?Section=Evolving_the_IAEA_State_Level_Concept&Template=/CM/ContentDisplay.cfm&ContentID=2971.

7. Jonathan B. Tucker, "Verifying the Chemical Weapons Ban: Missing Elements," *Arms Control Today*, Vol. 37, No. 1 (January-February, 2007), pp. 6–13, www.armscontrol.org/act/2007_01-02/Tucker; Ellen Tauscher, "Preventing Biological Weapons Proliferation and Bioterrorism," Address to the Annual Meeting of the States Parties to the Biological Weapons Convention, Geneva, Switzerland, December 9, 2009, www.state.gov/t/us/133335.htm.

8. Nackaerts, "Towards More Effective Safeguards," p. 1.

9. For a detailed study of the A. Q. Khan smuggling network, see David Albright, "Libya: A Major Sale at Last," ISIS Special Report, Institute for Science and International Security, http://isis-online.org/uploads/isis-reports/documents/Libya_and_the_Khan_Network_1Dec2010.pdf.

10. For a fuller discussion of second-tier suppliers, see Chaim Braun and Christopher F. Chyba, "Proliferation Rings: New Challenges to the Nuclear Nonproliferation Regime," *International Security*, Vol. 29, No. 2 (Fall 2004), pp. 5–49.

11. Nackaerts, "Towards More Effective Safeguards," p. 2.

12. Ibid.

13. For the text of Obama's Prague speech, see Remarks by President Barack Obama, Hradcany Square, Prague, Czech Republic, April 5, 2009, www.whitehouse.gov/the_press _office/Remarks-By-President-Barack-Obama-In-Prague-As-Delivered.

14. For a detailed discussion of the reception by other nuclear powers and other obstacles that have arisen to President Obama's vision of a nuclear free world, see Michael Nacht, "The Global Nuclear Environment: President Obama's Vision Amid Emerging Nuclear Threats," in Joseph F. Pilat and Nathan E. Busch, eds., *Routledge Handbook on Nuclear Proliferation and Policy* (New York: Routledge Press, 2015).

15. Joseph Cirincione, "How We Dodged Libya's Nuclear Bullet," *Huffington Post*, March 11, 2011, www.huffingtonpost.com/joe-cirincione/how-we-dodged-libyas-nucl_b _829669.html; Thomas Pickering, comments in panel session on "Preventing a Nuclear-Armed Iran," Arms Control Association Annual Meeting, Carnegie Endowment for International Peace, Washington, DC, June 4, 2012, www.armscontrol.org/events/ Join-ACA-June-4-Our-Annual-Meeting%20#panel2; Hans Blix, interviewed in "Blix Speaks with Reporters," CNN, January 23, 2003, http://transcripts.cnn.com/TRAN SCRIPTS/0301/23/se.05.html.

16. In this context, one might recall Jessica Mathews's description of the international inspection process in Iraq as "a success, a rather striking international success, that stands out in the record of recent decades. . . . While the international intelligence services were getting it wrong, the United Nations inspectors were getting the picture largely right." See Jessica Tuchman Mathews, "What Happened in Iraq? The Success Story of United Nations Inspections," Keynote Speech to the International Peace Academy, March 5, 2004, www.carnegieendowment.org/publications/index.cfm?fa=view&id=1471.

17. Examples of this could be seen in Mohammed ElBaradei's downplaying the seriousness of Iranian noncompliance in IAEA reports, or lowering standards for verification in Syria, in efforts to avoid war. See Jack Shenker, "Cautious Reports on Tehran Nuclear Programme 'Were Framed to Avoid War,'" *Guardian*, March 31, 2010, www.guardian.co.uk/world/2010/mar/31/iran-nuclear-programme-cautious-language; James M. Acton, Mark Fitzpatrick, and Pierre Goldschmidt, "The IAEA Should Call for a Special Inspection in Syria," *Proliferation Analysis*, Carnegie Endowment for International Peace, February 26, 2009, www.carnegieendowment.org/publications/index.cfm ?fa=view&id=22791.

18. Tucker, "Verifying the Chemical Weapons Ban," pp. 6–13.

19. Yukiya Amano, "Challenges in Nuclear Verification: The IAEA's Role on the Iranian Nuclear Issue," Speech given at the Brookings Institution, Washington, DC, October 31, 2014, https://www.iaea.org/newscenter/statements/challenges-nuclear-verifica tion-iaea%E2%80%99s-role-iranian-nuclear-issue.

20. Organization for the Prohibition of Chemical Weapons Executive Council,

"Medium-Term Plan for the Period from 2013-2015," Seventy-Fourth Session, EC-70/S/1/Rev.1, October 8–11, 2013, p. 6, https://www.opcw.org/index.php?eID=dam_front end_push&docID=15942.

21. Amano, "Challenges in Nuclear Verification."

22. Laura Smith-Spark and Marilia Brocchetto, "U.N. Watchdog: We Need Money to Monitor Iran Nuclear Deal," CNN, August 25, 2015, www.cnn.com/2015/08/25/world/iaea-iran-nuclear-deal.

23. See Lewis A. Dunn and Patricia McFate, "Transparency Aspects, Prospects, and Implications," Briefing at Lawrence Livermore National laboratory, Livermore, CA, September 24, 1992.

24. Roy Godson and James J. Wirtz, "Strategic Denial and Deception," *International Journal of Intelligence and Counterintelligence*, Vol. 13 (2000), pp. 424–37.

25. Christopher Way and Jessica L. P. Weeks, "Making It Personal: Regime Type and Nuclear Proliferation," *American Journal of Political Science*, Vol. 58, No. 3 (July 2014), pp. 705–19.

26. Mitchell B. Reiss, "Foreword," in Nathan E. Busch and Daniel H. Joyner, eds., *Combating Weapons of Mass Destruction: The Future of International Nonproliferation Policy* (Athens: University of Georgia Press, 2009), pp. xiii–xiv.

27. Nuclear Energy Study Group, "Nuclear Power and Proliferation Resistance: Securing Benefits, Limiting Risk," American Physical Society Panel on Public Affairs, May 2005, p. 8, www.aps.org/policy/reports/popa-reports/proliferation-resistance/upload/proliferation.pdf. For a description of some international R&D efforts in this area, see the European Commission Joint Research Centre Institute for Transuranium Elements, "Nuclear Safeguards Research and Development," http://itu.jrc.ec.europa.eu/index.php?id=194.

28. "NNSA Next Generation Safeguards Initiative," Fact Sheet, National Nuclear Security Administration, Department of Energy, Jan 2, 2009, http://nnsa.energy.gov/mediaroom/factsheets/nextgenerationsafeguards.

29. Ibid.

30. Department of Defense, Defense Science Board, *Task Force Report: Assessment of Nuclear Monitoring and Verification Technologies*, January 2014, p. 1, www.acq.osd.mil/dsb/reports/NuclearMonitoringAndVerificationTechnologies.pdf.

31. Ibid., p. 19.

32. Nuclear Energy Study Group, "Nuclear Power and Proliferation Resistance," p. 8.

33. Nikolai Khlebnikov, David Parlse, and Julian Whichello, "Novel Technologies for the Detection of Undeclared Nuclear Activities," IAEA-CN-148/32, released by the Nonproliferation Policy Education Center on March 2007, www.npolicy.org/article_file/Novel_technologies_for_the_detection_of_undeclared_nuclear_activities.pdf; Joseph F. Pilat, "IAEA Safeguards: The Role of Advanced Safeguards Technologies

in Meeting Tomorrow's Challenges," Paper presented at the JAEA-IAEA Workshop on Advanced Safeguards Technology for the Future Nuclear Fuel Cycle. Ibaraki, Japan, November 13–16, 2007, pp. 1–12, http://www-pub.iaea.org/mtcd/meetings/PDFplus/2007/cn1073/Papers/3.3%20Ppr_%20Pilat%20-%20IAEA%20Safeguards%20The%20Role%20of%20Advanced%20Safeguards%20Technologies%20in%20Meeting%20Tomorrow.pdf.

34. Joseph F. Pilat and Nathan E. Busch, "WMD Monitoring and Verification Regimes: Lessons from Iraq," *Contemporary Security Policy*, Vol. 32, No. 2 (August 2011), p. 425.

35. See especially Frank V. Pabian, "Evidence from Imagery: The Iran and Syrian Nuclear Programs—An Open and Shut Case?" Lecture given at the James Martin Center for Nonproliferation Studies, Monterey, CA, October 28, 2009, www.youtube.fcom/watch?v=JkXbbHMKpHk.

36. See Admiral Richard C. Macke, Speech given at "Arms Control and the Revolution in Military Affairs," Defense Special Weapons Agency, June 8–11, 1998, www.ciaonet.org/conf/dsw01/dswa01j.html.

37. U.S. Department of Defense, *Nuclear Posture Review Report*, April 2010, www.defense.gov/npr/docs/2010%20nuclear%20posture%20review%20report.pdf.

38. Rose Gottemoeller, "The Vision of Prague Endures," Speech given at the Ministry of Foreign Affairs, Prague, Czech Republic, December 4, 2014, www.state.gov/t/us/2014/234675.htm.

39. See Steve Fetter, "Nuclear Archaeology: Verifying Declarations of Fissile Material Production," *Science & Global Security*, Vol. 3, Nos. 3–4 (1993), pp. 237–59.

40. George Perkovich and James M. Acton, "Verifying the Transition to Zero," in George Perkovich and James M. Acton, eds., *Abolishing Nuclear Weapons: A Debate* (Washington, DC: Carnegie Endowment for International Peace, 2009), p. 62, http://carnegieendowment.org/files/abolishing_nuclear_weapons_debate.pdf, accessed June 15, 2013; Steve Fetter, "Verifying Nuclear Disarmament," Report prepared for the Henry L. Stimson Center's Project on Eliminating Weapons of Mass Destruction, March 12, 1998, p. 18, accessed April 4, 2013, http://drum.lib.umd.edu/bitstream/1903/4023/1/1998-VerifyingNuclearDisarmament.pdf.

41. For a discussion of nuclear forensics, see Klaus Mayer and Alexander Glaser, "Nuclear Forensics," in Joseph F. Pilat and Nathan E. Busch, eds., *The Routledge Handbook of Nuclear Proliferation and Policy* (New York: Routledge, 2015).

42. For a discussion of current proliferation resistant technologies and those under development, see Yusuke Kuno, "Advances in Proliferation Resistant Technologies and Procedures," in Joseph F. Pilat and Nathan E. Busch, eds., *The Routledge Handbook of Nuclear Proliferation and Policy* (New York: Routledge, 2015).

43. For a discussion of various multinational approaches, see John Carlson, "Multinational Approaches to the Nuclear Fuel Cycle," in Joseph F. Pilat and Nathan E. Busch,

eds., *The Routledge Handbook of Nuclear Proliferation and Policy* (New York: Routledge, 2015).

44. Nackaerts, "Towards More Effective Safeguards," p. 3.

45. Gene Aloise, Government Accountability Office, "Nuclear Nonproliferation: IAEA Safeguards and Other Measures to Halt the Spread of Nuclear Weapons and Material," testimony before the Subcommittee on National Security, Emerging Threats, and International Relations, House of Representatives, September 26, 2006, www.gao.gov/new.items/do61128t.pdf.

46. For a similar assessment, see John Carlson, "IAEA Safeguards Additional Protocol," Department of Foreign Affairs and Trade, Australian Government, January 20, 2009, https://www.dfat.gov.au/asno/publications/iaea-safeguards-additional-protocol.html.

47. For a discussion of some of these initiatives, see Gregory D. Koblentz, "From Biodefense to Biosecurity: The Obama Administration's Strategy for Countering Biological Threats," *International Affairs*, Vol. 88, No. 1 (January 2012), pp. 131–48.

48. Olli Heinonen, "Verifying the Dismantlement of South Africa's Nuclear Weapons Program," in Henry Sokolski, ed., *Nuclear Weapons Materials Gone Missing: What Does History Teach?* (Arlington, VA: Nonproliferation Policy Education Center, March 2014), p. 94, http://npolicy.org/books/2014muf/Nuclear%20Weapons%20Materials%20Gone%20Missing.pdf.

49. See, for example, Uri Berliner, "Crippled By Sanctions, Iran's Economy Key In Nuclear Deal," *National Public Radio*, November 25, 2013, www.npr.org/2013/11/25/247077050/crippled-by-sanctions-irans-economy-key-in-nuclear-deal. For a list of the economic sanctions against Iran prior to the negotiation of the Interim Agreement, see Council on Foreign Relations, "Backgrounder: The Lengthening List of Iran Sanctions," October 14, 2013, www.cfr.org/iran/lengthening-list-iran-sanctions/p20258.

Bibliography

Government Documents, Primary Sources

Aloise, Gene. "Nuclear Nonproliferation: IAEA Safeguards and Other Measure to Halt the Spread of Nuclear Weapons and Material." Testimony before the Subcommittee on National Security, Emerging Threats, and International Relations, U.S. House of Representatives. September 26, 2006, http://www.gao.gov/new.items/d061128t.pdf.

Amano, Yukiya. IAEA Director General's Remarks to the Press on Visit to Iran. International Atomic Energy Agency. September 21, 2015, https://www.iaea.org/newscenter/statements/iaea-director-generals-remarks-press-visit-iran.

———. "IAEA Director General's Statement and Road-map for the Clarification of Past & Present Outstanding Issues regarding Iran's Nuclear Program." International Atomic Energy Agency. July 14, 2015, https://www.iaea.org/newscenter/statements/iaea-director-generals-statement-and-road-map-clarification-past-present-outstanding-issues-regarding-irans-nuclear-program.

Blair, Dennis C. "Annual Threat Assessment of the US Intelligence Community for the Senate Select Committee on Intelligence." Report by the Director of National Intelligence. February 2, 2010, http://www.intelligence.senate.gov/100202/blair.pdf.

Blix, Hans. "Briefing of the Security Council." February 14, 2003, http://www.un.org/Depts/unmovic/blix14Febasdel.htm.

———. "Oral Introduction of the 12th Quarterly Report of UNMOVIC." Report to the UN Security Council. March 7, 2003, http://www.un.org/Depts/unmovic/SC7asdelivered.htm.

———. "An Update on Inspection." Speech delivered to the UN Security Council. January 27, 2003, http://www.un.org/Depts/unmovic/Bx27.htm.

Bowlder, William. "Message to Botha by Ambassador Bowlder." Archived by the Cold War International History Project, Woodrow Wilson International Center for Scholars. August 18, 1977, http://www.wilsoncenter.org/program/cold-war-international-history-project.

DeSutter, Paula. "Re-cooperation in Libyan Dismantlement Efforts." Testimony at a Hearing before the Subcommittee on International Terrorism, Nonproliferation, and

Human Rights, Committee on International Relations, U.S. House of Representatives. September 22, 2004, http://www.state.gov/s/l/2004/78305.htm.

———. Testimony before the Committee on Foreign Relations, U.S. Senate. February 26, 2004, http://2001-2009.state.gov/t/vci/rls/rm/2004/29945.htm.

Deutch, John. "Worldwide Threat Assessment." Brief to the Senate Select Committee in Intelligence. February 22, 1996, http://fas.org/irp/cia/product/dci_speech_022296 .html.

Duelfer, Charles. *The Comprehensive Report of the Special Advisor to the DCI on Iraq's WMD, Vol. 2.* September 30, 2004, https://www.cia.gov/library/reports/general-reports -1/iraq_wmd_2004/.

———. "Scope Note." *The Comprehensive Report of the Special Advisor to the DCI on Iraq's WMD, Vol. 1.* September 30, 2004, https://www.cia.gov/library/reports/general -reports-1/iraq_wmd_2004/scope.html.

———. *Testimony of Charles Duelfer, Special Advisor to the DCI for Iraqi Weapons of Mass Destruction.* Report to the United States Congress. March 30, 2004, https://www.cia .gov/news-information/speeches-testimony/2004/tenet_testimony_03302004.html.

Duelfer Report. "Al Muthanna Chemical Weapons Complex: Iraq's Chemical Warfare Program—Annex B," https://www.cia.gov/library/reports/general-reports-1/iraq_wmd _2004.

Earnest, Josh. "Press Briefing by Press Secretary Josh Earnest." The White House, Office of the Press Secretary. July 22, 2015, https://www.whitehouse.gov/the-press-office /2015/07/22/press-briefing-press-secretary-josh-earnest-7222015.

ElBaradei, Mohamed. "The Status of Nuclear Inspections in Iraq." Report to the UN Security Council. January 27, 2003, www.un.org/News/dh/iraq/elbaradei27jan03.htm.

Ford, Christopher A. "Thinking about a Korean Denuclearization Treaty." Paper prepared for a "Track II" dialogue with North Korean officials, Aspen Institute Germany, Gut Klostermühle resort. Germany, March 31 and April 1, 2012. Reproduced by the Hudson Institute, http://www.hudson.org/content/researchattachments/attachment/1019/ christopherford—dprkpaper042012.pdf.

Ham, Carter. "Transcript: AFRICOM Commander Ham Discusses African Security with Defense Writers." US AFRICOM Public Affairs. September 15, 2011, http://www.afri com.mil/Newsroom/Article/8587/transcript-africom-commander-ham-discusses -african.

International Atomic Energy Agency. "Application of Safeguards in the Democratic People's Republic of Korea." Report by the Director General, GOV/2011/53-GC (55)/24, http://isis-online.org/uploads/isis-reports/documents/IAEA_DPRK_2Sept2011.pdf.

———. "Board of Governors General Conference." GOV/2816/Add.1-GC (39)/10/Add.1. September 4, 1995, http://www.iaea.org/About/Policy/GC/GC39/GC39Documents/ English/gc39-10-add1_en.pdf.

———. "Conclusion of Additional Protocols: Status as of 21 May 2014," http://www.iaea .org/safeguards/documents/AP_status_list.pdf.

———. "Conclusion of Additional Protocols: Status as of 31 December 2013." December 31, 2013, http://www.iaea.org/safeguards/documents/AP_status_list.pdf.

———. "The Denuclearization of Africa." Report by the Director at the 37th General Conference, GC (XXXVII)/1075. September 9, 1993, http://www.iaea.org/About/Pol icy/GC/GC37/GC37Documents/English/gc37-1075_en.pdf.

———. "Final Assessment on Past and Present Outstanding Issues regarding Iran's Nuclear Programme." Report by the Director General, GOV/2015/68. December 2, 2015, https://www.iaea.org/sites/default/files/gov-2015-68.pdf.

———. "IAEA and DPRK: Fact Sheet on DPRK Nuclear Safeguards." May 2003, http://www.iaea.org/newscenter/focus/iaeadprk/fact_sheet_may2003.shtml.

———. "Implementation of the NPT Safeguards Agreement and Relevant Provisions of Security Council Resolutions in the Islamic Republic of Iran." Report by the Director General, GOV/2013/56. November 14, 2013, http://www.iaea.org/Publications/Docu ments/Board/2013/gov2013-56.pdf.

———. "Implementation of the NPT Safeguards Agreement and Relevant Provisions of Security Council Resolutions in the Islamic Republic of Iran." Report by the Director General, GOV/2013/3. May 22, 2013, http://www.iaea.org/Publications/Documents/Board/2013/gov2013-6.pdf.

———. "Implementation of the NPT Safeguards Agreement and Relevant Provisions of Security Council Resolutions in the Islamic Republic of Iran." Report by the Director General, GOV/2012/9. February 24, 2012, http://www.iaea.org/Publications/Documents/Board/2012/gov2012-9.pdf.

———. "Implementation of the NPT Safeguards Agreement and Relevant Provisions of Security Council Resolutions in the Islamic Republic of Iran." Report by the Director General, GOV/2011/65. November 8, 2011, http://www.iaea.org/Publications/Docu ments/Board/2011/gov2011-65.pdf.

———. "Implementation of NPT Safeguards Agreement and Relevant Positions of Security Council Resolutions 1737 (2006), 1747 (2007), 1803 (2008) and 1835 (2008) in the Islamic Republic of Iran." GOV/2009/35. June 5, 2009, http://www.isisnucleariran .org/assets/pdf/IAEA_Report_Iran_Feb_2009.pdf.

———. "Implementation of the NPT Safeguards Agreement in the Islamic Republic of Iran." Report by the Director General, GOV/2005/67. September 2, 2005, http://www .iaea.org/Publications/Documents/Board/2005/gov2005-67.pdf.

———. "Implementation of the NPT Safeguards Agreement in the Islamic Republic of Iran." Report by the Director, GOV/2004/34. June 1, 2004, http://www.fas.org/nuke/guide/iran/iaea0604.pdf.

———. "Implementation of the NPT Safeguards Agreement in the Islamic Republic of Iran." Report by the Director General, GOV/2003/75. November 10, 2003, http://www.iaea.org/Publications/Documents/Board/2003/gov2003-75.pdf.

———. "Implementation of the NPT Safeguards Agreement in the Socialist People's

Libyan Arab Jamahiriya." Report by the Director General, GOV/2008/39, http://www.iaea.org/Publications/Documents/Board/2008/gov2008-39.pdf.

———. "Limits to the Safeguards System." In *Against the Spread of Nuclear Weapons: IAEA Safeguards in the 1990's* (booklet 93-04459). Vienna: International Atomic Energy Agency, December 1999, http://www.iaea.org/Publications/Booklets/Safeguards/pia3810.html.

———. "Model Protocol Additional to the Agreement(s) between State(s) and the International Atomic Energy Agency for the Application of Safeguards." INFCIRC/540 (Corrected), September 1997, http://www.iaea.org/Publications/Documents/Infcircs/1997/infcirc540c.pdf.

———. "Report by the Secretary General." Board of Governors General Conference, GOV/2816-GC (39)/10. August 2, 1995, http://www.iaea.org/About/Policy/GC/GC39/GC39Documents/English/gc39-10_en.pdf.

———. "South Africa's Nuclear Capabilities." Report presented at the 36th General Conference, GC(XXXVI)/1015. September 4, 1992, http://www.iaea.org/About/Policy/GC/GC36/GC36Documents/English/gc-1015_en.pdf.

———. "Status List: Conclusion of Safeguards Agreements, Additional Protocols and Small Quantities Protocols." February 20, 2012, http://www.iaea.org/OurWork/SV/Safeguards/documents/sir_table.pdf.

———. "The Structure and Content of Agreements between the Agency and States Required in Connection with the Treaty on the Non-Proliferation of Nuclear Weapons." INFCIRC/153, section I.7. June 1972, http://www.iaea.org/Publications/Documents/Infcircs/Others/infcirc153.pdf.

Joint Comprehensive Plan of Action. July 14, 2015, http://www.eeas.europa.eu/statements-eeas/docs/iran_agreement/iran_joint-comprehensive-plan-of-action_en.pdf.

Katzman, Kenneth. "Iraq: U.S. Regime Change Efforts and Post-Saddam Governance." Congressional Research Service Report to Congress. April 26, 2005, http://digital.library.unt.edu/govdocs/crs//data/2005/upl-meta-crs-6454/RL31339_2005Apr26.pdf.

Katzman, Kenneth and Paul Kerr. "Interim Agreement on Iran's Nuclear Program." Congressional Research Service. December 11, 2013, http://www.fas.org/sgp/crs/nuke/R43333.pdf.

Kay, David A. *Statement on the Interim Progress Report on the Activities of the Iraq Survey Group (ISG).* Speech before the House Permanent Select Committee on Intelligence, the House Committee on Appropriations, Subcommittee on Defense, and the Senate Select Committee on Intelligence. October 2, 2003, https://www.cia.gov/news-information/speeches-testimony/2003/david_kay_10022003.html.

Kerr, Paul. "Iran's Nuclear Program: Status." Congressional Research Service Report to Congress. November 20, 2008, http://www.fas.org/sgp/crs/nuke/RL34544.pdf.

Kerry, John. "Iran Nuclear Agreement Review." Testimony before the Senate Foreign Relations Committee. Washington, DC. July 23, 2015, http://www.state.gov/secretary/remarks/2015/07/245221.htm.

———. "The P5+1's First Step Agreement with Iran on Its Nuclear Program." Opening Remarks before the House Foreign Affairs Committee. Washington, DC. December 10, 2013, http://www.state.gov/secretary/remarks/2013/12/218578.htm.

———. "Secretary Kerry's Press Availability." Press Briefing. U.S. Department of State. June 16, 2015, http://www.state.gov/secretary/remarks/2015/06/243892.htm.

Ki-moon, Ban. "Off-the-Cuff: Secretary-General's Press Encounter on the Report of the Mission to Investigate Allegations of the Use of Chemical Weapons in the Syrian Arab Republic: Report on the Incident of 21 August 2013 in the Ghouta Area of Damascus." Secretary General, United Nations. September 16, 2013, http://www.un.org/sg/offthecuff/index.asp?nid=2985.

Levitt, Matthew. "The Implications of Sanctions Relief under the Iran Agreement." Testimony submitted to the Senate Committee on Banking, Housing, and Urban Affairs. August 5, 2015, https://www.washingtoninstitute.org/uploads/Documents/testimony/LevittTestimony20150805.pdf.

Lopez, Todd C. "Army to Destroy Syrian Chemical Weapons Aboard Ship." Army News Service, Department of Defense. January 3, 2014, http://www.defense.gov/news/news article.aspx?id=121428.

Macke, Richard C. "Arms Control and the Revolution in Military Affairs." Speech given for Defense Special Weapons Agency. June 8–11, 1998, http://www.ciaonet.org/conf/dswo1/dswao1j.html.

Mahley, Donald. "Biological Weapons Convention." Statement by the Ambassador of the United States to the Ad Hoc Group of Biological Weapons Convention States Parties, Geneva, Switzerland. July 25, 2001, http://2001-2009.state.gov/t/ac/rls/rm/58069.htm.

Menendez, Bob. "Menendez Delivers Remarks on Iran Nuclear Deal at Seton Hall University's School of Diplomacy and International Relations." Press Release. August 18, 2015, http://www.menendez.senate.gov/news-and-events/press/menendez-delivers-remarks-on-iran-nuclear-deal-at-seton-hall-universitys-school-of-diplomacy-and-international-relations.

Mikulak, Robert P. "Statement to the Fortieth Meeting of the Executive Council." U.S. Delegation to the Executive Council, The Hague, Netherlands. April 29, 2014, http:www.state.gov/t/avc/rls/2014/225340.htm.

Nikitin, Mary Beth, Andrew Feickert, and Paul K. Kerr. "Syrian Chemical Weapons: Issues for Congress." Congressional Research Service. May 31, 2013, http://www.fas.org/sgp/crs/nuke/R42848.pdf.

Niksch, Larry A. "North Korea's Nuclear Weapons Program." Congressional Research Service Issue Brief for Congress. December 6, 2001, http://www.fas.org/nuke/guide/dprk/nuke/nk1.pdf.

Obama, Barack. "Government Assessment of the Syrian Government's Use of Chemical Weapons on August 21, 2013." Office of the Press Secretary, The White House. August 30, 2013, http://www.whitehouse.gov/the-press-office/2013/08/30/government-assess ment-syrian-government-s-use-chemical-weapons-august-21.

———. *National Strategy for Countering Biological Threats.* National Security Council. November 2009, http://www.whitehouse.gov/sites/default/files/National_Strategy_ for_Countering_BioThreats.pdf.

———. "Official Statement at the G-20 Summit." Pittsburgh, PA. September 25, 2009, transcript posted at www.nytimes.com/2009/09/26/world/middleeast/26nuke.text .html.

———. Presidential Debate with Mitt Romney. Commission on Presidential Debates. October 22, 2012, http://debates.org/index.php?page=october-22-2012-the-third-obama -romney-presidential-debate.

———. "Press Conference by the President." Office of the Press Secretary, The White House. March 6, 2012, http:www.whitehouse.gov/the-press-office/2012/03/06/press -conference-president.

———. "Remarks by President Obama at the Brandenburg Gate—Berlin, Germany." Office of the Press Secretary, The White House. June 19, 2013, http://www.white house .gov/the-press-office/2013/06/19/remarks-president-obama-brandenburg-gate-berlin -germany.

———. "Remarks by President Barack Obama." Speech at Hradcany Square, Prague, Czech Republic. Office of the Press Secretary, The White House. April 5, 2009, http:// www.whitehouse.gov/the_press_office/Remarks-By-President-Barack-Obama-In -Prague-As-Delivered.

———. "Remarks by the President to the White House Press Corps." Office of the Press Secretary, The White House. August 20, 2012, http://www.whitehouse.gov/the-press -office/2012/08/20/remarks-president-white-house-press-corps.

———. "State of the Union Address." U.S. Capitol, Washington, DC. January 25, 2011, http://www.whitehouse.gov/state-of-the-union-2011.

———. "Statement by the President on Iran." The White House, Office of the Press Secretary. July 14, 2015, https://www.whitehouse.gov/the-press-office/2015/07/14/ statement-president-iran.

———. "Transcript: President Obama's Full NPR Interview on Iran Nuclear Deal." National Public Radio. April 07, 2015, http://www.npr.org/2015/04/07/397933577/tran script-president-obamas-full-npr-interview-on-iran-nuclear-deal.

Organization for the Prohibition of Chemical Weapons. "Letter dated 28 March 2016 from the Secretary-General addressed to the President of the Security Council." United Nations Security Council, S/2016/285. March 29, 2016, http://reliefweb.int/ sites/reliefweb.int/files/resources/N1608678.pdf.

Pelton, Erin. "United Nations Releases Report on the Use of Chemical Weapons in Syria."

White House Blog. September 18, 2013, http://www.whitehouse.gov/blog/2013/09/18/united-nations-releases-report-use-chemical-weapons-syria.

Perricos, Demetrius. "Acting Executive Chairman's Speaking Notes—Security Council, 29 June 2007." Briefing given to the UN Security Council. June 29, 2007, http://www.un.org/Depts/unmovic/new/pages/security_council_briefings.asp#11.

Pompeo, Mike, and Tom Cotton. "Pompeo, Cotton Urge Disclosure of Complete Iran Nuclear Deal." Press Release. July 21, 2015, http://pompeo.house.gov/news/document single.aspx?DocumentID=398509.

Psaki, Jen. "U.S. Department of State Daily Press Briefing." Washington, DC. May 29, 2014, http://www.state.gov/r/pa/prs/dpb/2014/05/226885.htm.

Rice, Susan. "Press Briefing by Press Secretary Josh Earnest." The White House, Office of the Press Secretary. July 22, 2015, https://www.whitehouse.gov/the-press-office/2015/07/22/press-briefing-press-secretary-josh-earnest-7222015.

Schwartz, Thomas A. Testimony before the Committee on Armed Services, U.S. Senate, 107th Congress. March 5, 2002, http://wfile.ait.org.tw/wf-archive/2002/020306/epf310.htm.

Sharp, Jeremy M., and Christopher M. Blanchard. "Armed Conflict in Syria: U.S. and International Response." Congressional Research Service. June 14, 2013, www.fas.org/sgp/crs/mideast/RL33487.pdf.

Spector, Leonard. "Minimizing Dangers Posed by Syria's Military Assets during and after the Current Civil Turmoil." Testimony before the Subcommittee on Terrorism, Nonproliferation, and Trade Committee on Foreign Affairs, U.S. House of Representatives. July 19, 2012, http://cns.miis.edu/stories/120719_syria_cw_spector_testimony.htm.

Squassoni, Sharon A. "Disarming Libya: Weapons of Mass Destruction." Congressional Research Service Report to Congress. September 22, 2006, http://fpc.state.gov/docu ments/organization/78338.pdf.

———. "Iraq: U.N. Inspections for Weapons of Mass Destruction." Congressional Research Service Report for Congress. October 7, 2003, http://isn.ethz.ch/Digital-Library/Publications/Detail/?ots591=0c54e3b3-1e9c-be1e-2c24-a6a8c7060233&lng=en&id=10266.

Tenet, George. "Current and Projected National Security Threats." Testimony before the Senate Select Committee on Intelligence, U.S. Senate, February 5, 1997, https://www.cia.gov/news-information/speeches-testimony/1997/dci_testimony_020597.html.

———. "Government Assessment of the Syrian Government's Use of Chemical Weapons on August 21, 2013." Office of the Press Secretary. August 30, 2013, http://www.whitehouse.gov/the-press-office/2013/08/30/government-assessment-syrian-government-s-use-chemical-weapons-august-21.

———. "The Worldwide Threat in 2003: Evolving Dangers in a Complex World." Speech delivered before the Senate Select Committee on Intelligence, U.S. Senate. February 11, 2003, http://www.cia.gov/cia/public_affairs/speeches/2003/dci_speech_02112003.html.

———. "The Worldwide Threat in 2000: Global Realities of Our National Security." Testimony before the Senate Foreign Relations Committee, U.S. Senate. March 21, 2000, https://www.cia.gov/news-information/speeches-testimony/2000/dci_speech_032 100.html.

United Kingdom Ministry of Defense. "The United-Kingdom—Norway Initiative: Further Research into Managed Access of Inspectors during Warhead Dismantlement Verification." March 31, 2010, https://www.gov.uk/government/uploads/system/up loads/attachment_data/file/28424/20120426_2010_ukni_man_access_exercise.pdf.

United Nations. *Final Report of the Panel of Disarmament and Current and Future Ongoing Monitoring and Verification Issues.* UNSCOM, S/1999/356. March 30, 1999, http://www.un.org/Depts/unmovic/documents/Amorim%20Report.htm, http://www.un .org/Depts/unmovic/.

———. "Letter Dated 15 December 1998 from the Secretary-General Addressed to the President of the Security Council." Distr. General S/1998/1172. December 15, 1998, http: //www.un.org/Depts/unscom/s98-1172.htm.

———. Office for Disarmament Affairs. "Treaty on the Non-Proliferation of Nuclear Weapons (NPT)." July 1, 1968, http://www.un.org/disarmament/WMD/Nuclear/NPT text.shtml.

———. "Press Encounter with Hans Blix and Mohamed ElBaradei." UN News Centre, January 9, 2003, http://www.iraqwatch.org/un/unmovic/unmovic-blixelbaradei -010903.htm.

———. Security Council. "Security Council Resolution 2118." September 27, 2013, http://www.securitycouncilreport.org/atf/cf/%7B65BFCF9B-6D27-4E9C-8CD3 -CF6E4FF96FF9%7D/s_res_2118.pdf.

———. Security Council. *Resolution 1696 (2006),* July 31, 2006, www.iaea.org/newscen ter/focus/iaeairan/unsc_res1696-2006.pdf.

———. Security Council. "Letter Dated 17 December 1997 from the Executive Chairman of the Special Commission Established by the Secretary-General Pursuant to Paragraph 9 (b) (i) of Security Council Resolution 687 (1991) Addressed to the President of the Security Council." S/1997/987. December 17, 1997.

———. Security Council. "Security Council Resolution 687." April 3, 1991, http://www2 .unog.ch/uncc/resolutio/res0687.pdf.

———. UN News Centre. "Secretary-General Receives Syria's Formal Accession to Treaty Banning Chemical Weapons." September 14, 2014, http://www.un.org/apps/news/ story.asp?NewsID=45852#.U72RdPldXhE.

———. UNMOVIC. *Compendium of Iraq's Proscribed Weapons Programmes in the Chemical, Biological and Missile Areas.* June 2007, http://www.un.org/depts/unmovic /new/pages/compendium.asp.

———. UNMOVIC. "Initial Comments on the Report of the US-Led Iraq Survey Group (ISG) Searching for WMD in Iraq." Document S/2004/924. November 2004,

http://www.un.org/Depts/unmovic/new/documents/technical_documents/s-2004
-924-comments_on_ISG.pdf.

———. UNMOVIC. "Unresolved Disarmament Issues: Iraq's Proscribed Weapons Programs." UNMOVIC Working Document. March 6, 2003, http://www.un.org/Depts/
unmovic/documents/UNMOVIC%20UDI%20Working%20Document%206%20
March%2003.pdf.

———. "UNSCOM: Chronology of Main Events," December 1999, http://www.un.org/
Depts/unscom/Chronology/resolution949.htm.

———. "UNSC Resolution 1441," November 8, 2002, http://www.un.org/Docs/scres/
2002/sc2002.htm.

———. *Verification in All Its Aspects: Study on the Role of the United Nations in the Field of
Verification.* A/45/372. August 28, 1990, https://disarmament-library.un.org/UNODA
/Library.nsf/a26a5d5f8f81a9088525755c00525c64/bd3b27bcc4f182d1852575670070d75a
/$FILE/a-45-372.pdf.

———. *Verification in All Its Aspects, including the Role of the United Nations in the
Field of Verification.* A/50/377, September 22, 1995, http://www.un.org/documents/ga/
docs/50/plenary/a50-377.htm.

UN Security Council. "Resolution 2231." S/RES/2231 (2015). July 20, 2015, http://www
.un.org/en/sc/inc/pages/pdf/pow/RES2231E.pdf.

U.S. Central Intelligence Agency. *Addendums to the Comprehensive Report of the Special
Advisor to the DCI on Iraq's WMD.* March 2005, https://www.cia.gov/library/reports/
general-reports-1/iraq_wmd_2004/addenda.pdf.

———. "Current and Projected National Security Threats to the United States and
Its Interests Abroad." Written responses to questions before the Select Committee
on Intelligence, U.S. Senate, Hearing 104-510. February 22, 1996, http://archive.org/
stream/currentprojectedoounit/currentprojectedoounit_djvu.txt.

———. Office of the Director of Central Intelligence. "Unclassified Report to Congress
on the Acquisition of Technology Relating to Weapons of Mass Destruction and Advanced Conventional Munitions, 1 January through 30 June 2003." November 2004,
https://www.cia.gov/library/reports/archived-reports-1/jan_jun2003.pdf.

———. "Prospects for Further Proliferation of Nuclear Weapons." Directorate of Intelligence. Classified interagency intelligence memorandum, partially declassified and
released. Digital National Security Archive. October 2, 1974, http://nsarchive.chad
wyk.com.

———. "South African Enrichment Program." Declassified document, National Security Archive. August 1977, http://www.gwu.edu/~nsarchiv/NSAEBB/NSAEBB181/
sa16.pdf.

U.S. Commission on the Intelligence Capabilities of the United States Regarding Weapons of Mass Destruction. "Report to the President of the United States." March 31,
2005, http://www.gpo.gov/fdsys/pkg/GPO-WMD/pdf/GPO-WMD-1-1.pdf.

U.S. Congress. "H.R.1191—Iran Nuclear Agreement Review Act of 2015." Public Law No. 114-17, 114th Congress. May 22, 2015, https://www.congress.gov/bill/114th-congress/house -bill/1191/text/pl.

U.S. Department of Defense. *Nuclear Posture Review Report.* April 2010, http://www .defense.gov/npr/docs/2010%20nuclear%20posture%20review%20report.pdf.

U.S. Department of Energy. National Nuclear Security Administration. "NNSA Next Generation Safeguards Initiative: Fact Sheet." January 2, 2009, http://nnsa.energy.gov /mediaroom/factsheets/nextgenerationsafeguards.

———. *Plutonium: The First Fifty Years: United States Plutonium Production, Acquisition and Utilization from 1944 to 1994.* Washington, DC, Department of Energy. February 1996, http://fissilematerials.org/library/doe96.pdf.

U.S. Department of State. "Adherence to and Compliance with Arms Control and Nonproliferation Agreements and Commitments." Washington, DC. 2001, http://www .state.gov/documents/organization/22466.pdf.

———. Office of the Secretary of Defense. "Proliferation: Threat and Response." April 1996, http://www.dod.mil/pubs/prolif.

———. Office of the Spokesperson. "Libya: Securing Stockpiles Promotes Security." Office of the Spokesperson, Washington, DC. August 26, 2011, http://www.state.gov/r/ pa/prs/ps/2011/08/171101.htm.

———. Office of the Spokesman. "North Korea—Denuclearization Action Plan." Washington, DC. February 13, 2007, http://www.state.gov/r/pa/prs/ps/2007/february /80479.htm.

———. "PAWG Draft Paper on South Africa's Nuclear Inventory." Declassified document, National Security Archive. August 26, 1992, http://nsarchive.gwu.edu/NSAEBB /NSAEBB181/sa30a.pdf.

———. "Saddam's Chemical Weapons Campaign: Halabja, March 16, 1988." Bureau of Public Affairs, Washington, DC. March 14, 2003, http://2001-2009.state.gov/r/pa/ei/ rls/18714.htm.

———. "South Africa: Case Closed?" Declassified document, National Security Archive, December 19, 1993, http://www.gwu.edu/~nsarchiv.

U.S. Director of Central Intelligence. *The 22 September 1979 Event.* Interagency intelligence assessment, declassified January 2003, National Security Archive, GWU. December 1979, http://www2.gwu.edu/~nsarchiv/NSAEBB/NSAEBB181/sa23.pdf.

———. *Unclassified Report to Congress on the Acquisition of Technology Relating to Weapons of Mass Destruction and Advanced Conventional Munitions, 1 July through 31 December 2003.* N.d., https://www.cia.gov/library/reports/archived-reports-1/721 report_july_dec2003.pdf.

U.S. Director of National Intelligence. "Background Briefing with Senior U.S. Officials on Syria's Covert Nuclear Reactor and North Korea's Involvement." April 24, 2008, http://www.cfr.org/syria/background-briefing-senior-us-officials-syrias-covert-nuclear-reactor-north-koreas-involvement/p16105.

———. *South Africa: Policy Considerations Regarding a Nuclear Test*. Interagency assessment, declassified document, National Security Archive. August 18, 1977, http://www2.gwu.edu/~nsarchiv/NSAEBB/NSAEBB181/sa18.pdf.

———. *Unclassified Report to Congress on the Acquisition of Technology Relating to Weapons of Mass Destruction and Advanced Conventional Munitions, Covering 1 January to 31 December 2011*. N.d., http: www.fas.org/irp/threat/wmd-acq2011.pdf.

U.S. Government Accounting Office. "Weapons of Mass Destruction: Effort to Reduce Russian Arsenals May Cost More, Achieve Less than Planned." Report to the Chairman and Ranking Minority Member, Committee on Armed Services, House of Representatives. April 1999, http://www.gao.gov/assets/230/227235.pdf.

U.S. Government Statement. "Public Points for Qom Disclosure." Posted at the "Nuclear Iran" site of the Institute for Science and International Security. September 25, 2009, http://www.isisnucleariran.org/assets/pdf/Official_Comments_Qom_Disclosure.pdf.

U.S. Office of Technological Assessment. *Verification Technologies: Cooperative Aerial Surveillance in International Agreements*. Washington, DC: US Government Printing Office, July 1991.

U.S. Office of the Press Secretary. Ben Rhodes. "Statement by Deputy National Security Advisor for Strategic Communications on Syrian Chemical Weapons Use." The White House. June 13, 2013, http://www.whitehouse.gov/the-press-office/2013/06/13/statement-deputy-national-security-advisor-strategic-communications-ben-.

———. "Statement by the Press Secretary." The White House. April 24, 2008, http://georgewbush-whitehouse.archives.gov/news/releases/2008/04/20080424-14.html.

The White House. "Fact Sheet: First Step Understandings Regarding the Islamic Republic of Iran's Nuclear Program." Office of the Press Secretary. November 23, 2013, http://www.whitehouse.gov/the-press-office/2013/11/23/fact-sheet-first-step-understandings-regarding-islamic-republic-iran-s-n.

———. "The Historic Deal That Will Prevent Iran from Acquiring a Nuclear Weapon." Fact Sheet. N.d., https://www.whitehouse.gov/issues/foreign-policy/iran-deal.

———. "The Iran Nuclear Deal: What You Need to Know." Fact Sheet. N.d., https://www.whitehouse.gov/sites/default/files/docs/jcpoa_what_you_need_to_know.pdf.

Wolf, John. "Remarks to the Second Meeting of the Preparatory Committee." The 2005 Review Conference of the Parties to the Treaty on the Non-Proliferation of Nuclear Weapons, Geneva, Switzerland. April 28, 2003, http://2001-2009.state.gov/t/isn/rls/rm/20034.htm.

Bibliography

News Sources

ABC News
Associated Press
BBC News
Boston Globe
CBS News
Channel 4 News
Christian Science Monitor
CNN
CNN.com
Daily Mail
Delaware Online
Guardian
Hill
Huffington Post
Los Angeles Times
MSNBC
National Public Radio
New York Times
PBS
Reuters
Sydney Morning Herald
Sunday Times
Telegraph
Times
USA Today
Wall Street Journal
Washington Post

Journals, Books, Internet Resources

Abdoul Enein, Sameh. "Middle East—Nuclear No-Go." *Diplomat.* May 2011, http://www.diplomatmagazine.com/issues/2011/may/452-middle-east-nuclear-no-go-v15-452.html.

———. "NPT 2010–2015: The Way Forward." *Proliferation Analysis*, Carnegie Endowment for International Peace. March 31, 2011, http://carnegieendowment.org/2011/03/31/npt-2010-2015-way-forward/10wh?reloadFlag=1.

Abrahams, Elliot. "Bombing the Syrian Reactor: The Untold Story." *Commentary Magazine.* February 2013, http://commentarymagazine.com/article/bombing-the-syrian-reactor-the-untold-story/.

Acton, James. "Can the IAEA Suspend Assistance to Syria?" Comments posted on Arms-ControlWonk.com. November 25, 2008, http://www.armscontrolwonk.com/2112/can-the-iaea-suspend-technical-cooperation-with-syria.

Acton, James M., Mark Fitzpatrick, and Pierre Goldschmidt. "The IAEA Should Call for a Special Inspection in Syria." *Proliferation Analysis*, Carnegie Endowment for International Peace. February 26, 2009, http://www.carnegieendowment.org/publications/index.cfm?fa=view&id=22791.

Alibek, Kenneth. *Biohazard*. New York: Random House, 1999.

Albright, David. "India's Military Plutonium Inventory, End 2004." Institute for Science and International Security. May 7, 2005, http://isis-online.org/uploads/isis-reports/documents/india_military_plutonium.pdf.

———. "Libya: A Major Sale at Last." Institute for Science and International Security. December 1, 2010, http://isis-online.org/uploads/isis-reports/documents/Libya_and_the_Khan_Network_1Dec2010.pdf.

———. "The Rocky Path to a Long-Term Settlement with Iran." Op-ed. *Washington Post*. November 25, 2013, http://www.washingtonpost.com/opinions/reaching-a-final-iran-deal-will-be-a-tough-road/2013/11/25/dcc2f752-55ef-11e3-ba82-16ed03681809_story.html.

———. "South Africa and the Affordable Bomb." *Bulletin of the Atomic Scientists*, Vol. 50, No. 4 (July–August 1994): 37–47.

———. "South Africa's Nuclear Weapons Program." Lecture given at the Massachusetts Institute of Technology. March 14, 2001, http://web.mit.edu/ssp/seminars/wed_archives01spring/albright.htm.

———. "South Africa's Secret Nuclear Weapons." Institute for Science and International Security. May 1, 1994, http://isis-online.org/isis-reports/detail/south-africas-secret-nuclear-weapons/13.

Albright, David, and Robert Avagyan. "Taking Stock and Moving Forward on the Issue of the Parchin High Explosives Test Site." Institute for Science and Global Security. January 25, 2013, http://isis-online.org/isis-reports/detail/taking-stock-and-moving-forward-on-the-issue-of-the-parchin-high-explosives/.

Albright, David, and Paul Brannan. "IAEA Report on Syria: Undeclared Uranium Particles Found in Hot Cell Facility in Damascus; Syria Not Answering IAEA's Questions." Institute for Science and International Security. June 5, 2009, http://isis-online.org/publications/syria/Syria_IAEA_Report_Analysis_5June2009.pdf.

———. "If Not Now, When? Time for an IAEA Special Inspection in Syria." Institute for Science and Global Security. September 6, 2010, http://isis-online.org/isis-reports/detail/if-not-now-when-time-for-an-iaea-special-inspection-in-syria/.

———. "The Al Kibar Reactor: Extraordinary Camouflage, Troubling Implications." Institute for Science and International Security. May 12, 2008, http://www.isis-online.org/publications/syria/SyriaReactorReport_12May2008.pdf.

———. "ISIS Analysis of IAEA Safeguards Report on the Democratic People's Republic of Korea from September 2, 2011." Institute for Science and International Security. September 2, 2011, http://isis-online.org/isis-reports/detail/isis-analysis-of-iaea-safeguards-report-on-the-democratic-peoples-republic-/.

———. "The New National Intelligence Estimate on Iran: A Step in the Right Direction." Institute for Science and International Security. March 22, 2012, http://isis-online.org/uploads/isis-reports/documents/The_New_National_Intelligence_Estimate_on_Iran_A_Step_in_the_Right_Direction_1.pdf.

———. "Satellite Image Shows Suspected Uranium Conversion Plant in Syria." Institute for Science and International Security. February 23, 2011, http://isis-online.org/isis-reports/detail/satellite-image-shows-suspected-uranium-conversion-plant-in-syria1/.

Albright, David, Paul Brannan, Zachary Laporte, Katherine Tajer, and Christina Walrond. "Rendering Useless South Africa's Nuclear Test Shafts in the Kalahari Desert." Institute for Science and International Security. November 30, 2011, http://isis-online.org/uploads/isis-reports/documents/Vastrap_30November2011.pdf.

Albright, David, Paul Brannan, and Jacqueline Shire. "Syria Update: Suspected Reactor Site Dismantled." Institute for Science and International Security. October 25, 2007, http://www.isis-online.org/publications/SyriaUpdate25October2007.pdf.

Albright, David, Mark Dubowitz, and Orde Kittrie. "Stopping an Undetectable Iranian Bomb." Institute for Science and International Security. March 27, 2013, http://isis-online.org/isis-reports/detail/stopping-an-undetectable-iranian-bomb/8.

Albright, David, Olli Heinonen, and Serena Kelleher-Vergantini. "IAEA Visit to the Parchin Site." ISIS Report, Institute for Science and International Security, September 22, 2015, http://isis-online.org/uploads/isis-reports/documents/IAEA_Visit_to_the_Parchin_Site_September_22_2015_Final_1.pdf.

Albright, David, and Corey Hinderstein. "Iran Building Nuclear Fuel Cycle Facilities: International Transparency Needed." ISIS Issue Brief, Institute for Science and International Security. December 12, 2002, http://www.isis-online.org/publications/iran/iranimages.html.

———. "The Iranian Gas Centrifuge Uranium Enrichment Plant at Natanz: Drawing from Commercial Satellite Images." Institute for Science and International Security. March 14, 2003, http://www.isis-online.org/publications/iran/natanz03_02.html.

———. "Pelindaba and Valindaba Facilities, South Africa." Institute for Science and International Security. October 26, 2000, http://isis-online.org/isis-reports/detail/pelindaba-and-valindaba-facilities-south-africa/13.

———. "South Africa's Weaponization Efforts: Success on a Small Scale." Institute for Science and International Security. September 13, 2011, http://isis-online.org/uploads/isis-reports/documents/safrica.pdf.

———. "Verifiable, Cooperative Dismantlement of the DPRK's Nuclear Weapons Program." Paper presented at the Institute for Nuclear Materials Management (INMM) Annual Meeting, Orlando, Florida. June 15, 2004, http://www.isis-online.org/publi cations/dprk/dprk_cooperative_dismantlement.html.

Albright, David, and Kevin O'Neill. "The North Korean Nuclear Program: Unresolved Issues." Institute for Science and International Security. June 6, 1994, http://isis-online .org/isis-reports/detail/the-north-korean-nuclear-program-unresolved-iussues/10.

———. *Solving the North Korean Nuclear Puzzle*. Washington, DC: Institute for Science and International Security, 2000.

Albright, David, and Jacqueline Shire. "Iran Installing More Advanced Centrifuges at Natanz Pilot Enrichment Plant: Factsheet on the P-2/IR-2 Centrifuge." Institute for Science and International Security. February 7, 2008, http://www.isis-online.org/ publications/iran/ISIS_Iran_P2_7Feb2008.pdf.

Albright, David, and Jacqueline Shire, with Paul Brannan and Andrea Scheel. "Nuclear Iran: Not Inevitable, Essential Background and Recommendations for the Obama Administration." Institute for Science and International Security. January 21, 2009, http://www.isisnucleariran.org/assets/pdf/Iran_paper_final_2.pdf.

Albright, David, and Andrea Stricker. "Burma's Nuclear Aspirations: Less Reason Now for Concern." Institute for Science and International Security. December 12, 2011, http:// isis-online.org/isis-reports/detail/burmas-nuclear-aspirations-less-reason-now-for -concern/.

———. "In Positive Move, Burma to Sign Additional Protocol." Institute for Science and International Security. November 19, 2012, http://isis-online.org/isis-reports/detail /in-positive-move-burma-to-sign-additional-protocol/.

———. "Major U.S. Sting Operation Arrests Iranian in Nuclear Smuggling Network." Institute for Science and International Security. August 12, 2012, http://isis-online. org/uploads/isis-reports/documents/US_case_gas_centrifuge_equipment.pdf.

———. "Myanmar Says Halted Nuclear Research Program: Verification Critical." In- stitute for Science and International Security. June 3, 2011, http://isis-online.org/ isis-reports/detail/myanmar-says-halted-nuclear-research-program-verification -critical/.

———. "Preliminary Assessment of the JCPOA Procurement Channel: Regulation of Iran's Future Nuclear and Civil Imports and Considerations for the Future." ISIS Report, Institute for Science and International Security. August 31, 2015, http:// isisonline.org/uploads/isisreports/documents/Procurement_Channel_JCPOA_ analysis_31Aug2015_final_1.pdf.

Albright, David, Andrea Stricker, Daniel Schnur, and Sarah Burkhard. "Additional Tai- wan-Based Element of Iranian Military Goods Procurement Network Exposed." ISIS Report, Institute for Science and International Security. September 16, 2015, http:// isis-online.org/uploads/isis-reports/documents/Hsieh_case_study_16Sept2015-final .pdf.

Albright, David, and Christina Walrond. "Iran's Critical Capability in 2014: Verifiably Stopping Iran from Increasing the Number and Quality of Its Centrifuges." Institute for Science and International Security. July 17, 2013, http://isis-online.org/uploads/isis-reports/documents/Iran_critical_capability_17July2013.pdf.

———. "Technical Note: Revisiting Bomb Reactors in Burma and an Alleged Burmese Nuclear Weapons Program." Institute for Science and International Security. April 11, 2011, http://isis-online.org/uploads/isis-reports/documents/Burma_Analysis_Bomb_Reactors_11April2011.pdf.

———. "Update on the Arak Reactor." Institute for Science and International Security. July 15, 2013, http://www.isis-online.org/uploads/isis-reports/documents/Iran_critical_capability_17July2013.pdf.

Albright, David, Christina Walrond, and Andrea Stricker. "ISIS Analysis of IAEA Iran Safeguards Report." Institute for Science and International Security. May 22, 2013, http://www.isis-online.org/uploads/isis-reports/documents/ISIS_Analysis_IAEA_safeguards_Report_21Feb2013.pdf.

Albright, David, Houston Wood, and Andrea Stricker. "Breakout Timelines under the Joint Comprehensive Plan of Action." ISIS Report, Institute for Science and International Security. August 18, 2015, http://www.isis-online.org/uploads/isis-reports/documents/Iranian_Breakout_Timelines_and_Issues_18Aug2015_final.pdf.

Allison, Graham, and Olli Heinonen. "Break the Silence on Syria's Nuclear Program." Op-ed. *Wall Street Journal.* December 4, 2010, http://online.wsj.com/news/articles/SB10001424052748703377504575651130446186898.

Altman, Jürgen, and Joseph Rotblat, eds. *Verification of Arms Reductions: Nuclear, Conventional and Chemical.* Berlin: Spriuger-Verlag, 1989.

Anderson, Jon Lee. "Obama's Syria Problem." *New Yorker,* December 14, 2012. http://www.newyorker.com/online/blogs/comment/2012/12/obamas-syria-problem.html.

Apt, Ken. "Verification of the Chemical Weapons Convention: Maximizing Technical Effectiveness." *Briefing,* Vol. 3, No. 3 (April 24, 1992), LA-UR-92-1187, Los Alamos National Laboratory, Center for National Security Studies.

Arms Control Association. "Biological Weapons Convention Signatories and States-Parties." http://www.armscontrol.org/factsheets/bwcsig.

———. "The Chemical Weapons Convention (CWC) at a Glance." September 2013, https://www.armscontrol.org/factsheets/cwcglance.

———. "Getting It Right The Next Time: An Interview with Hans Blix." June 19, 2004, http://www.armscontrol.org/interviews/20040619_Blix.asp.

———. "The 1997 IAEA Additional Protocol at a Glance." December 2012, http://www.armscontrol.org/factsheets/IAEAProtoco.

———. "The Presidential Nuclear Initiatives (PNIs) on Tactical Nuclear Weapons at a Glance." August 2012, https://www.armscontrol.org/factsheets/pniglance.

Asculai, Ephraim. *Verification Revisited: The Nuclear Case.* Washington, DC: Institute for Science and International Security Press, 2002.

Aung, Shwe. "Burma Preparing to Ratify Chemical Weapons Ban: Ye Htut." *DVB.* February 14, 2014, https://www.dvb.no/news/Burma-preparing-to-ratify-chemical-weapons -ban-ye-htut-burma-myanmar/37250.

Baeckmann, Adolf von, Gary Dillon, and Demetrius Perricos. "Nuclear Verification in South Africa." *IAEA Bulletin,* Vol. 37, No. 1 (1995): 42–48.

Bahgat, Gawdat. "Nonproliferation Success: The Libyan Model." *World Affairs,* Vol. 168, No. 1 (Summer 2005): 3–12.

Bale, Jeffrey M. "South Africa's Project Coast: 'Death Squads,' Covert State-Sponsored Poisonings, and the Dangers of CBW Proliferation." *Democracy and Security,* Vol. 2, No. 1 (January 2006): 27–59.

Barletta, Michael, and Christina Ellington. "South Africa's Nuclear-Related Facilities." James Martin Center for Nonproliferation Studies. March 1999, http://cns.miis.edu/ safrica/facil.htm.

Barnaby, Frank. *A Handbook of Verification Procedures.* London: Macmillan, 1990.

Barnes, Diane. "Kerry Says 'Raw Data' Points to New Syria Chemical Strikes." *Global Security Newswire.* May 15, 2014, http://www.nti.org/gsn/article/hagel-holds-off-en dorsing-claims-new-syria-chemical-strikes.

Barzashka, Ivanka. "Using Enrichment Capacity to Estimate Iran's Breakout Potential." Federation of the American Scientists, Issue Brief. January 21, 2011, http://www.fas .org/pubs/_docs/IssueBrief_Jan2011_Iran.pdf.

Bermudez Jr., Joseph. "The Democratic People's Republic of Korea and Unconventional Weapons." In *Planning the Unthinkable: How New Powers Will Use Nuclear, Biological, and Chemical Weapons.* Ithaca, NY: Cornell University Press, 2000.

Blix, Hans. "The A-Bomb Squad." *World Monitor: The Christian Science Monitor Monthly* (November 1991): 18–21.

———. *Disarming Iraq: The Search for Weapons of Mass Destruction.* Bloomsbury: Pantheon Books, 2004.

———. "Inspecting Fact in the Aftermath of War." Op-ed. *Scotsman,* http://www.scots man.com/news/inspecting-facts-in-aftermath-of-war-1-929453.

———. Interview transcript in "Blix Speaks with Reporters." *CNN.* January 23, 2003, http://transcripts.cnn.com/TRANSCRIPTS/0301/23/se.05.html.

———. Lecture given at the "Glocalisation, World Governance, and the Reform of the United Nations" Workshop, Turin, Italy. March 13–14, 2004, http://www.globuset locuseng.org/What_We_Do/Projects/Global_Governance/Documentation_Semi nar_2004.kl.

———. "Transcript of the Interview with IAEA Director General Mohamed ElBaradei and Dr. Hans Blix, Former Head of UNMOVIC." March 21, 2004, posted at http:// www.iaea.org/NewsCenter/Transcripts/2004/cnn21032004.html.

———. "Verifying Arms Control Agreements: An Interview with Hans Blix." *Arms Control Today,* Vol. 33, No. 6 (July–August 2003): 12.

Boese, Wade. "U.S. Points to Libya as Disarmament Model." *Arms Control Today,* Vol. 34, No. 3 (April 2004): 29.

Bollfrass, Alex. "Details Bedevil Libyan Grand Bargain." *Arms Control Today,* Vol. 37, No. 8 (October 2007): 33–34.

———. "Libya Backs Out of CW Destruction Agreement." *Arms Control Today,* Vol. 37, No. 6 (July–August 2007): 29.

Boureston, Jack, and Yana Feldman. "Verifying Libya's Nuclear Dismantlement." In Trevor Findlay, *Verification Yearbook 2004.* 2005, http://www.vertic.org/media/Archi ved_Publications/Yearbooks/2004/VY04_Boureston-Feldman.pdf.

Boureston, Jack, and Charles D. Ferguson. "Strengthening Nuclear Safeguards: Special Committee to the Rescue?" *Arms Control Today,* Vol. 35, No. 10 (December 2005): 17–22.

Bowen, Wyn Q. "Libya and Nuclear Proliferation." *Adelphi Paper,* Vol. 46, No. 380 (May 2006): 7–103.

Braun, Chaim, and Christopher F. Chyba. "Proliferation Rings: New Challenges to the Nuclear Nonproliferation Regime." *International Security,* Vol. 29, No. 2 (Fall 2004): 5–49.

Braut-Hegghammer, Malfrid. "Libya's Nuclear Intentions: Ambition and Ambivalence." *Strategic Insights,* Vol. 8, No. 2 (April 2009): 1–13, https://www.hsdl.org/?view&did =36072.

———. "Libya's Nuclear Turnaround: Perspectives from Tripoli." *Middle East Journal,* Vol. 62, No. 1 (Winter 2008): 55–72.

Bunn, Matthew. "International Safeguards: Summarizing 'Traditional' and 'New' Measures." MIT OpenCourseWare. January 25, 2013, http://ocw.mit.edu/courses/nuclear -engineering/22-812j-managing-nuclear-technology-spring-2004/lecture-notes/lec 16notes.pdf.

———. "ISIS Seizes Nuclear Material—But That's Not the Reason to Worry." Op-ed. *National Interest.* July 11, 2014, http://nationalinterest.org/feature/isis-seizes-nuclear -material-that's-not-the-reason-worry-10849.

Bunn, Matthew, Eben Harrell, and Martin B. Malin. "Progress on Securing Nuclear Weapons and Materials: The Four-Year Effort and Beyond." Project on Managing the Atom, Belfer Center for Science and International Affairs, Harvard Kennedy School. March 2012, http://nrs.harvard.edu/urn-3:HUL.InstRepos:10592471.

Burgess, Stephen, and Helen Purkitt. "The Rollback of South Africa's Chemical and Biological Warfare Program." USAF Counterproliferation Center, Air War College, Maxwell Air Force Base, Alabama. April 2001, http://www.au.af.mil/au/awc/awcgate/ cpc-pubs/southafrica.pdf.

———. "The Secret Program: South Africa's Chemical and Biological Weapons." In Barry R. Schneider and Jim A. Davis, eds., *The War Next Time: Countering Rogue*

States and Terrorists Armed with Chemical and Biological Weapons. Maxwell AFB, Alabama: USAF Counterproliferation Center, April 2004.

Busch, Nathan. *No End in Sight: The Continuing Menace of Nuclear Proliferation.* Lexington: University Press of Kentucky, 2004.

———. "Risks of Nuclear Terror: Vulnerabilities of Thefts and Sabotage at Nuclear Weapons Facilities." *Contemporary Security Policy,* Vol. 23, No. 3 (December 2002): 19–60.

———. "Russian Roulette: The Continuing Relevance of Russia to the Nuclear Proliferation Debate." *Security Studies,* Vol. 11, No. 3 (Spring 2002): 44–90.

Busch, Nathan E., and Joseph F. Pilat. "Disarming Libya? A Reassessment after the Arab Spring." *International Affairs,* Vol. 89, No. 2 (March 2013): 451–75.

Butler, Richard. *The Greatest Threat: Iraq, Weapons of Mass Destruction, and the Growing Crisis of Global Security.* New York: Public Affairs, 2000.

Byman, Daniel. "A Farewell to Arms Inspections." *Foreign Affairs,* Vol. 79, No. 1 (January–February 2000): 119–32.

Canadian Council on International Law and the Markland Group. *Treaty Compliance: Some Concerns and Remedies.* Nijhoff Law Specials, Vol. 32. London: Kluwer Law International, 1998.

Carlson, John. "IAEA Safeguards Additional Protocol." Department of Foreign Affairs and Trade, Australian Government. January 20, 2009, https://www.dfat.gov.au/asno/publications/iaea-safeguards-additional-protocol.html.

———. "Multinational Approaches to the Nuclear Fuel Cycle." In Joseph F. Pilat and Nathan E. Busch, eds., *The Routledge Handbook of Nuclear Proliferation and Policy.* New York: Routledge Press, 2015.

Carnegie Endowment for International Peace. "North Korea's Secret Nuclear Weapons Program: A Serious Violation of North Korea's International Commitments?" *Proliferation Analysis.* October 25, 2002, http://carnegieendowment.org/2002/10/25/north-korea-s-secret-nuclear-weapons-program-serious-violation-of-north-korea-s-international-commitments/25fg.

Center for Nonproliferation Studies. "ABACC." *Inventory of International Nonproliferation Organizations and Regime.* March 1, 2013, http://cns.miis.edu/inventory/pdfs/abacc.pdf.

———. "EURATOM." *Inventory of International Nonproliferation Organizations and Regimes.* December 17, 2012, http://cns.miis.edu/inventory/pdfs/euratom.pdf.

Chayes, Abram, and Antonia Handler Chayes. *The New Sovereignty: Compliance with International Regulatory Agreements.* Cambridge, MA: Harvard University Press, 1998.

Chubin, Shahram. *Whither Iran? Reform, Domestic Politics and National Security.* Adelphi Paper 342. New York: Oxford University Press, 2002.

Cirincione, Joseph, Jessica T. Mathews, and George Perkovich. "WMD in Iraq: Evidence and Implications." Carnegie Endowment for International Peace. January 2004, http://www.carnegieendowment.org/files/Iraq3FullText.pdf.

Cirincione, Joseph, Jon B. Wolfsthal, and Mirian Rajkumar. *Deadly Arsenals: Nuclear, Biological, and Chemical Threats.* Washington, DC: Carnegie Endowment for International Peace, 2005.

Cleminson, Frank Ronald. "International Verification of WMD Proliferation: Applying UNMOVIC's Legacy." *Journal of Military and Strategic Studies,* Vol. 9, No. 3 (Spring 2006–7), http://www.jmss.org/jmss/index.php/jmss/article/viewFile/104/114.

———. "What Happened to Saddam's Weapons of Mass Destruction?" *Arms Control Today,* Vol. 33, No. 7 (September 2003): 3–6.

Cliff, David. "Multilateral Approaches to Future Dismantlement Verification." Paper presented at the UK PONI Annual Conference, Nuclear Stability: From the Cuban Crisis to the Energy Crisis, Royal United Services Institute, Great Britain. May 10, 2012, http://www.rusi.org/downloads/assets/UK_PONI_2012_-_Cliff_-_Multilateral _Disarmament_Verification.pdf.

Cliff, David, Hassan Elbahtimy, and Andreas Persbo. "Verifying Warhead Dismantlement: Past, Present, Future." *Verification Matters,* VERTIC Research Reports No. 9. September 2010, http://www.vertic.org/media/assets/Publications/VM9.pdf.

Cochran, Thomas. "Highly Enriched Uranium Production for South African Nuclear Weapons." *Science and Global Security,* Vol. 4, No. 2 (Summer 1994): 33–48.

Commission on Presidential Debates. "Transcript of the First Bush-Kerry Presidential Debate." Transcript of a debate at the University of Miami. September 30, 2004, http://www.debates.org/index.php?page=september-30-2004-debate-transcript.

Committee on International Security and Arms Control. *Monitoring Nuclear Weapons and Nuclear-Explosive Materials.* National Academy of Sciences. Washington, DC: National Academies Press, 2005.

Cordesman, Anthony H. *Iraq and the War of Sanctions: Conventional Threats and Weapons of Mass Destruction.* Westport, CT: Praeger Publishers, 1999.

Cordesman, Anthony H., and Adam C. Seitz. "Iranian Weapons of Mass Destruction: Biological Weapons Programs." Center for Strategic and International Studies. October 28, 2008, http://csis.org/files/media/csis/pubs/081028_iranbw_chapterrev.pdf.

Council on Foreign Relations. "Backgrounder: The Lengthening List of Iran Sanctions." October 14, 2013, http://www.cfr.org/iran/lengthening-list-iran-sanctions/p20258.

Crail, Peter. "IAEA Lays Out Iran Weapons Suspicions." *Arms Control Today.* December 2011, http://www.armscontrol.org/print/5154.

———. "IAEA Sends Syria Nuclear Case to the UN." *Arms Control Today.* July–August 2011, http://www.armscontrol.org/print/4948.

———. "Report Alleges Secret Myanmar Nuclear Work." *Arms Control Today,* Vol. 40, No. 6 (July–August, 2010): 44.

Cserveny, Vilmos, Josef Goldblat, Faawzy Hussein Hamad, Hannelore Hoppe, Jez Littlewood, Ibrahim Othman, Enrique Roman Morey, and Mohammed Kadry Said. "Building a Weapons of Mass Destruction Free Zone in the Middle East: Global

Non-Proliferation Regimes and Regional Experiences." UN Institute for Disarmament Research (UNIDIR), UNIDIR/2004/24, 2004, http://www.baselpeaceoffice.org /sites/default/files/imce/menwfz/building_a_wmd_free_zone_in_the_middle_east_ unidir.pdf.

Dagres, Holly. "Viewpoint: Three Years In, Is Iran's Green Revolution Still Going?" *Middle East Voices*. June 13, 2009, http://middleeastvoices.com/2012/06/viewpoint-three -years-in-is-irans-green-revolution-still-going.

Dahlitz, Julie. *Avoidance and Settlement of Arms Control Disputes: Follow-up Studies Subsequent to the Symposium on the International Law of Arms Control and Disarmament*. New York: United Nations, 1994.

Daifallah, Adam. "General Strike Set in Iran in Bid to Topple Mullahs." *New York Sun*, April 24, 2003, p. A1.

Davis, Jay. "Technical and Policy Issues for Nuclear Weapons Reductions." *APS Physics*, Forum on Physics and Society. January 2012, http://www.aps.org/units/fps/newslet ters/201201/davis.cfm.

DeSutter, Paula. "Libya, WMDs, and Musa Kusa." *National Review Online*. April 4, 2011, http://www.nationalreview.com/articles/263744/libya-wmds-and-musa-kusa-paula -desutter.

———. Quotation in Wade Boese. "U.S. Points to Libya as Disarmament Model: An Interview with Assistant Secretary of State Paula DeSutter." *Arms Control Today*. April 2004, http://www.armscontrol.org/act/2004_04/DeSutter.asp.

Dill, Catherine, and Jeffrey Lewis. "Suspect Defense Facility in Myanmar." James Martin Center for Nonproliferation Studies. May 9, 2014, http://www.nonproliferation.org/ suspect-defense-facility-in-myanmar.

Downes, Mark. *Iran's Unresolved Revolution*. Aldershot: Ashgate Publishing Company, 2002.

Duelfer, Charles. "Extremists at Former Saddam CW Facility." Duelfer Blog. June 19, 2014, http://www.charlesduelfer.com/blog/.

———. *Hide and Seek: The Search for Truth in Iraq*. New York: Public Affairs, 2009.

———. "The Inevitable Failure of Inspections in Iraq." *Arms Control Today*, Vol. 32, No. 7 (September 2002): 8–11, http://www.armscontrol.org/act/2002_09/duelfer_sept02.

———. Interview on *NewsHour with Jim Lehrer*. April 27, 2005, http://www.pbs.org/ newshour/bb/middle_east/jan-june05/duelfer_4-27.html.

Ekaiser, Ernesto. "Interview with Hans Blix." *El Pais*. April 9, 2003, http://www.globalpolicy .org/security/issues/iraq/unmovic/2003/0409lostpatience.htm.

Ekeus, Rolf. "Reassessment: The IISS Strategic Dossier on Iraq's Weapons of Mass Destruction." *Survival*, Vol. 46, No. 2 (Summer 2004): 73–88.

ElBaradei, Mohamed. Interview by the Academy of Achievement. *Academy of Achievement*, Washington, DC. June 3, 2006, http://www.achievement.org/autodoc/page/ elboint-1.

———. "Interview on *Hard Talk*." *BBC News.* August 29, 2003, http://news.bbc.co.uk/1/hi/programmes/hardtalk/3190731.stm.

———. Interview with Charlie Rose. *The Charlie Rose Show.* October 30, 2007, http://www.iaea.org/newscenter/transcripts/2007/cr301007.html.

———. Quotation in *Online News Hour*. PBS. October 7, 2005, http://www.pbs.org/newshour/updates/nobel_10-07-05.html.

———. "Transcript of ElBaradei's U.N. Presentation." Transcript, *CNN*. March 7, 2003, http://www.cnn.com/2003/US/03/07/sprj.irq.un.transcript.elbaradei/.

Elleman, Michael, Dina Esfandiary, and Emile Hokayem. "Syria's Proliferation Challenge and the European Union's Response." EU Non-Proliferation Consortium, *Nonproliferation Papers*, No. 20. July 2012, http://www.sipri.org/research/disarmament/eu-consortium/publications/Nonproliferation-paper-20.

Esposito, John L. "Introduction: From Khomeini to Khatami." In John L. Esposito and R. K. Ramazani, eds., *Iran at the Crossroads*. New York: Palgrave, 2001.

European Commission Joint Research Centre Institute for Transuranium Elements. "Nuclear Safeguards Research and Development." N.d., http://itu.jrc.ec.europa.eu/index.php?id=194.

Feaver, Peter D. "Command and Control in Emerging Nuclear Nations." *International Security*, Vol. 17, No. 3 (Winter 1992–93): 160–87.

Fetter, Steve. "Nuclear Archaeology: Verifying Declarations of Fissile Material Production." *Science and Global Security*, 3, nos. 3–4 (1993): 237–59.

———. "Stockpile Declarations." In Nicholas Zarimpas, ed., *Transparency in Nuclear Warheads and Materials: The Political and Technical Dimensions*. Oxford: Oxford University Press, 2003.

———. "Verifying Nuclear Disarmament." Report prepared for the Henry L. Stimson Center's Project on Eliminating Weapons of Mass Destruction. March 12, 1998, http://drum.lib.umd.edu/bitstream/1903/4023/1/1998-VerifyingNuclearDisarmament.pdf.

Findlay, Trevor. "LOOKING BACK: The UN Monitoring, Verification, and Inspection Commission." *Arms Control Today*, Vol. 35, No. 7 (September 2005): 45–48.

———. "Preserving UNMOVIC: The Institutional Possibilities." *Disarmament Diplomacy*, No. 76 (March–April 2004), http://www.acronym.org.uk/dd/dd76/76tf.htm.

Findlay, Trevor, and Ben Mines. "UNMOVIC in Iraq: Opportunity Lost." In Trevor Findlay, ed., *Verification Yearbook 2003*. London: VERTIC, 2003, http://www.vertic.org/media/Archived_Publications/Yearbooks/2003/VY03_Findlay-Mines.pdf.

Firsing, Scott. "South Africa's Nuclear Dismantlement Continues to Astonish." *LSE Ideas*, London School of Economics and Political Science. December 2011, http://blogs.lse.ac.uk/ideas/2011/12/south-africa%E2%80%99s-nuclear-dismantlement-continues-to-astonish-2/.

Fischer, David. *History of the International Atomic Energy Agency: The First Forty Years.*

International Atomic Energy Agency. 1997, http://www-pub.iaea.org/mtcd/publica tions/pdf/pub1032_web.pdf.

Fisher, Max. "A Nuclear Standoff with Libya." *Atlantic*. November 2010, http://www.the atlantic.com/international/archive/2012/11/a-nuclear-standoff-with-libya/67076.

Ford, Christopher A. "Deterrence to—and through—'Zero': Challenges of Disarma- ment and Proliferation." Presented to the Nonproliferation Forum, sponsored by the Woodrow Wilson Center and the Los Alamos National Laboratory, Ronald Reagan International Building, Washington, DC. November 14, 2008, http://www.hudson .org/files/documents/Wilson%20Center%20FINAL2.pdf.

———. "Why Not Nuclear Disarmament?" *New Atlantis*, No. 27 (Spring 2010): 3–20, http://www.thenewatlantis.com/publications/why-not-nuclear-disarmament.

Fradkin, Hillel, and Lewis Libby. "Enforcing the Iran Deal: Another Gaping Hole." Hud- son Institute. August 25, 2015, http://www.hudson.org/research/11556-enforcing-the -iran-deal-another-gaping-hole.

Frayman, Amir. "Iran's Nuclear Program—Lessons from the South African Model." In- ternational Institute for Counter-Terrorism. September 15, 2005, http://www.ict.org .il/Article/932/Iran.

Fuller, James. "Verification on the Road to Zero: Issues for Nuclear Warhead Dismantle- ment." *Arms Control Association*, Vol. 40, No. 10. December 2010, http://www.arms control.org/act/2010_12/%20Fuller.

Gallagher, Nancy W. *The Politics of Verification*. Baltimore, MD: Johns Hopkins Univer- sity Press, 1999.

Gerdes, Eric R., Roger G. Johnston, and James E. Doyle. "A Proposed Approach for Monitoring Nuclear Warhead Dismantlement." *Science and Global Security*, Vol. 9 (2001): 113–41.

Gill, Bates. "China's Role in Nonproliferation." In Nathan E. Busch and Daniel H. Joyner, eds., *Combating Weapons of Mass Destruction: The Future of International Nonprolif- eration Policy*. Athens: University of Georgia Press, 2009.

Glaser, Alexander. "Facilitating Nuclear Disarmament: Verified Declarations of Fissile Material Stocks and Production." *Nonproliferation Review*, Vol. 19, No. 1 (June 2012): 125–35.

Global Security. "Attacking Iraq: Countdown Timeline." *Global Security*, http://www .globalsecurity.org/military/ops/iraq-timeline.htm.

Global Security Newswire. "ElBaradei Lashes Critics of Syrian Nuclear Aid Request." November 25, 2008, http://www.globalsecuritynewswire.org/gsn/nw_20081125_8832 .php.

———. "Fidelity of Syrian Chemical Disclosure Questioned." November 1, 2013, http:// www.nti.org/gsn/article/questions-remain-about-fidelity-syrian-chemical-disclo sure/.

———. "France: Assad Launched 14 Chemical Strikes since October." May 14, 2014,

http://www.nti.org/gsn/article/france-assad-launched-14-chemical-strikes-after
-september.

———. "Iran Reduces Sensitive Uranium Stocks by Half, Envoys say." April 16, 2014,
http://nti.org/gsn/article/iran-slashes-sensitive-uranium-half.

———. "Iran's Uranium Stocks Could Grow under Nuclear Accord." January 22, 2014,
http://www.nti.org/gsn/article/iran-uranium-stocks-could-grow-under-interim
-accord.

———. "Key Envoy: Iran Talks May Drag into 2015." June 10, 2014, http://www.nti.org/
gsn/article/iran-talks-may-drag-2015-key-envoy-says/?mgs1=d8c9gbrDRS.

———. "Myanmar Brushes Off Analysis of Alleged Chemical-Arms Site." May 19, 2014,
http://www.nti.org/gsn/article/myanmar-expert-concerns-alleged-chemical-arms
-site.

———. "Syria Chemical Fears Linger after Disarmament Milestone." June 24, 2014,
http://www.nti.org/gsn/article/syria-chemical-fears-linger-after-disarmament-step/.

———. "U.S. Insiders: Assad Turns Last Chemical Arms into Bargaining Chip." May
1, 2014, http://www.nti.org/gsn/article/us-insiders-assad-turns-last-chemical-arms
-bargaining-chip.

———. "Weapons Stocks Still a Worry in Post-Qadhafi Libya." October 21, 2011, http://
www.nti.org/gsn/article/weapons-stocks-still-a-worry-in-post-qadhafi-libya/.

Godson, Roy, and James Wirtz, eds. *Strategic Denial and Deception: The Twenty-First
Century Challenge.* New Brunswick, NJ: Transaction Publishers, 2002.

Goldblat, Joseph. *Ways to Improve the Implementation and Enforcement of Arms Control
Agreements: Role of Verification.* Geneva Centre for Security Policy, Occasional Paper
Series, No. 19, August 2000.

Gould, Chandré, and Peter I. Folb. *Project Coast: Apartheid's Chemical and Biological Warfare Program.* UN Institute for Disarmament Research (UNIDIR) and the Centre for
Conflict Resolution (South Africa). 2002, http://www.unidir.org/files/publications/
pdfs/project-coast-apartheid-s-chemical-and-biological-warfare-programme-296.pdf.

———. "The South African Chemical and Biological Warfare Program: An Overview."
Nonproliferation Review, Vol. 7, No. 3 (Fall–Winter 2000): 10–23.

Graham, Bob, Jim Talent, Graham Allison, Robin Cleveland, Steve Rademaker, Tim Roemer, Wendy Sherman, Henry Sokolski, and Rich Verma. *World at Risk: The Report of
the Commission on the Prevention of WMD Proliferation and Terrorism.* New York:
Vintage Books, 2008.

Häckel, Erwin, and Gotthard Stein, eds. *Tightening the Reins: Towards a Strengthened
International Nuclear Safeguards System.* German Society for Foreign Affairs. Berlin:
Springer, 2000.

Hanson, Douglas. "Case Not Closed: Iraq's WMD Stockpiles." *American Thinker.* March 2,
2004, http://www.americanthinker.com/2004/03/case_not_closed_iraqs_wmd_stoc
.html.

Harris, Elisa D. "Threat Reduction and North Korea's CBW Programs." *Nonproliferation Review,* Vol. 11, No. 3 (February 2004): 86–109.

Harris, Verne, Sello Hatang, and Peter Liberman. "Unveiling South Africa's Nuclear Past." *Journal of Southern African Studies,* Vol. 30, No. 3 (September 2004): 457–75.

Hart, John, and Vitali Fedchenko. "Inspection and Verification Regimes." In Nathan E. Busch and Daniel H. Joyner, eds., *Combating Weapons of Mass Destruction: The Future of International Nonproliferation Policy.* Athens: University of Georgia Press, 2009.

Hecker, Siegfried S. "What I Found in North Korea." *Foreign Affairs.* December 9, 2010, http://www.foreignaffairs.com/articles/67023/siegfried-s-hecker/what-i-found-in -north-korea.

Heinonen, Olli. "The Case for an Immediate IAEA Special Inspection in Syria." *Policy Watch.* November 5, 2010, http://www.washingtoninstitute.org/policy-analysis/view/ the-case-for-an-immediate-iaea-special-inspection-in-syria.

———. "IAEA Safeguards—Evolving to Meet Today's Verification Undertakings." Conference Paper, Belfer Center for Science and International Affairs. July 12, 2013, http://belfercenter.ksg.harvard.edu/publication/23241/iaea_safeguards_evolving_ to_meet_todays_verification_undertakings.html.

———. Interview in Raphael Ahren, "Parchin Inspection Plan Won't Work, IAEA's Credibility on the Line, Says Ex-Deputy." *Times of Israel.* September 4, 2015, http:// www.timesofisrael.com/parchin-inspection-plan-flawed-iaeas-credibility-on-the -line-says-ex-deputy.

———. "Uranium Particles at Parchin Indicate Possible Undeclared Iranian Nuclear Activities." Foundation for Defense of Democracies. July 1, 2016, http://www.defend democracy.org/media-hit/olli-heinonen1-uranium-particles-at-parchin-indicate -possible-undeclared-iranian-nuclear-a.

———. "The Verification Devil in the Details." Belfer Center for Science and International Affairs. November 26, 2013, http://iranmatters.belfercenter.org/blog/verification -devil-details.

———. "Verifying the Dismantlement of South Africa's Nuclear Weapons Program." In Henry Sokolski, ed., *Nuclear Weapons Materials Gone Missing: What Does History Teach?* Arlington, VA: Nonproliferation Policy Education Center, March 2014, p. 95, http://npolicy.org/books/2014muf/Nuclear%20Weapons%20Materials%20Gone %20Missing.pdf.

Heinonen, Olli, and Simon Henderson. "On Iran." Op-ed. *Economist.* July 6, 2013, http:// belfercenter.ksg.harvard.edu/publication/23213/on_iran.html.

Heinonen, Olli, and Orde Kittrie. "Iran Plays Games with the Geneva Deal." Op-Ed. *Arms Control and Regional Security for The Middle East.* December 19, 2013, http:// belfercenter.ksg.harvard.edu/publication/23769/iran_plays_games_with_the_ge neva_deal.html.

Henderson, Barney. "Syria Civil War Death Toll Passes 100,000 People." *Telegraph.* July 25, 2013, http://www.telegraph.co.uk/news/worldnews/middleeast/Syria/10202616/ Syria-civil-war-death-toll-passes-100000-people.html.

Hibbs, Mark. "The Unspectacular Future of the IAEA Additional Protocol." *Proliferation Analysis*, Carnegie Endowment for International Peace. April 26, 2012, http://carne gieendowment.org/2012/04/26/unspectacular-future-of-iaea-additional-protocol/ ahhz.

Hirsch, Theodore. "The IAEA Additional Protocol: What It Is and Why It Matters." *Non-proliferation Review*, Vol. 11, No. 13 (Fall–Winter 2004): 140–66.

Hochman, Dafna. "Rehabilitating a Rogue: Libya's WMD Reversal and Lessons for U.S. Policy." *Parameters*, Vol. 36, No. 1 (Spring 2006): 63–77.

Hoffman, Mike. "Syria Airstrike in Iraq Complicates ISIL Equation." DefenseTech. June 25, 2014, http://defensetech.org/2014/06/25/syria-airstrike-in-iraq-complicates-isil -equation.

Horner, Daniel. "U.S. Revisits Plutonium Disposition Plan." *Arms Control Today*, Vol. 43, No. 4. May 2013, http://www.armscontrol.org/print/5770.

Ifft, Edward. "Iraq and the Value of On-Site Inspections." *Arms Control Today*, Vol. 34, No. 9 (November 2004): 21–27.

Iklé, Fred Charles. "After Detection—What?" *Foreign Affairs*, Vol. 39, No. 2 (January 1961): 208–20.

Institute for Science and International Security. "United Nations Security Council Reso-lutions." NuclearIran, N.d., http://www.isisnucleariran.org/documents/unscr.

———. "Verification of the Joint Comprehensive Plan of Action." ISIS Report. July 28, 2015, http://isis-online.org/uploads/isis-reports/documents/Verification_of_Iran_JCPOA _Final.pdf.

International Institute for Strategic Studies. "North Korea Digs In." *Strategic Comments*, Vol. 14, No. 10 (November 2008): 2.

International Panel on Fissile Materials. *Global Fissile Material Report 2009: A Path to Nuclear Disarmament.* October 2009, http://fissilematerials.org/library/gfmr09.pdf.

———. *Global Fissile Material Report 2007.* October 2007, http://fissilematerials.org/ library/gfmr07.pdf.

James Martin Center for Nonproliferation Studies. "The Moscow Summit: Mayak Fis-sile Material Storage Facility." N.d., http://cns.miis.edu/archive/summit/mayak.htm.

Jasani, Bhupendra, Irmgard Niemeyer, Sven Nussbaum, Bernd Richter, and Gotthard Stein, eds. *International Safeguards and Satellite Imagery: Key Features of the Nuclear Fuel Cycle and Computer-Based Analysis.* Berlin: Springer, 2009.

Jasani, Bhupendra, Martino Pesaresi, Stefan Schneiderbauer, and Gunter Zeug, eds. *Remote Sensing from Space: Supporting International Peace and Security.* Berlin: Springer, 2009.

Jasani, Bhupendra and Toshibomi Sakata, eds. *Satellites for Arms Control and Crisis Monitoring.* Oxford: Oxford University Press for SIPRI, 1987.

Jentleson, Bruce W., and Christopher A. Whytock. "Who 'Won' Libya?: The Force-Diplomacy Debate and Its Implications for Theory and Policy." *International Security*, Vol. 30, No. 3 (Winter 2005–6): 47–86.

Jeon, Jei Guk. "North Korean Leadership: Kim Jong Il's Balancing Act in the Ruling Circle." *Third World Quarterly*, Vol. 21, No. 5 (October 2000): 761–79.

Jofi, Joseph. "Challenges in Extending the Joint Plan of Action." Iran Matters, Belfer Center for Science and International Affairs. June 25, 2014, http://iranmatters.belfer center.org/blog/challenges-extending-joint-plan-action.

Joseph, Robert G. *Countering WMD: The Libyan Experience*. Fairfax, VA: National Institute Press, 2009.

Joshi, Sharad. "Playing Politics: How the Regional Context Impedes Confronting Myanmar's Alleged Nuclear Program." *Nuclear Threat Initiative*, Issue Brief. February 4, 2011, http://www.nti.org/e_research/e3_myanmar.html.

Joyner, Daniel H. "More Gold from Blix on the IAEA's Use of Information from National Intelligence Agencies." Arms Control Law blog. March 8, 2013, http://armscontrol law.com/2013/03/08/more-gold-from-blix-on-the-iaeas-use-of-information-from -national-intelligence-agencies/.

Kahn, Laura H. "The Biological Weapons Convention: Proceeding without a Verification Protocol." *Bulletin of the Atomic Scientists.* May 9, 2011, http://thebulletin.org/ biological-weapons-convention-proceeding-without-verification-protocol.

Kawashima, Yuta. "Timeline of Syrian Chemical Weapons Activity, 2012–2014." Arms Control Association. June 2014, https://www.armscontrol.org/factsheets/Timeline -of-Syrian-Chemical-Weapons-Activity.

Kay, David A. "Denial and Deception Practices of WMD Proliferators: Iraq and Beyond." *Washington Quarterly*, Vol. 18, No. 1 (Winter 1995): 85–105.

Kerr, Paul. "Commission Slams WMD Intelligence." *Arms Control Today*, Vol. 35, No. 4 (May 2005): 27–29.

———. "The IAEA's Report on Iran: An Analysis." *Arms Control Today*, Vol. 33, No. 10 (December 2003): 32–33, http://www.armscontrol.org/act/2003_12/IAEAreport.

———. "Iran's Nuclear Program: Status." CRS Report to Congress. Congressional Research Service. November 20, 2008, http://www.fas.org/sgp/crs/nuke/RL34544.pdf.

———. "Libya to Keep Limited Missile Force." *Arms Control Today*, Vol. 34, No. 4 (May 2004): 28.

———. "Libya's Disarmament: A Model for U.S. Policy?" *Arms Control Today*, Vol. 34, No. 5 (June 2004): 34–38.

———. "North Korea Admits Secret Nuclear Weapons Program." *Arms Control Today*, Vol. 32, No. 9 (November 2002): 19, 24, http://www.armscontrol.org/act/2002_11/ nkoreanov02.

Khajehpour, Bijan. "Iran's Economy: Twenty Years after the Islamic Revolution." In John L. Esposito and R. K. Ramazani, eds., *Iran at the Crossroads*. New York: Palgrave, 2001.

Khlebnikov, Nikolai, David Parlse, and Julian Whichello. "Novel Technologies for the Detection of Undeclared Nuclear Activities." IAEA-CN-148/32, released by the Nonproliferation Policy Education Center. March 2007, http://www.npolicy.org/article_file/Novel_technologies_for_the_detection_of_undeclared_nuclear_activities.pdf.

Kimball, Daryl G. "Myanmar Vows to Upgrade IAEA Safeguards." *Arms Control Today.* December 2012, http//www.armscontrol.org/print/5603.

———. "Nuclear Disarmament: the South African Example." *Arms Control Now.* July 8, 2011, http://armscontrolnow.org/2011/07/08/nuclear-disarmament-the-south-african -example.

Kimball, Daryl, and Kelsey Davenport. "Chemical Weapons: Frequently Asked Questions." Arms Control Association. October 2013, http://www.armscontrol.org/fact sheets/Chemical-Weapons-Frequently-Asked-Questions.

Klerk, F. W. de. Quoted in J. W. de Villiers, Roger Jardine, and Mitchell Reiss. "Why South Africa Gave up the Bomb." *Foreign Affairs,* Vol. 72, No. 5 (November–December 1993): 98–109.

Klinginger, Bruce, and Walter Lohman. "Securing U.S. Objectives in North Korea: A Memo to President-Elect Obama." Heritage Foundation. January 6, 2009, http: heri tage.org/Research/AsiaandthePacific/sr0037.cfm.

Koblentz, Gregory D. "From Biodefense to Biosecurity: The Obama Administration's Strategy for Countering Biological Threats." *International Affairs,* Vol. 88, No. 1 (January 2011): 131–48.

———. "Pathogens as Weapons: The International Security Implications of Biological Warfare." *International Security,* Vol. 28, No. 3 (Winter 2003–4): 84–122.

Krass, Allan S. *Verification: How Much is Enough?* London: Taylor and Francis, 1985.

Kuno, Yusuke. "Advances in Proliferation Resistant Technologies and Procedures." In Joseph F. Pilat and Nathan E. Busch, eds., *The Routledge Handbook of Nuclear Proliferation and Policy.* New York: Routledge Press, 2015.

Lentzos, Filippa. "Hard to Prove: The Verification Quandary of the Biological Weapons Convention." *Nonproliferation Review,* Vol. 18, No. 3 (November 2011): 571–82.

Levite, Ariel E. "Never Say Never Again: Nuclear Reversal Revisited." *International Security,* Vol. 27, No. 3 (Winter 2002–3): 59–88.

Lewis, Jeffrey. "Libya's Scud-B Force." Arms Control Wonk. August 22, 2011, http://lewis .armscontrolwonk.com/archive/4383/libyas-scud-b-force.

———. "Note from a Small Organization." Arms Control Wonk. May 16, 2014, http:// lewis.armscontrolwonk.com/archive/7328/note-from-a-small-organization.

Lewis, Jeffrey, and Catherine Dill. "Myanmar's Unrepentant Arms Czar." *Foreign Policy.* May 9, 2014, http://www.foreignpolicy.com/articles/2014/05/09/myanmar_north_korea _thein_htay_chemical_weapons.

Lewis, Patricia. "Verification, Compliance, and Enforcement." In George Perkovich and James M. Acton, eds., *Abolishing Nuclear Weapons: A Debate.* Carnegie Endowment

for International Peace. 2009, http://carnegieendowment.org/files/abolishing_nuclear
_weapons_debate.pdf.

Liberman, Peter. "Rise and Fall of the South African Bomb." *International Security,* Vol. 26, No. 2 (Fall 2001): 45–86.

———. "Unveiling South Africa's Nuclear Past." *Journal of Southern African Studies,* Vol. 30, No. 3 (September 2004): 459.

Lieberman, Jodi. "Dismantling the South African Nuclear Weapons Program: Lessons Learned and Questions Unresolved." In Henry Sokolski, ed., *Nuclear Weapons Materials Gone Missing: What Does History Teach?* Arlington, VA: Nonproliferation Policy Education Center, March 2014, p. 85, http://npolicy.org/books/2014muf/Nuclear%20Weapons%20Materials%20Gone%20Missing.pdf.

Litwak, Robert. *Regime Change: U.S. Strategy through the Prism of 9/11.* Washington, DC: Woodrow Wilson Center Press, 2007.

Lodgaard, Sverre. *Nuclear Disarmament and Non-Proliferation: Towards a Nuclear-Weapon-Free World?* New York: Routledge, 2011.

Lopez, George A., and David Cortright. "Containing Iraq: Sanctions Worked." *Foreign Affairs,* Vol. 83, No. 4 (July–August 2004): 90–103.

Lorber, Eric, and Peter Feaver. "Do the Iran Deal's 'Snapback' Sanctions Have Teeth?" *Foreign Policy.* July 21, 2015, http://foreignpolicy.com/2015/07/21/do-the-iran-deals-snap back-sanctions-have-teeth.

Louw, P. Eric. *The Rise, Fall, and Legacy of Apartheid.* Westport, CT: Praeger Publishers, 2004.

Lynch, Colum. "Shutting Down Iran's Nuclear Smugglers." *Foreign Policy.* July 1, 2015, http://foreignpolicy.com/2015/07/01/shutting-down-irans-tehran-nuclear-smug glers-security-council-united-nations.

Lynch, Colum, John Hudson, and Yochi Dreazen. "Exclusive: Syria Pushes to Keep Its Chemical Weapons Factories." *Foreign Policy.* October 31, 2013, http://thecable.foreign policy.com/posts/2013/10/31/exclusive_syria_tries_to_hold_on_to_its_chemical_ weapons_factories#sthash.74Fx6MXX.dpbs.

Manthorpe, Jonathan. "Anger at Clerics Threatens to Bring Iran to the Boil." *Vancouver Sun.* November 23, 2002, p. A27.

Masiza, Zondi. "A Chronology of South Africa's Nuclear Program." *Nonproliferation Review,* Vol. 1, No. 1 (Fall 1993): 35–55.

Mathews, Jessica T. "We Can Stop Syria by Using Lessons from Iraq." Op-ed. *Washington Post.* September 13, 2013, http://www.carnegie-mec.org/2013/09/13/we-can-stop -syria-by-using-lessons-from-iraq/gn63?reloadFlag=1.

———. "What Happened in Iraq? The Success Story of United Nations Inspections." Keynote speech to the International Peace Academy. March 5, 2004, http://carnegie endowment.org/2004/03/10/wmd-and-united-nations/2f99.

May, Michael, ed. *Verifying the Agreed Framework.* A joint report by the Centre for International Security and Cooperation (CISAC) and the Center for Global Security Research (CGSR). April 2001, http://fsi.stanford.edu/publications/verifying_the_agreed_framework/.

Mayer, Klaus, and Alexander Glaser. "Nuclear Forensics." In Joseph F. Pilat and Nathan E. Busch, eds., *The Routledge Handbook of Nuclear Proliferation and Policy*. New York: Routledge Press, 2015.

Mazarr, Michael J., ed. *Nuclear Weapons in a Transformed World: The Challenge of Virtual Nuclear Arsenals*. New York: St. Martin's Press, 1997.

McCarthy, Timothy V., and Jonathan B. Tucker. "Saddam's Toxic Arsenal: Chemical and Biological Weapons in the Gulf Wars." In Peter R. Lavoy, Scott D. Sagan, and James J. Wirtz, eds., *Planning the Unthinkable: How New Powers Will Use Nuclear, Biological, and Chemical Weapons*. Ithaca, NY: Cornell University Press, 2000.

McNaugher, Thomas L. "Ballistic Missiles and Chemical Weapons: The Legacy of the Iran-Iraq War." *International Security*, Vol. 15, No. 2 (Autumn 1990): 5–34.

Mian, Zia, and Frank N. von Hippel. "Policy and Technical Issues Facing a Fissile Material (Cutoff) Treaty." In Joseph F. Pilat and Nathan E. Busch, eds., *The Routledge Handbook of Nuclear Proliferation and Policy*. New York: Routledge Press, 2015.

Milani, Mohsen. "Reform and Resistance in the Islamic Republic of Iran." In John L. Esposito and R. K. Ramazani, eds., *Iran at the Crossroads*. New York: Palgrave, 2001.

Milhollin, Gary. "The Iraqi Bomb." *New Yorker* (February 1, 1993): 47–56.

Missile Technology Control Regime. "MTCR Guidelines and the Equipment, Software and Technology Annex." Missile Technology Control Regime, http://www.mtcr.info/english/guidelines.html.

Moodie, Michael, and Amy Sands. "New Approaches to Compliance with Arms Control and Nonproliferation Agreements." *Nonproliferation Review*, Vol. 8, No. 1 (Spring 2001): 1–9.

Moon, Duk-ho. "North Korea's Nuclear Weapons Program: Verification Priorities and New Challenges." Cooperative Monitoring Center Occasional Paper #32. December 2003, http://www.sandia.gov/cooperative-monitoring-center/_assets/documents/sand 2003-4558.pdf.

Müller, Harald. "Compliance Politics: A Critical Analysis of Multilateral Arms Control Treaty Enforcement." *Nonproliferation Review*, Vol. 7, No. 2 (Summer 2000): 77–90.

———. "The NPT Review Process and Strengthening the Treaty: Disarmament." EU Non-Proliferation Consortium, Non-Proliferation Papers, No. 10. February 2012, http://www.nonproliferation.eu/documents/nonproliferationpapers/haraldmuller 4f797b677acbf.pdf.

Munoz, Carlo. "US Should Help Secure Libyan WMD, House Intel Chief Says." *AolDefense*. September 16, 2011, http://defense.aol.com/2011/09/16/u-s-should-help-secure -libyan-wmd-house-intel-chief-says/.

Nacht, Michael. "The Global Environment: President Obama's Vision amid Emerging

Nuclear Threats." In Joseph F. Pilat and Nathan E. Busch, eds., *The Routledge Handbook of Nuclear Proliferation and Policy*. New York: Routledge Press, 2015.

Nackaerts, Herman. "A Changing Nuclear Landscape: Preparing for Future Verification Challenges." International Forum on Peaceful Use of Nuclear Energy and Nuclear Non-Proliferation, Vienna, Austria. February 2, 2011, www.iaea.org/newscenter/statements/ddgs/2011/nackaerts020211.html.

———. "IAEA Safeguards: Cooperation as the Key to Change." Keynote address, Institute for Nuclear Materials Management 52nd Annual Meeting. July 18, 2011, www.iaea.org/safeguards/statements-repository/Key_to_Change.pdf.

———. "Towards More Effective Safeguards: Learning Hard Lessons." Opening Plenary Address, INMM Annual Meeting. July 18, 2011, http://www.inmm.org/AM/Template.cfm?Section=Evolving_the_IAEA_State_Level_Concept&Template=/CM/ContentDisplay.cfm&ContentID=2971.

Noland, Marcus. "Why North Korea Will Muddle Through." *Foreign Affairs*, Vol. 76, No. 4 (July–August 1997): 105–18.

Norwegian Nobel Committee. "The Nobel Peace Prize for 2009." October 9, 2009, http://www.nobelprize.org/nobel_prizes/peace/laureates/2009/press.html.

Nuclear Energy Study Group. "Nuclear Power and Proliferation Resistance: Securing Benefits, Limiting Risk." American Physical Society Panel on Public Affairs. May 2005, http://www.aps.org/policy/reports/popa-reports/proliferation-resistance/upload/proliferation.pdf .

Nuclear Proliferation International History Project. "NPIHP Releases 20 Documents on the South African Nuclear Program." Woodrow Wilson International Center for Scholars. February 1, 2012, http://www.wilsoncenter.org/article/npihp-releases-20-documents-the-south-african-nuclear-program.

Nuclear Threat Initiative. "Conference on Disarmament (CD)." Updated June 2014, http://www.nti.org/treaties-and-regimes/conference-on-disarmament.

———. "CWC: Key Challenges and the Road Ahead." WMD411. July 2010, http://www.nti.org/f_wmd411/f203.html.

———. "Iran: Biological." Country Profiles. February 2013, http://www.nti.org/country-profiles/iran/biological/.

———. "Iran: Chemical." Country Profiles. February 2013, http://www.nti.org/country-profiles/iran/chemical/.

———. "Iraq Nuclear Chronology: 1990–2002." http://www.nti.org/e_research/profiles/Iraq/Nuclear/2121_3293.html.

———. "Myanmar Overview." July 2013, http://www.nti.org/country-profiles/myanmar/.

———. "South Africa Profile: Nuclear Overview." February 2013, http://www.nti.org/e_research/profiles/SAfrica/Nuclear/index.html.

Nussbaum, Sven, and Irmgard Niemeyer. "Automated Extraction of Change Information from Multispectral Satellite Imagery." *ESARDA Bulletin*, Vol. 36 (July 2007): 19–25.

Ogilvie-White, Tanya, and David Santoro. "Disarmament and Non-Proliferation: Towards More Realistic Bargains." *Survival*, Vol. 53, No. 3 (June 2011): 101–18.

Organization for the Prohibition of Chemical Weapons. "The Chemical Weapons Convention." N.d., http://www.opcw.org/chemical-weapons-convention.

———. "Guidelines for Schedules of Chemicals." N.d., http://www.opcw.org/?52,15,02 ,01,04,2007.

———. "Non-Member States." N.d., http://www.opcw.org/about-opcw/non-member-states.

———. "OPCW Inspectors Verify Newly Declared Chemical Weapons Materials in Libya." January 20, 2012, www.opcw.org/news/article/opcw-inspectors-verify-newly-declared-chemical-weapons-materials-in-libya.

———. "Syria Completes Destruction Activities to Render Inoperable Chemical Weapons Production Facilities and Mixing/Filling Plants." Press Release, OPCW Website. October 31, 2013, http://www.opcw.org/news/article/syria-completes-destruction-activities-to-render-inoperable-chemical-weapons-production-facilities-a/.

———. "Syria Submits Its Initial Declaration and a General Plan of Destruction of Its Chemical Weapons Programme." OPCW Website. October 27, 2013, http://www.opcw.org/index.php?id=242&tx_ttnews%5Btt_news%5D=1776&cHash=02aaddb97 0a75957d30033ec257b66c6.

Pabian, Frank V. "Evidence from Imagery: The Iran and Syrian Nuclear Programs— An Open and Shut Case?" Lecture given at the James Martin Center for Nonproliferation Studies, Monterey, CA. October 28, 2009, http://www.youtube.fcom/watch ?v=JkXbbHMKpHk.

———. "The South African Denuclearization Exemplar: Insights for Nonproliferation." Los Alamos Unclassified Report, LA-UR # 12-25213. December 2012.

Paul, T. V. *Power vs. Prudence: Why States Forgo Nuclear Weapons*. Montreal: McGill-Queen's University Press, 2000.

Pavey, Rob. "Layoff Notices Coming for MOX Workers." *Augusta Chronicle*. June 3, 2013, http://chronicle.augusta.com/news/metro/2013-06-03/layoff-notices-coming-mox -workers?v=1370305450.

Pearson, Graham S. *The Search for Iraq's Weapons of Mass Destruction: Inspection, Verification, and Nonproliferation*. New York: Palgrave Macmillan, 2005.

———. *The UNSCOM Saga: Chemical and Biological Weapons Non-Proliferation*. Basingstoke: Palgrave, 2000.

Perkovich, George, and James M. Acton. "Verifying the Transition to Zero." In George Perkovich and James M. Acton, eds., *Abolishing Nuclear Weapons: A Debate*. Carnegie Endowment for International Peace. 2009, http://carnegieendowment.org/files/ abolishing_nuclear_weapons_debate.pdf.

Perricos, Demetrius. "Understanding the Lessons of Nuclear Inspections and Monitoring in Iraq: A Ten-Year Review: Perricos." Conference hosted by the Institute for Science and International Security. June 14–15, 2001 (transcript date, August 28, 2001), http://isis-online.org/perricos.

Phillips, Melanie. "I Found Saddam's WMD Bunkers." *Spectator.* April 20, 2007, http://www.melaniephillips.com/i-found-saddams-wmd-bunkers.

Pickering, Thomas. "Preventing a Nuclear-Armed Iran." Comments in a panel session at the Arms Control Association Annual Meeting, Carnegie Endowment for International Peace, Washington, DC. June 4, 2012, http://www.armscontrol.org/events/Join-ACA-June-4-Our-Annual-Meeting%20>.

Pilat, Joseph F. "Arms Control, Verification, and Transparency." In Jeffrey A. Larsen and Gregory J. Rattray, eds., *Arms Control Toward the 21st Century.* Boulder, CO: Lynne Rienner Publishers, 1996.

———. "IAEA Safeguards: The Role of Advanced Safeguards Technologies in Meeting Tomorrow's Challenges." Paper presented at the JAEA-IAEA Workshop on Advanced Safeguards Technology for the Future Nuclear Fuel Cycle, Ibaraki, Japan, November 13–16, 2007, http://www-pub.iaea.org/mtcd/meetings/PDFplus/2007/cn1073/Papers /3.3 %20Ppr_%20Pilat%20-%20IAEA%20Safeguards%20The%20Role%20of%20Advanced%20Safeguards%20Technologies%20in%20Meeting%20Tomorrow.pdf.

———. "Verification and Transparency: Relics or Future Requirements?" in Jeffrey A. Larsen, ed., *Arms Control: Cooperative Security in a Changing Environment.* Boulder, CO: Lynne Rienner Publishers, 2002.

Pilat, Joseph F., and Nathan E. Busch. "WMD Monitoring and Verification Regimes: Lessons from Iraq." *Contemporary Security Policy,* Vol. 32, No. 2 (August 2011): 401–31.

Podvig, Patel. "Disposition of Excess Military Nuclear Material." UN Institute for Disarmament, http://www.unidir.org/files/publications/pdfs/dispositions-of-excess-military -nuclear-material-388.pdf.

Pollack, Kenneth M. *The Threatening Storm: The Case for Invading Iraq.* New York: Random House, 2002.

Potter, William C. *The Politics of Nuclear Renunciation: The Cases of Belarus, Kazakhstan, and Ukraine.* Occasional Paper No. 22. Washington, DC: Henry L. Stimson Center, 1995.

Purkitt, Helen, and Stephan Burgess. *South Africa's Weapons of Mass Destruction.* Bloomington: Indiana University Press, 2005.

Putin, Vladimir. "A Plea for Caution from Russia." Op-ed. *New York Times.* September 11, 2013, http://www.nytimes.com/2013/09/12/opinion/putin-plea-for-caution-from -russia-on-syria.html.

Reilly, Jill. "Revealed: International Inspectors Discover Gaddafi's Secret Stockpile of Chemical Weapons." *Daily Mail.* January 21, 2012, http://www.dailymail.co.uk/news/ article-2089436/Revealed-Gaddafis-secret-stockpile-chemical-weapons.html.

Reiss, Mitchell. *Bridled Ambition: Why Countries Constrain Their Nuclear Capabilities.* Baltimore, MD: Johns Hopkins University Press, 1995.

———. "Foreword." In Nathan E. Busch and Daniel H. Joyner, eds., *Combating Weapons of Mass Destruction: The Future of International Nonproliferation Policy*, xiii–xiv. Athens: University of Georgia Press, 2009.

Robinson, Paul. "A New Path Forward for the CTBT." In Joseph F. Pilat and Nathan E. Busch, eds., *The Routledge Handbook of Nuclear Proliferation and Policy*. New York: Routledge Press, 2015.

Rockwood, Laura. "The IAEA and International Safeguards." In Joseph F. Pilat and Nathan E. Busch, eds., *The Routledge Handbook of Nuclear Proliferation and Policy*. New York: Routledge Press, 2015.

Rogers, Mike. "The Evolution of American Intelligence and National Security in the Decade since 9/11." Speech at the American Enterprise Institute. September 16, 2011, http://www.aei.org/article/foreign-and-defense-policy/defense/the-evolution-of -american-intelligence-and-national-security-in-the-decade-since-911-speech/.

Rubin, Michael. "Enough with the Iran Deal 'Most Intrusive Inspections' Canard." *Commentary*. August 10, 2015, https://www.commentarymagazine.com/foreign-policy/ middle-east/iran/iran-inspections-canard.

Saab, Bilal Y. "Can Libya Be Locked Down?: In a Post-Qaddafi Era, Who Will Secure Libya's Chemical and Biological Weapons Materials?" *WMD Junction*, James Martin Center for Nonproliferation Studies. September 22, 2011, http://cns.miis.edu/wmd junction/110922_libya_lockdown.htm.

Sada, Georges. *Saddam's Secrets: How an Iraqi General Defied and Survived Saddam Hussein*. Brentwood, TN: Integrity Publishers, 2006.

Sagan, Scott D. "Nuclear Latency and Nuclear Proliferation." In William Potter and Gaukhar Mukhatzhanova, eds., *Forecasting Nuclear Proliferation in the 21st Century*. Stanford: Stanford University Press, 2010.

Salama, Sammy. "Was Libyan WMD Disarmament a Significant Success for Nonproliferation?" Center for Nonproliferation Studies Monterey Institute of International Studies. September 2004, http://www.nti.org/analysis/articles/was-libyan-wmd-dis armament-success/.

Salama, Sammy, and Cameron Hunter. "Iraq's WMD Scientists in the Crossfire." *Nuclear Threat Initiative*. May 2006, http://www.nti.org/analysis/articles/iraqs-wmd-scientists -crossfire/.

Samore, Gary. "Will Iran Strike a Nuclear Deal by July?" *Politico Magazine*. June 2, 2014, http://www.politico.com/magazine/story/2014/06/will-iran-strike-a-nuclear-deal -by-july-107250.html.

Samore, Gary, et al. *The Iran Nuclear Deal: A Definitive Guide*. Belfer Center for Science and International Affairs. August 2015, http://belfercenter.ksg.harvard.edu/files/Iran DealDefinitiveGuide.pdf.

Saunders, Emily C., Ariana N. Rowley, and Bryan L. Feary. "Towards a Tactical Nuclear Weapons Treaty." Paper presented at the Midwest Political Science Association Annual Conference. April 13, 2013.

Sayler, Kelly. "Malaysia, Export Controls, and the Nuclear Black Market." *Center for Strategic and International Studies.* March 24, 2011, http://csis.org/blog/malaysia-export-controls-and-nuclear-black-market.

Schneidmiller, Chris. "No Sign of Changes to Libyan Chemical Arms Security after Benghazi Attack." *Global Security Newswire.* September 14, 2012, http://www.nti.org/gsn/article/no-sign-changes-libya.

———. "OPCW Verifies Secret Libyan Chemical Arms." *Global Security Newswire.* January 20, 2012, http://www.nti.org/gsn/article/opcw-verifies-secret-libyan-chemical-arms/.

Schulte, Gregory L. "Strengthening the IAEA: How the Nuclear Watchdog Can Regain Its Bark." *Strategic Forum* 253. March 2010, http://www.nuclearfiles.org/menu/key-issues/nuclear-energy/issues/iaea/Strenthening-the-IAEA.pdf.

Scoblic, J. Peter, and Matthew Rice. "Shifting Priorities: UNMOVIC and the Future of Inspections in Iraq, An Interview with Ambassador Rolf Ekeus." *Arms Control Today,* Vol. 30, No. 2 (March 2000): 3–6.

Seongwhun, Cheon, and Tatsujiro Suzuki. "The Tripartite Nuclear-Weapon-Free Zone in Northeast Asia: A Long-Term Objective of the Six-Party Talks." *International Journal of Korean Unification Studies,* Vol. 12, No. 2 (December 2003): 41–68.

Shea, Thomas E. "The Trilateral Initiative: A Model for the Future?" *Arms Control Association,* Vol. 38, No. 4. May 2008, www.armscontrol.org/act/2008_05/PersboShea.

Sherman, Wendy. Quoted in "Lead Negotiator: U.S. Would Consider Limited Enrichment by Iran with Conditions." Public Broadcasting Service. December 4, 2013, http://www.pbs.org/newshour/bb/world-july-dec13-sherman_12-04.

Shultz, George P., William J. Perry, Henry A. Kissinger, and Sam Nunn. "Deterrence in the Age of Proliferation." *Wall Street Journal.* March 7, 2011, http://online.wsj.com/article/SB10001424052748703300904576178760530169414.html.

———. "Toward a Nuclear-Free World." *Wall Street Journal.* January 15, 2008, http://www.nuclearsecurityproject.org/publications/toward-a-nuclear-free-world.

———. "A World Free of Nuclear Weapons." *Wall Street Journal.* January 4, 2007, http://www.nuclearsecurityproject.org/publications/a-world-free-of-nuclear-weapons.

Sinai, Joshua. "Libya's Pursuit of Weapons of Mass Destruction." *Nonproliferation Review,* Vol. 4, No. 3 (Spring–Summer 1997): 92–100, http://cns.miis.edu/npr/pdfs/sinai43.pdf.

Singh, Michael. "Syria's Lessons for the Iran Nuclear Talks." *Policy Analysis,* Washington Institute for Near East Policy. September 20, 2013, https://www.washingtoninstitute.org/policy-analysis/view/syrias-lessons-for-the-iran-nuclear-talks.

Snyder, Scott. "North Korea's Challenge of Regime Survival: Internal Problems and the Implications for the Future." *Pacific Affairs,* Vol. 73, No. 4 (Winter 2000–2001): 517–33.

Sokolski, Henry. "The Iran Deal: An Omission We Still Can Fix." Nonproliferation Policy Education Center. October 15, 2015, http://www.npolicy.org/article.php?aid=1295&tid=4.

Sokova, Elena. "Plutonium Disposition." *Nuclear Threat Initiative.* September 16, 2010, http://www.nti.org/analysis/articles/plutonium-disposition-14.

Solingen, Etel. "The Political Economy of Nuclear Restraint." *International Security,* Vol. 19, No. 2 (Fall 1994): 126–69.

Spector, Leonard S. "Assad's Chemical Romance." *Foreign Policy.* August 23, 2011, http://www.foreignpolicy.com/articles/2011/08/23/assads_chemical_romance.

———. "Repentant Nuclear Proliferants." *Foreign Policy* Vol. 88 (Fall 1992): 3–20.

Squassoni, Sharon A. "The Iranian Nuclear Program." In Nathan E. Busch and Daniel H. Joyner, eds., *Combating Weapons of Mass Destruction: The Future of International Nonproliferation Policy.* Athens: University of Georgia Press, 2009.

———. "Iraq: U.N. Inspections for Weapons of Mass Destruction." Congressional Research Service Report for Congress. October 7, 2003, http://isn.ethz.ch/Digital-Library/Publications/Detail/?ots591=0c54e3b3-1e9c-be1e-2c24-a6a8c7060233&lng=en&id=10266.

Steavenson, Wendell. "Iranian Protest Widens: 10,000 at Demo." *Gazette* (Montreal, Quebec). December 9, 2002, p. A13.

Stein, Peter, and Peter D. Feaver. *Assuring Control of Nuclear Weapons: The Evolution of Permissive Action Links.* Lanham, MD: University Press of America, 1987.

Stockholm International Peace Research Institute. "Iraq: The UNSCOM Experience." SIPRI Fact Sheet. October 1998, http://books.sipri.org/files/FS/SIPRIFS9810.pdf.

Stoll, Ira. "Saddam's WMD Moved to Syria, An Israeli Says." *New York Sun.* December 15, 2005, http://www.nysun.com/article/24480.

Stone, Richard. "U.N. Inspectors Find Wisps of Smoke but No Smoking Guns." *Science,* Vol. 299 (March 28, 2003): 1967–69.

Stricker, Andrea. "Case Study: United States Busts Likely North Korean Transshipment Scheme." Institute for Science and International Security. May 24, 2013, http://isis-online.org/isis-reports/detail/case-study-united-states-busts-likely-north-korean-transshipment-scheme/.

———. "United States Prosecutes U.S.-Based Smuggler Working for Iran." Institute for Science and International Security. October 26, 2012, http://isis-online.org/isis-reports/detail/united-states-prosecutes-u.s.-based-smuggler-working-for-iran/.

Stricker, Andrea, and Serena Kelleher-Vergantini. "Myanmar Government Must Close Down Military Ties with North Korea." Institute for Science and International Security. July 5, 2013, http://isis-online.org/isis-reports/detail/myanmar-government-must-close-down-military-ties-with-north-korea/.

Stumpf, Waldo. "Birth and Death of the South African Nuclear Weapons Programme." Presentation at "50 Years After Hiroshima" Conference, hosted by the Union Scienziati per in Disarm, Castiglioncello, Italy. September 28–October 2, 1995, http://fas.org/nuke/guide/rsa/nuke/stumpf.htm.

———. "South Africa's Nuclear Weapons Program: From Deterrence to Dismantlement." *Arms Control Today,* Vol. 25, No. 10 (December 1995–January 1996): 3–8.

Sublette, Carey. "Report on the 1979 Vela Incident." *Nuclear Weapon Archive.* September 1, 2001, http://nuclearweaponarchive.org/Safrica/Vela.html.

Tauscher, Ellen. "Preventing Biological Weapons Proliferation and Bioterrorism." Address to the Annual Meeting of the States Parties to the Biological Weapons Convention, Geneva, Switzerland. December 9, 2009, http://www.state.gov/t/us/133335.htm.

Taylor, Terrence. "Building on the Experience: Lessons from UNSCOM and UNMOVIC." *Disarmament Diplomacy,* No. 75 (January–February 2004), http://www.acronym.org.uk/dd/dd75/75tt.htm.

Tenet, George J. "Remarks as Prepared for Delivery at Georgetown University." February 5, 2004, https://www.cia.gov/news-information/speeches-testimony/2004/tenet_georgetownspeech_02052004.html.

Tobey, William H. "Testing a Nuclear Deal with Tehran." Op-ed. *Foreign Policy.* November 13, 2013, http://belfercenter.ksg.harvard.edu/publication/23616/testing_a_nuclear_deal_with_tehran.html.

Trevan, Tim. *Saddam's Secrets: The Hunt for Iraq's Hidden Weapons.* London: Harper Collins Publishers, 1999.

Tsipis, Kostas, et al. *Arms Control Verification: The Technologies that Make It Possible.* Washington, DC: Pergamon-Brassey's, 1986.

Tucker, Jonathan B. "Growing Together: Biological and Chemical Threats." *Science Progress.* February 2, 2011, http://scienceprogress.org/2011/02/growing-together/.

———. "Monitoring and Verification in a Noncooperative Environment: Lessons from the U.N. Experience in Iraq." *Nonproliferation Review,* Vol. 3, No. 3 (Spring–Summer 1996): 1–14.

———. "Putting Teeth in the Biological Weapons Convention." *Issues in Science and Technology,* Vol. 18, No. 3. Spring 2002, http://issues.org/18-3/tucker.

———. "Re-envisioning the Chemical Weapons Convention." *Bulletin of the Atomic Scientists.* May 2, 2011, http://thebulletin.org/re-envisioning-chemical-weapons-convention.

———. "The Rollback of Libya's Chemical Weapons Program." *Nonproliferation Review,* Vol. 16, No. 3 (November 2009): 363–84, http://www.tandfonline.com/doi/pdf/10.1080/10736700903255060.

———. "Seeking Biosecurity without Verification: The New U.S. Strategy on Biothreats." *Arms Control Today,* Vol. 40, No. 1 (January–February 2010): 8–14.

———. "Strengthening the Biological Weapons Convention." *Arms Control Today,* Vol. 25, No. 3 (April 1995): 9–12.

———. "Verifying the Chemical Weapons Ban: Missing Elements." *Arms Control Today,* Vol. 37, No. 1 (January–February 2007): 6–13.

———. ed. *The Chemical Weapons Convention: Implementation Challenges and Solutions.* Monterey, CA: Centre for Non-Proliferation Studies, Monterey Institute of International Studies, April 2001.

Üzümcü, Ahmet. "Announcement to Media on Last Consignment of Chemicals Leaving

Syria." Organization for the Prohibition of Chemical Weapons. June 23, 2014, http://www.opcw.org/news/article/announcement-to-media-on-last-consignment-of-chemicals-leaving-syria/.

———. "Organisation for the Prohibition of Chemical Weapons." John Gee Memorial Lecture, Australian National University, Canberra, Australia. July 26, 2012, http://www.opcw.org/index.php?eID=dam_frontend_push&docID=15594.

Walker, Paul F. "Myanmar Ratifies Chemical Weapons Convention." *Arms Control Now.* January 28, 2015, https://www.armscontrol.org/blog/ArmsControlNow/2015-01-28/Myanmar-Ratifies-Chemical-Weapons-Convention.

Waller, Douglas. "Ready to Implode?" *Time,* Vol. 149, No. 18 (May 5, 1997).

Webb, Greg. "IAEA Issues Tough Report on Alleged Syrian Nuclear Site." *Global Security Newswire.* November 19, 2008, http://www.globalsecuritynewswire.org/gsn/ts_2008 1119_9297.php.

Weber, Andrew C., and Anya Erokhina. "Cooperative Threat Reduction and Its Lessons." In Joseph F. Pilat and Nathan E. Busch, eds., *The Routledge Handbook of Nuclear Proliferation and Policy.* New York: Routledge, 2015.

Wehrfritz, George, and Hideko Takayama. "Riding the Seoul Train: An Underground Railroad Leads North Korean Refugees to the South." *Newsweek International.* March 5, 2001, www.newsweek.com/riding-seoul-train-148821.

Weiss, Lauran. "UN Security Council Resolutions on Iran." Arms Control Association. August 2012, http://www.armscontrol.org/factsheets/Security-Council-Resolutions-on-Iran.

White, Jeffery. "The Assad Regime Winning by Inches?" *PolicyWatch2221*, Washington Institute. March 11, 2014, http://www.washingtoninstitute.org/policy-analysis/view/the-assad-regime-winning-by-inches.

Wit, Joel. "Dealing with North Korea's Nuclear Weapons Program." *Policy Forum* 98-13B. November 18, 1998, http://nautilus.org/napsnet/napsnet-policy-forum/napsnet-forum-23-future-of-agreed-framework-2.

World Nuclear Association. "Nuclear Power in South Africa." February 2013, http://www.world-nuclear.org/info/Country-Profiles/Countries-O-S-/South-Africa.

Zanders, Jeawn Pascal. "Destroying Libya's Chemical Weapons: Deadlines and Delays." *WMD Junction*, James Martin Center for Nonproliferation Studies. May 19, 2011, http://cns.miis.edu/wmdjunction/110519_destroying_libya_cw.htm.

Index

and, 172–73; nuclear weapons, 49, 139, 142, 172; Operation Desert Fox, 37, 87; Plutonium Management and Disposition Agreement, 150–51; reconnaissance satellites, 51; research and development, 248–50; sanctions on Iran, 6, 184, 189–90, 196–97, 254; South African disarmament and, 56, 63, 66, 68; South African nuclear program and, 58–59, 273n47; Syrian chemical weapons and, 210, 211–12, 214, 216, 217, 220; Syrian civil war and, 326n215; Trilateral Initiative, 145, 146–47, 148–49, 150, 151; wargames, 225. *See also* Bush administration; Joint Commission; Obama administration; Operation Iraqi Freedom; P5+1

United States Department of Defense, 118, 248

United States Department of Energy, 248

United States Department of Justice, 161

United States Department of State, 58–59, 100, 115–16, 118, 121, 124, 250

UNMOVIC, *see* United Nations Monitoring Verification and Inspection Commission

UNSCOM, *see* United Nations Special Commission on Iraq

Uranium: Iraqi material, 101; Libyan facilities and stocks, 117, 121; materials unaccounted for, 67; South African production, 49. *See also* Fissile material

Uranium enrichment: by Iran, 1–2, 179, 180, 184, 186–88, 200, 204–5, 231; multinational control, 251; by North Korea, 173, 174, 237; by South Africa, 49–50, 57–59, 61–62, 65–67, 69, 157; waste byproducts, 157. *See also* Highly enriched uranium; Low-enriched uranium

Üzümcü, Ahmet, 214

Varjoranta, Tero, 195

Verification: goals, 17; as political process, 17, 19–20, 25; transparency and, 18, 131, 153. *See also* Monitoring and verification processes

Viljoen, Constand, 51

WAES, *see* Wide-area environmental sampling

Weapons of mass destruction (WMD): cooperation among proliferating states, 238–39; preventive strikes issue, 219–20. *See also* Biological weapons; Chemical weapons; Global disarmament; Latent capabilities; Monitoring and verification; Nuclear weapons

Weber, Andrew C., 123

Wide-area environmental sampling (WAES), 25, 130, 160, 243, 244, 249

WMD, *see* Weapons of mass destruction

Yip, Susan, 161